The Autobiography of a Meskwaki Woman

A New Edition and Translation

Ives Goddard

Petoskey, Michigan

A Mundart Press Reprint

2022

Mundart Press, Petoskey MI 49770

This Mundart Press edition is an unaltered reprint of *The Autobiography of a Meskwaki Woman: A New Edition and Translation*, originally published under the editorship of John D. Nichols and H.C. Wolfart as *Algonquian and Iroquoian Linguistics, Memoir 18* (Winnipeg, 2006). It is a photographic scan of the original, with typographical design by A.C. Ogg. Reprinted with permission.

The original manuscript edited and translated here is in the National Anthropological Archives of the Department of Anthropology, Smithsonian Institution. It is posted online at: https://collections.si.edu/search/detail/ead_collection:sova-naa-ms2999.

A publication of the Recovering Voices Program of the Smithsonian Institution, supported in part by a gift from the Shoniya Fund.

Publisher's Cataloguing-in-Publication Data

Names: Goddard, Ives, 1941- editor, translator.
Title: The autobiography of a Meskwaki woman : a new edition and translation. Ives Goddard.
Description: Facsimile reprint edition. | Petoskey, Michigan : A Mundart Press Reprint, 2022. | Originally written in 1918 by an anonymous Meskwaki woman from the Meskwaki settlement in Tama County, Iowa. | "This Mundart Press edition is an unaltered reprint ... originally published under the editorship of John D. Nichols and H.C. Wolfart as 'Algonquian and Iroquoian Linguistics, Memoir 18' (Winnipeg, 2006)."--Title page verso. | Includes bibliographical references and appendix: "Analysis of Inflections". | Audience: the Sac and Fox Tribe of the Mississippi in Iowa and scholars and linguists studying their language. | "A publication of the Recovering Voices Program of the Smithsonian Institution, supported in part by a gift from the Shoniya Fund."--Title page verso. | Text in Meskwaki and English.
Identifiers: ISBN: 9780990334484 | LCCN: 2022905371
Subjects: LCSH: Fox language--Iowa--Tama County--Texts. | Fox women--Iowa--Tama County-- Biography. | Fox women--Iowa--Tama County--Social life and customs. | Fox Indians--Iowa-- Tama County--Social life and customs.
Classification: LCC: PM1195.Z9 G63 2022 | DDC: 497/.314--dc23

Contents

Introduction

This is an edition and translation of an autobiographical account written in the Meskwaki language by a Meskwaki Indian woman in the second decade of the twentieth century.

The Writer

The writer's name was "withheld by agreement" (Michelson 1925:295), and her identity is not known. She lived on the Meskwaki Settlement in Tama County, Iowa, and was apparently in her late middle age when she wrote the account in 1918. She uses no names of people or places, and the most concrete clue to who she was is her mention of the drum society she joined with her second husband (see lines 162C-D in the edition). This has been taken to refer to events of October, 1896, when a drum with the associated Drum Dance worship was brought to the Meskwakis by Wisconsin Potawatomis (Michelson 1925:344). The Meskwaki historian Charley H. Chuck gave the names of the first Meskwakis to join this drum (Chuck 1907:42), but a review of this information with the late Adeline Wanatee established that none of the women he named had life histories that match that of the writer.

The Manuscript

The account was written in pencil on 194 pages from cheap school tablets of three different sizes. It is preserved in the National Anthropological Archives of the Department of Anthropology, Smithsonian Institution, in the Museum Support Center in Suitland, Maryland (NAA ms. 2999). It was obtained for Truman Michelson of the Bureau of American Ethnology by Harry Lincoln, his Meskwaki-speaking linguistic assistant, in the summer of 1918. Michelson had been paying Meskwaki speakers to write literary and ethnographic texts in Meskwaki since 1911, and the writer would have written her account expressly for Michelson as part of his long-term project to document the language. Michelson turned the written text over to Horace Poweshiek, a bilingual, school-educated Meskwaki, who wrote out an English translation (NAA ms. 3009). Then, in June 1920, Michelson had the text read out loud to him by Harry Lincoln's wife, Shapochiwa, and wrote a phonetic transcription from her dictation (NAA ms. 3001). Shapochiwa skipped a few passages that involved topics which it would have been indecent for her to speak about to Michelson, and these were read for him by Harry Lincoln. Michelson's edition, which he submitted for publication in January, 1921, consisted of the phonetic text he had recorded from Shapochiwa and Harry Lincoln, his revision of Horace Poweshiek's translation, and ethnographic and linguistic notes. It appeared in the *Fortieth Annual Report of the Bureau of American Ethnology* for the fiscal year 1918-1919 (Michelson 1925). Some short sections relating to menstruation and sexual behavior were omitted from both the Meskwaki and English versions, in some cases without indication.

The Edition

The present edition has been completely redone from the original autograph manuscript, and a fresh translation has been prepared based on this. I wish, however, to acknowledge that this edition naturally relies heavily on the earlier one and on the contributions of those named in the preceding paragraph. I reviewed much of the text with Adeline Wanatee (1910-1996) in 1990, and examined many remaining uncertainties in 2001 with Everett Kapayou (1933-2006). I did not go over every line of the text with these speakers, however, and any remaining errors must be considered my responsibility.

The Meskwaki Writing System

The version of the Great Lakes Algonquian alphabetic syllabary that the Meskwakis use and some aspects of how they use it have been described elsewhere (Walker 1996:168-171; Goddard 1996). It writes all the distinctions of the language except vowel length and *h*, and there is no punctuation except for a word divider, which is often used sparingly (as in the present text) or not at all. These features may make syllabic writing difficult to read, even for native speakers, but they also make the syllabary easy to write fluently, and written Meskwaki usually provides an accurate rendering of the complex structures of the oral language. The syllabary does not, however, represent some features of colloquial pronunciation, notably the loss of many intervocalic semivowels and the elision of final vowels (Voorhis 1971:74-75; Goddard 1988). It generally represents the most deliberate and explicit pronunciation used in the community in earlier years.

Editorial Conventions

Editing Meskwaki syllabic texts entails restoring the missing phonemic features and word breaks and marking sentence boundaries, quoted speech or thought, and sentence-internal structural units with appropriate punctuation. Also, all identified writing errors, which are relatively infrequent, are emended, and all such emendations are registered in the critical apparatus ("Textual Notes," pp. 179-195). The editing conventions used are intended to make the editing explicit and in principle reversible. A word divider is rendered as a space or, if the divider separates the components of compound word, as a hyphen. A ligature under a space (‿) or hyphen (-̮) indicates that the word boundary was not marked by a word divider; in this text the ligature is not written between a word-final and a word-initial vowel, since the lack of elision points unambiguously to the presence of a word boundary and since this writer writes so few word dividers in such cases. A bar (|) indicates the lack of a word divider at a line end in the manuscript, where the use of word dividers is less common than within lines. A double bar (‖) indicates the end of the manuscript page; a page end in the middle of a word is not indicated in the edition but only in the textual notes.

Intonation patterns that alter the word stress are analyzed as separate morphemes and marked with special punctuation. The question mark (?) is used in Meskwaki only to mark the interrogative intonation; questions that use question words, which lack this intonation, are marked with a period.

The numbers in the left margin refer to the pages of the manuscript, which are those of the writer for pages 1-63 and the corrected numbers added by Michelson for pages 64-194. Capital letters are assigned to the lines of the edition, which were arrived at by analysis of patterns of syntax and discourse organization. All words in a line of the edition that continues onto a second page in the manuscript are referred to by the number of the manuscript page that the line begins on.

Clitics and Elision

A clitic boundary (▪) is marked before an enclitic or cliticized word, which draws the non-distinctive main stress to the preceding vowel (Goddard 1991:163-165). If an ostensible cliticized word has more than three syllables it does not affect the placement of the stress, and the clitic boundary is used simply to mark the presence of vowel elision. The clitic boundary is also used after the proclitic preverbs to aid in segmentation, although these are accented as if part of the following word.

A final short vowel is elided before the initial vowel (other than /i/ or /i·/) of an enclitic, a cliticized word, or a longer word in close juncture. In such combinations word-initial /i/ and /i·/ are elided after any vowel, with the transfer of the vowel length of /i·/ to the preceding vowel. A vowel resulting from the elision of word initial /i/ or /i·/ is written as part of the preceding word. Where an apparent elision of initial /i/ in a non-enclitic is preceded by (unwritten) /h/, however, it is usually assumed that the word-final /i/ of the preceding word has been left unwritten after /h/, according to the usual practice of the writer, and the edition writes the /i/ as part of the following word. The final vowel of a non-particle that is not written after /h/ before the initial consonant of an enclitic is not restored in the edition (60A, 95G, 185C); the omission in such cases is either an infelicitous writing or the indication of an anomalously modern pronunciation.

Interlinear Analysis

The interlinear analysis in this edition breaks down inflected words into stems and inflections and provides glosses (conventionalized translations or labels) for these components. The glosses do not cover the whole range of meanings, especially in the case of particles and enclitics. Alternate glosses are separated by a comma with no space, and multiple-word glosses are linked by periods with no spaces. Curly braces ({...}) mark the gloss of a valence for an oblique complement of the type indicated, as "{so}" for a manner oblique, "{smwh}" (i.e., "{somewhere}") for a locative oblique, and so forth. The elements bearing these valences are those referred to as relative roots.

The inflection at the end of a word is given in the interlinear analysis as an unanalyzed ending preceded by a plus sign (+). Pronominal prefixes and the abstract representations of reduplication (CV, CVCV, etc.) and initial change (IC), a process of vowel replacement, are followed by a plus sign. The gloss of an ending includes the pronominal prefix, aorist proclitic preverb *e·h▪* AOR, or initial change, if one of these is part of the inflected form, and the morpheme for initial change is otherwise glossed only as "xx." The breakdown of the numerous endings into their component suffixes will be given Goddard (forthcoming). A comprehensive general account of Meskwaki verbal affixes is in Goddard (2004); additional discussion is in Goddard (2005).

One-syllable reduplication (CV+, etc.) is glossed "RED1," and two-syllable reduplication (CVCV+) is glossed "RED2"; their uses, which overlap, are described in Dahlstrom (1997; forthcoming) and Goddard (forthcoming).

Dependent nouns, which always require a pronominal prefix, are given in the interlinear analysis with a preceding hyphen (-).

Enclitics are given in the interlinear analysis with a preceding clitic boundary (▪), but cliticized independent words are given without this.

The Translation

The translation is intended to read smoothly in English while at the same time following the Meskwaki as closely as possible. Where the word order of the two languages is radically different compromises have sometimes been made. For example, a verb of quotation after a long section of direct discourse is usually translated as a separate, resumptive sentence. An example is "So he said to me then." (88C), which translates a Meskwaki clause that is syntactically linked to the preceding quote and is so punctuated in the Meskwaki text.

The use of polite language for sexual matters follows the style of the writer. Although she was quite frank in mentioning such topics, she always used proper expressions for them. (See also the textual note to 112B.)

Most of the words in the text may be found in Goddard (1994). In some cases the present translation improves on the translations given in that source.

Proximate and Obviative

The use of the proximate and obviative categories is fundamental to the organization of Meskwaki discourse but nearly impossible to translate into English. The proximate is a first-ranked third person and the obviative is a second-ranked third person (Goddard 1990; Thomason 2003). To aid in tracking these categories, which are often not marked by specific suffixes, they are indicated in the translation as follows: animate proximate ($^{(P)}$); animate obviative ($^{(O)}$); inanimate proximate ($^{(p)}$); inanimate obviative ($^{(o)}$). Obviative is not indicated in the translation where it is not overtly marked anywhere in the Meskwaki as distinct from proximate, even if it would predictably be revealed by agreement.

ACKNOWLEDGMENTS

I am indebted to Adeline Wanatee, Everett Kapayou, and all those who contributed to Michelson's edition (see *The Manuscript* and *The Edition*, above). Leonard Bloomfield's lexicon (Goddard 1994) was also extremely useful. The bulk of the work of inserting the interlinear glosses was done by Patricia O. Afable under a Research Initiatives Grant from the Smithsonian Institution using Shoebox 2.0 software. Lucy Thomason was immensely helpful as a research assistant and colleague.

References

[Chuck, Charley H.] "Cha kă ta ko si." 1907. A collection of Meskwaki manuscripts. Iowa City: The State Historical Sciety of Iowa.

Dahlstrom, Amy. 1997. Fox (Mesquakie) reduplication. *International Journal of American Linguistics* 63:205-226.

Dahlstrom, Amy. Forthcoming. Morphology and syntax of the Fox (Mesquakie) language.

Goddard, Ives. 1988. Stylistic dialects in Fox linguistic change. *Historical Dialectology*, ed. by Jacek Fisiak, pp. 193-209. Berlin: Mouton de Gruyter.

Goddard, Ives. 1990. Aspects of the topic structure of Fox narratives: proximate shifts and the use of overt and inflectional NPs. *International Journal of American Linguistics* 56:317-340.

Goddard, Ives. 1991. Observations regarding Fox (Mesquakie) phonology. *Papers of the 22nd Algonquian Conference*, ed. by William Cowan, pp. 157-181. Ottawa: Carleton University.

Goddard, Ives. 1994. *Leonard Bloomfield's Fox lexicon. Critical edition.* Algonquian and Iroquoian Linguistics Memoir 12. Winnipeg: University of Manitoba.

Goddard, Ives. 1996. Writing and reading Mesquakie (Fox)," *Papers of the 27th Algonquian Conference*, ed. by David H. Pentland, pp. 117-134. Winnipeg: University of Manitoba.

Goddard, Ives. 2004. Meskwaki verbal affixes. *Papers of the 35th Algonquian Conference*, ed. by H.C. Wolfart, pp. 97-123. Winnipeg: University of Manitoba.

Goddard, Ives. 2005. Modal attraction and other cases of functional overlap in Meskwaki modes. *Papers of the 36th Algonquian Conference*, ed. by H.C. Wolfart, pp. 207-221. Winnipeg: University of Manitoba.

Goddard, Ives. Forthcoming. Meskwaki grammar.

Michelson, Truman. 1925. The autobiography of a Fox Indian woman. *Annual Report of the Bureau of American Ethnology*, vol. 40, pp. 291-349. Washington.

Thomason, Lucy Grey. 2003. The proximate and obviative contrast in Meskwaki. Ph.D. dissertation, University of Texas at Austin.

Voorhis, Paul H. 1971. New notes on the Mesquakie (Fox) language. *International Journal of American Linguistics* 37:63-75.

Walker, Willard B. 1996. Native writing systems, *Handbook of North American Indians*, ed. Ives Goddard, vol. 17: *Languages*, pp. 290-323. Washington: Smithsonian Institution.

Abbreviations

´	(in glosses) obviative
´	(in transcriptions and interlinears) unpredictable stress
0	third person inanimate
0p	third person inanimate plural
0s	third person inanimate singular
0´	third person inanimate obviative
0´p	third person inanimate obviative plural
0´s	third person inanimate obviative singular
Ø	zero (ending or suffix that is not phonetically overt)
1	first person
1p	first person plural exclusive
1s	first person singular
12	first person plural inclusive
2	second person
2p	second person plural
2s	second person singular
3	third person animate
3p	third person animate plural
3s	third person animate singular
3´	third person animate obviative
3´p	third person animate obviative plural
3´s	third person animate obviative singular
ANpl	animate plural
ANsg	animate singular
AOR	aorist conjunct
AOR.INT	aorist interrogative
CC	changed conjunct
CH.INT	changed interrogative
CH.PRI	changed prioritive
CONJ	plain conjunct
DIM	diminutive
DUB	independent dubitative
ECM	second member of exocentric particle compound
EMPH	emphatic; emphatic intonation (stress shift)
EN	expressive negative intonation

EXPL	mild expletive
HRSY	hearsay (evidential)
IC	initial change (change of first vowel: *i*, *e*, *a* → *e·*; *o* → *we·*; irregularly, addition of *e·*)
IMP	imperative
IND	independent indicative
INpl	inanimate plural
INsg	inanimate singular
INT	plain interrogative
INTERJ	interjectional intonation
INT.PPL	interrogative participle
ITER	conjunct iterative
LOC	locative
loc.obl	with locative oblique head
loc.obl.pl	with locative oblique plural head
NEG	conjunct negative
O2	secondary object (of AI or TA)
obl	with oblique head
obl.pl	with oblique plural head
OBVpl	animate obviative plural
OBVsg	animate obviative singular
PERF	perfective
pl.	plural
PN	prenoun
POT	potential
PP	preparticle
PPL	conjunct participle
PRET	preterite
PROH	prohibitive
PV	preverb
Q	interrogative intonation
REL	relational
smth	something
smwh	somewhere
SUBJ	conjunct subjunctive
VOCsg	vocative singular
X	indefinite person
3p–0	third plural animate subject and inanimate object
3s(-0)	third singular animate subject of objectless TI verb
3p(INpl)	third plural animate possessor with inanimate plural noun
PPL(INpl)	participle with inanimate plural head
PPL(obl)	participle with oblique head

The Autobiography of a Meskwaki Woman

1

A kaho·ni=yá·pi wi·h=a·totama·ni e·šawiya·ni.
kaho·ni =ya·pi ´ wi·h= a·tot +ama·ni IC+ išawi +ya·ni
so.then =here.I,we.go EMPH FUT+ tell.of +1s-0/AOR xx+ do.{so} +1s/PPL(obl)
So, now I shall tell the story of my life.

B me·kwe·h=ča·hi| nekotwa·šika e·h=taswipepo·nwe·ya·ni očiwe·pi e·h=we·pi‿kehke·netama·ni,
me·kwe·he =ča·hi nekotwa·šika e·h= taswipepo·nwe· +ya·ni očiwe·pi
I.believe =so six AOR+ be.{so.many}.years.old +1s/AOR from.{smth}.on

e·h= we·pi kehke·net +ama·ni
AOR+ begin/PV know +1s-0/AOR
Well, I believe it's from the time that I was six years old that my recollections begin,

C a·kwi=wi·n=e·yi·ki=pe·hki.‿
a·kwi =wi·na e·yi·ki pe·hki
not =but as.well really
but at the same time they're not complete.

D newaniwani·hke a·ya·wasi ne·kotawahi·nakahkini peteki=’ši.
ne+ CVCV+ wani·hke· +Ø a·ya·wasi IC+ nekotawahi·nakat +kini peteki iši
1+ RED2+ forget +1s/IND here.and.there xx+ be.one.year +0/ITER back {so}
I forget bits and pieces every year[P] back.

E kaho·ni e·h=taši·hka·noya·ni, ni·ča·paki| e·h=ašihaki,
kaho·ni e·h= taši·hka·no +ya·ni ni·ča·p +aki e·h= aših +aki
so.then AOR+ play +1s/AOR doll +ANpl AOR+ make +1s-3/AOR
So then, when I played, I made dolls[P]

F e·h=wi·če·nomaki=ta·taki.
e·h= wi·če·nom +aki ta·taki
AOR+ join.in.play +1s-3/AOR in.a.way
and pretended that we were all playing together.

G nekot=a·pehe kehči‿ni·ča·pa netašiha·wa.
nekoti =a·pehe kehči ni·ča·p +a ne+ aših +a·wa
one =usually great/PN doll +ANsg 1+ make +1s-3s/IND
I usually made one larger doll[P],

2

A o·n=a·peh=na·hka apeno·haki=ta·taki, ma·ne=meko.
o·ni =a·pehe na·hka apeno·h +aki ta·taki ma·ne =meko
and,then =usually also,again child +ANpl in.a.way much,many =EMPH
and there would also be pretend children[P], many of them.

B o·n=a·pehe e·h=wača·hoči ta·tak=a·pehe i·na‿meši‿ni·ča·pa,
o·ni =a·pehe e·h= wača·ho +či ta·taki =a·pehe i·na meši
and,then =usually AOR+ cook +3s/AOR in.a.way =usually that/ANsg big/PN

ni·ča·p +a
doll +ANsg
And that big doll[P] would do the cooking, I pretended,

C ni·na=ke·h=meko=wi·n=a·pehe| newača·ho·hka·no.
ni·na =ke·hi =meko =wi·na =a·pehe ne+ wača·ho·hka·no +Ø
1s/EMPH =moreover =EMPH =but =usually 1+ play.at.cooking +1s/IND
but actually I̲ would act out the cooking.

D o·n=a·pehe e·h=wi·seniya·ke e·h=ma·no·hpoya·ke e·h=išiwe·pi·hka·noya·ni.
o·ni =a·pehe e·h= wi·seni +ya·ke e·h= ma·no·hpo +ya·ke
and,then =usually AOR+ eat +1p/AOR AOR+ many.eat.together +1p/AOR

e·h= išiwe·pi·hka·no +ya·ni
AOR+ pretend.{so} +1s/AOR
And then I would pretend that we ate, a lot of us eating together.

E na·hka wi·kiya·pe·hani netašihašihto, ni·ča·paki e·h=owi·kihaki.
na·hka wi·kiya·pe·h +ani ne+ CVCV+ ašiht +o ni·ča·p +aki
also,again house/DIM +INpl 1+ RED2+ make +1s-0/IND doll +ANpl

e·h= owi·kih +aki
AOR+ to.dwell.{smwh}].cause +1s-3/PPL(loc.obl)
I also used to make little houses where I had the dolls[P] live.

* * *

F no·hika e·h=taswipepo·nwe·ya·ni me·kwe·he e·h=we·pi-kokwe·čikwa·sikawaki neni·ča·paki.
no·hika e·h= taswipepo·nwe· +ya·ni me·kwe·he
seven AOR+ be.{so.many}.years.old +1s/AOR I.believe

e·h= we·pi CV_Ye·+ kočikwa·sikaw +aki ne+ ni·ča·p +aki
AOR+ begin/PV RED1+ try.to.sew.for +1s-3/AOR 1+ doll +ANpl
When I was seven years old, I believe, I began to practice doing sewing for my dolls[P].

3

A šewe·=pe·hki nemya·še·wi.
šewe·na pe·hki ne+ mya·še·wi· +Ø
but really 1+ do.task.badly +1s/IND
But I did a really poor job of it.

B nemayomayo·taneko e·h=pwa·wi‿nahikwa·soya·ni.
ne+ CVCV+ mayo·taneko +Ø e·h= pwa·wi nahikwa·so +ya·ni
1+ RED2+ cry.while.working +1s/IND AOR+ NEG/PV know.how.to.sew +1s/AOR
I used to cry as I worked because I couldn't do a competent job of sewing.

C a·kwi=’yo=ke·h=a·pehe kaškowe·ya·nini,| “ašihtawino,” e·h=inaki‿nekya.|
a·kwi =iyo =ke·hi =a·pehe kaškowe· +ya·nini ašihtaw +ino
not =for =moreover =usually persuade.people +1s/NEG make.O2.for +2s-1s/IMP

e·h= iN +aki ne+ -ky +a
AOR+ say.{so}.to +1s-3/AOR 1+ mother +ANsg
You understand that, when I asked my mother[P] to do it for me, I could never persuade her.

D “ke·keya·h=ma·h‿ki·h=nahihto.
ke·keya·hi =ma·hi ke+ wi·h= nahiht +o
eventually =you.see 2+ FUT+ know.how.to.make +2s-0/IND
“You see, in time you'll know how to do it.

E wi·h=nahikwa·soyani=ma·hi we·či‿pwa·wi-ašihto·na·ni.
wi·h= nahikwa·so +yani =ma·hi
FUT+ know.how.to.sew +2s/AOR =you.see

IC+ oči pwa·wi ašihtaw +ena·ni
xx+ from.{smth}/PV NEG/PV make.O2.for +1s-2s/PPL(obl)
The reason I don't do it for you is so you'll learn how to sew.

4

A i·ni=ma·hi‿we·či|-nahikwa·soki,
i·ni =ma·hi IC+ oči nahikwa·so +eki
that/INsg =you.see xx+ from.{smth}/PV know.how.to.sew +X/PPL(obl)
See, that's how we learn to sew,

B e·h=kokwe·čikwa·sikawoči oni·ča·pinawaki.
e·h= CV_Ye·+ kočikwa·sikaw +eči o+ ni·ča·p +inawaki
AOR+ RED1+ try.to.sew.for +X-3/AOR 3+ doll +X(ANpl)
by practicing sewing for our dolls[P].

C i·ni=ke·h=we·či-oni·ča·piki.‿
i·ni =ke·hi IC+ oči oni·ča·pi +eki
that/INsg =moreover xx+ from.{smth}/PV have.doll +X/PPL(obl)
That's why we have dolls, actually.

D ča·ki=meko ke·ko·h ašihtawa·pi oto·šehki·ta·kanwa·wi,
ča·ki =meko ke·ko·h +i ašihtaw +a·pi o+ ošehki·ta·kan +wa·wi
all =EMPH thing +INsg make.O2.for +X-3/IND 3+ clothing +3p(INsg)
We make every part of their clothing for them[P],

E omahkese·hwa·wani=ke·hi."
o+ mahkese·h +wa·wani =ke·hi
3+ moccasin +3p(INpl) =moreover
including their moccasins."

F o·ni=ča·h=a·pehe ahpene·či=meko e·h=kokwe·čikwa·sikawaki neni·ča·paki.
o·ni =ča·hi =a·pehe ahpene·či =meko e·h= CV_Ye·+ kočikwa·sikaw +aki
and,then =so =usually every.time =EMPH AOR+ RED1+ try.to.sew.for +1s–3/AOR
ne+ ni·ča·p +aki
1+ doll +ANpl
So then I would practice doing sewing for my dolls[P] all the time.

* * *

5
A kaho·ni šwa·šika me·kwe·he e·h=taswipepo·nwe·ya·ni,
kaho·ni šwa·šika me·kwe·he e·h= taswipepo·nwe· +ya·ni
so.then eight I.believe AOR+ be.{so.many}.years.old +1s/AOR
And then, I believe when I was eight years old,

B e·h=we·pi_mata·kwe·netama·ni e·h=anehanenwi·ya·ni.
e·h= we·pi mata·kwe·net +ama·ni e·h= CVCV+ anenwi· +ya·ni
AOR+ begin/PV enjoy +1s–0/AOR AOR+ RED2+ swim +1s/AOR
I began to be fond of swimming.

C ki·hpene=meko| ašiči e·h=pema·pye·ki si·po·wi e·h=owi·kiya·kini,
ki·hpene =meko ašiči e·h= pema·pye· +ki si·po·w +i
in.the.event.that =EMPH near AOR+ flow.past +0/AOR river +INsg
e·h= owi·ki +ya·kini
AOR+ dwell.{smwh} +1p/PPL(loc.obl.pl)
All it took was for there to be a river[P] near where our lodges were,

D neta·hpeč_anenwi·pena iškwe·se·haki.
ne+ a·hpeči anenwi· +pena iškwe·se·h +aki
1+ permanently/PV swim +1p/IND girl +ANpl
and we girls[P] were forever swimming.

E nema·ne·pen=a·pehe.|
ne+ ma·ne· +pena =a·pehe
1+ be.much,many +1p/IND =usually
There would be a lot of us.

F neneškimeko·pena=ke·h=wi·n=a·pehe,
ne+ neškim +eko·pena =ke·hi =wi·na =a·pehe
1+ forbid,admonish +X–1p/IND =moreover =but =usually
Actually, we would be told not to,

6

A šewe·na ke·ški‿ki·mi·ya·kini=meko·=’ni e·h=maw‿anenwi·ya·ke.
šewe·na IC+ kaški ki·mi· +ya·kini =meko
but xx+ able.to/PV sneak.away +1p/ITER =EMPH
i·ni e·h= mawi anenwi· +ya·ke
then AOR+ go.and/PV swim,bathe +1p/AOR
but whenever we were able to sneak away, we went to swim.

B a·net=a·peh ki·ški·škatahwa·pi e·h=pwa·wi‿nenoše·wa·či.
a·neta =a·pehe Ci·h+ ki·škatahw +a·pi e·h= pwa·wi nenoše· +wa·či
some =usually RED1+ whip +X-3/IND AOR+ NEG/PV heed +3p/AOR
Some[P] would be whipped for not listening.

C ni·na=wi·na, a·kwi=nana·ši ki·ški·škatahwikini;
ni·na =wi·na a·kwi nana·ši Ci·h+ ki·škatahw +ikini
1s/EMPH =but not (ever) RED1+ whip +X-1s/NEG
But as for me, I was never whipped.

D ’še=ma·h‿nenekotiheko·pi| e·h=iškwe·se·hiya·ni.
iše =ma·hi ne+ nekotih +eko·pi e·h= iškwe·se·hi +ya·ni
just =you.see 1+ have.one +X-1s/IND AOR+ be.girl +1s/AOR
You see, I was the only girl in the family.

E še·ški nekehči‿neškimeko·p=a·pehe || e·h=pwa·wi‿kaškimiki.
še·ški ne+ kehči neškim +eko·pi =a·pehe e·h= pwa·wi kaškim +iki
only 1+ greatly/PV admonish +X-1s/IND =usually AOR+ NEG/PV persuade +X-1s/AOR
I would only be severely scolded for not minding.

7

A ne·škimikini na·hka nemahkate·wi·neko·pi.
IC+ neškim +ikini na·hka ne+ mahkate·wi·N +eko·pi
xx+ forbid,admonish +X-1s/ITER also,again 1+ to.fast].cause +X-1s/IND
And whenever I was scolded I was also made to fast.

B pwa·wi‿nenoše·ya·nini na·hka neneškimeko·pi kotakaki wi·h=ki·wi·‿’te·maki iškwe·se·haki.
IC+ pwa·wi nenoše· +ya·nini na·hka ne+ neškim +eko·pi kotak +aki
xx+ NEG/PV heed +1s/ITER also,again 1+ forbid,admonish +X-1s/IND other +ANpl
wi·h= ki·wi wi·te·m +aki iškwe·se·h +aki
FUT+ around/PV accompany +1s-3/AOR girl +ANpl
And also, when I didn’t listen, I was forbidden to go around with the other girls[P].

C “po·si‿wa·waneška·haki a·šihenakiče.
po·si wa·waneška·h +aki a·ših +enakiče
extreme/PN misbehaver +ANpl get.into.bad.habits +3-2s/PROH
“The ones[P] that behave the worst might get you into their bad habits.

D a·kwi=ma·hi·=’niki ke·ko·h=wi·h=nahihto·wa·čini anemi‿ki·šiki·hiwa·te,
a·kwi =ma·hi i·niki ke·ko·h +i wi·h= nahiht +o·wa·čini
not =you.see that/ANpl something +INsg FUT+ know.how.to.make +3p–0/NEG

anemi ki·šiki·hi +wa·te
go.on/PV grow.up/DIM +3p/SUBJ
You see, those[P] girls aren’t going to know how to make things as they grow older,

8

A pwa·wi-‿ke·ko·h -nahi‿kočihto·wa·te.
pwa·wi ke·ko·h +i nahi kočiht +o·wa·te
NEG/PV something +INsg be.given.to/PV try.to.make +3p–0/SUBJ
if they never try to make anything.

B i·ni=ke·h‿wi·h=išawiyani,
i·ni =ke·hi IC+ wi·h= išawi +yani
that/INsg =moreover xx+ FUT+ do.{so} +2s/PPL(obl)
And that’s the way you’ll be, too,

C pwa·wi‿nahi‿kočihto·yane ke·ko·hi,
pwa·wi nahi kočiht +o·yane ke·ko·h +i
NEG/PV be.given.to/PV try.to.make +2s–0/SUBJ thing +INsg
if you never try to make things

D še·ški| ki·wi‿tanenekoyane,” neteko·p=a·pehe.
še·ški ki·wi taneneko +yane ne+ iN +eko·pi =a·pehe
only around/PV thrash,fool.around +2s/SUBJ 1+ say.{so}.to +X–1s/IND =usually
and just fool around,” I would be told.

E e·h=mahkate·wi·šiki‿na·wahkwe·kini‿netašameko·pi.
e·h= mahkate·wi·N +iki IC+ na·wahkwe· +kini ne+ ašam +eko·pi
AOR+ to.fast].cause +X–1s/AOR xx+ be.noon +0/ITER 1+ give.to.eat.to +X–1s/IND
When I was made to fast I was fed every noon.

F šewe·na pa·pekwa=meko na·htasokonakato·hikini i·ni=meko‖ e·h=ki·ši-wani·hke·ya·ni e·ši‿neškimikini.
šewe·na pa·pekwa =meko IC+ na·htasokonakato·hi +kini i·ni =meko
but right.away =EMPH xx+ be.a.few.days/DIM +0/ITER then =EMPH

e·h= ki·ši wani·hke· +ya·ni IC+ iši neškim +ikini
AOR+ PERF/PV forget.O2 +1s/AOR xx+ {so}/PV forbid,admonish +X–1s/PPL(obl.pl)
But right away after a few days I had already forgotten the things I had been forbidden to do.

9

A na·hka, “ka·ta nekotahi nahi-nepe·wowe·hkani.
na·hka ka·ta nekotahi nahi nepe·wowe· +hkani
also,again don’t somewhere given.to/PV sleep.at.house.of.people +2s/PROH
Also, “Don’t ever spend the night someplace else.

B wi·če·nomačini iškwe·se·haki, aya·pami͜pya·no| e·h=owi·ke·hiyakwe.
IC+ wi·če·nom +ačini iškwe·se·h +aki
xx+ join.in.play +2s-3/ITER girl +ANpl

aya·pami pya· +no e·h= owi·ke·hi +yakwe
back/PV come +2s/IMP AOR+ dwell.{smwh}/DIM +12/PPL(loc.obl)
Whenever you play with the other girls[P]*, be sure and come back to our camp.*

C e·ye·h͜wa·se·ya·ki ki·h=ki·ši͜pya.
IC+ aye·hi wa·se·ya· +ki ke+ wi·h= ki·ši pya· +Ø
xx+ continue.to/PV be.light +0/CC 2+ FUT+ PERF/PV come +2s/IND
You must be back while it's still light.

D ka·ta pehkote·nemihkani nekotah=taši.
ka·ta pehkote·nemi +hkani nekotahi taši
don't be.overtaken.by.night +2s/PROH somewhere {smwh}
Don't be caught out after dark someplace else.

E a·yaškači͜wi·če·nomi," neteko·pi.
CV+ aškači wi·če·nom +i ne+ iN +eko·pi
RED1+ later join.in.play +2s-3/IMP 1+ say.{so}.to +X-1s/IND
And don't play with them too often," I was told.

* * *

F kaho·ni ša·ka e·h=taswipepo·nwe·ya·ni,
kaho·ni ša·ka e·h= taswipepo·nwe· +ya·ni
so.then nine AOR+ be.{so.many}.years.old +1s/AOR
And then, when I was nine years old,

10

A e·h=anemi|-kaški-asemihaki=nekya.
e·h= anemi kaški asemih +aki ne+ -ky +a
AOR+ go.on/PV able.to/PV help +1s-3/AOR 1+ mother +ANsg
I went on to being able to help my mother[P].

B me·no·hkami·kini we·pi-ahčike·kini,|
IC+ meno·hkami· +kini IC+ we·pi ahčike· +ekini
xx+ be.spring +0/ITER xx+ begin/PV plant +X/ITER
Whenever spring planting began,

C "ke·ko·he·hi ahčike·no wi·h=ota·hwi·hemiyani," e·h=išiki.
ke·ko·he·h +i ahčike· +no
something/DIM +INsg plant.02 +2s/IMP

IC+ wi·h= ota·hwi·hemi +yani e·h= iN +iki
xx+ FUT+ have.02.as.possession +2s/PPL(INsg) AOR+ say.{so}.to +X-1s/AOR
I was told, "Plant a little something to be your own."

D ke·hten=a·pehe| e·h=ahčike·ya·ni.
ke·htena =a·pehe e·h= ahčike· +ya·ni
truly =usually AOR+ plant.02 +1s/AOR
And I really would plant something.

E we·pi-tatakohamekini e·hčike·ki,
IC+ we·pi tatakoh +amekini IC+ ahčike· +eki
xx+ begin/PV clear.by.tool +X-0/ITER xx+ plant.02 +X/PPL(INsg)
And whenever the crops began to be weeded,

F "ši·´, ki·na=wi·na=ne·h ketahki tatakohano," e·h=išiki.
ši·´ ki·na =wi·na =ne·hi ke+ ahky +i tatakoh +ano
Say! 2s/EMPH =but =too 2+ earth +INsg clear.by.tool +2s-0/IMP

e·h= iN +iki
AOR+ say.{so}.to +X-1s/AOR
I was told, "Say, make sure you hoe the weeds in *<u>your</u>* *garden, too."*

G čaki-mo·naha·ka·h netomo·naha·kani.
čaki mo·naha·ka·h +i ne+ omo·naha·kani +Ø
small/PN hoe/DIM +INsg 1+ have.02.as.hoe +1s/IND
I had little hoe of my own.

11

A kapo·twe=na·hk=a·peh e·h=po·ni-mo·naškahike·ki,
kapo·twe na·hka =a·pehe e·h= po·ni mo·naškahike· +eki
at.some.point also,again =usually AOR+ cease/PV do.weeding +X/AOR
And when the time came to quit hoeing,

B nemi·ša·te·nem=a·pehe e·h=ki·ši-wayači-po·ni·hkameki e·hčike·ki.
ne+ mi·ša·te·nemo +Ø =a·pehe
1+ be.pleased +1s/IND =usually

e·h= ki·ši wayači po·ni·hk +ameki IC+ ahčike· +eki
AOR+ PERF/PV already/PV cease.dealing.with +X-0/AOR xx+ plant.02 +X/PPL(INsg)
I would be happy to have the work on the garden crops over and done with.

C neša·kwe·nemo='yo=ke·h=a·pehe ke·ko·h| wi·h=iši·hta·ya·ni.
ne+ ša·kwe·nemo +Ø =iyo =ke·hi =a·pehe ke·ko·h +i
1+ be.unwilling +1s/IND =for =moreover =usually something +INsg

wi·h= iši·hta· +ya·ni
FUT+ work.{so} +1s/AOR
I always hated to do any kind of work, you understand.

D šewe·n=a·pehe, "mani ki·ši-'ši·hta·yane,
šewe·na =a·pehe mani ki·ši iši·hta· +yane
but =usually this/INsg PERF/PV work.{so} +2s/SUBJ
But when I was told, "After you get done with this,

E meše·=’nah ki·h=mawi·_’če·noma·waki iškwe·se·haki,” e·h=išik=a·pehe,
meše·=’nahi ke+ wi·h= mawi wi·če·nom +a·waki iškwe·se·h +aki
as.may.be 2+ FUT+ go.and/PV join.in.play +2s-3p/IND girl +ANpl

e·h= iN +iki =a·pehe
AOR+ say.{so}.to +X-1s/AOR =usually
you may go and play with the other girls[P],”

F i·n=e·h=anwa·či·ya·ni.‖
i·ni e·h= anwa·či· +ya·ni
then AOR+ consent +1s/AOR
then I would be willing.

12
A ke·hten=a·pehe·=’ni e·h=kehči_wi·če·nomaki apeno·haki.
ke·htena =a·pehe i·ni e·h= kehči wi·če·nom +aki apeno·h +aki
truly =usually then AOR+ greatly/PV join.in.play +1s-3/AOR child +ANpl
And in fact I would play with the other children[P] a lot then.

B e·h=ma·mi·hko·hiya·ke e·ši|-mata·kwe·netama·ke.
e·h= ma·mi·hko·hi +ya·ke IC+ iši mata·kwe·net +ama·ke
AOR+ play.tag +1p/AOR xx+ {so}/PV enjoy +1p-0/PPL(obl)
Our favorite game was tag.

C na·hina·h=na·hka e·hčike·ya·ke ki·šikekini,
na·hina·hi na·hka IC+ ahčike· +ya·ke IC+ ki·šiken +kini
time,distance also,again xx+ plant +1p/PPL(INsg) xx+ be.full.grown +0/ITER
And again, at the times when our crops had ripened,

D “ši·´, koči_wača·hono=wi·na=ki·na ki·šikihto·yani,” e·h=išiki.
ši·´ koči wača·ho +no =wi·na ki·na IC+ ki·šikiht +o·yani
Say! try.to/PV cook.O2 +2s/IMP =but 2s/EMPH xx+ to.grow].cause +2s-0/PPL(INsg)

e·h= iN +iki
AOR+ say.{so}.to +X-1s/AOR
I would be told, “Say, why don’t you try and cook what you’ve raised, yourself?”

E ke·hten=a·peh ni·na·=’ni e·h=koči_wača·hoya·ni.
ke·htena =a·pehe ni·na i·ni e·h= koči wača·ho +ya·ni
truly =usually 1s/EMPH then AOR+ try.to/PV cook.O2 +1s/AOR
Then I would, in fact, try to cook some,

F ki·šesama·nini e·h=kotatamowa·či nemeso·ta·naki,
IC+ ki·šes +ama·nini e·h= kotat +amowa·či ne+ -meso·ta·n +aki
xx+ finish.cooking +1s-0/ITER AOR+ taste +3p-0/AOR 1+ parent +ANpl
and after I had cooked it, my parents[P] would taste it

13
A “pe·hki_wi·kaniwi,” e·h=išiwa·či, “ki·šikihto·či.”
pe·hki wi·kan   +niwi   e·h= iN   +iwa·či
really be.good.tasting +0´s/IND AOR+ say.{so}.to +3p-1s/AOR

IC+ ki·šikiht   +o·či
xx+ to.grow].cause +3s-0/PPL(INsg)
and would talk about me and say, “It(0) tastes really good, what she(P) has raised.”

B “pe·hki=ke·h=mek=e·yi·ki wi·kese·hkwe·wa,” neteko·k=a·pehe.
pe·hki =ke·hi   =meko e·yi·ki wi·kese·hkwe·   +wa
really =moreover =EMPH as.well cook.good.tasting.food +3s/IND

ne+ iN   +eko·ki   =a·pehe
1+ say.{so}.to +3p-1s/IND =usually
They(P) would say about me, “And she(P)'s a really good cook, as well.”

C nemi·ša·te·nemo| i·n=e·šiwa·čini.
ne+ mi·ša·te·nemo +Ø   i·ni   IC+ iN   +iwa·čini
1+ be.pleased   +1s/IND that/INsg xx+ say.{so}.to +3p-1s/ITER
I felt proud whenever they(P) said that about me.

D keye·hapa=ke·h=wi·na iše=meko e·šimikehe wi·h=nahese·hkwe·ya·ni e·h=ine·nemiki.
keye·hapa   =ke·hi   =wi·na iše =meko IC+ išim   +ikehe
it.turned.out =moreover =but   just =EMPH xx+ speak.{so}.to +X-1s/CH.PRET

wi·h= nahese·hkwe·   +ya·ni e·h= ine·nem   +iki
FUT+ know.how.to.cook +1s/AOR AOR+ think.about.{so} +X-1s/AOR
Actually, though, I was just being told that out of a desire that I would become a competent cook.

E o·ni=ni·na, “ke·htena=ye·toke,” e·h=išite·he·ya·ni.
o·ni   ni·na   ke·htena =ye·toke e·h= išite·he· +ya·ni
and,then 1s/EMPH truly   =it.seems AOR+ think.{so} +1s/AOR
And here, I was thinking that it was probably the truth.

* * *

14
A kaho·ni me·ta·swipepo·nwe·ya·ni,
kaho·ni IC+ meta·swipepo·nwe· +ya·ni
so.then xx+ be.ten.years.old +1s/CC
And then, when I reached ten years of age,

B i·niye·ka·=’ni ni·ča·paki e·h=po·ni-mata·kwe·nemaki.
i·niye·ka   i·ni ni·ča·p +aki   e·h= po·ni   mata·kwe·nem +aki
that/ABS(ANpl) then doll   +ANpl AOR+ cease/PV enjoy   +1s-3/AOR
I lost my interest in the dolls(P) I'd had.

C i·ni=wi·na‿ke·waki=meko nemata·kwe·neta e·h=anenwi·ya·ni.

```
i·ni      =wi·na ke·waki      =meko ne+ mata·kwe·net +a
that/INsg =but   as.yet,still =EMPH 1+  enjoy        +1s-0/IND

e·h= anenwi·    +ya·ni
AOR+ swim,bathe +1s/AOR
```

I was still fond of my swimming, though,

D šewe·na·=’ni, “ni·h=maw‿anenwi?” e·nakini nekya,

```
šewe·na i·ni ne+ wi·h= mawi      anenwi·    +Ø      ?
but     then 1+  FUT+  go.and/PV swim,bathe +1s/IND Q

IC+ iN            +akini      ne+ -ky    +a
xx+ say.{so}.to +1s-3/ITER 1+  mother +ANsg
```

but then, whenever I asked my mother[P] if I could go swimming,

E “hao·ʔ,” e·h=išiči.

```
hao·ʔ          e·h= iN          +iči
alright,hello AOR+ say.{so}.to +3s-1s/AOR
```

she[P] told me, “Alright.”

F “ko·hkomesa ki·h=ko·kenamawa·wa opi·sehka·hani,

```
ke+ -o·hkomes    +a    ke+ wi·h= ko·kenamaw   +a·wa       o+ pi·sehka·h +ani
2+  grandmother +ANsg 2+  FUT+  wash.O2.for +2s-3s/IND 3+ blouse     +INpl
```

“You may wash your grandmother[P]’s blouses,

15

A ni·na=ke·h=e·yi·ki ki·h=ko·kenamawi,” e·h=išiki.

```
ni·na    =ke·hi     e·yi·ki ke+ wi·h= ko·kenamaw  +i
1s/EMPH =moreover as.well 2+  FUT+  wash.O2.for +2s-1s/IND

e·h= iN          +iki
AOR+ say.{so}.to +X-1s/AOR
```

and you may wash mine also,” I was told.

B pe·pi·wikeno·hiki=we·=meko| e·h=anohka·šiki| wi·h=ko·kenama·ni.

```
IC+ papi·wikeno·hi      +ki            =we·na   =meko e·h= anohka·N      +iki
xx+ be.small.(pl.)/DIM +0/PPL(INsg) =in.fact =EMPH AOR+ give.task.to +X-1s/AOR

wi·h= ko·ken +ama·ni
FUT+  wash    +1s-0/AOR
```

And in fact I was given the job of washing any small article of clothing[p].

C ke·htena=mek=a·pehe nemečime·nemo, “ni·h=maw‿anenwi?”‿wi·h=iya·ni,

```
ke·htena =meko =a·pehe   ne+ mečime·nemo +Ø      ne+ wi·h= mawi
truly    =EMPH =usually 1+  hesitate    +1s/IND 1+  FUT+  go.and/PV

anenwi·    +Ø      ? wi·h= i        +ya·ni
swim,bathe +1s/IND Q FUT+  say.{so} +1s/AOR
```

To tell the truth, I would hesitate to ask if I could go swimming,

D e·h=kohtama·ni wi·h=ko·kenike·ya·ni.‿
e·h= koht +ama·ni wi·h= ko·kenike· +ya·ni
AOR+ fear +1s-0/AOR FUT+ do.washing +1s/AOR
as I dreaded doing the washing.

E keye·hapa=ke·h=wi·na wi·h=nahi‿ko·kenike·ya·ni e·h=ine·nemiki we·či‿to·tawikehe.
keye·hapa =ke·hi =wi·na wi·h= nahi ko·kenike· +ya·ni
it.turned.out =moreover =but FUT+ know.how.to/PV do.washing +1s/AOR

e·h= ine·nem +iki IC+ oči to·taw +ikehe
AOR+ think.about.{so} +X-1s/AOR xx+ from.{smth}/PV treat.{so} +X-1s/PRET.PPL(obl)
I later realized, though, that I was treated like that out of a desire that I would learn to do the washing.

16
A ke·htena=meko nenahi‿ko·kenike kapo·twe.
ke·htena =meko ne+ nahi ko·kenike· +Ø kapo·twe
truly =EMPH 1+ know.how.to/PV do.washing +1s/IND at.some.point
And sure enough, I did learn how to do the washing after a time.

B "i·ni=ma·h=ki·na we·či‿to·to·na·ni:
i·ni =ma·hi ki·na IC+ oči to·taw +ena·ni
that/INsg =you.see 2s/EMPH xx+ from.{smth}/PV treat.{so} +1s-2s/PPL(obl)
"There, you see, that's why I treated you like that:

C wi·h=nahi‿ko·kenike·yani," netekwa=nekya.
wi·h= nahi ko·kenike· +yani ne+ iN +ekwa
FUT+ know.how.to/PV do.washing +2s/AOR 1+ say.{so}.to +3s-1s/IND

ne+ -ky +a
1+ mother +ANsg
so you'd learn to do the washing," my mother[P] told me.

D "a·kwi=kohi ka·kike·wi-anemi-pemeniwe·čini owiye·ha.‿
a·kwi =kohi ka·kike·wi anemi pemeniwe· +čini owiye·h +a
not =certainly forever/PV go.on/PV take.care.of.people +3s/NEG someone +ANsg
"You surely know that nobody[P] goes on taking care of us forever.

E kapo·twe=koh pye·čise·wi e·taši|-pemeniwa·ta‖ e·h=pana·pameči.
kapo·twe =kohi pye·čisa· +wi
at.some.point =certainly time.comes +0s/IND

IC+ taši pemeniwe· +ta e·h= pana·pam +eči
xx+ be.engaged.in/PV take.care.of.people +3/PPL(ANsg) AOR+ lose.sight.of +X-3/AOR
Without a doubt, the time comes some day when we lose sight of the one[P] that's taking care of us.

17

A ni·na='yo‿nekya a·kwi te·pahkwi‿kehke·nemakini e·šina·kosikwe·ni.
ni·na =iyo ne+ -ky +a a·kwi te·pahkwi kehke·nem +akini
1s/EMPH =for 1+ mother +ANsg not attain/PV know +1s-3/NEG

IC+ išina·kosi +kwe·ni
xx+ look.{so} +3s,0/INT.PPL(obl)
Like me, I never got to know what my mother[P] looked like.

B nesekwisa neki·šikenekwa.
ne+ -sekwis +a ne+ ki·šiken +ekwa
1+ cross-aunt +ANsg 1+ raise +3s-1s/IND
My father's sister[P] raised me.

C i·ni=ča·h‿e·to·tawiči i·noki e·to·to·na·ni.
i·ni =ča·hi IC+ to·taw +iči i·noki
that/INsg =so xx+ treat.{so} +3s-1s/PPL(obl) now

IC+ to·taw +ena·ni
xx+ treat.{so} +1s-2s/PPL(obl)
And the way I'm treating you now is the way she[P] treated me.

D a·kwi‿še·ški| wi·h=tanenekoya·ni‿wi·to·hkawičini.
a·kwi še·ški wi·h= taneneko +ya·ni wi·to·hkaw +ičini
not only FUT+ fool.around +1s/AOR allow +3s-1s/NEG
She[P] didn't allow me to just be fooling around.

E apina=mo·hči=ni·na‿šwa·šika e·h=taswipepo·nwe·ya·ni, pe·hki=meko e·h=nahese·hkwe·ya·ni. ‖
apina mo·hči ni·na šwa·šika e·h= taswipepo·nwe· +ya·ni
even even 1s/EMPH eight AOR+ be.{so.many}.years.old +1s/AOR

pe·hki =meko e·h= nahese·hkwe· +ya·ni
really =EMPH AOR+ know.how.to.cook +1s/AOR
Why, I even knew how to cook really well when I was only eight years old.

18

A ke·ko·h‿e·ši-otamesičini nesekwisa, e·h=wača·hoya·ni," ‿netekwa.
ke·ko·h +i IC+ iši otamesi +čini ne+ -sekwis +a
something +INsg xx+ {so}/PV be.busy +3s/ITER 1+ cross-aunt +ANsg

e·h= wača·ho +ya·ni ne+ iN +ekwa
AOR+ cook +1s/AOR 1+ say.{so}.to +3s-1s/IND
Whenever my aunt[P] was busy with something, I did the cooking," she[P] told me.

B neta·nwe·htawa·wa i·n=e·h=iči.‿
ne+ a·nwe·htaw +a·wa i·ni e·h= i +či
1+ disbelieve +1s-3s/IND that/INsg AOR+ say.{so} +3s/AOR
I didn't believe her[P] when she[P] said that.

C ni·na·'yo=ke·h i·ni e·h=meta·swipepo·nwe·ya·ni,

```
ni·na     =iyo =ke·hi     i·ni e·h= meta·swipepo·nwe·  +ya·ni
1s/EMPH =for =moreover then AOR+ be.ten.years.old  +1s/AOR
```

Understand that I was then ten years old,

D ača·hmeko e·h=anemi|- pe·hki‿-nahese·hkwe·hiya·ni,

```
ača·hmeko e·h= anemi    pe·hki nahese·hkwe·hi         +ya·ni
only.then AOR+ go.on/PV really know.how.to.cook/DIM +1s/AOR
```

and I was only then getting to know how to do a bit of cooking competently,

E na·hka e·h=nahikwa·so·hiya·ni.

```
na·hka      e·h= nahikwa·so·hi       +ya·ni
also,again AOR+ know.how.to.sew/DIM +1s/AOR
```

and also I could to sew a little.

F šewe·na nemya·še·wi.

```
šewe·na ne+ mya·še·wi·    +Ø
but     1+  do.task.badly +1s/IND
```

Yet I did a poor job of it.

G na·hka i·nina·h=meko na·hina·h=to·hki·čini nekya,‿"to·hki·no'. nepi=ki·h=na·te," e·h=išiči.

```
na·hka      i·nina·hi      =meko na·hina·hi     IC+ to·hki· +čini
also,again at.that.time =EMPH time,distance xx+ wake.up +3s/ITER

ne+ -ky     +a     to·hki· +no      ′
1+   mother +ANsg wake.up +2s/IMP INTERJ

nepy  +i     ke+ wi·h= na·t       +Ø         e·h= iN            +iči
water +INsg 2+  FUT+  go.to.get +2s-0/IND AOR+ say.{so}.to +3s-1s/AOR
```

Also at that same time, when my mother(P) woke up she(P) would tell me, "Wake up! You have to go after water.

19

A "na·hka pi·we·hkenese·no wi·h=peškone·nawačike·yakwini," e·h=išiči.

```
na·hka      pi·we·hkenese· +no     IC+ wi·h= peškone·nawačike· +yakwini
also,again get.dry.sticks +2s/IMP xx+ FUT+  get.fire.started  +12/PPL(INpl)

e·h= iN            +iči
AOR+ say.{so}.to +3s-1s/AOR
```

And also get some dry sticks for us to kindle the fire with."

B e·h=ša·kwe·nemoya·n=a·pehe neki·hki·hkimeko·pi=meko.

```
e·h= ša·kwe·nemo  +ya·ni  =a·pehe  ne+ ki·hki·hkim         +eko·pi   =meko
AOR+ be.unwilling +1s/AOR =usually 1+  order.against.will +X-1s/IND =EMPH
```

When I didn't want to, I would be made to anyway.

C i·ni=meko ahpene·či e·to·tawiki.
i·ni =meko ahpene·či IC+ to·taw +iki
that/INsg =EMPH every.time xx+ treat.{so} +X-1s/PPL(obl)
That's how I was always treated.

D kapo·twe=na·hka, "mani=ke·h| kepapakye·hi," neteko·pi.
kapo·twe na·hka mani =ke·hi ke+ papakye·h +i
at.some.point also,again this/INsg =moreover 2+ hatchet +INsg

ne+ iN +eko·pi
1+ say.{so}.to +X-1s/IND
At some point also I was told, "Here's your hatchet."

E pye·to·ki papakye·he·hi‿če·ka·heno·hiki.
IC+ pye·t +o·ki papakye·he·h +i IC+ čaka·heno·hi +ki
xx+ bring +X-0/PPL(INsg) hatchet/DIM +INsg xx+ be.small/DIM +0/PPL(INsg)
A little hatchet[P] is what I'd been brought.

F nemi·ša·te·nemo.
ne+ mi·ša·te·nemo +Ø
1+ be.pleased +1s/IND
I was delighted.

G "mani=ke·h ketapihka·ni," neteko·pi.
mani =ke·hi ke+ apihka·n +i ne+ iN +eko·pi
this/INsg =moreover 2+ tumpline +INsg 1+ say.{so}.to +X-1s/IND
And I was told, "Here's your tumpline."

20

A e·h=manese·ya·k=a·pehe nekya,
e·h= manese· +ya·ke =a·pehe ne+ -ky +a
AOR+ cut.firewood +1p/AOR =usually 1+ mother +ANsg
When my mother[P] and I went to cut firewood,

B ni·na=ke·h netanemo·ta ki·šahama·nini papi·wi‿mese·he·hani.
ni·na =ke·hi ne+ anemo·t +a IC+ ki·šah +ama·nini
1s/EMPH =moreover 1+ carry.away.on.back +1s-0/IND xx+ chop/PERF +1s-0/PPL(INpl)

papi·wi mese·he·h +ani
small.(pl.)/PN piece.of.firewood/DIM +INpl
I would carry home on my back the little sticks of wood I had chopped.

C wi·n=a·pehe nenana·hiwanehka·kwa,
wi·na =a·pehe ne+ nana·hiwanehkaw +ekwa
3s/EMPH =usually 1+ arrange.back-load.for +3s-1s/IND
But she[P] would arrange my load for me

D e·h=a·čimohiči‿wi·h=inapito·ya·ni.
e·h= a·čimoh +iči IC+ wi·h= inapit +o·ya·ni
AOR+ inform +3s-1s/AOR xx+ FUT+ tie.so +1s-0/PPL(obl)
and tell me how to tie it.

E ke·keya·h=meko·=’ni e·h=we·pi‿neši‿manese·ya·ni kehčine.
ke·keya·hi =meko i·ni e·h= we·pi neši manese· +ya·ni kehčine
eventually =EMPH then AOR+ begin/PV alone/PV cut.firewood +1s/AOR nearby
Then eventually I began to cut firewood by myself nearby.

* * *

F kaho·ni meta·swi‿nekoti e·h=taswipepo·nwe·ya·ni,
kaho·ni meta·swi nekoti e·h= taswipepo·nwe· +ya·ni
so.then ten one AOR+ be.{so.many}.years.old +1s/AOR
And then, when I was eleven years old,

21
A na·hka maškimote·hani e·h=ašihto·č=a·pehe e·h=wa·pawa·pamaki.
na·hka maškimote·h +ani e·h= ašiht +o·či =a·pehe
also,again bag +INpl AOR+ make +3s-0/AOR =usually

e·h= CVCV+ wa·pam +aki
AOR+ RED2+ look.at +1s-3/AOR
I would always watch her[(P)] as she[(P)] made bags, also.

B “nahi´,| ki·h=kočihto,” netekwa.
nahi´ ke+ wi·h= kočiht +o ne+ iN +ekwa
Well! 2+ FUT+ try.to.make +2s-0/IND 1+ say.{so}.to +3s-1s/IND
“Alright, you must try and make one,” she[(P)] told me.

C nekoti·=’ni e·h=ni·pitawiči, čaki‿maškimote·he·hi,
nekoti i·ni e·h= ni·pitaw +iči čaki maškimote·he·h +i
one then AOR+ set.up.warp.of.02.for +3s-1s/AOR small/PN bag/DIM +INsg
Then she[(P)] got one started for me to weave, a little bag,

D e·h=kehkahamawiči wi·h=išihto·ya·ni.
e·h= kehkahamaw +iči IC+ wi·h= išiht +o·ya·ni
AOR+ designate.02.for +3s-1s/AOR xx+ FUT+ make.{so} +1s-0/PPL(obl)
and showed me how to make it.

E ke·htena| nekatawi‿=meko‿-nahihto,
ke·htena ne+ katawi =meko nahiht +o
truly 1+ almost =EMPH know.how.to.make +1s-0/IND
Sure enough, I came close to knowing how to make it,

F šewe·=pe·hki=meko| nemya·še·wi. ‖
šewe·na pe·hki =meko ne+ mya·še·wi· +Ø
but really =EMPH 1+ do.task.badly +1s/IND
but I did a really poor job.

22
A na·hkači=meko,| "kotaki ki·h=ašihto,"‿neteko·pi.
na·hkači =meko kotak +i ke+ wi·h= ašiht +o ne+ iN +eko·pi
also,again =EMPH other +INsg 2+ FUT+ make +2s-0/IND 1+ say.{so}.to +X-1s/IND
Again I was told, "You should make another one."

B a·wasi·me·h=meko·=’ni e·nekihkwa·ki.
a·wasi·me·hi =meko i·ni IC+ inekihkwa· +ki
more/DIM =EMPH that/INsg xx+ be.{so}.big +0/PPL(INsg)
It was one[p] that was a little bigger.

C o·ni=pe·hki=kapo·twe e·h=nahihto·ya·ni.
o·ni pe·hki kapo·twe e·h= nahiht +o·ya·ni
and,then really at.some.point AOR+ know.how.to.make +1s-0/AOR
And after a time I reached the point where I was able to make them well.

D ke·hten=a·peh i·n=e·h=ša·kwe·nemoya·ni wi·h=ašihto·ya·ni.|
ke·htena =a·pehe i·ni e·h= ša·kwe·nemo +ya·ni wi·h= ašiht +o·ya·ni
truly =usually then AOR+ be.unwilling +1s/AOR FUT+ make +1s-0/AOR
To tell the truth, I then wouldn't want to make them.

E aškiča·h=ke·h‿netanwa·či e·h=ašihto·ya·ni,
aškiča·hi =ke·hi ne+ anwa·či· +Ø e·h= ašiht +o·ya·ni
at.first =moreover 1+ consent +1s/IND AOR+ make +1s-0/AOR
And here at first I had made them willingly,

F e·ye·h‿pwa·wi- pe·hki‿-nahihto·ya·ni.|
IC+ aye·hi pwa·wi pe·hki nahiht +o·ya·ni
xx+ continue.to/PV NEG/PV really know.how.to.make +1s-0/CC
as long as I didn't know how to make them well.

G šewe·na neki·hki·hkimeko·pi=meko‿wi·h=ašihašihto·ya·ni.
šewe·na ne+ ki·hki·hkim +eko·pi =meko wi·h= CVCV+ ašiht +o·ya·ni
but 1+ persuade.against.will +X-1s/IND =EMPH FUT+ RED2+ make +1s-0/AOR
But I was made to keep on making them anyway.

23
A pe·po·kini·=’ni pe·hki e·h=ašihašihto·ya·ni.
IC+ pepo· +kini i·ni pe·hki e·h= CVCV+ ašiht +o·ya·ni
xx+ be.winter +0/ITER then really AOR+ RED2+ make +1s-0/AOR
In the winters[p] is when I would really be making them continually.

B kaho·ni na·hka i·nina·h=meko apahko·haya če·keši·he·hita e·h=ni·pitawiki.|
kaho·ni na·hka i·nina·hi =meko apahko·hay +a
so.then also,again at.that.time =EMPH cattail-reed.mat/DIM +ANsg

IC+ čakeši·he·hi +ta e·h= ni·pitaw +iki
xx+ be.small/DIM +3/PPL(ANsg) AOR+ set.up.warp.of.O2.for +X-1s/AOR
And then, it was also at that time that a little cattail-reed mat(P) was started for me to weave.

C “ašihi=mana,” e·h=išiki,
aših +i mana e·h= iN +iki
make +2s-3/IMP this/ANsg AOR+ say.{so}.to +X-1s/AOR
“Make this(P),” I was told,

D e·h=kočihaki.
e·h= kočih +aki
AOR+ try.to.make +1s-3/AOR
and I tried to make it(P).

E ke·keya·h=meko neki·šiha·wa.
ke·keya·hi =meko ne+ ki·ših +a·wa
eventually =EMPH 1+ finish.making +1s-3s/IND
Eventually I finished it(P).

F neki·ša·koči_mya·še·wi.
ne+ ki·ša·koči mya·še·wi· +Ø
1+ extremely/PV do.task.badly +1s/IND
I did the poorest job imaginable.

G ke·keya·h=meko·=’ni e·h=we·pi-asemihaki_nekya,
ke·keya·hi =meko i·ni e·h= we·pi asemih +aki ne+ -ky +a
eventually =EMPH then AOR+ begin/PV help +1s-3/AOR 1+ mother +ANsg
Then, in time, I began to help my mother(P),

24

A ki·ši_nahapahkwa·ke·ya·ni.
IC+ ki·ši nahapahkwa·ke· +ya·ni
xx+ PERF/PV know.how.to.make.cattail-reed.mats +1s/CC
after I knew how to make cattail-reed mats.

B pe·hki| mi·ša·te·nemow=a·pehe ke·ko·h| ki·ši_nahihto·ya·nini.
pe·hki mi·ša·te·nemo +wa =a·pehe ke·ko·h +i
really be.pleased +3s/IND =usually something +INsg

IC+ ki·ši nahiht +o·ya·nini
xx+ PERF/PV know.how.to.make +1s-O/ITER
She(P) would really be pleased whenever I had learned to make something.

C “i·ni=ma·h=ki·na.
i·ni =ma·hi ki·na
that/INsg =you.see 2s/EMPH
“There, you see!

D ki·na·kwi| wi·h=ašihta·tisoyani ki·ši-neši‿pemenetisoyane we·či|-ki·hki·hkimena·ni wi·h=ašihto·yani ke·ko·hi.|
ki·na·kwi wi·h= ašihta·tiso +yani ki·ši neši
confidently FUT+ make.O2.for.self +2s/AOR PERF/PV alone/PV

pemenetiso +yane IC+ oči ki·hki·hkim +ena·ni
take.care.of.self +2s/SUBJ xx+ from.{smth}/PV order.against.will +1s-2s/PPL(obl)

wi·h= ašiht +o·yani ke·ko·h +i
FUT+ make +2s-O/AOR thing +INsg
The reason I insist that you make things is so you'll have the confidence to make them for yourself after you're taking care of yourself on your own.

E a·kwi=ke·h ketema·kihena·nini| e·h=kaka·to·nena·ni‿ke·ko·h‿wi·h=nahihto·yani.
a·kwi =ke·hi ketema·kih +ena·nini e·h= kaka·to·N +ena·ni
not =moreover ill-treat +1s-2s/NEG AOR+ urge +1s-2s/AOR

ke·ko·h +i wi·h= nahiht +o·yani
something +INsg FUT+ know.how.to.make +2s-O/AOR
And I'm not being cruel to you when I push you to learn to make something.

25

A kwaye·ši ki·ši‿ča·ki‿nahihto·yane‿ke·ko·hi po·ni‿ne·wiyane,|
kwaye·ši ki·ši ča·ki nahiht +o·yane ke·ko·h +i
that.way PERF/PV all/PV know.how.to.make +2s-O/SUBJ thing +INsg

po·ni ne·w +iyane
cease/PV see +2s-1s/SUBJ
That way, if you already know how to make everything when you cease to see me,

B a·kwi‿ke·ko·h‿wi·h=iši-sanakihto·yanini.
a·kwi ke·ko·h +i wi·h= iši sanakiht +o·yanini
not something +INsg FUT+ {so}/PV have.hard.time +2s(-O)/NEG
you won't have a hard time with anything.

C ki·h=ašihto wi·h=ota·hwi·hemiyani.
ke+ wi·h= ašiht +o IC+ wi·h= ota·hwi·hemi +yani
2+ FUT+ make +2s-O/IND xx+ FUT+ have.O2.as.possession +2s/PPL(INsg)
You'll make your own things.

D ni·na·'yo·'ni e·to·tawiči_pe·menita nesekwisa,
ni·na =iyo i·ni e·h= to·taw +iči
1s/EMPH =for that/INsg AOR+ treat.{so} +3s-1s/AOR

IC+ pemen +ita ne+ -sekwis +a
xx+ take.care.of +3-1s/PPL(ANsg) 1+ cross-aunt +ANsg
Like me, that was how I was treated by my aunt[P] *who took care of me,*

E we·či_nahihto·ya·ni ke·ko·he·hi.
IC+ oči nahiht +o·ya·ni ke·ko·he·h +i
xx+ from.{smth}/PV know.how.to.make +1s-0/PPL(obl) something/DIM +INsg
which is why I know how to make any little thing.

26
A 'neketema·kihekw=a·peh,' netešite·he,
ne+ ketema·kih +ekwa =a·pehe ne+ išite·he· +Ø
1+ ill-treat +3s-1s/IND =usually 1+ think.{so} +1s/IND
I always thought she[P] *was being cruel to me,*

B e·h=anohka·šiči| ke·ko·h_ahpene·či.|
e·h= anohka·N +iči ke·ko·h +i ahpene·či
AOR+ give.task.to +3s-1s/AOR thing +INsg every.time
giving me things to do all the time.

C keye·hapa=ke·h=wi·na me·nwi_to·tawitehe.
keye·hapa =ke·hi =wi·na IC+ menwi to·taw +itehe
it.turned.out =moreover =but xx+ well/PV treat.{so} +3s-1s/CH.PRET
I later realized, though, that she[P] *was being good to me.*

D ki·ši|-kehke·netama·ni=ča·h=ni·na,
IC+ ki·ši kehke·net +ama·ni =ča·hi ni·na
xx+ PERF/PV know +1s(-0)/CC =so 1s/EMPH
And after I understood

E 'we·nah=menwi_to·tawikwe·ni,' netešite·h=a·pehe.
we·nahi menwi to·taw +ikwe·ni ne+ išite·he· +Ø =a·pehe
I.see.now well/PV treat.{so} +3s-1s/INT 1+ think.{so} +1s/IND =usually
I would think, 'Well, I can see now that actually she[P] *was being good me.'*

F o·ni·'noki=ki·na i·ni_we·či|- i·ni=meko_-to·to·na·ni.
o·ni i·noki ki·na
and,then now 2s/EMPH

i·ni IC+ oči i·ni =meko to·taw +ena·ni
that/INsg xx+ from.{smth}/PV that/INsg =EMPH treat.{so} +1s-2s/PPL(obl)
And that's why I treat you that same way now.

G i·ni=ke·h=ye·toke=ne·h=ki·na e·ne·nemiyani.
i·ni =ke·hi =ye·toke ne·hi ki·na IC+ ine·nem +iyani
that/INsg =moreover =it.seems too 2s/EMPH xx+ think.about.{so} +2s-1s/PPL(obl)
What's more, that's quite likely what you think of me, too.

H 'neketema·kihekwa,' ketešite·he·petoke.
ne+ ketema·kih +ekwa ke+ išite·he· +petoke
1+ ill-treat +3s-1s/IND 2+ think.{so} +2s/DUB
You probably think I'm being cruel to you.

27

A e·h=tepa·nena·ni=kohi we·či- wi·h=nahi·hka·noyani -ine·nemena·ni.
e·h= tepa·N +ena·ni =kohi IC+ oči
AOR+ love +1s-2s/AOR =certainly xx+ from.{smth}/PV

wi·h= nahi·hka·no +yani ine·nem +ena·ni
FUT+ know.how.to.do.things +2s/AOR think.about.{so} +1s-2s/PPL(obl)
I promise you, though, that it's because I love you that I want you to know how to do things.

B o=pwa·wi‿=ke·h -tepa·nena·neh, awita‿nahi‿ki·w‿anohka·nenaka·h,
o pwa·wi =ke·hi tepa·N +ena·nehe awita nahi ki·wi
or NEG/PV =moreover love +1s-2s/SUBJ.PRET not/POT given.to/PV around/PV

anohka·N +enaka·ha
give.task.to +1s-2s/POT
If I didn't love you, I would never ask you to go around doing things,

C 'wi·h=to·tawaki!?' ine·nemena·neh.
IC+ wi·h= to·taw +aki !? ine·nem +ena·nehe
xx+ FUT+ treat.{so} +1s-3/PPL(obl) EN think.about.{so} +1s-2s/SUBJ.PRET
if I thought, 'What do I care about her(P)?'

D nepwa·hka·yane=ča·h ki·šikiyane,
nepwa·hka· +yane =ča·hi ki·šiki +yane
be.smart +2s/SUBJ =so grow.up +2s/SUBJ
So, if you have good sense when you grow up,

E peteki iši-mehkwe·netamane e·to·to·na·ni,
peteki iši mehkwe·net +amane IC+ to·taw +ena·ni
back {so}/PV remember +2s-0/SUBJ xx+ treat.{so} +1s-2s/PPL(obl)
and you think back about how I treated you,

F 'we·nah=menwi‿to·tawikwe·ni nekya,' ki·h=išite·he.
we·nahi menwi to·taw +ikwe·ni ne+ -ky +a
I.see.now well/PV treat.{so} +3s-1s/INT 1+ mother +ANsg

ke+ wi·h= išite·he· +Ø
2+ FUT+ think.{so} +2s/IND
you'll think, 'Well, I can see now that actually my mother(P) was being good me.'

28

A o=wa·waneška·hiyane=ke·h,
o wa·waneška·hi +yane =ke·hi
or be.bad +2s/SUBJ =moreover
But if you turn bad,

B a·kwi| wi·h=nahi‿mehkwe·nemiyanini ki·ši|-ašenoya·ne.
a·kwi wi·h= nahi mehkwe·nem +iyanini ki·ši ašeno +ya·ne
not FUT+ given.to/PV remember +2s-1s/NEG PERF/PV be.absent +1s/SUBJ
you'll never remember me after I'm gone.

C na·hka=mani:
na·hka mani
also,again this/INsg
And here's another thing:

D e·h=nahihto·yani ke·ko·h‿a·kwi wi·h=ašihto·yanini.
e·h= nahiht +o·yani ke·ko·h +i a·kwi wi·h= ašiht +o·yanini
AOR+ know.how.to.make +2s-0/AOR thing +INsg not FUT+ make +2s-0/NEG
While knowing how to make things, you won't make them.

E i·ni‿wi·h=išawiyani wa·waneška·hiyane.
i·ni IC+ wi·h= išawi +yani wa·waneška·hi +yane
that/INsg xx+ FUT+ do.{so} +2s/PPL(obl) be.bad +2s/SUBJ
That's how you'll be if you're badly behaved.

F a·kwi=ke·hi·=’ni iši‿natawe·nemena·nini wi·h=išawiyani.
a·kwi =ke·hi i·ni iši natawe·nem +ena·nini wi·h= išawi +yani
not =moreover that/INsg {so}/PV seek +1s-2s/NEG FUT+ do.{so} +2s/AOR
And, frankly, I don't want you to be that way.

G mahkwa·či=meko wi·h=anemi|-pemenetisoyani ketene·nemene,"
mahkwa·či =meko wi·h= anemi pemenetiso +yani
quietly,calmly =EMPH FUT+ go.on/PV take.care.of.self +2s/AOR

ke+ ine·nem +ene
2+ think.about.{so} +1s-2s/IND
I want you to just go on taking care of yourself quietly."

29

A netekwa nekya.
ne+ iN +ekwa ne+ -ky +a
1+ say.{so}.to +3s-1s/IND 1+ mother +ANsg
So my mother[P] told me.

* * *

B o·ni=na·hka meta·swi‿ni·šwi e·h=taswipepo·nwe·ya·ni,
o·ni na·hka meta·swi ni·šwi e·h= taswipepo·nwe· +ya·ni
and,then also,again ten two AOR+ be.{so.many}.years.old +1s/AOR
And then again when I was twelve years old,

C "nahi´, ma·hani kočihto·no," neteko·pi,
nahi´ ma·hani kočiht +o·no ne+ iN +eko·pi
Well! this/INpl try.to.make +2s-0/IMP 1+ say.{so}.to +X-1s/IND
I was told, "Alright now, try and make these,"

D nemahkese·hani.
ne+ mahkese·h +ani
1+ moccasin +INpl
referring to my moccasins.

E "ki·h=natawi‿we·pi-ašihta·tiso| ki·ši‿nahihto·yane.‿
ke+ wi·h= natawi we·pi ašihta·tiso +Ø
2+ FUT+ seek/PV begin/PV make.02.for.self +2s/IND
ki·ši nahiht +o·yane
PERF/PV know.how.to.make +2s-0/SUBJ
"You must try to start making them for yourself after you know how to make them.

F keki·ši‿=koči‿-kehke·neta keni·ča·paki e·šihišihtawači.‿
ke+ ki·ši =koči kehke·net +a
2+ PERF/PV =you.know know +2s-0/IND
ke+ ni·ča·p +aki IC+ CVCV+ išihtaw +ači
2+ doll +ANpl xx+ RED2+ make.02.{so}.for +2s-3/PPL(obl)
After all, you already know about how to make them for your dolls[P].

G i·ni=koči wi·h=išihto·yani," neteko·pi.
i·ni =koči IC+ wi·h= išiht +o·yani ne+ iN +eko·pi
that/INsg =you.know xx+ FUT+ make.{so} +2s-0/PPL(obl) 1+ say.{so}.to +X-1s/IND
So that's the way you must make them," I was told.

30

A še·ški·=’ni e·h=anešamawiki.
še·ški i·ni e·h= anešamaw +iki
only then AOR+ cut.02.to.shape.for +X-1s/AOR
Then they were cut out for me, but nothing more.

B pe·hčihto·ya·nini=na·hka e·h=peneškenamawiki,
IC+ pehčiht +o·ya·nini na·hka e·h= peneškenamaw +iki
xx+ make.mistakenly +1s-0/ITER also,again AOR+ undo.02.for +X-1s/AOR
Also, whenever I made a mistake it was ripped out for me,

C “mani=kohi‿wi·h=išihto·yani,”| e·h=išiki.‿
mani =kohi IC+ wi·h= išiht +o·yani e·h= iN +iki
this/INsg =certainly xx+ FUT+ make.{so} +2s-0/PPL(obl) AOR+ say.{so}.to +X-1s/AOR
and I was told, “This is how you have to make it.”

D ke·keya·h=meko‿ke·htena| nenahihto.
ke·keya·hi =meko ke·htena ne+ nahiht +o
eventually =EMPH truly 1+ know.how.to.make +1s-0/IND
Eventually I really did learn how to make them.

E o·ni=na·hka meškwa·swa·wa če·keši·he·hita| e·h=ana·hkwa·tamawiki.
o·ni na·hka meškwa·swa·w +a IC+ čakeši·he·hi +ta
and,then also,again yarn-belt +ANsg xx+ be.small/DIM +3/PPL(ANsg)
e·h= ana·hkwa·tamaw +iki
AOR+ string.yarn.for.O2.through.heddle.for +X-1s/AOR
And then also the yarn for a small yarn-belt[P] was set up on a heddle for me.

F anehki·hi·=’ni| e·h=kehkihtawiki,
anehki·hi i·ni e·h= kehkihtaw +iki
little,few then AOR+ start.O2.as.demonstration.for +X-1s/AOR
Then a little of it was started to show me,

G “nahi′,‿mana‿koči-ašihi,” e·h=išiki.
nahi′ mana koči aših +i e·h= iN +iki
Well! this/ANsg try.to/PV make +2s-3/IMP AOR+ say.{so}.to +X-1s/AOR
and I was told, “Alright now, try and make this[P].”

H e·h=we·pi‿kočihaki.
e·h= we·pi kočih +aki
AOR+ begin/PV try.to.make +1s-3/AOR
And I began to try to make it[P].

31
A ke·htena=meko ke·keya·h| nenahiha·wa.
ke·htena =meko ke·keya·hi ne+ nahih +a·wa
truly =EMPH eventually 1+ know.how.to.make +1s-3s/IND
I really did learn how to make it[P] eventually.

B o·ni| e·h=ašihašihaki meškwa·swa·waki.
o·ni e·h= CVCV+ aših +aki meškwa·swa·w +aki
and,then AOR+ RED2+ make +1s-3/AOR yarn-belt +ANpl
And then I would make yarn-belts[P].

C te·pesiwa=meko nekya ke·ko·h_ki·ši_nahihto·ya·nini.

```
te·pesi      +wa      =meko ne+ -ky     +a    ke·ko·h   +i
be.grateful +3s/IND =EMPH 1+   mother +ANsg something +INsg

IC+ ki·ši   nahiht           +o·ya·nini
xx+ PERF/PV know.how.to.make +1s-0/ITER
```

My mother[P] was very appreciative whenever I had learned how to make something.

D i·nina·h=ke·h=meko·='ni_pe·hki e·h=nahese·hkwe·ya·ni._

```
i·nina·hi    =ke·hi     =meko i·ni pe·hki e·h= nahese·hkwe·     +ya·ni
at.that.time =moreover =EMPH then really AOR+ know.how.to.cook +1s/AOR
```

And by that time I was a really competent cook.

E nekotah_e·ya·čini nekya,

```
nekotahi  IC+ iha·       +čini    ne+ -ky     +a
somewhere xx+ go.{smwh} +3s/ITER 1+   mother +ANsg
```

Whenever my mother[P] went anywhere,

F "ki·h=wača·ho," e·h=išiči.

```
ke+ wi·h= wača·ho +Ø      e·h= iN           +iči
2+  FUT+  cook    +2s/IND AOR+ say.{so}.to +3s-1s/AOR
```

she said to me, "You cook."

G na·hka ana·hkanani e·h=ašihto·či,

```
na·hka     ana·hkan  +ani  e·h= ašiht +o·či
also,again fiber.mat +INpl AOR+ make  +3s-0/AOR
```

And also when she made fiber mats,

H ni·n=a·pehe| e·h=wača·hoya·ni.|

```
ni·na   =a·pehe  e·h= wača·ho +ya·ni
1s/EMPH =usually AOR+ cook    +1s/AOR
```

I̲ would do the cooking.

I "ki·h=nakači_wača·ho.

```
ke+ wi·h= nakači          wača·ho +Ø
2+  FUT+  be.used.to/PV cook    +2s/IND
```

"You must get used to cooking.

32

A i·ni=ma·h_e·h=katawi_pye·čisa·ki sa·kiči_wi·h=awiyani.|

```
i·ni =ma·hi   e·h= katawi    pye·čisa·  +ki     sa·kiči wi·h= awi        +yani
then =you.see AOR+ almost/PV time.comes +0/AOR outside FUT+  be.{smwh} +2s/AOR
```

You see, the time is now almost here when you'll have a period.

B ki·h=wača·hetiso=ma·hi‿sa·kič=awiyane,"| neteko·p=a·pehe.‿
ke+ wi·h= wača·hetiso +Ø =ma·hi sa·kiči awi +yane
2+ FUT+ cook.for.self +2s/IND =you.see outside be.{smwh} +2s/SUBJ

ne+ iN +eko·pi =a·pehe
1+ say.{so}.to +X-1s/IND =usually
See, you must cook for yourself when you have a period," I would be told.

C kapo·twe·=’ni‿“nahi´‿we·pi|-kočipani·no.
kapo·twe i·ni nahi´ we·pi kočipani· +no
at.some.point then Well! begin/PV try.mat.weaving +2s/IMP
Some time after that I was told, "Alright, start trying some mat-weaving.

D ki·h=natawi‿nahihto=na·hka‿ma·hani ana·hkanani," e·h=iširki.
ke+ wi·h= natawi nahiht +o na·hka
2+ FUT+ seek/PV know.how.to.make +2s-0/IND also,again

ma·hani ana·hkan +ani e·h= iN +iki
this/INpl fiber.mat +INpl AOR+ say.{so}.to +X-1s/AOR
It's time for you to begin learning how to make these fiber mats also."

E e·h=we·pi‿kočipani·ya·ni.
e·h= we·pi kočipani· +ya·ni
AOR+ begin/PV try.mat.weaving +1s/AOR
I started trying to weave mats.

F ke·keya·h=meko pe·hki·=’ni e·h=nahipani·ya·ni.
ke·keya·hi =meko pe·hki i·ni e·h= nahipani· +ya·ni
eventually =EMPH really then AOR+ know.how.to.do.mat.weaving +1s/AOR
And in time, then, I knew how to weave them correctly.

G e·h=we·pi-asehasemihaki nekya. ‖
e·h= we·pi CVCV+ asemih +aki ne+ -ky +a
AOR+ begin/PV RED2+ help +1s-3/AOR 1+ mother +ANsg
And I started helping my mother(P) *regularly.*

33
A mi·ša·te·nemowa| e·h=anemi‿=meko‿-nahihto·ya·ni ke·ko·hi.
mi·ša·te·nemo +wa
be.pleased +3s/IND

e·h= anemi =meko nahiht +o·ya·ni ke·ko·h +i
AOR+ go.on/PV =EMPH know.how.to.make +1s-0/AOR thing +INsg
She(P) *was proud as I kept learning to make things.*

* * *

B o·ni=na·hka meta·swi-neswi e·h=taswipepo·nwe·ya·ni,
o·ni na·hka meta·swi neswi e·h= taswipepo·nwe· +ya·ni
and,then also,again ten three AOR+ be.{so.many}.years.old +1s/AOR
And then again when I was thirteen years old,

C "nahi′‿na·katawe·netisono.|
nahi′ na·katawe·netiso +no
Well! follow.self.mentally +2s/IMP
"Now, watch yourself.

D i·ni=yá·pi e·h=katawi-aškihkwe·wiyani.‿
i·ni =ya·pi ′ e·h= katawi aškihkwe·wi +yani
then =here.I,we.go EMPH AOR+ almost/PV have.first.period +2s/AOR
Here, it's almost time for you to have your first period.

E ka·ta‿wani·hke·hkani| mani| e·na·čimohena·ni.
ka·ta wani·hke· +hkani mani IC+ ina·čimoh +ena·ni
don't forget.O2 +2s/PROH this/INsg xx+ inform.{so} +1s-2s/PPL(obl)
Don't forget these instructions that I'm giving you.

F nešiwana·čihiye·kani‿ketawe·ma·waki pwa·wi‿wi·ke·siyane.
nešiwana·čih +iye·kani ke+ -tawe·ma·w +aki pwa·wi wi·ke·si +yane
ruin +2s-3/PROH 2+ woman's.brother +ANpl NEG/PV be.careful +2s/SUBJ
You might ruin things for your brothers(P) if you aren't careful.

G mya·netwi=ma·hi·=’ni aškihkwe·wiweni.
mya·net +wi =ma·hi i·ni aškihkwe·wiwen +i
be.bad +0s/IND =you.see that/INsg menarche +INsg
See, having a first period is an evil condition.

34

A maneto·waki neškinamo·ki·=’ni.
maneto·w +aki neškin +amo·ki i·ni
spirit +ANpl hate +3p-0/IND that/INsg
The manitous(P) hate that.

B owiye·ha e·h=ketemina·koči maneto·wani, e·škihkwe·winičini| e·h=wi·hpoma·či,
owiye·h +a e·h= keteminaw +ekoči maneto·w +ani
someone +ANsg AOR+ bless +3′-3s/AOR spirit +OBVsg

IC+ aškihkwe·wi +ničini e·h= wi·hpom +a·či
xx+ have.first.period +3′/PPL(OBVsg) AOR+ eat.with +3s-3′/AOR
When someone(P) is blessed by a manitou(O) and eats with someone(O) having her first period,

C i·n=e·h=neškina·koči ke·temina·kočini,
i·ni e·h= neškinaw +ekoči IC+ keteminaw +ekočini
then AOR+ hate +3′-3s/AOR xx+ bless +3′-3s/PPL(OBVsg)
then the one(O) who blessed him(P) takes a dislike to him(P)

D e·h=po·ni‿nenehke·nemekoči.
e·h= po·ni nenehke·nem +ekoči
AOR+ cease/PV think.about +3′-3s/AOR
and stops thinking of him[P].

E i·ni=ča·h, 'wi·ke·sino´,' we·či-iti·ki,
i·ni =ča·hi wi·ke·si +no ´
that/INsg =so be.careful +2s/IMP INTERJ

IC+ oči iti· +eki
xx+ from.{smth}/PV say.{so}.to.each.other +X/PPL(obl)
So that's why we're told to be careful,

F we·či‿pako·ši‿=meko -wi·tama·ti·ki. ‖
IC+ oči pako·ši =meko wi·tama·ti· +eki
xx+ from.{smth}/PV ahead.of.time =EMPH tell.each.other +X/PPL(obl)
and why we're told well ahead of time.

35
A ki·na=’yo na·hina·h| aškihkwe·wiyane,
ki·na =iyo na·hina·hi aškihkwe·wi +yane
2s/EMPH =for time,distance have.first.period +2s/SUBJ
Like you, at the time when you first have your period,

B e·h=taši‿=meko -aškihkwe·wiwane·ni i·ni=meko wi·h=kahkisoyani.
e·h= taši =meko aškihkwe·wi +wane·ni
AOR+ {smwh}/PV =EMPH have.first.period +2s/INT.PPL(loc.obl)

i·ni =meko IC+ wi·h= kahkiso +yani
that/INsg =EMPH xx+ FUT+ hide +2s/PPL(loc.obl)
you must hide yourself at once, right wherever you are when you have it.

C ka·ta=ke·h‿wi·kiya·peki pya·hkani.
ka·ta =ke·hi wi·kiya·p +eki pya· +hkani
don't =moreover house +LOC come.{smwh} +2s/PROH
And specifically don't come to the main house.

D i·ni wi·h=išawiyani," netekwa nekya.
i·ni IC+ wi·h= išawi +yani ne+ iN +ekwa
that/INsg xx+ FUT+ do.{so} +2s/PPL(obl) 1+ say.{so}.to +3s-1s/IND

ne+ -ky +a
1+ mother +ANsg
That's what you must do," my mother[P] *told me.*

E nese·kimekwa.
ne+ se·kim +ekwa
1+ frighten.by.speech +3s-1s/IND
She[P] *frightened me with what she told me.*

F ke·htena=či·h=meko meta·swi-neswi a·pehtawi e·h=taswipepo·nwe·ya·ni.
ke·htena =či·hi =meko meta·swi neswi a·pehtawi
truly =it.was.discovered =EMPH ten three half

e·h= taswipepo·nwe· +ya·ni
AOR+ be.{so.many}.years.old +1s/AOR
And when I was thirteen and a half it suddenly really did happen to me.

G "mese·hani na·to·tano,"| neteko·pi.
mese·h +ani na·to·t +ano ne+ iN +eko·pi
piece.of.firewood +INpl go.to.carry.on.back +2s-O/IMP 1+ say.{so}.to +X-1s/IND
I was told, "Go get a back-load of firewood."

H ke·tawi͜na·wahkwe·ki e·h=na·kwa·ya·ni.
IC+ katawi na·wahkwe· +ki e·h= na·kwa· +ya·ni
xx+ almost/PV be.noon +0/CC AOR+ leave +1s/AOR
When it was almost noon[(p)] *I started out.*

36

A i·ya·h=nekotah͜e·nemehka·ya·ni
i·ya·hi nekotahi IC+ anemehka· +ya·ni
yonder somewhere xx+ walk.on +1s/CC
As I was walking along off someplace,

B ke·ko·h=meko͜neteši͜pehki·na·ko·tiso,
ke·ko·h +i =meko ne+ iši pehki·na·ko·tiso +Ø
something +INsg =EMPH 1+ {so}/PV feel.a.difference.in.self +1s/IND
I felt something different about myself,

C e·h=sa·kiči·ya·ni.
e·h= sa·kiči· +ya·ni
AOR+ go.out,to.toilet +1s/AOR
and I urinated.

D ki·ši͜sa·kiči·ya·ni,͜e·h=wa·patama·ni e·h=taši͜sa·kiči·ya·ni.
IC+ ki·ši ṣa·kiči· +ya·ni e·h= wa·pat +ama·ni
xx+ PERF/PV go.out,to.toilet +1s/CC AOR+ look.at +1s-0/AOR

e·h= taši sa·kiči· +ya·ni
AOR+ {smwh}/PV go.out,to.toilet +1s/PPL(loc.obl)
And after urinating, I looked at the place where I had urinated.

E kaši´͜meškowiwi=či·h.
kaši´ meškowi +wi =či·hi
Why! be.bloody +0s/IND =it.was.discovered
Why, here I saw that it[(p)] *was bloody.*

F neki·ša·koči|-se·kesi.
ne+ ki·ša·koči se·kesi +Ø
1+ extremely/PV be.frightened +1s/IND
I was terribly frightened.

G ača·hmeko=’yo=ke·hi·=’ni i·n=e·h=išawiya·ni.
ača·hmeko =iyo =ke·hi i·ni i·ni e·h= išawi +ya·ni
only.then =for =moreover then that/INsg AOR+ do.{so} +1s/AOR
Remember, that was the first time this had happened to me.

H a·kwi=meko‿kehke·netama·nini e·šiwe·pawiwa·ne·ni.‿
a·kwi =meko kehke·net +ama·nini IC+ išiwe·pawi +wa·ne·ni
not =EMPH know +1s-0/NEG xx+ be,act.somehow.signifying.{so} +1s/INT.PPL(obl)
I didn’t comprehend what the thing I was experiencing was all about.

37
A “mani=ye·toke·=’ni e·wotamawiki e·h=a·čimohiki,” netešite·he.
mani =ye·toke i·ni IC+ awotamaw +iki
this/INsg =it.seems that/INsg xx+ refer.to.02.for +X-1s/PPL(INsg)

e·h= a·čimoh +iki ne+ išite·he· +Ø
AOR+ inform +X-1s/AOR 1+ think.{so} +1s/IND
I thought, “This is probably what was being referred to when I was instructed.”

B i·nah=meko·=’ni na·wi‿pi·kwa·we e·h=mawi‿šekišekišina·ni.
i·nahi =meko i·ni na·wi pi·kwa·we e·h= mawi CVCV+ šekišin +a·ni
there =EMPH then in.middle/PP thicket/ECM AOR+ go.and/PV RED2+ lie.down +1s/AOR
Then I went to lie down right there in the middle of the thicket.

C netahitanwe·kesi e·h=se·kesiya·ni.
ne+ CVCV+ tanwe·kesi +Ø e·h= se·kesi +ya·ni
1+ RED2+ be.crying +1s/IND AOR+ be.frightened +1s/AOR
I was crying because I was frightened.

D kwi·yena=ke·hi·=’nina·h| katawi‿ni·penwi,|
kwi·yena =ke·hi i·nina·hi katawi ni·pen +wi
exactly =moreover at.that.time almost/PV be.harvest.time +0s/IND
Now, right then it[(p)] *was almost harvest time for the garden crops,*

E ki·ši‿ča·ki‿nekwačihike·ya·ke.‿
IC+ ki·ši ča·ki nekwačihike· +ya·ke
xx+ PERF/PV all/PV hill.corn +1p/CC
after we had done all our hilling.

F aškači·meki·h kapo·twe=ye·toke e·h=aškačipwi·hiteh nekya,
aškači·meki·hi kapo·twe =ye·toke e·h= aškačipwi·h +itehe
later/DIM at.some.point =it.seems AOR+ tire.of.waiting.for +3s-1s/AOR.PRET

ne+ -ky +a
1+ mother +ANsg
After quite a while at some point my mother[(P)] apparently got tired of waiting for me,

G e·h=pye·či‿‖natone·hwitehe.
e·h= pye·či natone·hw +itehe
AOR+ coming/PV look.for +3s-1s/AOR.PRET
and she[(P)] came looking for me.

38
A kapo·twe·=’ni e·h=mehkawiči.
kapo·twe i·ni e·h= mehkaw +iči
at.some.point then AOR+ find +3s-1s/AOR
And soon she[(P)] found me.

B ni·na=ke·hi·=’ni‿pe·hki e·h=kehči‿mayo·ya·ni.‿
ni·na =ke·hi i·ni pe·hki e·h= kehči mayo· +ya·ni
1s/EMPH =moreover then really AOR+ greatly/PV cry +1s/AOR
That’s when I really cried hard.

C “nahi′, po·nwe·kesino.
nahi′ po·nwe·kesi +no
Well! stop.crying +2s/IMP
“Now, now! Stop crying.

D iše=ma·hi·=’n=e·šawiki e·h=ihkwe·wiki.‿
iše =ma·hi i·ni IC+ išawi +eki e·h= ihkwe·wi +eki
just =you.see that/INsg xx+ do.{so} +X/PPL(obl) AOR+ be.woman +X/AOR
You see, that’s just what happens to us in being women.

E iše išikiheti·pi i·ni‿wi·h=išawiki.
iše išikiheti· +pi i·ni wi·h= išawi +eki
just to.be.{so}].cause.each.other +X/IND that/INsg FUT+ do.{so} +X/AOR
For that to happen to us is just the way we’re made.

F a·kwi=ke·h‿ke·ko·h wi·h=išawiyanini.
a·kwi =ke·hi ke·ko·h +i wi·h= išawi +yanini
not =moreover something +INsg FUT+ do.{so} +2s/NEG
But actually nothing serious will happen to you.

G i·ni=ma·h=mani wi·h=ki·ši‿kwayahkwe·netamani e·h=naha·wiki i·n=e·h=išawiyani.
```
i·ni =ma·hi    =mani             wi·h= ki·ši     kwayahkwe·net +amani
then =you.see =as.it.is.now FUT+  PERF/PV get.over       +2s-0/AOR

e·h= naha·win +ki     i·ni       e·h= išawi    +yani
AOR+ be.warm  +0/AOR that/INsg AOR+ do.{so} +2s/AOR
```
You see, now you're going to be through with being that way in warm weather[p].

H pepo·kehe=mata, sanakihto·hkapa.
```
pepo·      +kehe            =mata            sanakiht        +o·hkapa
be.winter +0/SUBJ.PRET =alternatively have.hard.time +2s(-0)/POT
```
If it[p] had been winter instead, you would have had a hard time.

39

A nepačihkapa anenwi·yanehe.
```
nepači   +hkapa  anenwi·     +yanehe
be.cold +2s/POT swim,bathe +2s/SUBJ.PRET
```
You would have gotten cold when you swam.

B pe·pye·hči=’yo=ke·h=meko nye·wenwi čapo·kisahohkapa.
```
pe·pye·hči =iyo =ke·hi     =meko nye·wenwi  čapo·kisaho          +hkapa
have.to     =for =moreover =EMPH four.times enter.water.quickly +2s/POT
```
Bear in mind, you would have been required to take four quick dips under the water.

C iše=meko·=’ni| e·šawiki=’pi mani e·h=aški·‿=’ni=‿’šawiki.
```
iše  =meko i·ni        IC+ išawi    +eki          =ipi  mani
just =EMPH that/INsg xx+ do.{so} +X/PPL(obl) =HRSY as.it.is.now

e·h= aški     i·ni       išawi    +eki
AOR+ first/PV that/INsg do.{so} +X/AOR
```
That's just what we're supposed to do the first time what just happened to you happens to us.

D i·noki=wi·na mani e·h=naha·wiki,
```
i·noki =wi·na mani            e·h= naha·win +ki
now    =but   as.it.is.now AOR+ be.warm  +0/AOR
```
But as it is, since it[p]'s warm weather now,

E meše=meko opye·ni ki·h=anenwi na·hina·h| e·nenwi·wane·ni," neteko·pi.
```
meše   =meko opye·ni ke+ wi·h= anenwi·     +Ø
freely =EMPH slowly  2+  FUT+  swim,bathe +2s/IND

na·hina·hi     IC+ anenwi·     +wane·ni    ne+ iN            +eko·pi
time,distance xx+ swim,bathe +2s/CH.INT 1+  say.{so}.to +X-1s/IND
```
you'll be able to take your time swimming, if you want, at the time you bathe," I was told.

F "matamatakwišineno=meko.
```
CVCV+ matakwišin      +no      =meko
RED2+ lie.covered.up +2s/IMP =EMPH
```
"Keep lying there all covered up.

G ka·ta‖ natawa·pihkani.|
```
ka·ta natawa·pi   +hkani
don't try.to.see +2s/PROH
```
Don't look around.

40

A ki·h=mawi-ašiko·ne," neteko·pi.
```
ke+ wi·h= mawi       ašikaw           +ene        ne+ iN            +eko·pi
2+  FUT+  go.and/PV make.house.for +1s-2s/IND 1+  say.{so}.to +X-1s/IND
```
I'll go and make a house for you," I was told.

B pe·hki=meko ni·na·=ʼni e·h=taši‿kotakesoya·ni,
```
pe·hki =meko ni·na   i·ni e·h= taši                 kotakeso          +ya·ni
really =EMPH 1s/EMPH then AOR+ be.engaged.in/PV suffer.from.heat +1s/AOR
```
Meanwhile, I was suffering a great deal from the heat.

C na·wi|-pi·kwaški=ʼyo=ke·hi,‿
```
na·wi          pi·kwaški       =iyo =ke·hi
in.middle/PP thick.weeds/ECM =for =moreover
```
Remember, it was in the middle of thick weeds,

D na·hka| pe·hki wi·šate·wi.|
```
na·hka      pe·hki wi·šate·        +wi
also,again really be.hot.weather +0s/IND
```
and it[(p)] was also a really hot day.

E e·na·kwi·hiki=meko·=ʼni,
```
IC+ ana·kwi·hi      +ki    =meko i·ni
xx+ be.evening/DIM +0/CC =EMPH then
```
Then early that evening[(p)] I heard,

F "i·ni=yá·pi e·h=na·nena·ni.
```
i·ni =ya·pi            ´     e·h= na·N      +ena·ni
then =here.I,we.go EMPH AOR+ go.after +1s-2s/AOR
```
"Alright now, I'm here to get you.

G e·h=ki·šiko·na·ni wi·h=owi·kiyani.
```
e·h= ki·šikaw                           +ena·ni
AOR+ finish.making.02.as.house.for +1s-2s/AOR

IC+ wi·h= owi·ki        +yani
xx+ FUT+  dwell.{smwh} +2s/PPL(loc.obl)
```
I've made you a place to live in.

H matako·hkwe·hono.
```
matako·hkwe·ho +no
cover.head      +2s/IMP
```
Cover your head with something.

I ka·ta=meko nekotah‿wi·h=iši-natawa·piyani išite·he·hkani,"‖
ka·ta =meko nekotahi wi·h= iši natawa·pi +yani išite·he· +hkani
don't =EMPH somewhere FUT+ {so}/PV try.to.see +2s/AOR think.{so} +2s/PROH
Don't even think of trying to look around anywhere."

41

A neteko·pi.‿
ne+ iN +eko·pi
1+ say.{so}.to +X-1s/IND
So I was told.

B i·ya·hi·=’n=e·h=pye·šiki.
i·ya·hi i·ni e·h= pye·N +iki
yonder then AOR+ bring +X-1s/AOR
Then I was brought over there.

C čaki|-wi·kiya·pe·hi.
čaki wi·kiya·pe·h +i
small/PN house/DIM +INsg
It was a little house.

D kaho·ni=na·hka kepiwani ki·hka=meko‿nekepi·hoko·pi.
kaho·ni na·hka kepiw +ani ki·hka =meko ne+ kepi·hw +eko·pi
so.then also,again piece.of.brushwood +INpl around =EMPH 1+ fence.in +X-1s/IND
And then I was also fenced in with brush all around.

E a·ya·kwači=meko wi·h=iši‿pwa·wi|-tahpa·pata·niki| ina·kwate·wani.|
CV+ a·kwači =meko IC+ wi·h= iši pwa·wi tahpa·pata·ni +ki
RED1+ in.pile =EMPH xx+ FUT+ {so}/PV NEG/PV can.be.seen.through +0/PPL(obl)

ina·kwate· +wani
be.piled.{so} +0p/IND
It[(p)] was piled up in heaps in such a way that it[(p)] couldn't be seen through.

F ke·sipi=meko e·h=owi·ke·hiya·ni tawa·hiwi,
ke·sipi =meko e·h= owi·ke·hi +ya·ni tawa·hi +wi
only.(that,those) =EMPH AOR+ dwell.{smwh}.DIM +1s/PPL(loc.obl) be.space/DIM +0s/IND
There was only just enough room[(p)] for my little house

G wi·h=taši‿wača·hoya·ni sa·kiči·me·hi.
IC+ wi·h= taši wača·ho +ya·ni sa·kiči·me·hi
xx+ FUT+ {smwh}/PV cook +1s/PPL(loc.obl) outside/DIM
and a place for me to cook right outside.

H i·ni=ke·h‿ni·ki še·ški=meko wi·h-inekihkwišina·ke no·hkomesa inekihkwihto·kwe·ni nekya.
i·ni =ke·hi ne+ -i·k +i še·ški =meko
that/INsg =moreover 1+ lodge +INsg only =EMPH

IC+ wi·h= inekihkwišin +a·ke ne+ -o·hkomes +a
xx+ FUT+ lie.over.{such}.area +1p/PPL(obl) 1+ grandmother +ANsg

inekihkwiht +o·kwe·ni ne+ -ky +a
make.{so}.big +3s-0/INT 1+ mother +ANsg
What's more, my mother[P] had made that house of mine only big enough for Grandmother[P] and me to lie down in.

42
A "ko·hkomesa·='ni‿wi·h=na·naki, ayo·h‿wi·h=taši‿wi·čihehki," netekwa nekya.
ke+ -o·hkomes +a i·ni wi·h= na·N +aki ayo·hi
2+ grandmother +ANsg then FUT+ go.after +1s-3/AOR this/LOC

wi·h= taši wi·čih +ehki ne+ iN +ekwa ne+ -ky +a
FUT+ {smwh}/PV live.with +3-2s/AOR 1+ say.{so}.to +3s-1s/IND 1+ mother +ANsg
"Now I'll go get your grandmother[P] to stay here with you," my mother[P] told me.

B kotaka=ma·h=wi·na=meko metemo·he·ha.‿
kotak +a =ma·hi =wi·na =meko metemo·he·h +a
other +ANsg =you.see =but =EMPH old.woman/DIM +ANsg
But, you understand, it was a different old lady[P].

C keye·hapa='yo‿wi·h=taši‿kekye·hkimiči i·na we·či‿pye·neči.
keye·hapa =iyo wi·h= taši kekye·hkim +iči
it.turned.out =for FUT+ be.engaged.in/PV teach +3s-1s/AOR

i·na IC+ oči pye·N +eči
that/ANsg xx+ from.{smth}/PV bring +X-3/PPL(obl)
And as I found out, she[P] was brought over to be teaching me.

D e·h=pwa·wi‿=ni·na·='ni‿-wi·seniya·ni nehkaniki·šekwe.
e·h= pwa·wi ni·na i·ni wi·seni +ya·ni nehkaniki·šekwe
AOR+ NEG/PV 1s/EMPH then eat +1s/AOR all.day.long
Meanwhile, all that day I didn't eat.

E "wa·pake ki·h=na·to·nepena‿wi·h=ayo·yanini wača·hoyane," neteko·pi.
wa·pan +ke ke+ wi·h= na·taw +enepena
be.morning +0/SUBJ 2+ FUT+ go.after.02.for +1p-2/IND

IC+ wi·h= ayo· +yanini wača·ho +yane ne+ iN +eko·pi
xx+ FUT+ use +2s-0/PPL(INpl) cook +2s/SUBJ 1+ say.{so}.to +X-1s/IND
"Tomorrow we'll go get you things to use when you cook," I was told.

F a·kwi wi·ša·pene·ya·nini, e·h=se·kesiya·ni.
a·kwi wi·ša·pene· +ya·nini e·h= se·kesi +ya·ni
not be.hungry +1s/NEG AOR+ be.frightened +1s/AOR
I wasn't hungry, since I was frightened.

43
A wa·paniki·=’ni no·hkomesa e·h=mawi-wi·seniči.
wa·pan +niki i·ni ne+ -o·hkomes +a e·h= mawi wi·seni +či
be.morning +0′/CC then 1+ grandmother +ANsg AOR+ go.and/PV eat +3s/AOR
The next day Grandmother[P] went to eat.

B še·ški=meko e·hpi·hči-mawi·-’seničini, nešihka·=’ni i·nah=e·h=taši-kohta·čiya·ni.
še·ški =meko IC+ ahpi·hči mawi wi·seni +čini
only =EMPH xx+ in.process.of/PV go.and/PV eat +3s/ITER

nešihka i·ni i·nahi e·h= taši kohta·či +ya·ni
alone then that/LOC AOR+ {smwh}/PV be.afraid +1s/AOR
For only as long as she[P] went to eat each time was I alone and frightened there.

C e·na·kwiki=meko·=’ni e·h=pye·tawiki mahkahko·hani,
IC+ ana·kwi +ki =meko i·ni e·h= pye·taw +iki mahkahko·h +ani
xx+ be.evening +0/CC =EMPH then AOR+ bring.O2.to +X-1s/AOR box,pail/DIM +INpl
And then that evening[p] pots were brought to me,

D wi·h=wača·hoya·ni·=’nahi ke·ko·he·hi mi·čiwa·hi,
IC+ wi·h= wača·ho +ya·ni =i·nahi ke·ko·he·h +i mi·čiwa·h +i
xx+ FUT+ cook.O2 +1s/PPL(INsg) =with.that something/DIM +INsg food/DIM +INsg
and some things in the way of food for me to cook,

E nepi=na·hka, mese·hani.
nepy +i na·hka mese·h +ani
water +INsg also,again piece.of.firewood +INpl
and also water and firewood.

F ača·hmeko·=’ni e·h=wača·hoya·ni.
ača·hmeko i·ni e·h= wača·ho +ya·ni
only.then then AOR+ cook +1s/AOR
Only then did I cook a meal.

44
A o·ni=ča·h=a·pehe no·hkomesa e·h=taši-kekye·hkimiči,
o·ni =ča·hi =a·pehe ne+ -o·hkomes +a e·h= taši
and,then =so =usually 1+ grandmother +ANsg AOR+ be.engaged.in/PV

kekye·hkim +iči
teach +3s-1s/AOR
So then Grandmother[P] would be teaching me,

B e·h=a·čimohiči e·ši‿menwiweto·weči owi·ya·ninawi.
e·h= a·čimoh +iči IC+ iši menwiwet +o·weči
AOR+ inform +3s-1s/AOR xx+ {so}/PV lead.well +X-0/REL/PPL(obl)

o+ -i·yaw +inawi
3+ body,self +X(INsg)
instructing me about how a person leads a good life.

C pe·hki=’yo=ke·h=meko‿ke·htena‿metemo·he·hiwa.‿
pe·hki =iyo =ke·hi =meko ke·htena metemo·he·hi +wa
really =for =moreover =EMPH truly be.old.woman/DIM +3s/IND
She[P] *was truly a very old lady, you understand.*

D ke·htena=ča·h=meko‿te·pwe·toke e·nahina·čimohiči.
ke·htena =ča·hi =meko te·pwe· +wetoke IC+ CVCV+ ina·čimoh +iči
truly =so =EMPH speak.the.truth +3s/DUB xx+ RED2+ inform.{so} +3s-1s/PPL(obl)
And that being the case, she[P] *truly must have been right in her instructions to me.*

E “noši·hi,” netekw=a·peh,
ne+ -o·šisem +Ø ne+ iN +ekwa =a·pehe
1+ grandchild +VOCsg 1+ say.{so}.to +3s-1s/IND =usually
“Grandchild,” she[P] *would say to me,*

F “kapo·twe‿wi·h=a·čimohena·ni e·ši‿pešikwiweto·ki owi·ya·ninawi.
kapo·twe wi·h= a·čimoh +ena·ni
at.some.point FUT+ inform +1s-2s/AOR

IC+ iši pešikwiwet +o·ki o+ -i·yaw +inawi
xx+ {so}/PV lead.straight +X-0/PPL(obl) 3+ body,self +X(INsg)
“Presently I’ll instruct you in how a person leads an upright life.

G i·noki=mani‿kene·wi e·hpi·hči‿kehkya·ya·ni.
i·noki =mani ke+ ne·w +i
now =as.it.is.now 2+ see +2s-1s/IND

IC+ ahpi·hči kehkya· +ya·ni
xx+ to.{such}.degree/PV be.old +1s/PPL(obl)
You see now how <u>*old*</u> *I am.*

45

A e·šimikini=ča·h e·h=išawiya·ni,
IC+ išim +ikini =ča·hi e·h= išawi +ya·ni
xx+ speak.{so}.to +X-1s/PPL(obl.pl) =so AOR+ do.{so} +1s/AOR
Well, it’s because I did the things I was told to do

B e·h=kočawiya·ni=meko e·h=na·katawe·netama·ni wi·h=iši‿pešikwiweto·wa·ne·ni| ni·yawi.‿
e·h= kočawi +ya·ni =meko e·h= na·katawe·net +ama·ni
AOR+ try +1s/AOR =EMPH AOR+ follow.mentally +1s-0/AOR

wi·h= iši pešikwiwet +o·wa·ne·ni ne+ -i·yaw +i
FUT+ {so}/PV lead.straight +1s-0/INT.PPL(obl) 1+ body,self +INsg
and really tried to keep my mind on how I might lead an upright life.

C ke·htena=meko‿nete·pahkoška‿kehkye·weni," netekwa.|
ke·htena =meko ne+ te·pahkošk +a kehkye·wen +i ne+ iN +ekwa
truly =EMPH 1+ attain +1s-0/IND old.age +INsg 1+ say.{so}.to +3s-1s/IND
It has indeed come true that I have attained old age," she(P) said to me.

D "i·ni=ča·h‿a·mi‿'šawiyani‿
i·ni =ča·hi IC+ a·mi išawi +yani
that/INsg =so xx+ POT/PV do.{so} +2s/PPL(obl)
"By the same token, that's the way you can be

E pesetawiyane| e·nahina·čimohena·nini.
pesetaw +iyane IC+ CVCV+ ina·čimoh +ena·nini
listen.to +2s-1s/SUBJ xx+ RED2+ inform.{so} +1s-2s/PPL(obl.pl)
if you listen to the things I instruct you to do.

F mana=wi·na‿kekya, e·ye·h‿no·te·kiči, ne·we·hiya·nin=a·pehe neta·ya·čimoha·wa.
mana =wi·na ke+ -ky +a IC+ aye·hi no·te·ki +či
this/ANsg =but 2+ mother +ANsg xx+ continue.to/PV not.be.old.enough +3s/CC

IC+ ne·w +e·hiya·nini =a·pehe ne+ CV+ a·čimoh +a·wa
xx+ see +1s-3/DIM/ITER =usually 1+ RED1+ inform +1s-3s/IND
In the case of your mother(P) now, before she(P) understood things, every time I merely saw her, I would instruct her(P).

46

A e·h=či·nawe·maki=ke·h‿we·či-a·ya·čimohaki,
e·h= či·nawe·m +aki =ke·hi
AOR+ be.related.to +1s-3/AOR =moreover

IC+ oči CV+ a·čimoh +aki
xx+ from.{smth}/PV RED1+ inform +1s-3/PPL(obl)
It was simply because she(P) was my relative that I instructed her(P),

B koči·h‿osekwisani menwi‿to·ta·kwa| e·h=pemenekoči.
koči·hi o+ -sekwis +ani menwi to·taw +ekwa
although 3+ cross-aunt +OBVsg well/PV treat.{so} +3′-3s/IND

e·h= pemen +ekoči
AOR+ take.care.of +3′-3s/AOR
even though, of course, her aunt(O) treated her(P) well in raising her(P).

C i·ni‿we·či‿nahihto·či ki·na·na e·h=ihkwe·wiyakwe kemi·hkeče·wi·wenena·ni.|
i·ni IC+ oči nahiht +o·či ki·na·na
that/INsg xx+ from.{smth}/PV know.how.to.make +3s–0/PPL(obl) 12/EMPH

e·h= ihkwe·wi +yakwe ke+ mi·hkeče·wi·wen +ena·ni
AOR+ be.woman +12/AOR 2+ work +12(INsg)
That's why she[P] knows how to make the things that are the work of us women.

D kehkinawa·pamate=ča·h e·šihto·čini ke·ko·h‿menwawihkapa‿kekya, noši·hi.
kehkinawa·pam +ate =ča·hi IC+ ašiht +o·čini ke·ko·h +i
watch.to.learn +2s–3/SUBJ =so xx+ make +3s–0/ITER something +INsg

menwawi +hkapa ke+ -ky +a ne+ -o·šisem +Ø
do.well +2s/POT 2+ mother +ANsg 1+ grandchild +VOCsg
So whenever your mother[P] makes anything, you'd do well to watch and learn from her[P], grandchild.

E "na·hka=mani‿ni·na·na e·hpi·hčikiya·ke,
na·hka mani ni·na·na IC+ ahpi·hčiki +ya·ke
also,again this/INsg 1p/EMPH xx+ be.{so}.old +1p/CC
"And also when we reached your age,

F i·ni=ča·h e·h=iši‿‖aškihkwe·wiya·ke,
i·ni =ča·hi e·h= iši aškihkwe·wi +ya·ke
that/INsg =so AOR+ {so}/PV have.first.period +1p/AOR
and so, like you, had our first period,

47

A nemahkate·wi·pena.
ne+ mahkate·wi· +pena
1+ fast +1p/IND
we had to fast.

B mama·nokoni·pi.
Ca+ ma·nokoni· +pi
RED1+ fast.many.days +X/IND
The fasts would go for many days.

C a·neta meta·sokoni·waki,| a·neta nye·wi, nya·nanwi; a·čipanakiči=meko.
a·neta meta·sokoni· +waki a·neta nye·wi nya·nanwi a·čipanakiči =meko
some fast.for.ten.days +3p/IND some four five all.kinds =EMPH
Some fasted for ten days, some for four or five; it varied.

D i·noki=wi·na·=’ni e·h=anemi‿pehki·nikeki.
i·noki =wi·na i·ni e·h= anemi pehki·niken +ki
now =but then AOR+ go.on/PV be.different +0/AOR
But nowadays it[p]'s getting to be different.

E ni·na e·h=aškihkwe·wiya·ni, šwa·šika netasokoni.
```
ni·na    e·h= aškihkwe·wi        +ya·ni  šwa·šika ne+ tasokoni·            +Ø
1s/EMPH AOR+ have.first.period +1s/AOR eight    1+  fast.{so.many}.days +1s/IND
```
When I had my first period, I had to fast for eight days.

F iše=mo·hči=meko neta·hpeči‿ma·mahkate·wi·pena,
```
iše  mo·hči =meko ne+ a·hpeči          CV+   mahkate·wi· +pena
just even   =EMPH 1+ permanently/PV RED1+ fast          +1p/IND
```
It was just taken for granted that we would fast regularly,

G pa·ši=meko e·h=kehči‿ki·šikiya·ke,"‖ netekwa‿no·hkomesa.|
```
pa·ši                =meko e·h= kehči       ki·šiki +ya·ke  ne+ iN           +ekwa
continuing.(until) =EMPH AOR+ greatly/PV grow.up +1p/AOR 1+  say.{so}.to +3s-1s/IND

ne+ -o·hkomes    +a
1+   grandmother +ANsg
```
right up until we were fully grown," Grandmother[(P)] told me.

48

A nekya=ke·h‿še·ški·=’ni e·h=pe·pye·či-nepina·tawiči,
```
ne+ -ky     +a    =ke·hi      še·ški i·ni e·h= CV+   pye·či
1+   mother +ANsg =moreover only   then AOR+ RED1+ coming/PV

nepina·taw          +iči
go.after.water.for +3s-1s/AOR
```
My mother[(P)], on the other hand, would only come to get water for me then,

B mese·hani=na·hka‿wi·h=pehtawe·ya·nini we·ča·hoya·nini.
```
mese·h             +ani  na·hka      IC+ wi·h= pehtawe·   +ya·nini
piece.of.firewood +INpl also,again xx+ FUT+  make.fire +1s/PPL(INpl)

IC+ wača·ho +ya·nini
xx+ cook    +1s/ITER
```
and also wood for me to make a fire with whenever I cooked.

C na·hka‿netanahanahtaki·pena.
```
na·hka      ne+ CVCV+ anahtaki·    +pena
also,again 1+  RED2+ braid.string +1p/IND
```
And [Grandmother] and I also used to braid strings.

D mani e·šawiya·kini,
```
mani       IC+ išawi    +ya·kini
this/INsg xx+ do.{so} +1p/ITER
```
Whenever we did this, she would tell me,

E "ka·ta=ke·h| me·šenakani‿ki·nesani.
```
ka·ta =ke·hi     me·šen +akani      ke+ -i·nes         +ani
don't =moreover touch  +2s-0/PROH 2+   hair.of.head +INpl
```
"And another thing is, don't touch your hair.

F čaꞏkeškaꞏhkiče.
čaꞏkeškaꞏ +hkiče
fall.to.pieces +0/PROH
It might all fall out.

G naꞏhka‿kaꞏta‿wiꞏškopanohikeꞏhkani eꞏyiꞏkiꞏ=ʼni.
naꞏhka kaꞏta wiꞏškopanohikeꞏ +hkani eꞏyiꞏki iꞏni
also,again don't put.sugar.on.things +2s/PROH as.well then
And also don't use sugar in your food either then.

H aꞏhkwihpokwatoꞏhiki eꞏh=miꞏčiki,
IC+ aꞏhkwihpokwatoꞏhi +ki eꞏh= miꞏči +eki
xx+ have.strong.taste/DIM +0/PPL(INsg) AOR+ eat +X-0/AOR
When people eat anything with a strong taste

I owiꞏpičinawani čaꞏkeškeꞏwani, inaꞏčimopi,
o+ -iꞏpit +inawani čaꞏkeškaꞏ +wani inaꞏčimo +pi
3+ teeth +X(INpl) fall.to.pieces +0p/IND narrate.{so} +X/IND
their teeth go all to pieces, so they say,

49

A weꞏči‿kohtameki| wiꞏškopanoꞏhiki=keꞏh| wiꞏh=miꞏčiki,"
IC+ oči koht +ameki
xx+ from.{smth}/PV fear +X-0/PPL(obl)

IC+ wiꞏškopanoꞏhi +ki =keꞏhi wiꞏh= miꞏči +eki
xx+ be.sweet.tasting/DIM +0/PPL(INsg) =moreover FUT+ eat +X-0/AOR
which is why they're afraid to eat anything sweet(p), in particular."

B netekwa noꞏhkomesa.
ne+ iN +ekwa ne+ -oꞏhkomes +a
1+ say.{so}.to +3s-1s/IND 1+ grandmother +ANsg
So Grandmother(P) told me.

C ahpeneꞏči=meko netaꞏyaꞏčimohekwa eꞏši‿menwikeniki.
ahpeneꞏči =meko ne+ CV+ aꞏčimoh +ekwa IC+ iši menwiken +niki
every.time =EMPH 1+ RED1+ inform +3s-1s/IND xx+ {so}/PV be.good +0′/PPL(obl)
She(P) instructed me about what was good(o) all the time.

D "nahiʹ, naꞏhka=mani:
nahiʹ naꞏhka mani
Well! also,again this/INsg
"Well, here's another thing:

E i·ni wi·h=ki·šikiwe·nemehki neniwaki, e·h=ki·ši-aškihkwe·wiyani.
i·ni wi·h= ki·šikiwe·nem +ehki neniw +aki
then FUT+ think.mature +3–2s/AOR man +ANpl

e·h= ki·ši aškihkwe·wi +yani
AOR+ PERF/PV have.first.period +2s/AOR
Men[(P)] will now think that you're grown up, since you've had your first period.

F i·ni=meko wi·h=we·pi̯natawe·nemehki wi·h=mi·hkemehki.
i·ni =meko wi·h= we·pi natawe·nem +ehki wi·h= mi·hkem +ehki
then =EMPH FUT+ begin/PV seek +3–2s/AOR FUT+ court +3–2s/AOR
After this, they'll begin to want to court you.

G pwa·wi̯=ča·h=meko -ki·wi̯me·nešite·he·yane,
pwa·wi =ča·hi =meko ki·wi me·nešite·he· +yane
NEG/PV =so =EMPH around/PV be.bashful +2s/SUBJ
Well, if you don't go around being bashful,

50
A a·kwi ašitahi‿wi·h=mačino·hkini wi·h=mi·hkemehki.‿
a·kwi ašitahi wi·h= mačinaw +ehkini wi·h= mi·hkem +ehki
not for.a.long.time FUT+ dare.with.regard.to +3–2s/NEG FUT+ court +3–2s/AOR
they won't have the nerve to court you for some time to come.

B ni·miheti·kini=ke·h ma·ne·wa·čini kwi·yese·haki,
IC+ ni·miheti· +ekini =ke·hi IC+ ma·ne· +wa·čini kwi·yese·h +aki
xx+ dance.together +X/ITER =moreover xx+ be.much,many +3p/ITER boy +ANpl
And when there are lots of boys[(P)] at dances,

C a·čipanakiči taši̯'ši-e·nihe·nikowe·wa·te,
a·čipanakiči taši iši CVCV+ e·nikowe· +wa·te
all.kinds be.engaged.in/PV {so}/PV RED2+ say.funny.things.to.people +3p/SUBJ
and they[(P)]'re saying all sorts of funny things to people,

D pwa·wi̯=meko -ki·w̯ame·na·kosiyane,
pwa·wi =meko ki·wi ame·na·kosi +yane
NEG/PV =EMPH around/PV show.reaction.on.face +2s/SUBJ
you'll do better never to show any reaction by your expression,

E na·pi=meko| kenwe·ši ki·h=koseta·ko·ki.
na·pi =meko kenwe·ši ke+ wi·h= kosetaw +eko·ki
for.the.better =EMPH long.time 2+ FUT+ fear.to.approach +3p–2s/IND
as they[(P)]'ll be afraid to approach you for a long time.

F e·nihe·nikehtawate=wi·na, a·kwi wi·h=ke·ko·he·nemehkini.
CVCV+ e·nikehtaw +ate =wi·na
RED2+ listen.to.with.laughter +2s-3/SUBJ =but

a·kwi wi·h= ke·ko·he·nem +ehkini
not FUT+ think.something.of +3-2s/NEG
But if you always laugh at what they[(P)] say, they won't respect you.

51
A i·ni=meko wi·h=we·pi·hko·hki.
i·ni =meko wi·h= we·pi·hkaw +ehki
then =EMPH FUT+ begin.dealing.with +3-2s/AOR
They'll make a move on you right away.

B wa·waneška·hiyane,
wa·waneška·hi +yane
be.bad +2s/SUBJ
If you're badly behaved,

C ketawe·ma·waki| wi·h=me·nešite·he·waki, na·hka kešise·haki.
ke+ -tawe·ma·w +aki wi·h= me·nešite·he· +waki
2+ woman's.brother +ANpl FUT+ be.bashful +3p/IND

na·hka ke+ -šise·h +aki
also,again 2+ cross-uncle +ANpl
your brothers[(P)] will be ashamed, and also your mother's brothers[(P)].

D mahkwa·či=ča·h| ki·wita·yane, wi·h=mi·ša·te·nemowaki.
mahkwa·či =ča·hi ki·wita· +yane wi·h= mi·ša·te·nemo +waki
quietly,calmly =so stay.around +2s/SUBJ FUT+ be.pleased +3p/IND
By the same token, if you stay at home quietly, they[(P)]'ll be pleased.

E ki·h=tepa·neko·ki.
ke+ wi·h= tepa·N +eko·ki
2+ FUT+ love +3p-2s/IND
They[(P)]'ll be fond of you.

F še·ški=meko ke·ko·h e·ye·niwe e·h=owi·kiye·kwe_taši-ašihašihto·yane,
še·ški =meko ke·ko·h +i e·ye·niwe e·h= owi·ki +ye·kwe
only =EMPH thing +INsg staying.the.same AOR+ dwell.{smwh} +2p/AOR

taši CVCV+ ašiht +o·yane
{smwh}/PV RED2+ make +2s-0/SUBJ
If all you do is stay at home, where all of you live, making things,

G ki·h=ma·mi·neko·ki_ke·ko·hi we·tehtenamowa·čini.
ke+ wi·h= CV+ mi·N +eko·ki ke·ko·h +i IC+ otehten +amowa·čini
2+ FUT+ RED1+ give.O2.to +3p-2s/IND thing +INsg xx+ get +3p-0/ITER
they[(P)]'ll give you things whenever they get them.

52

A na·hka‿ke·ko·h e·načini, ki·h=te·pwe·hta·ko·ki ketawe·ma·waki.
```
na·hka        ke·ko·h    +i     IC+ iN            +ačini
also,again something +INsg xx+ say.{so}.to +2s-3/ITER

ke+ wi·h= te·pwe·htaw                       +eko·ki    ke+ -tawe·ma·w       +aki
2+  FUT+  believe,agree.to.request.of +3p-2s/IND 2+   woman's.brother +ANpl
```
And whenever you ask your brothers[P] to do anything, they[P]'ll do it for you.

B i·n=e·šawiki mahkwa·či e·h=ki·wita·ki.‿
```
i·ni        IC+ išawi    +eki           mahkwa·či       e·h= ki·wita·    +eki
that/INsg xx+ do.{so} +X/PPL(obl) quietly,calmly AOR+ stay.around +X/AOR
```
That's how it is with a person when she stays at home quietly.

C tepa·šiwe·waki oteneni·minawaki.
```
tepa·šiwe·   +waki    o+ neniw +eminawaki
love.people +3p/IND 3+ man   +X(ANpl)
```
The men[P] in her family are fond of her.

D "o=mani=na·hka:
```
o  mani        na·hka
or this/INsg also,again
```
"And here's another thing:

E owi·či-iškwe·se·hinawaki a·neta wa·waneška·hiwaki.
```
o+ -i·či    iškwe·se·h +inawaki a·neta wa·waneška·hi +waki
3+  fellow girl        +X(ANpl) some   be.bad          +3p/IND
```
Some of the girls[P] in anyone's generation are badly behaved.

F i·niki=ča·h| ka·ki·wi·-'te·mete wa·waneška·haki,
```
i·niki     =ča·hi CV+    ki·wi        wi·te·m    +ete       wa·waneška·h +aki
that/ANpl =so     RED1+ around/PV accompany +X-3/SUBJ bad.one        +ANpl
```
Well, if a someone goes around with those bad ones[P],

G a·šihiwe·wa·sa ‖ e·hpi·hči‿pwa·wi‿pe·hki -ki·ši‿nepwa·hka·ki.
```
a·šihiwe·                     +wa·sa
get.people.into.bad.habits +3p/POT

IC+ ahpi·hči          pwa·wi pe·hki ki·ši    nepwa·hka· +eki
xx+ in.process.of/PV NEG/PV really PERF/PV be.smart    +X/CC
```
they[P] would get her into their bad habits while she has still not yet really developed good sense.

53

A ka·ta=ča·h nahi-ki·wi·-'te·miye·kani wa·waneška·hiwičiki, noši·hi,"
ka·ta =ča·hi nahi ki·wi wi·te·m +iye·kani
don't =so given.to/PV around/PV accompany +2s-3/PROH

IC+ wa·waneška·hiwi +čiki ne+ -o·šisem +Ø
xx+ be.bad +3/PPL(ANpl) 1+ grandchild +VOCsg
So, grandchild, never go around with the bad ones[P]."

B netekwa no·hkomesa.
ne+ iN +ekwa ne+ -o·hkomes +a
1+ say.{so}.to +3s-1s/IND 1+ grandmother +ANsg
So Grandmother[P] told me.

C "na·hka=mani:
na·hka mani
also,again this/INsg
"And here's another thing:

D meše=meko·='nahi ke·hkya·ta ki·h=menwi-to·tawa·wa.
meše=meko·='nahi IC+ kehkya· +ta ke+ wi·h= menwi to·taw +a·wa
any xx+ be.old +3/PPL(ANsg) 2+ FUT+ well/PV treat.{so} +2s-3s/IND
You must be good to any old person[P].

E maneto·wani=koh wa·pamekwa,
maneto·w +ani =kohi wa·pam +ekwa
spirit +OBVsg =certainly look.at +3'-3s/IND
There's no doubt the manitou[O] has regard for them[P],

F we·či-te·pahkwi-kehkya·či, e·h=wi·ke·čiweto·či owi·yawi.
IC+ oči te·pahkwi kehkya· +či
xx+ from.{smth}/PV attain/PV be.old +3s/PPL(obl)

e·h= wi·ke·čiwet +o·či o+ -i·yaw +i
AOR+ lead.carefully +3s-0/AOR 3+ body,self +INsg
which is why they[P] reached old age, leading their lives with care.

G "ka·ta owiye·ha ta·tašimiye·kani.
ka·ta owiye·h +a CV+ tašim +iye·kani
don't someone +ANsg RED1+ talk.about +2s-3/PROH
"Don't talk about anyone[P].

54

A ka·ta pašipašitowe·hkani.
ka·ta CVCV+ pašitowe· +hkani
don't RED2+ tell.lie +2s/PROH
Don't tell lies.

B ka·ta nahi‿kemo·tehkani.
ka·ta nahi   kemo·t +hkani
don't given.to/PV steal +2s/PROH
Don't ever steal.

C nahi‿kemo·teyane, ki·h=ketema·kesi.
nahi   kemo·t +yane   ke+ wi·h= ketema·kesi   +Ø
given.to/PV steal +2s/SUBJ 2+ FUT+ be.miserable,poor +2s/IND
If you're given to stealing, you'll become poor.

D ka·ta.|
ka·ta
don't
Don't do it.

E keta·hwi·hemi tepa·tamane,
ke+ -ta·hwi·hem   +i   tepa·t +amane
2+ thing,possession +INsg love   +2s-0/SUBJ
If you're tight with your possessions,

F ahkwiya·h=meko a·kwi‿ke·ko·h wi·h=nahi-otehtenamanini ke·ko·hi.
ahkwiya·hi   =meko a·kwi ke·ko·h   +i   wi·h= nahi   otehten +amanini
especially,more.so =EMPH not   something +INsg FUT+ given.to/PV get   +2s-0/NEG

ke·ko·h +i
thing   +INsg
it will all the more be the case that you never receive any kinds of things,

G še·še·hkosiyane=ke·h,
še·še·hkosi +yane   =ke·hi
be.generous +2s/SUBJ =moreover
while if you're generous,

H ki·h=nahi-otehtena ke·ko·h.
ke+ wi·h= nahi   otehten +a   ke·ko·h +i
2+ FUT+ given.to/PV get   +2s-0/IND thing   +INsg
you'll always receive things.

I na·hka ka·ta owiye·ha ki·wi-nasata·winohkatawiye·kani.‖
na·hka   ka·ta owiye·h +a   ki·wi   nasata·winohkataw   +iye·kani
also,again don't someone +ANsg around/PV act.unfriendly.toward +2s-3/PROH
And also, don't be aloof and unfriendly toward anyone[(P)]*.*

55

A a·hpene=meko ki·h=ahpi·hči-keša·čiha·wa ke·hčikita.
a·hpene =meko ke+ wi·h= ahpi·hči keša·čih +a·wa
all.alike =EMPH 2+ FUT+ to.{such}.degree/PV be.kind.to +2s-3s/IND

IC+ kehčiki +ta
xx+ be.old +3/PPL(ANsg)
You must be equally kind to every older person[(P)].

B i·ni, noši·hi, e·ši-menwikeki e·h=išawiki,"
i·ni ne+ +o·šisem +Ø IC+ iši menwiken +ki
that/INsg 1+ grandchild +VOCsg xx+ {so}/PV be.good +0/PPL(obl)

e·h= išawi +eki
AOR+ do.{so} +X/AOR
That, grandchild, is the good way[(P)] *to be."*

C netekwa no·hkomesa.
ne+ iN +ekwa ne+ -o·hkomes +a
1+ say.{so}.to +3s-1s/IND 1+ grandmother +ANsg
So Grandmother[(P)] *told me.*

D ahpene·či=meko netahitana·čimohekwa wi·h=išawiya·ni.
ahpene·či =meko ne+ CVCV+ tana·čimoh +ekwa wi·h= išawi +ya·ni
every.time =EMPH 1+ RED2+ be.informing +3s-1s/IND FUT+ do.{so} +1s/AOR
She[(P)] *was always giving me instructions about what I should do.*

E kapo·twe·='ni meta·sokoni i·nah e·h=ki·ši-owi·kiya·ni.
kapo·twe i·ni meta·sokoni i·nahi e·h= ki·ši owi·ki +ya·ni
at.some.point then for.ten.days that/LOC AOR+ PERF/PV dwell.{smwh} +1s/AOR
At some point I had been living there for ten days.

F "nahi·='ni=yá·pi wi·h=mawi-anenwi·yani," i·n=e·h=iši či nekya.
nahi´ i·ni =ya·pi ´ wi·h= mawi anenwi· +yani i·ni
Well! then =here.I,we.go EMPH FUT go.and/PV swim,bathe +2s/AOR then

e·h= iN +iči ne+ -ky +a
AOR+ say.{so}.to +3s-1s/AOR 1+ mother +ANsg
And it was then my mother[(P)] *told me, "Alright, now it's time for you to go and bathe."*

G e·h=na·kwa·ya·ke si·po·ki.
e·h= na·kwa· +ya·ke si·po·w +eki
AOR+ leave +1p/AOR river +LOC
And we went off to the river.

56

A “ketenano·=’nahi kepi·sehka·hi,” neteko·pi.
```
keten    +ano      =i·nahi     ke+ pi·sehka·h +i     ne+ iN          +eko·pi
take.off +2s-0/IMP =with.that 2+  blouse     +INsg 1+  say.{so}.to +X-1s/IND
```
“Now take off your blouse,” I was told.

B ki·ši|-ketenama·ni·=’ni e·h=čapo·kisahoya·ni.
```
IC+ ki·ši   keten    +ama·ni  i·ni e·h= čapo·kisaho        +ya·ni
xx+ PERF/PV take.off +1s-0/CC then AOR+ jump.into.the.water +1s/AOR
```
After taking it off, I jumped into the water.

C “o·ni wi·h=pe·hpe·šona·ni,” neteko·pi.
```
o·ni     wi·h= pe·hpe·šw +ena·ni   ne+ iN          +eko·pi
and,then FUT+  scarify   +1s-2s/AOR 1+ say.{so}.to +X-1s/IND
```
“And now I’m going to scarify your skin,” I was told.

D meso·te·wi=meko nepe·hpe·šoko·pi.
```
meso·te·wi  =meko ne+ pe·hpe·šw +eko·pi
universally =EMPH 1+  scarify   +X-1s/IND
```
Little cuts were sliced in me all over.

E “o·ni=na·hka ahkiki,” neteko·pi.|
```
o·ni     na·hka      ahkiki     ne+ iN          +eko·pi
and,then also,again down.below 1+  say.{so}.to +X-1s/IND
```
“And now down below also,” I was told.

F “še·ški ota·siya·nenano keko·te·hi,”| e·h=išiki.
```
še·ški ota·siya·nen         +ano      ke+ -ko·te·h  +i    e·h= iN          +iki
only   use.as.breechclout +2s-0/IMP 2+  skirt     +INsg AOR+ say.{so}.to +X-1s/AOR
```
And I was told, “Only, hold your skirt like a breechclout.”

G nepwa·meki na·hka e·h=pe·hpe·šwiki.
```
ne+ -pwa·m  +eki na·hka      e·h= pe·hpe·šw +iki
1+   thigh  +LOC also,again AOR+ scarify   +X-1s/AOR
```
And I was also scarified on my thighs.

H “wi·h=pwa·wi_nahi-kehči_mya·no·te·yani,
```
wi·h= pwa·wi  nahi         kehči       mya·no·te· +yani
FUT+  NEG/PV given.to/PV greatly/PV menstruate +2s/AOR
```
“It’s so you’ll never have heavy periods,

57

A kehči-ačika·ke meškwi,” neteko·pi.
```
kehči      ačika·     +ke      meškw +i     ne+ iN          +eko·pi
greatly/PV flow,drip +0/SUBJ blood +INsg 1+  say.{so}.to +X-1s/IND
```
if there’s a heavy flow of blood now,” I was told.

B pe·hki=meko nekotakiheko·pi.
pe·hki =meko ne+ kotakih +eko·pi
really =EMPH 1+ cause.to.suffer +X-1s/IND
I was really made to suffer.

C kotakani·=’ni e·h=ošehki·tama·ni,
kotak +ani i·ni e·h= ošehki·t +ama·ni
other +INpl then AOR+ wear.(as).clothing +1s-0/AOR
Then I put on other clothes

D i·nini·=’ni e·h=pakitama·ni ki·wi-ošehki·tama·nini=’yo·we.
i·nini i·ni e·h= pakit +ama·ni
that/INpl then AOR+ discard,release +1s-0/AOR

IC+ ki·wi ošehki·t +ama·nini =iyo·we
xx+ around/PV wear.(as).clothing +1s-0/PPL(INpl) =PAST
and threw away the ones I had been wearing.

E ača·hmeko·=’ni e·h=natawa·piya·ni.
ača·hmeko i·ni e·h= natawa·pi +ya·ni
only.then then AOR+ try.to.see +1s/AOR
Only at that point did I look around.

F o·ni na·hka meta·sokoni e·h=neši|-wača·hoya·ni=meko sa·kiči taši.|
o·ni na·hka meta·sokoni e·h= neši wača·ho +ya·ni =meko
and,then also,again for.ten.days AOR+ alone/PV cook +1s/AOR =EMPH

sa·kiči taši
outside {smwh}
And then for another ten days I had to cook outdoors by myself.

G me·ta·sokonakahki=na·hka·=’ni e·h=mawi-anenwi·ya·ni.
IC+ meta·sokonakat +ki na·hka i·ni e·h= mawi anenwi· +ya·ni
xx+ be.ten.days +0/CC also,again then AOR+ go.and/PV swim,bathe +1s/AOR
And after the ten days[P], I had to go and bathe again.

58

A o·ni=ča·h ača·hmeko e·h=we·pi-wi·hpoke·ya·ni pi·tike.
o·ni =ča·hi ača·hmeko e·h= we·pi wi·hpoke· +ya·ni pi·tike
and,then =so only.then AOR+ begin/PV eat.with.people +1s/AOR inside
And when that was done, only then did I begin to eat inside again with the others.

B nekya·=’ni e·h=a·čimohaki.
ne+ -ky +a i·ni e·h= a·čimoh +aki
1+ mother +ANsg then AOR+ inform +1s-3/AOR
And I informed my mother[P] then.

C “pe·hki=koči no·hkomesa neta·hpeči-a·ya·čimohekwa wi·h=išawiya·ni,” netena·wa.

```
pe·hki =koči      ne+ -o·hkomes     +a     ne+ a·hpeči
really =you.know 1+   grandmother +ANsg 1+  permanently/PV

CV+    a·čimoh +ekwa        wi·h= išawi    +ya·ni  ne+ iN           +a·wa
RED1+ inform  +3s-1s/IND FUT+  do.{so} +1s/AOR 1+  say.{so}.to +1s-3s/IND
```

“You know, Grandmother[P] really kept instructing me all the time about what I should do,” I told her[P].

D apahapane·niwa.

```
CVCV+ apane·ni +wa
RED2+ smile    +3s/IND
```

She[P] laughed.

E “i·ni=ma·h we·či-a·pi|-na·naki,

```
i·ni      =ma·hi   IC+ oči               a·pi                 na·N     +aki
that/INsg =you.see xx+ from.{smth}/PV have.gone.and/PV go.after +1s-3/PPL(obl)
```

“Well, you see, that’s why I went to get her[P],

F wi·h=a·ya·čimohehki pe·hki e·ši-menwikeniki,

```
wi·h= CV+    a·čimoh +ehki      pe·hki IC+ iši      menwiken +niki
FUT+  RED1+ inform  +3-2s/AOR really xx+ {so}/PV be.good  +0′/PPL(obl)
```

so she[P] would give you serious advice about the good way[o],

G ‘na·pi=ke·h pesetawa·hkiče,’ e·h=ine·nemena·ni.”

```
na·pi            =ke·hi    pesetaw   +a·hkiče        e·h= ine·nem          +ena·ni
for.the.better =moreover listen.to +3s-3′/FUT.IMP AOR+ think.about.{so} +1s-2s/AOR
```

as I hoped you might listen to her[P].”

59

A o·ni=ča·h=pe·hki a·wasi=meko·=’ni e·h=we·pi|-iši-a·hpečimiki| ke·ko·h=meko wi·h=iši·hta·ya·ni.

```
o·ni     =ča·hi pe·hki a·wasi =meko i·ni e·h= we·pi    iši
and,then =so    really more   =EMPH then AOR+ begin/PV {so}/PV

a·hpečim          +iki       ke·ko·h +i     =meko wi·h= iši·hta·  +ya·ni
tell.constantly +X-1s/AOR thing   +INsg =EMPH FUT+  work.{so} +1s/AOR
```

So after that, I really began to be constantly asked more than ever to do things.

B pe·škitye·ni na·hka·=’ni e·šihto·čini,

```
pe·škity +ani  na·hka       i·ni IC+ ašiht +o·čini
basket   +INpl also,again then xx+ make  +3s-0/ITER
```

And also, then, whenever she[P] made baskets

C “ki·na=ne·hi,” e·h=išiči.

```
ki·na    =ne·hi e·h= iN          +iči
2s/EMPH =too   AOR+ say.{so}.to +3s-1s/AOR
```

she[P] would say to me, “You try too.”

D papi·wi‿pe·škiti·han=a·pehe netašihto.
papi·wi pe·škiti·h +ani =a·pehe ne+ ašiht +o
small.(pl.)/PN basket/DIM +INpl =usually 1+ make +1s-0/IND
I would make small baskets.

E ke·keya·h=meko meme·ša·hiwani ki·šihto·ya·nini.
ke·keya·hi =meko IC+ Ce_e·+ meša·hi +wani IC+ ki·šiht +o·ya·nini
eventually =EMPH xx+ RED1+ be.large/DIM +0p/IND xx+ make +1s-0/PPL(INpl)
And in time the ones[(p)] *I made were larger.*

* * *

F kaho·ni meta·swi-nya·nanwi e·h=taswipepo·nwe·ya·ni‿
kaho·ni meta·swi nya·nanwi e·h= taswipepo·nwe· +ya·ni
so.then ten five AOR+ be.{so.many}.years.old +1s/AOR
So then, when I was fifteen years old, I was told,

60
A "nahi′‿pena′, kokwe·čikwa·sono pi·wa·hani, se·nipa·h=ke·hi.
nahi′ pena′ CV_Ye·+ kočikwa·so +no pi·wa·h +ani se·nipa·h +i =ke·hi
Well! please RED1+ try.to.sew.02 +2s/IMP bead +INpl ribbon +INsg =moreover
"Alright, why don't you try to sew beadwork, or ribbon appliqué.

B keta·hwi·hemani ki·h=ašihašihto nahikwa·soyane ni·miyanini wi·h=ayo·yani.
ke+ -ta·hwi·hem +ani ke+ wi·h= CVCV+ ašiht +o
2+ thing,possession +INpl 2+ FUT+ RED2+ make +2s-0/IND
nahikwa·so +yane IC+ ni·mi +yanini wi·h= ayo· +yani
know.how.to.sew +2s/SUBJ xx+ dance +2s/ITER FUT+ use +2s-0/AOR
If you know how to sew [those], you can make all your own things to wear when you dance.

C kwaye·ši, ki·ši‿=ke·h -nahikwa·soyane kehke·nemeneke, ki·h=anohanohka·neko·pi.
kwaye·ši ki·ši =ke·hi nahikwa·so +yane kehke·nem +eneke
that.way PERF/PV =moreover know.how.to.sew +2s/SUBJ know +X-2s/SUBJ
ke+ wi·h= CVCV+ anohka·N +eko·pi
2+ FUT+ RED2+ give.task.to +X-2s/IND
That way, when people know that you've become good at sewing, you'll be asked to make things.

D a·kwi=ke·h=še·ški.
a·kwi =ke·hi še·ški
not =moreover only
And not only that.

E ki·h=tepahoko·pi.
ke+ wi·h= tepahw +eko·pi
2+ FUT+ pay +X-2s/IND
You'll get paid.

F ki·h=mese·neta=meko nahikwa·soyane,"
ke+ wi·h= mese·net +a =meko nahikwa·so +yane
2+ FUT+ benefit.from +2s-0/IND =EMPH know.how.to.sew +2s/SUBJ
You'll really benefit from it if you know how to sew."

61
A netekwa nekya.
ne+ iN +ekwa ne+ -ky +a
1+ say.{so}.to +3s-1s/IND 1+ mother +ANsg
So my mother[P] told me.

B o·ni=ča·h e·h=we·pi-kokwe·čikwa·soya·ni.
o·ni =ča·hi e·h= we·pi CV_Ye·+ kočikwa·so +ya·ni
and,then =so AOR+ begin/PV RED1+ try.to.sew.02 +1s/AOR
So then I began to practice sewing [beads and ribbon appliqué].

C kenwe·ši=ča·h=meko nepemi·hka| wi·h=wi·ke·siya·ni.
kenwe·ši =ča·hi =meko ne+ pemi·hk +a
long.time =so =EMPH 1+ be.busy.at.through.time +1s-0/IND

wi·h= wi·ke·si +ya·ni
FUT+ be.careful +1s/AOR
And it took me a long time to be proficient.

D nekotah=meko ni·šwawahi·me nepemi·hka wi·h=wi·ke·siya·ni.
nekotahi =meko ni·šwawahi·me ne+ pemi·hk +a
somewhere =EMPH two.years 1+ be.busy.at.through.time +1s-0/IND

wi·h= wi·ke·si +ya·ni
FUT+ be.careful +1s/AOR
It must have taken me about two years to be proficient.

E i·ni=meko| očiwe·pi ahpene·či ke·ko·h e·h=ašihto·ya·ni.
i·ni =meko očiwe·pi ahpene·či ke·ko·h +i e·h= ašiht +o·ya·ni
then =EMPH from.{smth}.on every.time thing +INsg AOR+ make +1s-0/AOR
And from then on I was always making things.

* * *

F meta·swi-kotwa·šika e·h=taswipepo·nwe·ya·ni,
meta·swi kotwa·šika e·h= taswipepo·nwe· +ya·ni
ten six AOR+ be.{so.many}.years.old +1s/AOR
When I was sixteen years old,

G e·h=pena·wiki ana·hkanani e·h=ašihašihto·ya·ke,
e·h= pena·wi +ki ana·hkan +ani e·h= CVCV+ ašiht +o·ya·ke
AOR+ be.summer +0/AOR fiber.mat +INpl AOR+ RED2+ make +1p-0/AOR
we used to make fiber mats in the warm months[p],

62

A pe·po·kini maškimote·hani na·hka meškwa·swa·waki,
IC+ pepo· +kini maškimote·h +ani na·hka meškwa·swa·w +aki
xx+ be.winter +0/ITER bag +INpl also,again yarn-belt +ANpl
and in the winters[P] bags and also yarn belts[P],

B e·h=se·nipa·hikwa·soya·ke, e·h=pi·wa·hikwa·soya·ke.
e·h= se·nipa·hikwa·so +ya·ke e·h= pi·wa·hikwa·so +ya·ke
AOR+ sew.ribbon-appliqué +1p/AOR AOR+ sew.beadwork +1p/AOR
and we sewed ribbon appliqué and beadwork.

C ke·htena=či·h=meko netanohanohka·neko·pi ke·ko·hi,
ke·htena =či·hi =meko ne+ CVCV+ anohka·N +eko·pi
truly =it.was.discovered =EMPH 1+ RED2+ give.task.to +X-1s/IND

ke·ko·h +i
thing +INsg
Sure enough, I found that I kept being asked to make things,

D netepahoko·pi=mek=a·pehe.
ne+ tepahw +eko·pi =meko =a·pehe
1+ pay +X-1s/IND =EMPH =usually
and I would get paid for them.

E "i·ni=ma·h=ki·na," neteko·p=a·pehe,
i·ni =ma·hi ki·na ne+ iN +eko·pi =a·pehe
that/INsg =you.see 2s/EMPH 1+ say.{so}.to +X-1s/IND =usually
"You see," I would be told,

F "we·či-anemi-a·čimohena·ni wi·h=nahihto·yani ke·ko·h.
IC+ oči anemi a·čimoh +ena·ni
xx+ from.{smth}/PV go.on/PV inform +1s-2s/PPL(obl)

wi·h= nahiht +o·yani ke·ko·h +i
FUT+ know.how.to.make +2s-0/AOR thing +INsg
"that's the reason I keep instructing you to learn to make things.

G i·na·ma·hani ana·hkanani ki·šihto·kini owiye·ha e·h=mi·neči,
i·na·ma·hani ana·hkan +ani IC+ ki·šiht +o·kini
that.other.(away)/INpl fiber.mat +INpl xx+ make +X-0/PPL(INpl)

owiye·h +a e·h= mi·N +eči
someone +ANsg AOR+ give.to +X-3/AOR
When we give anyone[P] some of those fiber mats you were doing that we've made,

63

A kapo·twe=meko a·šitami mi·šiwe·wa ke·ko·hi.

```
kapo·twe      =meko a·šitami  mi·šiwe·             +wa      ke·ko·h +i
at.some.point =EMPH in.return give.02.to.people +3s/IND thing   +INsg
```

sometime later they[P] give us things in return.

B na·hka ma·hani maškimote·hani, e·yi·ki=meko e·h=mi·neči,

```
na·hka      ma·hani   maškimote·h +ani  e·yi·ki =meko e·h= mi·N        +eči
also,again this/INpl bag          +INpl as.well =EMPH AOR+ give.02.to +X-3/AOR
```

And also the bags, when we give them to someone[P] as well,

C a·šitami mi·neti·pi_ke·ko·hi.

```
a·šitami  mi·neti·                +pi    ke·ko·h +i
in.return give.02.to.each.other +X/IND thing   +INsg
```

we're given things in return.

D otehtena·pi=meko ke·ko·h.

```
otehten +a·pi     =meko ke·ko·h +i
get     +X-0/IND =EMPH thing   +INsg
```

We do get things.

E i·ni we·či-anwa·či·ki e·h=ašihašihto·ki ke·ko·hi,

```
i·ni      IC+ oči           anwa·či· +eki          e·h= CVCV+ ašiht +o·ki
that/INsg xx+ from.{smth}/PV consent  +X/PPL(obl) AOR+ RED2+ make  +X-0/AOR

ke·ko·h +i
thing   +INsg
```

That's why we're always willing to make things,

F e·h=mese·netameki ki·šihto·kini," neteko·pi.

```
e·h= mese·net     +ameki  IC+ ki·šiht +o·kini        ne+ iN           +eko·pi
AOR+ benefit.from +X-0/AOR xx+ make    +X-0/PPL(INpl) 1+  say.{so}.to +X-1s/IND
```

because we benefit from the things we make," I was told.

64

A kaši´, ke·htena=či·h=meko, e·h=we·pi-mi·na·we·netama·ni, te·pwe·pi e·nahina·čimohikini.

```
kaši´ ke·htena =či·hi             =meko
Why!  truly    =it.was.discovered =EMPH

e·h= we·pi    mi·na·we·net        +ama·ni  te·pwe·          +pi
AOR+ begin/PV think.seriously.of +1s-0/AOR speak.the.truth +X/IND

IC+ CVCV+ ina·čimoh    +ikini
xx+ RED2+ inform.{so} +X-1s/PPL(obl.pl)
```

Indeed, when I began to give serious thought to it, I realized the things I was always told were really true.

* * *

B o·ni=ča·hi no·hikanesiya·ni a·wasi·me·hi,
o·ni =ča·hi IC+ no·hikanesi +ya·ni a·wasi·me·hi
and,then =so xx+ be.seventeen.years.old +1s/CC more/DIM
So then, sometime after I turned seventeen,

C nekotahi‿sa·kiči| e·h=awiya·ni,
nekotahi sa·kiči e·h= awi +ya·ni
somewhere outside AOR+ be.{smwh} +1s/AOR
when I was staying outside somewhere during my period,

D ni·šokonakahki=ča·h‿meše·='nah,
IC+ ni·šokonakat +ki =ča·hi meše·='nahi
xx+ be.two.days +0/CC =so as.may.be
after maybe two days there,

E kapo·twe aškačitepehki e·ye·ši‿nepa·ya·ni,
kapo·twe aškačitepehki IC+ aye·ši nepa· +ya·ni
at.some.point late.at.night xx+ continue.to/PV sleep +1s/CC
sometime late at night while I was sleeping,

F "to·hki·no´," netekwa=nekoti.
to·hki· +no ´ ne+ iN +ekwa nekoti
wake.up +2s/IMP INTERJ 1+ say.{so}.to +3s-1s/IND one
someone[(P)] said to me, "Wake up!"

G aškote·hka·ni‖ ki·wi‿so·kenamwa,| e·h=wa·se·šawe·či,
aškote·hka·n +i ki·wi so·ken +amwa e·h= wa·se·šawe· +či
match +INsg around/PV hold +3s-0/IND AOR+ have.a.light +3s/AOR
The person[(P)] was holding a match as a light,

65

A neniwa=či·h‿e·h=wa·pamaki.
neniw +a =či·hi e·h= wa·pam +aki
man +ANsg =it.was.discovered AOR+ look.at +1s-3/AOR
and I saw that it was a man[(P)], when I looked at him[(P)].

B kaši´,‿pe·hki=meko neki·ša·koči-se·kesi.
kaši´ pe·hki =meko ne+ ki·ša·koči se·kesi +Ø
Why! really =EMPH 1+ extremely/PV be.frightened +1s/IND
Why, I was absolutely just as frightened as I could be.

C apina=meko nenenekapiso e·h=se·kesiya·ni,
apina =meko ne+ nenekapiso +Ø e·h= se·kesi +ya·ni
even =EMPH 1+ tremble +1s/IND AOR+ be.frightened +1s/AOR
I was even trembling from my fright.

D e·h=mi·wešihwaki=ke·h,

```
e·h= mi·wešihw  +aki       =ke·hi
AOR+ drive.away +1s-3/AOR =moreover
```

What's more, when I ordered him[P] away,

E a·kwi‿meči|-kwi·yena iššišimoya·nini.

```
a·kwi meči      kwi·yena iššišimo                    +ya·nini
not   quite/PP exactly  speak.with.{such}.voice +1s/NEG
```

my voice didn't sound quite right.

F masa·či=ke·h=meko nekaški‿kano·na·wa.

```
masa·či           =ke·hi     =meko ne+ kaški       kano·N     +a·wa
with.difficulty =moreover =EMPH 1+  able.to/PV speak.to +1s-3s/IND
```

In fact, I was barely able to speak to him[P].

G o·ni=ča·h| očiwe·pi a·yahpi·hčina·h=meko·=’ni‖ e·h=pye·či-koči-pye·notawiwa·či neniwaki.

```
o·ni      =ča·hi očiwe·pi          a·yahpi·hčina·hi     =meko i·ni
and,then =so     from.{smth}.on every.now.and.then =EMPH then

e·h= pye·či      koči        pye·notaw +iwa·či     neniw +aki
AOR+ coming/PV try.to/PV come.to    +3p-1s/AOR man    +ANpl
```

So then, from then on, every once in a while men[P] came and tried to approach me.

66

A ahpene·či=’yo=ke·h=meko nekekye·hkimeko·pi e·ši‿menwikeki.|

```
ahpene·či   =iyo =ke·hi      =meko ne+ kekye·hkim +eko·pi
every.time =for =moreover =EMPH 1+  teach         +X-1s/IND

IC+ iši       menwiken +ki
xx+ {so}/PV be.good   +0/PPL(obl)
```

For I had always been taught the right way.

B na·hka kapo·twe=’ni e·h=kehke·nemiki e·h=we·pi-koči-mi·hkema·soya·ni.

```
na·hka        kapo·twe         i·ni e·h= kehke·nem +iki
also,again at.some.point then AOR+ know          +X-1s/AOR

e·h= we·pi       koči        mi·hkema·so +ya·ni
AOR+ begin/PV try.to/PV be.courted   +1s/AOR
```

And at some point then also, it became known that attempts to court me had begun.

C o·ni| e·h=a·čimohiki.

```
o·ni        e·h= a·čimoh +iki
and,then AOR+ inform   +X-1s/AOR
```

And then I was instructed.

D "nahi′‿ni·šwa·pitakesiyane i·ni wi·h=natawi-ona·pe·miyani.

```
nahi′ ni·šwa·pitakesi      +yane     i·ni wi·h= natawi   ona·pe·mi     +yani
Well! be.twenty.years.old +2s/SUBJ then FUT+  seek/PV have.husband +2s/AOR
```

"Well now, when you're twenty you must try to get married.

E wi·h=ona·pe·miwane·na=ke·h=meko·='na wi·h=kakano·neti·hata mehteno·hi,

```
IC+ wi·h= ona·pe·mi          +wane·na          =ke·hi     =meko i·na
xx+ FUT+  have.O2.as.husband +2s/INT.PPL(ANsg) =moreover =EMPH that/ANsg

IC+ wi·h= kakano·neti·h +ata              mehteno·hi
xx+ FUT+  converse.with +2s-3/PPL(ANsg) only
```

And whoever(P) it may be that you're going to marry should be the only one(P) you have conversations with,

67

A we·pi-kakano·neti·yane.

```
we·pi     kakano·neti· +yane
begin/PV converse      +2s/SUBJ
```

when you begin to have conversations with men.

B ka·ta=wi·na meše=meko·='nah ma·ne kakano·neti·hiye·kani.

```
ka·ta =wi·na meše=meko·='nahi ma·ne      kakano·neti·h +iye·kani
don't =but   any                much,many converse.with +2s-3/PROH
```

Don't have conversations aimlessly with many different ones(P).

C a·kwi menwikekini i·n=e·h=išawiwa·či ihkwe·waki.

```
a·kwi menwiken +kini  i·ni      e·h= išawi    +wa·či  ihkwe·w +aki
not   be.good  +0/NEG that/INsg AOR+ do.{so} +3p/AOR woman   +ANpl
```

It(p)'s not a good thing when women(P) do that.

D e·h=ma·ne·ha·wa·či owi·hka·nwa·wahi,

```
e·h= ma·ne·h   +a·wa·či   o+ -i·hka·n  +wa·wahi
AOR+ have.many +3p-3'/AOR 3+  friend   +3p(OBVpl)
```

When they(P) have many friends(O),

E a·kwi| menwi-to·ta·kowa·čini we·na·pe·miwa·čini,

```
a·kwi menwi    to·taw     +ekowa·čini IC+ ona·pe·mi          +wa·čini
not   well/PV treat.{so} +3'-3p/NEG   xx+ have.O2.as.husband +3p/PPL(OBVsg)
```

their(P) husbands(O) don't treat them(P) well,

F e·h=kya·we·niči e·h=kehke·nemekowa·či e·šawiwa·či.

```
e·h= kya·we·     +niči    e·h= kehke·nem +ekowa·či  IC+ išawi    +wa·či
AOR+ be.jealous +3'/AOR AOR+ know        +3'-3p/AOR xx+ do.{so} +3p/PPL(obl)
```

as they(O)'re jealous when they(O) learn about what they(P) did.

G i·ni=ča·h|| we·či-neškiti·ki wi·h=ma·ne·heči owi·hka·ninawaki,"

```
i·ni      =ča·hi IC+ oči               neškiti·                +eki
that/INsg =so    xx+ from.{smth}/PV admonish.each.other +X/PPL(obl)

wi·h= ma·ne·h   +eči     o+ -i·hka·n  +inawaki
FUT+  have.many +X-3/AOR 3+  friend   +X(ANpl)
```

So that's why we're forbidden to have a lot of friends(P)."

68

A i·n=e·h=išiki.

    i·ni e·h= iN   +iki
    then AOR+ say.{so}.to +X-1s/AOR

So I was told then.

* * *

B o·ni=kapo·twe meta·swi‿šwa·šika e·h=taswipepo·nwe·ya·ni, e·h=meno·hkami·ki,|

    o·ni   kapo·twe   meta·swi šwa·šika e·h= taswipepo·nwe·   +ya·ni
    and,then at.some.point ten   eight   AOR+ be.{so.many}.years.old +1s/AOR

    e·h= meno·hkami· +ki
    AOR+ be.spring   +0/AOR

And then sometime later when I was eighteen, in early summer[P],

C na·hina·h=ča·h ahte·himinani e·h=we·pi·hkameki,

    na·hina·hi   =ča·hi ahte·himin +ani e·h= we·pi·hk   +ameki
    time,distance =so   strawberry +INpl AOR+ begin.dealing.with +X-0/AOR

so at the beginning of strawberry season,

D nekoti·=’ni ihkwe·he·ha e·h=wi·te·maki e·h=ahte·himinehke·ya·ke.

    nekoti i·ni ihkwe·he·h +a   e·h= wi·te·m   +aki
    one   then woman/DIM +ANsg AOR+ accompany +1s-3/AOR

    e·h= ahte·himinehke·   +ya·ke
    AOR+ pick.strawberries +1p/AOR

I went picking strawberries with a certain young woman[P].

E “ki·h=ne·wa·pena=ke·h nekoti,” netekw=a·pehe.

    ke+ wi·h= ne·w +a·pena   =ke·hi   nekoti ne+ iN   +ekwa   =a·pehe
    2+ FUT+ see +12-3/IND =moreover one   1+ say.{so}.to +3s-1s/IND =usually

“Actually, we’re going to meet someone[P]*,” she*[P] *kept telling me.*

F “iše=ma·h ketešimene,” o·n=a·peh‿e·h=išiči.

    iše =ma·hi   ke+ išim   +ene
    just =you.see 2+ speak.{so}.to +1s-2s/IND

    o·ni   =a·pehe e·h= iN   +iči
    and,then =usually AOR+ say.{so}.to +3s-1s/AOR

And then she[P] *would say to me, “You understand, I’m just kidding you.”*

69

A keye·hapa=ke·h=wi·na ki·šiti·wa·tehe nekoti oškinawe·hani i·ya·h‿wi·h=ne·woti·wa·či.

    keye·hapa   =ke·hi   =wi·na IC+ ki·šiti·   +wa·tehe   nekoti
    it.turned.out =moreover =but   xx+ agree.on.plan +3p/CH.PRET one

    oškinawe·h +ani   i·ya·hi wi·h= ne·woti·   +wa·či
    young.man +OBVsg yonder FUT+ see.each.other +3p/AOR

It turned out, however, she[P] *and a certain young man*[O] *had agreed to meet over there.*

B kapo·twe i·ya·h‿pye·nota·kwa.
kapo·twe i·ya·hi pye·notaw +ekwa
at.some.point yonder come.to +3′-3s/IND
After a time, he[O] came to see her[P] over there.

C pe·hki=či·h=meko po·so·te·wi-keša·čiheti·waki.
pe·hki =či·hi =meko po·so·te·wi keša·čiheti· +waki
really =it.was.discovered =EMPH profoundly/PV be.kind.to.each.other +3p/IND
I could see from their friendliness to each other that they[P] were well acquainted.

D asemihekwa=meko e·h=ahte·himinehke·či.
asemih +ekwa =meko e·h= ahte·himinehke· +či
help +3′-3s/IND =EMPH AOR+ pick.strawberries +3s/AOR
He[O] helped her[P] as she[P] picked strawberries.

E nepe·pye·či‿=mek=a·peh -nawasehka·kwa nekotah wi·h=a·ya·ke.
ne+ CV+ pye·či =meko =a·pehe nawasehkaw +ekwa
1+ RED1+ coming/PV =EMPH =usually invite.along +3s-1s/IND

nekotahi wi·h= iha· +ya·ke
somewhere FUT+ go.{smwh} +1p/AOR
She[P] would always come after me to get me to go someplace with her.

F kapo·twe=meko·=’ni kotakani·=’ni e·h=pe·pye·či‿wi·te·ma·či·=’na, owi·či-oškinawe·hani.
kapo·twe =meko i·ni kotak +ani i·ni e·h= CV+ pye·či
at.some.point =EMPH then other +OBVsg then AOR+ RED1+ coming/PV

wi·te·m +a·či i·na o+ -i·či oškinawe·h +ani
accompany +3s-3′/AOR that/ANsg 3+ fellow young.man +OBVsg
And at some point that fellow[P] started coming with someone else[O] then, another young man[O].

70

A o·ni=ni·na·=’na| ihkwe·he·ha e·h=taši·hkawiči wi·h=kakano·neti·hemaki.
o·ni ni·na i·na ihkwe·he·h +a e·h= taši·hkaw +iči
and,then 1s/EMPH that/ANsg woman/DIM +ANsg AOR+ be.dealing.with +3s-1s/AOR

wi·h= kakano·neti·h +emaki
FUT+ converse.with +1s-3′/AOR
And then that young woman[P] tried to persuade <u>me</u> to have conversations with <u>him</u>[O].

B “a·kwi=ma·h‿ke·ko·h wi·h=išawičini.
a·kwi =ma·hi ke·ko·h +i wi·h= išawi +čini
not =you.see something +INsg FUT+ do.{so} +3s/NEG
“Mind you, he[P] won’t do anything.

C mahkwa·či=ma·h=meko ki·h=kakano·neti·pwa," netekwa i·na ihkwe·wa.
mahkwa·či =ma·hi =meko ke+ wi·h= kakano·neti· +pwa
quietly,calmly =you.see =EMPH 2+ FUT+ converse +2p/IND

ne+ iN +ekwa i·na ihkwe·w +a
1+ say.{so}.to +3s-1s/IND that/ANsg woman +ANsg
I mean, you and he can just have conversations together nicely," that woman[P] told me.

D e·taswi-͜nekotah͜-iha·ya·kini,
IC+ taswi nekotahi iha· +ya·kini
xx+ {so.much,many}/PV somewhere go.{smwh} +1p/ITER
Every time she and I went anywhere,

E pye·waki=meko i·niki neniwaki.‖
pya· +waki =meko i·niki neniw +aki
come +3p/IND =EMPH that/ANpl man +ANpl
here, those guys[P] turned up.

71
A ke·keya·h=meko·=’ni ke·htena e·h=we·pi͜-kaški͜-kano·naki i·na oškinawe·ha.
ke·keya·hi =meko i·ni ke·htena e·h= we·pi kaški kano·N +aki
eventually =EMPH then truly AOR+ begin/PV able.to/PV speak.to +1s-3/AOR

i·na oškinawe·h +a
that/ANsg young.man +ANsg
And in time, then, I really did begin to be able to speak to that young man[P].

B o·ni=ča·h=pe·hki| e·h=ka·ki·wi͜-nye·wiya·ke.
o·ni =ča·hi pe·hki e·h= CV+ ki·wi nye·wi +ya·ke
and,then =so really AOR+ RED1+ around/PV be.four +1p/AOR
So then it was always just the four of us anywhere.

C kaši´͜pe·hki=či·h=meko ke·htena meta·tehtawa·pi.
kaši´ pe·hki =či·hi =meko ke·htena meta·tehtaw +a·pi
Why! really =it.was.discovered =EMPH truly enjoy.hearing +X-3/IND
Why, I found it truly was really enjoyable to hear them[P] talk.

D e·nihe·nikowe·waki.
CVCV+ e·nikowe· +waki
RED2+ say.funny.things.to.people +3p/IND
They[P] would always say funny things.

E i·ni=meko=ni·na e·h=a·hpeči͜-natawe·nemaki wi·h=ne·waki.
i·ni =meko ni·na e·h= a·hpeči natawe·nem +aki wi·h= ne·w +aki
then =EMPH 1s/EMPH AOR+ permanently/PV seek +1s-3/AOR FUT+ see +1s-3/AOR
For me it got to where I constantly wanted to see him[P].

F pa·pekwa nekotah e·ya·ya·nini e·h=ki·ši‿ne·waki.
pa·pekwa nekotahi IC+ iha· +ya·nini e·h= ki·ši ne·w +aki
right.away somewhere xx+ go.{smwh} +1s/ITER AOR+ PERF/PV see +1s-3/AOR
And whenever I went someplace, I would see him[P] right away.

72
A ma·ne=wi·na=meko netaši·hka·ko·ki neniwaki‿wi·h=kakano·neti·haki.
ma·ne =wi·na =meko ne+ taši·hkaw +eko·ki neniw +aki
much,many =but =EMPH 1+ be.dealing.with +3p-1s/IND man +ANpl

wi·h= kakano·neti·h +aki
FUT+ converse.with +1s-3/AOR
There were, however, many men[P] trying to persuade me to have conversations with them[P].

B kapo·twe·=’ni e·h=kehke·nemiki.
kapo·twe i·ni e·h= kehke·nem +iki
at.some.point then AOR+ know +X-1s/AOR
Then and at some point I was found out.

C kaši′‿pe·hki=či·h=meko nekehči‿neškimeko·pi.
kaši′ pe·hki =či·hi =meko ne+ kehči neškim +eko·pi
Why! really =it.was.discovered =EMPH 1+ greatly/PV forbid,admonish +X-1s/IND
My, but I was, unexpectedly, really scolded severely.

D kotaka=či·h=meko nekehkahama·ko·pi oškinawe·h wi·h=ona·pe·miya·ni.
kotak +a =či·hi =meko ne+ kehkahamaw +eko·pi
other +ANsg =it.was.discovered =EMPH 1+ designate.O2.for +X-1s/IND

oškinawe·h +a wi·h= ona·pe·mi +ya·ni
young.man +ANsg FUT+ have.O2.as.husband +1s/AOR
And a different young man[P] I never even expected was named for me to marry.

E nekwaya·ši‿=ke·h‿ni·na·na -anehka·ti·pena.|
ne+ kwaya·ši =ke·hi ni·na·na anehka·ti· +pena
1+ irreversibly/PV =moreover 1p/EMPH be.acquainted.with.each.other +1p/IND
And here [this other one] and I were already acquainted beyond undoing.

F o·ni, “natawa·či=meko ki·h=ona·pe·mi=kekeni,” neteko·pi.
o·ni natawa·či =meko ke+ wi·h= ona·pe·mi +Ø kekeni
and,then resolving.accordingly =EMPH 2+ FUT+ have.husband +2s/IND quickly

ne+ iN +eko·pi
1+ say.{so}.to +X-1s/IND
And then I was told, “Given all this, you’d better get married right away.

73

A “ ‘ni·šwa·pitakesiyane‿ki·h=ona·pe·mi,’ ketene=’yo·we, e·h=a·čimohena·ni,” neteko·pi.

```
ni·šwa·pitakesi     +yane     ke+ wi·h= ona·pe·mi     +Ø
be.twenty.years.old +2s/SUBJ 2+   FUT+  have.husband +2s/IND

ke+ iN            +ene        =iyo·we e·h= a·čimoh +ena·ni
2+  say.{so}.to +1s-2s/IND =PAST   AOR+ inform  +1s-2s/AOR

ne+ iN            +eko·pi
1+  say.{so}.to +X-1s/IND
```

“I told you before, when I instructed you, that you should get married when you were twenty,” I was told.

B “na·hka| keneškimene=’yo·we wa·waneška·haki wi·h=ka·ki·wi·‿’te·mači.

```
na·hka        ke+ neškim            +ene         =iyo·we
also,again 2+  forbid,admonish +1s-2s/IND =PAST

wa·waneška·h +aki   wi·h= CV+   ki·wi      wi·te·m    +ači
bad.one        +ANpl FUT+  RED1+ around/PV accompany +2s-3/AOR
```

“And I also warned you not to go around with bad girls(P).

C ke·htena·=’nah=mani:|

```
ke·htena =i·nahi     mani
truly    =with.that this/INsg
```

The fact of the matter is this:

D i·ni=meko e·h=ki·ši‿pwa·wi‿kwi·yena·hiyani.

```
i·ni =meko e·h= ki·ši   pwa·wi kwi·yena·hi +yani
then =EMPH AOR+ PERF/PV NEG/PV act.right   +2s/AOR
```

Already you’re not doing right.

E e·ye·h‿ne·se·ya·ni=’yo·we ketaka·wa·nene

```
IC+ aye·hi          ne·se·  +ya·ni =iyo·we ke+ aka·wa·N +ene
xx+ continue.to/PV live.on +1s/CC =PAST   2+  desire   +1s-2s/IND
```

It was my desire that while I was still living

74

A wi·h=ki·ši‿te·pahkwi-menwi‿wa·pamena·ni wi·h=iši|-menwi-ona·pe·miyani.

```
wi·h= ki·ši    te·pahkwi menwi    wa·pam  +ena·ni
FUT+  PERF/PV attain/PV well/PV look.at +1s-2s/AOR

IC+ wi·h= iši     menwi   ona·pe·mi    +yani
xx+ FUT+  {so}/PV well/PV have.husband +2s/PPL(obl)
```

I would get to enjoy the sight of you being happily married.

B i·noki=wi·na a·kwi=meko tane·nemena·nini wi·h=nekoti‿menwi-ona·pe·miyani.
i·noki =wi·na a·kwi =meko tane·nem +ena·nini
now =but not =EMPH expect +1s-2s/NEG

wi·h= nekoti menwi ona·pe·mi +yani
FUT+ in.one.go/PV well/PV have.husband +2s/AOR
But now I don't expect you to be married right, once and for all.

C "pe·hki=ma·h=wi·na·=’na| ke·kano·neti·yana o·sani| mya·šawiniwani.
pe·hki =ma·hi =wi·na i·na IC+ kakano·neti· +yana
really =you.see =but that/ANsg xx+ converse.with.O2 +2s/PPL(ANsg)

o+ -o·s +ani mya·šawi +niwani
3+ father +OBVsg be.bad +3´s/IND
"See, the father$^{(O)}$ of that one$^{(P)}$ you're having conversations with is not a good person.

D ne·nesenesa=meko.
CV+ neS +enesa =meko
RED1+ kill +3-2s/POT =EMPH
He'd beat you for sure.

E i·n=e·šawiniči o·sani.
i·ni IC+ išawi +niči o+ -o·s +ani
that/INsg xx+ do.{so} +3´/PPL(obl) 3+ father +OBVsg
That's how his$^{(P)}$ father$^{(O)}$ is.

75

A nahi‿we·pi·hkwe·we·niwani.
nahi we·pi·hkwe·we· +niwani
given.to/PV beat.own.wife +3´s/IND
He$^{(P)}$ beats his wife.

B ke·ko·h=na·hka e·ši‿ma·mata·nahkiwinikini
ke·ko·h +i na·hka IC+ iši ma·mata·nahkiwi +nikini
something +INsg also,again xx+ {so}/PV entertainment.goes.on +0´/ITER
And also, whenever any kind of public entertainment$^{(o)}$ is going on,

C a·kwi wi·to·hkawa·čini i·tepi wi·h=a·niči owi·wani·=’na neniwa.
a·kwi wi·to·hkaw +a·čini i·tepi wi·h= iha· +niči o+ -i·w +ani
not allow +3s-3´/NEG to.there FUT+ go.{smwh} +3´/AOR 3+ wife +OBVsg

i·na neniw +a
that/ANsg man +ANsg
that man$^{(P)}$ doesn't allow his$^{(P)}$ wife$^{(O)}$ to go there.

D na·hka pe·hki=meko na·ni·kihto·hiwa.
na·hka pe·hki =meko na·ni·kihto·hi +wa
also,again really =EMPH be.lazy +3s/IND
And also he$^{(P)}$'s really very lazy.

E i·ni=ča·h=meko ni·na·=ʼna e·ne·nemaki wi·h=išawiči okwisema·wa.
i·ni =ča·hi =meko ni·na i·na IC+ ine·nem +aki
that/INsg =so =EMPH 1s/EMPH that/ANsg xx+ think.about.{so} +1s-3/PPL(obl)

wi·h= išawi +či okwisema·w +a
FUT+ do.{so} +3s/AOR son +ANsg
So, that's exactly how I think the son[P] *will be.*

F asa·mi=meko‿še·ški a·hpetose·wa.
asa·mi =meko še·ški a·hpetose· +wa
too.much =EMPH only walk.all.the.time +3s/IND
Too much of the time all he[P] *does is just constantly walk around.*

76
A a·kwi=meko ni·na kehke·nemakini‿ke·ko·h‿wi·h=iši‿mi·hkeče·wi·či.
a·kwi =meko ni·na kehke·nem +akini
not =EMPH 1s/EMPH know +1s-3/NEG

ke·ko·h +i wi·h= iši mi·hkeče·wi· +či
something +INsg FUT+ {so}/PV work +3s/AOR
I've never known him[P] *to do any kind of work.*

B wa·šipaka=meko=ki·na taši‿pemeniye·kapa, ona·pe·miyane.
wa·šipaka =meko ki·na taši pemen +iye·kapa
instead.of.the.other =EMPH 2s/EMPH be.engaged.in/PV take.care.of +2s-3/POT

ona·pe·mi +yane
have.O2.as.husband +2s/SUBJ
You'd be the one taking care of him, if you married him.

C wanine·honesa.
wanine·hw +enesa
cheat +3-2s/POT
He would cheat you.

D ki·na=ʼyo=ke·h=mani keki·ši‿ča·ki‿nahihto kemi·hkeče·wi·wenena·ni e·h=ihkwe·wiyakwe.
ki·na =iyo =ke·hi =mani ke+ ki·ši ča·ki nahiht +o
2s/EMPH =for =moreover =as.it.is.now 2+ PERF/PV all/PV know.how.to.make +2s-0/IND

ke+ mi·hkeče·wi·wen +ena·ni e·h= ihkwe·wi +yakwe
2+ work +12(INsg) AOR+ be.woman +12/AOR
Remember, you now already know how to make all the things that are the work of us women.

E a·kwi=ča·hi·=ʼna‿wi·h=ona·pe·miyanini. ‖
a·kwi =ča·hi i·na wi·h= ona·pe·mi +yanini
not =so that/ANsg FUT+ have.O2.as.husband +2s/NEG
So in short, you mustn't marry him[P].

77

A kotaka‿ki·h=ona·pe·mi ni·na ne·he·netamo·na·na| wi·h=wi·čawiwači.|
kotak +a ke+ wi·h= ona·pe·mi +Ø
other +ANsg 2+ FUT+ have.O2.as.husband +2s/IND

ni·na IC+ nahe·netamaw +ena·na wi·h= wi·čawiw +ači
1s/EMPH xx+ think.O2.proper.for +1s-2s/PPL(ANsg) FUT+ be.with +2s-3/AOR
You must marry the other one(P) who I think will be the right one(P) for you to be married to.

B "ki·h=po·ni̯=ke·hi·=’na -kakano·neti·ha·wa keme·nawa·ta·kana.
ke+ wi·h= po·ni =ke·hi i·na kakano·neti·h +a·wa
2+ FUT+ cease/PV =moreover that/ANsg converse.with +2s-3s/IND

ke+ me·nawa·ta·kan +a
2+ object.of.affection +ANsg
"What's more, you must stop having conversations with the one(P) you're stuck on.

C ki·hpene=ke·h kehke·nemena·ne na·hka| kakano·neti·hate,
ki·hpene =ke·hi kehke·nem +ena·ne
in.the.event.that =moreover know +1s-2s/SUBJ

na·hka kakano·neti·h +ate
also,again converse.with +2s-3/SUBJ
And if I ever find out that you've been having conversations with him(P) again,

D i·ni wi·h=po·ni̯=we·we·ne·netamani keke·ko·hemena·ni.
i·ni wi·h= po·ni we·we·ne·net +amani ke+ ke·ko·h +emena·ni
then FUT+ cease/PV have.control.over +2s-0/AOR 2+ thing +12(INsg)
then you won't have any more claim on our things.

E a·kwi| wi·h=te·pwe·hena·nini ke·ko·h=e·šiyanini.
a·kwi wi·h= te·pwe·h +ena·nini
not FUT+ believe,agree.to.request.of +1s-2s/NEG

ke·ko·h +i IC+ iN +iyanini
something +INsg xx+ say.{so}.to +2s-1s/ITER
And I won't agree to your requests.

78

A iše=’yo=mani| peteki kepye·či̯=meko -kehke·nemene e·h=pesetawiyani e·ši-wi·tamo·na·nini.
iše =iyo =mani peteki ke+ pye·či =meko kehke·nem +ene
just =for =as.it.is.now back 2+ coming/PV =EMPH know +1s-2s/IND

e·h= pesetaw +iyani IC+ iši wi·tamaw +ena·nini
AOR+ listen.to +2s-1s/AOR xx+ {so}/PV tell +1s-2s/PPL(obl.pl)
After all, I know that, as it has been up to now, you have listened to the things I told you to do.

B i·ni we·či˭te·pwe·hena·ni ke·ko·h=e·šiyanini.
i·ni IC+ oči te·pwe·h +ena·ni
that/INsg xx+ from.{smth}/PV believe,agree.to.request.of +1s-2s/PPL(obl)

ke·ko·h +i IC+ iN +iyanini
something +INsg xx+ say.{so}.to +2s-1s/ITER
That's why I agreed to your requests.

C "na·hka=mani:
na·hka mani
also,again this/INsg
"And here's another thing:

D taswi˭ne·hihto·hiya·ni| ke·ko·hi e·h·ki·ši˭nahihto·yani pe·hki nemi·ša·te·nemo.
taswi IC+ nahiht +o·hiya·ni ke·ko·h +i
{so.much,many} xx+ know.how.to.make +1s-0/DIM/PPL(obl) thing +INsg

e·h= ki·ši nahiht +o·yani pe·hki ne+ mi·ša·te·nemo +Ø
AOR+ PERF/PV know.how.to.make +2s-0/AOR really 1+ be.pleased +1s/IND
I'm really proud now that you know how to make everything I may know how to make.

E i·ni=ke·h=a·peh we·či˭neškimena·ke wa·waneška·haki|| wi·h=ka·ki·wi-wi·te·mači.
i·ni =ke·hi =a·pehe IC+ oči neškim +ena·ke
that/INsg =moreover =usually xx+ from.{smth}/PV forbid,admonish +1p-2/PPL(obl)

wa·waneška·h +aki wi·h= CV+ ki·wi wi·te·m +ači
bad.one +ANpl FUT+ RED1+ around/PV accompany +2s-3/AOR
That's actually the reason why we would forbid you to go around with the bad actors[(P)].

79
A ke·htena·='nah=mani:
ke·htena =i·nahi mani
truly =with.that this/INsg
The fact of the matter is this:

B na·hina·h=meko we·pi˭ka·ki·wi-˭'te·mači e·h=kehke·nemena·ke,
na·hina·hi =meko IC+ we·pi CV+ ki·wi wi·te·m +ači
time,distance =EMPH xx+ begin/PV RED1+ around/PV accompany +2s-3/CC

e·h= kehke·nem +ena·ke
AOR+ know +1p-2/AOR
Just as soon as you started going around with them[(P)] *we knew it,*

C e·h=po·ni˭kosači neniwaki.
e·h= po·ni koS +ači neniw +aki
AOR+ cease/PV fear +2s-3/AOR man +ANpl
since you were no longer afraid of men[(P)].

D i·ye·me·h=ke·h=a·peh kekosa·waki nekotah_wi·h=a·yani,
i·ye·me·hi =ke·hi =a·pehe ke+ koS +a·waki
a.while.back/DIM =moreover =usually 2+ fear +2s-3p/IND

nekotahi wi·h= iha· +yani
somewhere FUT+ go.{smwh} +2s/AOR
Here, not so long ago you would be afraid to go anywhere because of them[P],

E i·noki=ke·h ketaka·wa·ta=meko_nekotah_wi·h=a·yani ahpene·či.
i·noki =ke·hi ke+ aka·wa·t +a =meko
now =moreover 2+ desire +2s-0/IND =EMPH

nekotahi wi·h= iha· +yani ahpene·či
somewhere FUT+ go.{smwh} +2s/AOR every.time
while now you're eager to go places all the time.

F "a·kwi=ma·h| wi·h=ke·ko·he·neta·kosiyanini wa·waneška·hiyane. ||
a·kwi =ma·hi wi·h= ke·ko·he·neta·kosi +yanini wa·waneška·hi +yane
not =you.see FUT+ be.thought.to.be.something +2s/NEG be.bad +2s/SUBJ
"Don't you see, you won't be respected if you're badly behaved.

80

A mahkwa·či=ma·h_ki·wita·ničini e·ka·wa·na·wa·čih neniwaki wi·h=wi·čawiwa·wa·či.
mahkwa·či =ma·hi IC+ ki·wita· +ničini
quietly,calmly =you.see xx+ stay.around +3′/PPL(OBVsg)

IC+ aka·wa·N +a·wa·čihi neniw +aki wi·h= wi·čawiw +a·wa·či
xx+ desire +3p-3′/PPL(OBVpl) man +ANpl FUT+ be.with +3p-3′/AOR
Mind you, the ones[O] who stay home quietly are the ones[O] men[P] desire to be married to.

B o=wa·waneška·hahi=ke·hi, še·ški=meko_wi·h=wa·pašiha·wa·či we·či-mata·kwi·hkawa·wa·či.
o wa·waneška·h +ahi =ke·hi še·ški =meko wi·h= wa·paših +a·wa·či
or bad.one +OBVpl =moreover only =EMPH FUT+ waste,spoil +3p-3′/AOR

IC+ oči mata·kwi·hkaw +a·wa·či
xx+ from.{smth}/PV enjoy.frequenting +3p-3′/PPL(obl)
But as for the bad actors[O], they[P] like to go to them[O] only to deprave them[O].

C a·kwi=ke·h_wi·h=owi·wiwa·či oči_taši·hkawa·wa·čini.
a·kwi =ke·hi wi·h= owi·wi +wa·či
not =moreover FUT+ have.O2.as.wife +3p/AOR

oči taši·hkaw +a·wa·čini
from.{smth}/PV be.dealing.with +3p-3′/NEG
They[P] aren't after them[O] in order to marry them[O].

D “ki·h=kekeni‿=ča·h=meko -ona·pe·mi| a·šimena·na kwayahkwi,” neteko·pi.
ke+ wi·h= kekeni =ča·hi =meko ona·pe·mi +Ø
2+ FUT+ quickly/PV =so =EMPH have.O2.as.husband +2s/IND

IC+ a·šim +ena·na kwayahkwi ne+ iN +eko·pi
xx+ urge.O2.on +1s-2s/PPL(ANsg) prudently 1+ say.{so}.to +X-1s/IND
“So under the circumstances you’d better marry the one[P] *I’m urging you to right away,” I was told.*

E meta·swi‿ša·ka e·h=taswipepo·nwe·ya·ni.
meta·swi ša·ka e·h= taswipepo·nwe· +ya·ni
ten nine AOR+ be.{so.many}.years.old +1s/AOR
I was nineteen.

* * *

81
A o·ni| natawa·či a·šimika e·h=we·pi‿kakano·neti·haki.
o·ni natawa·či IC+ a·šim +ika
and,then resolving.accordingly xx+ urge.O2.on +X-1s/PPL(ANsg)

e·h= we·pi kakano·neti·h +aki
AOR+ begin/PV converse.with +1s-3/AOR
And then, deciding there was nothing else for it, I began having conversations with the one[P] *being urged on me.*

B a·kwi=meko meči-kwi·yena ine·nemakini.
a·kwi =meko meči kwi·yena ine·nem +akini
not =EMPH quite exactly think.about.{so} +1s-3/NEG
I had my doubts about him[P]*.*

C i·niya=meko kotaka a·wasi‿neteši-nenehke·nema·wa.
i·niya =meko kotak +a a·wasi ne+ iši nenehke·nem +a·wa
that/ABS(ANsg) =EMPH other +ANsg more 1+ {so}/PV think.about +1s-3s/IND
My mind was more on the other one[P]*.*

D ahpene·či=meko, “ta·ni·=’nah‿kakano·neti·ya·ne,”‿netešite·h=a·pehe.
ahpene·či =meko ta·ni =i·nahi kakano·neti· +ya·ne
every.time =EMPH how =with.that converse.with.O2 +1s/SUBJ

ne+ išite·he· +Ø =a·pehe
1+ think.{so} +1s/IND =usually
All the time I would think, “I wish I could talk with him.”

E a·kwi=meko kaški|-‿pe·hki‿-po·ni‿kakano·neti·hakini.|
a·kwi =meko kaški pe·hki po·ni kakano·neti·h +akini
not =EMPH able.to/PV really cease/PV converse.with +1s-3/NEG
I couldn’t completely stop having conversations with him[P]*.*

F netotehte·nema·wa=meko.
ne+ otehte·nem +a·wa =meko
1+ be.concerned.about +1s-3s/IND =EMPH
I just couldn't get him[P] out of my mind.

82

A o·ni·=’na a·šimika_na·hka e·h=ka·ki·wi·-’te·maki| nekotah_e·ya·ya·nini.
o·ni i·na IC+ a·šim +ika na·hka
and,then that/ANsg xx+ urge.O2.on +X-1s/PPL(ANsg) also,again

e·h= CV+ ki·wi wi·te·m +aki nekotahi IC+ iha· +ya·nini
AOR+ RED1+ around/PV accompany +1s-3/AOR somewhere xx+ go.{smwh} +1s/ITER
And then next I went around with the one[P] being urged on me whenever I went anywhere.

B ke·keya·h=meko·=’ni e·h=anehkawaki.‿
ke·keya·hi =meko i·ni e·h= anehkaw +aki
eventually =EMPH then AOR+ get.acquainted.with +1s-3/AOR
In time then, I became acquainted with him[P].

C šewe·na kotaka=meko a·wasi neteši-a·hpeči-nenehke·nema·wa, ne·škinamawika.
šewe·na kotak +a =meko a·wasi ne+ iši a·hpeči nenehke·nem +a·wa
but other +ANsg =EMPH more 1+ {so}/PV permanently/PV think.about +1s-3s/IND

IC+ neškinamaw +ika
xx+ hate.O2.for +X-1s/PPL(ANsg)
But I continually thought more about the other one[P] who wasn't liked for me.

D o·ni=ča·h=kapo·twe a·šimika e·h=we·pi·hkawiči owi·kewa·ki wi·h=iši-wi·te·maki.|
o·ni =ča·hi kapo·twe IC+ a·šim +ika
and,then =so at.some.point xx+ urge.O2.on +X-1s/PPL(ANsg)

e·h= we·pi·hkaw +iči
AOR+ begin.dealing.with +3s-1s/AOR

o+ -i·k +wa·ki wi·h= iši wi·te·m +aki
3+ lodge +3p(LOC) FUT+ {so}/PV accompany +1s-3/AOR
And so then, at some point the one[P] urged on me began to try to get me to go with him[P] to his family's house.

E ahpene·či=meko·=’n=e·h=taši·hkawiči wi·h=wi·te·maki e·taswi-ne·wakini.
ahpene·či =meko i·ni e·h= taši·hkaw +iči
every.time =EMPH then AOR+ be.dealing.with +3s-1s/AOR

wi·h= wi·te·m +aki IC+ taswi ne·w +akini
FUT+ accompany +1s-3/AOR xx+ {so.much,many}/PV see +1s-3/ITER
He[P] was always after me then to go with him[P] every time I saw him[P].

83

A o·ni, “nahi´,| pe·hki=ma·h=ni·na‿nekosetawa·waki| kemeso·ta·naki,” netena·wa.

```
o·ni      nahi´ pe·hki =ma·hi    ni·na    ne+ kosetaw              +a·waki
and,then Well! really =you.see 1s/EMPH 1+  fear.to.approach +1s-3p/IND

ke+ -meso·ta·n  +aki  ne+ iN           +a·wa
2+   parent     +ANpl 1+  say.{so}.to +1s-3s/IND
```

And then I told him(P), “Well, see, I’m really shy about being around your parents(P).”

B “o·´,‿ki·na=ta·ni e·h=owi·kiye·kwe‿ki·h=iši‿wi·te·mene,”‿netekwa.

```
o·´ ki·na    =ta·ni          e·h= owi·ki        +ye·kwe
Oh  2s/EMPH =if.you.agree AOR+ dwell.{smwh} +2p/PPL(loc.obl)

ke+ wi·h= iši      wi·te·m    +ene        ne+ iN            +ekwa
2+  FUT+  {so}/PV accompany +1s-2s/IND 1+  say.{so}.to +3s-1s/IND
```

“Oh, then let me go with you to <u>your</u> family’s house,” he(P) said to me.

C “a·kwi=ma·h‿pe·pehki·na·towe·yakwini.

```
a·kwi =ma·hi    CV+   pehki·na·towe·              +yakwini
not   =you.see RED1+ speak.different.language +12/NEG
```

“I mean, we don’t speak different languages.

D a·kwi=ča·h‿wi·h=koseta·ti·yakwe išikekini.

```
a·kwi =ča·hi wi·h= koseta·ti·                        +yakwe  išiken  +kini
not   =so     FUT+  fear.to.approach.each.other +12/AOR be.{so} +0/NEG
```

So there’s no basis for us to be shy of each other.

E ni·na=’yo a·kwi‿kosetawakini‿kemeso·ta·naki.

```
ni·na    =iyo a·kwi kosetaw            +akini     ke+ -meso·ta·n +aki
1s/EMPH =for not   fear.to.approach +1s-3/NEG 2+   parent     +ANpl
```

Like me, <u>I’m</u> not shy about being around <u>your</u> parents(P).

F ta·ni!?

```
ta·ni !?
how   EN
```

Why should I be?

G a·kwi| ke·ko·h iši‿wa·waneška·hi‿to·to·na·nini|| nehki pye·či‿kakano·neti·yakwe.

```
a·kwi ke·ko·h    +i     iši     wa·waneška·hi +Ø       to·taw      +ena·nini
not   something +INsg {so}/PV badly/PV       +1s/IND treat.{so} +1s-2s/NEG

nehki           IC+ pye·či    kakano·neti· +yakwe
for.{so}.long xx+ coming/PV converse.     +12/PPL(obl)
```

I haven’t done anything wrong to you for as long as we’ve been having conversations with each other.

84

A mahkwa·či=meko_ketaši·hko·ne.

```
mahkwa·či       =meko ke+ taši·hkaw       +ene
quietly,calmly =EMPH 2+  be.dealing.with +1s-2s/IND
```

I've been very reserved towards you.

B kekehke·neta=ké·hi.

```
ke+ kehke·net +a          =ke·hi    ´
2+  know      +2s-0/IND  =moreover EMPH
```

You know that.

C nekekye·htena·mite·he=meko_wi·h=wi·čawi·ti·yakwe mahkwa·či.

```
ne+ kekye·htena·mite·he· +Ø       =meko wi·h= wi·čawi·ti·          +yakwe
1+  think.seriously      +1s/IND =EMPH FUT+  be.with.each.other +12/AOR

mahkwa·či
quietly,calmly
```

I'm very serious that we should have a quiet marriage together.

D 'ta·ni·=’nahi anwa·či·te,' netešite·h=ahpene·či.

```
ta·ni =i·nahi     anwa·či· +te        ne+ išite·he·  +Ø      ahpene·či
how   =with.that consent  +3s/SUBJ 1+  think.{so} +1s/IND every.time
```

I hope every time that you'll consent.

E ki·na=meko_mehteno·hi i·n=e·šite·he·ya·ni wi·h=wi·čawi·na·ni.

```
ki·na    =meko mehteno·hi i·ni       IC+ išite·he·  +ya·ni
2s/EMPH =EMPH only       that/INsg xx+ think.{so} +1s/PPL(INsg)

wi·h= wi·čawiw +ena·ni
FUT+  be.with  +1s-2s/AOR
```

You're the only one I want to be married to.

F pe·hki=ke·h=meko_ki·h=menwi_to·to·ne.

```
pe·hki =ke·hi     =meko ke+ wi·h= menwi    to·taw     +ene
really =moreover =EMPH 2+  FUT+  well/PV treat.{so} +1s-2s/IND
```

What's more, I'll really treat you well.

G e·šimiyanini=meko ni·h=išawi. ‖

```
IC+ išim            +iyanini               =meko ne+ wi·h= išawi    +Ø
xx+ speak.{so}.to +2s-1s/PPL(obl.pl) =EMPH 1+  FUT+  do.{so} +1s/IND
```

I'll do the things you tell me to.

85

A na·hka ahpene·či=meko_ni·h=mi·hkeče·wi.

```
na·hka       ahpene·či  =meko ne+ wi·h= mi·hkeče·wi· +Ø
also,again every.time =EMPH 1+  FUT+  work          +1s/IND
```

And also I'll always work.

B ma·haki=na·hka kemeso·ta·naki, a·kwi‿wi·h=neškinamo·na·nini.
ma·haki na·hka ke+ -meso·ta·n +aki a·kwi wi·h= neškinamaw +ena·nini
this/ANpl also,again 2+ parent +ANpl not FUT+ hate.O2.for +1s-2s/NEG
And I won't hate your parents(P).

C a·kwi=ke·hi=’še=’šimena·nini.‿
a·kwi =ke·hi iše išim +ena·nini
not =moreover just speak.{so}.to +1s-2s/NEG
I'm not kidding you, either.

D mani·=’noki e·nena·ni ke·htena=meko i·ni‿wi·h=išawiya·ni," netekwa.
mani i·noki IC+ iN +ena·ni ke·htena =meko i·ni
this/INsg now xx+ say.{so}.to +1s-2s/PPL(obl) truly =EMPH that/INsg

IC+ wi·h= išawi +ya·ni ne+ iN +ekwa
xx+ FUT+ do.{so} +1s/PPL(obl) 1+ say.{so}.to +3s-1s/IND
What I'm telling you right now is really what I will do," he(P) told me.

E kapo·twe·=’ni e·h=anwa·či·ya·ni.
kapo·twe i·ni e·h= anwa·či· +ya·ni
at.some.point then AOR+ consent +1s/AOR
At some point then I consented.

F pe·hkote·ki·=’ni e·h=na·kwa·ya·ke,
IC+ pehkote· +ki i·ni e·h= na·kwa· +ya·ke
xx+ be.night +0/CC then AOR+ leave +1p/AOR
We started out after dark,

G e·h=me·nešite·he·ya·ni e·h=wa·se·ya·ki i·ya·h‿wi·h=pakami·‿’te·maki e·h=owi·kiya·ke.
e·h= me·nešite·he· +ya·ni e·h= wa·se·ya· +ki
AOR+ be.bashful +1s/AOR AOR+ be.light +0/AOR

i·ya·hi wi·h= pakami wi·te·m +aki e·h= owi·ki +ya·ke
yonder FUT+ arriving/PV accompany +1s-3/AOR AOR+ dwell.{smwh} +1p/PPL(loc.obl)
as I was embarrassed to arrive over at our house with him(P) while it(P) was daylight.

86

A o·ni ača·hmeko e·h=wi·hpe·ti·ya·ke.
o·ni ača·hmeko e·h= wi·hpe·ti· +ya·ke
and,then only.then AOR+ sleep.with.each.other +1p/AOR
And then we slept together for the first time.

B a·kwi=meko=ni·na kaški-nepa·ya·nini,
a·kwi =meko ni·na kaški nepa· +ya·nini
not =EMPH 1s/EMPH able.to/PV sleep +1s/NEG
For my part, I just couldn't sleep,

C neniwa e·h=wi·hpe·maki.
neniw +a e·h= wi·hpe·m +aki
man +ANsg AOR+ sleep.with +1s-3/AOR
since I was sleeping with a man[P].

D nehkanitepehkwe newa·wani·wesi.
nehkanitepehkwe ne+ wa·wani·wesi +Ø
all.night.long 1+ not.know.how +1s/IND
I couldn't get used to it all night.

E wa·paki·-’ni e·h=ne·woči.
IC+ wa·pan +ki i·ni e·h= ne·w +eči
xx+ be.morning +0/CC then AOR+ see +X-3/AOR
The next morning people saw him[P].

F pe·hki=meko ke·htena ki·wi_menwi_to·tawa·pi,
pe·hki =meko ke·htena ki·wi menwi to·taw +a·pi
really =EMPH truly around/PV well/PV treat.{so} +X-3/IND
Sure enough, they went around really treating him[P] well,

G me·nwe·netamawika e·h=ona·pe·miya·ni.
IC+ menwe·netamaw +ika e·h= ona·pe·mi +ya·ni
xx+ like.O2.for +X-1s/PPL(ANsg) AOR+ have.O2.as.husband +1s/AOR
since I had married the one[P] they liked for me.

H o·ni_nesokoni_ki·ši-wi·hpe·maki,
o·ni nesokoni IC+ ki·ši wi·hpe·m +aki
and,then for.three.days xx+ PERF/PV sleep.with +1s-3/CC
And then after I had slept with him[P] for three nights,

I kapo·twe e·škačitepehki·niki newe·pi_wi·kawihekwa,‖
kapo·twe IC+ aškačitepehki· +niki ne+ we·pi wi·kawih +ekwa
at.some.point xx+ late.at.night +0′/CC 1+ begin/PV bother +3s-1s/IND
sometime late at night[O] he[P] began to bother me.

87
A kapo·twe·-’ni e·h=we·pi·hkawiči ke·ko·h_wi·h=to·tawiči.
kapo·twe i·ni e·h= we·pi·hkaw +iči
at.some.point then AOR+ begin.dealing.with +3s-1s/AOR

ke·ko·h +i wi·h= to·taw +iči
something +INsg FUT+ treat.{so} +3s-1s/AOR
Then at some point he[P] started in with me to make love to me.

B neša·kwe·nemo.
ne+ ša·kwe·nemo +Ø
1+ be.unwilling +1s/IND
I didn't want to.

C na·hka=meko pe·hkote·ki i·ni=meko=na·hka e·h=we·pi·hkawiči.
na·hka =meko IC+ pehkote· +ki i·ni =meko na·hka
also,again =EMPH xx+ be.night +0/CC then =EMPH also,again

e·h= we·pi·hkaw +iči
AOR+ begin.dealing.with +3s-1s/AOR
The following night(P) he(P) started in with me again right away.

D e·škačitepehki·niki,
IC+ aškačitepehki· +niki
xx+ late.at.night +0′/CC
Late at night he(P) said to me,

E "a·kwi=ma·h=ki·na·na·=’ni wi·h=neši ’šawiyakwini.
a·kwi =ma·hi ki·na·na i·ni wi·h= neši išawi +yakwini
not =you.see 12/EMPH that/INsg FUT+ alone/PV do.{so} +12/NEG
"You realize you and I won't be the only ones to do that.

F i·ni=ma·h e·šahišawiwa·či kekimesi| we·wi·weti·čiki.
i·ni =ma·hi IC+ CVCV+ išawi +wa·či kekimesi
that/INsg =you.see xx+ RED2+ do.{so} +3p-0/PPL(obl) each.one

IC+ owi·weti· +čiki
xx+ marry.each.other +3/PPL(ANpl)
I mean, that's what all married couples(P) do.

G a·kwi=ke·h ki·wa·čimowa·čini
a·kwi =ke·hi ki·wa·čimo +wa·čini
not =moreover go.around.narrating +3p/NEG
It's just that they(P) don't go around talking about what they do,

H we·či pwa·wi kehke·nemakwe," netekwa.
IC+ oči pwa·wi kehke·nem +akwe ne+ iN +ekwa
xx+ from.{smth}/PV NEG/PV know +12-3/PPL(obl) 1+ say.{so}.to +3s-1s/IND
which is why we don't know about them(P).

I "ki·na·na=’yo=mani, a·kwi wi·h=kehke·nemenakwini owiye·ha.
ki·na·na =iyo =mani a·kwi wi·h= kehke·nem +enakwini owiye·h +a
12/EMPH =for =as.it.is.now not FUT+ know +3,X-12/NEG someone +ANsg
"So as for you and me now, no one(P) will know about us.

88

A mo·hči=meko=nekoti a·kwi=nana·ši wi·h=a·čimohakwini.
mo·hči =meko nekoti a·kwi nana·ši wi·h= a·čimoh +akwini
even =EMPH one not (ever) FUT+ inform +12-3/NEG
We'll never inform even one person(P).

B ki·na·na=meko ke·sipi| ki·h=kehke·neta·pena e·šawiwakwe·ni,"
```
ki·na·na =meko ke·sipi               ke+ wi·h= kehke·net +a·pena
12/EMPH  =EMPH only.(that,those) 2+  FUT+  know      +12-0/IND

IC+ išawi    +wakwe·ni
xx+ do.{so} +12/INT.PPL(obl)
```
Only you and I will know about whatever we do."

C i·n=e·h=išiči.
```
i·ni e·h= iN            +iči
then AOR+ say.{so}.to +3s-1s/AOR
```
So he[P] said to me then.

D ke·keya·hi·=’ni e·h=anwa·či·ya·ni,
```
ke·keya·hi i·ni e·h= anwa·či· +ya·ni
eventually then AOR+ consent  +1s/AOR
```
Eventually then I consented

E e·h=a·htawa·šimiki.
```
e·h= a·htawa·šim +iki
AOR+ lay.on.back +X-1s/AOR
```
and was put on my back.

F kaho·ni| mani e·ši-‿ke·ko·h‿-to·tawiki,
```
kaho·ni mani       IC+ iši      ke·ko·h    +i     to·taw      +iki
so.then this/INsg xx+ {so}/PV something +INsg treat.{so} +X-1s/CC
```
So then, just as I was being made love to,

G kaši´‿pe·hki=či·h=meko ki·ša·koči‿wi·sakamata·pi.
```
kaši´ pe·hki =či·hi                 =meko ki·ša·koči    wi·sakamat  +a·pi
Why!  really =it.was.discovered =EMPH extremely/PV suffer.pain +X(-0)/IND
```
why, I abruptly learned that it's really extremely painful for a person.

89

A a·kwi| kaški-‿ke·ko·h -išawiya·kini pe·hki.
```
a·kwi kaški       ke·ko·h   +i     išawi    +ya·kini pe·hki
not   able.to/PV something +INsg do.{so} +1p/NEG  really
```
We were unable to make love successfully.

B ke·keya·h nemi·wisaha·wa,
```
ke·keya·hi ne+ mi·wisah   +a·wa
eventually 1+  push.away +1s-3s/IND
```
Eventually I pushed him[P] away,

C ki·h‿meči-wi·sakamačihiči.
```
IC+ ki·h     meči     wi·sakamačih              +iči
xx+ PERF/PV quite/PV to.suffer.pain].cause +3s-1s/CC
```
after he[P]'d caused me quite a lot of pain.

D na·hka=meko| wa·paki‿pe·hkote·ki, na·hka=meko nekočawipena.
```
na·hka       =meko IC+ wa·pan      +ki    IC+ pehkote· +ki
also,again =EMPH xx+ be.morning +0/CC xx+ be.night +0/CC

na·hka       =meko ne+ kočawi +pena
also,again =EMPH 1+   try     +1p/IND
```
The next night[P] *we tried again.*

E a·kwi=meko kaški- i·ni=‿’šawiya·kini.
```
a·kwi =meko kaški         i·ni        išawi    +ya·kini
not    =EMPH able.to/PV that/INsg do.{so} +1p/NEG
```
We just couldn't do it.

F nesenwi i·n=e·šawiya·ke,
```
nesenwi      i·ni        IC+ išawi    +ya·ke
three.times that/INsg xx+ do.{so} +1p/CC
```
When we did it three times,

G ača·hmeko·=’ni e·h=kaški-‿pe·hki·=’ni=‿’šawiya·ke.
```
ača·hmeko i·ni e·h= kaški       pe·hki i·ni        išawi    +ya·ke
only.then then AOR+ able.to/PV really that/INsg do.{so} +1p/AOR
```
then we were able to do it successfully.

H šewe·=ni·na kenwe·ši=meko nepemi|-wi·sakamata‿ke·ko·h=e·šawiya·kini.
```
šewe·na ni·na    kenwe·ši   =meko ne+ pemi       wi·sakamat   +a
but      1s/EMPH long.time =EMPH 1+  along/PV suffer.pain +1s(-0)/IND

ke·ko·h    +i     IC+ išawi    +ya·kini
something +INsg xx+ do.{so} +1p/ITER
```
But for a long while it kept hurting me whenever we made love.

90

A o·ni otaye·ni e·h=mi·šiči,
```
o·ni      o+ -tay +ani   e·h= mi·N        +iči
and,then 3+  pet +OBVsg AOR+ give.02.to +3s-1s/AOR
```
And then he[P] *gave me his*[P] *horse*[O]*,*

B na·hka oto·šehki·ta·kani‿ni·mičini e·yohayo·či mi·ša·tesiweni.
```
na·hka       o+ ošehki·ta·kan +i    IC+ ni·mi +čini
also,again 3+ clothing        +INsg xx+ dance +3s/ITER

IC+ CVCV+ ayo· +či              mi·ša·tesiwen +i
xx+ RED2+ use  +3s-0/PPL(INsg) finery          +INsg
```
and also his clothes, the fancy ones he[P] *wore when he*[P] *danced.*

C o·ni=ni·na·=’ni| netawe·ma·waki e·h=mi·naki,
```
o·ni      ni·na    i·ni       ne+ -tawe·ma·w        +aki  e·h= mi·N        +aki
and,then 1s/EMPH that/INsg 1+   woman's.brother +ANpl AOR+ give.02.to +1s-3/AOR
```
And then I gave them to my brothers[P]*,*

D i·nini=na·hka kato·škaša·hani.
i·nini na·hka kato·škaša·h +ani
that/OBVsg also,again horse +OBVsg
and also that horse[O].

E kapo·twe=na·hka no·hkoma| nepye·či̲natomekwa.
kapo·twe na·hka ne+ -o·hkom +a
at.some.point also,again 1+ mother-in-law +ANsg

ne+ pye·či natom +ekwa
1+ coming/PV ask.to.come +3s-1s/IND
At some point also, my mother-in-law[P] *came and asked me to come over.*

F "i·tepi='ha·no," netekwa=nekya,
i·tepi iha· +no ne+ iN +ekwa ne+ -ky +a
to.there go.{smwh} +2s/IMP 1+ say.{so}.to +3s-1s/IND 1+ mother +ANsg
My mother[P] *told me to go there,*

G e·h=na·kwa·ya·ni.
e·h= na·kwa· +ya·ni
AOR+ leave +1s/AOR
and I set out.

91

A i·ya·h_pye·ya·ya·ni,
i·ya·hi IC+ pya· +ya·ni
yonder xx+ come.{smwh} +1s/CC
When I arrived over there,

B "ayo·h=kohi´," neteko·pi.
ayo·hi =kohi ´ ne+ iN +eko·pi
this/LOC =certainly INTERJ 1+ say.{so}.to +X-1s/IND
"Right over here," I was told.

C "či·tapino," neteko·pi,
či·tapi +no ne+ iN +eko·pi
sit.up +2s/IMP 1+ say.{so}.to +X-1s/IND
"Sit down," I was told,

D e·h=nana·hapiya·ni.
e·h= nana·hapi +ya·ni
AOR+ sit.down +1s/AOR
and I took my seat.

E kaši´, newe·pi̲=či·h -mi·ša·čiheko·pi.|
kaši´ ne+ we·pi =či·hi mi·ša·čih +eko·pi
Why! 1+ begin/PV =it.was.discovered dress.in.finery +X-1s/IND
Why, to my surprise, I was soon being dressed in fancy clothes.

F kekimesi=meko neča·ki‿mi·ša·čiheko·pi.|
kekimesi =meko ne+ ča·ki mi·ša·čih +eko·pi
each.one =EMPH 1+ all/PV dress.in.finery +X-1s/IND
I was dressed in all fancy clothes from top to toe.

G o·ni=na·hka, "mana=ke·h wi·h=awanata| še·šketo·ha," neteko·pi.
o·ni na·hka mana =ke·hi IC+ wi·h= awaN +ata
and,then also,again this/ANsg =moreover xx+ FUT+ take.away +2s-3/PPL(ANsg)

še·šketo·h +a ne+ iN +eko·pi
kettle +ANsg 1+ say.{so}.to +X-1s/IND
And then also I was told, "And here, this kettle[P] is for you to take home with you."

H e·yi·ki=meko i·nah=ahte·wi‿mača·hi·ni,
e·yi·ki =meko i·nahi ahte· +wi mača·hi·n +i
as.well =EMPH that/LOC be.{smwh} +0s/IND dry.goods +INsg
There were dry goods[p] as well in the kettle,

I na·hka‿saketone·pičikani·=’nah=ahte·wi še·šketo·heki.‖
na·hka saketone·pičikan +i i·nahi ahte· +wi še·šketo·h +eki
also,again bridle +INsg that/LOC be.{smwh} +0s/IND kettle +LOC
and there was also a bridle[p] in it.

92
A pe·hki=meko ni·na| netanemi-makinehpaši e·h=na·kwa·ya·ni.
pe·hki =meko ni·na ne+ anemi makinehpaši +Ø
really =EMPH 1s/EMPH 1+ go.on/PV have.load.piled.high.on.back +1s/IND

e·h= na·kwa· +ya·ni
AOR+ leave +1s/AOR
Going home, off I went with a huge load piled high on my back.

B nepakami‿mi·ša·tesi e·h=owi·kiya·ke,
ne+ pakami mi·ša·tesi +Ø e·h= owi·ki +ya·ke
1+ arrive/PV dress.up +1s/IND AOR+ dwell.{smwh} +1p/PPL(loc.obl)
I arrived at our house clad in fancy clothes,

C e·h=wa·pataki=nekya.
e·h= wa·pat +aki ne+ -ky +a
AOR+ look.at +3s-0/AOR 1+ mother +ANsg
and my mother[P] looked it all over.

D e·h=ne·taki saketone·pičikani,
e·h= ne·t +aki saketone·pičikan +i
AOR+ see +3s-0/AOR bridle +INsg
Seeing the bridle she[P] [said],

E “i·ni=ma·h=ki·na.
i·ni =ma·hi ki·na
that/INsg =you.see 2s/EMPH
“There, you see!

F ni·šwi·='ni e·h=otehtenači kato·škaša·haki.
ni·šwi i·ni e·h= otehten +ači kato·škaša·h +aki
two then AOR+ get +2s-3/AOR horse +ANpl
Now you've received two horses[P].

G i·na='h=we·na=kotaka!? ona·pe·miyanehe!? i·ni| ke·ko·h_iši_mi·nenene·ha!?”
i·na =ihi =we·na kotak +a ona·pe·mi +yanehe
that/ANsg =NEG =in.fact other +ANsg have.O2.as.husband +2s/SUBJ.PRET

i·ni ke·ko·h +i iši mi·N +enene·ha !?
that/INsg something +INsg {so}/PV give.O2.to +X-2s/POT EN
If you'd married that other one[P]*, do you think you would have been given anything like that!”*

H kapo·twe·='ni=na·hka=ni·na, “nahi´,‖ mani awata·ke·ko,” e·h=išiki.
kapo·twe i·ni na·hka ni·na
at.some.point then also,again 1s/EMPH

nahi´ mani awata·ke· +ko e·h= iN +iki
Well! this/INsg take.O2.to.people +2p/IMP AOR+ say.{so}.to +X-1s/AOR
Then next, at some point, I was told, “Alright, take this over there, the two of you.”

93

A wi·seniweni maškimote·heki ahtohahto·pi,| ana·hkanani=na·hka.
wi·seniwen +i maškimote·h +eki CVCV+ aht +o·pi ana·hkan +ani na·hka
food +INsg bag +LOC RED2+ have +X-0/IND fiber.mat +INpl also,again
Food was put into yarn bags, and there were also fiber mats.

B na·htaswi=meko meškwa·swa·waki so·kiso·kihčike·pi.
na·htaswi =meko meškwa·swa·w +aki CVCV+ so·kihčike· +pi
several =EMPH yarn-belt +ANpl RED2+ tie.things +X/IND
Several yarn-belts[P] *were used to tie them.*

C i·n=e·h=ki·še·wi·ya·ke.
i·ni e·h= ki·še·wi· +ya·ke
then AOR+ finish.task +1p/AOR
Then we were through with the formalities.

D o·ni=ča·h=še·ški e·h=ma·mi·šiwa·či| ke·ko·hi‿či·nawe·ma·čiki wi·čawiwomakini,‿mača·hi·ni ta·taki.

```
o·ni      =ča·hi še·ški e·h= CV+   mi·N          +iwa·či     ke·ko·h +i
and,then =so    only   AOR+ RED1+ give.O2.to +3p-1s/AOR thing   +INsg

IC+ či·nawe·m      +a·čiki          IC+ wi·čawiw +emakini
xx+ be.related.to +3-3′/PPL(ANpl) xx+ be.with  +1s-3′/PPL(OBVsg)

mača·hi·n +i    ta·taki
dry.goods +INsg in.a.way
```

And then, after that, my husband(O)'s relatives(P) would give me things informally, like dry goods.

E o·ni=ni·na‿wi·seniweni – maškoči·sa,‖ wa·pikonani – nekoti‿=meko‿-maškimote·h=a·pehe ahkwa·wi, pe·škiti·ki=ke·h=a·pehe, e·h=awata·ke·ya·ni,

```
o·ni      ni·na    wi·seniwen +i    maškoči·s +a    wa·pikon +ani
and,then 1s/EMPH food        +INsg beans     +ANsg pumpkin  +INpl

nekoti  =meko maškimote·he =a·pehe  ahkwa·wi
one/PP =EMPH bag/ECM      =usually to.full.amount

pe·škity +eki =ke·hi      =a·pehe  e·h= awata·ke·          +ya·ni
basket   +LOC =moreover =usually AOR+ take.O2.to.people +1s/AOR
```

And for my part, I would take over some food, beans(P) and squashes, usually one full bag or basket of them,

94

A ana·hkanani, mesi·kwaki.

```
ana·hkan   +ani  mesi·kw     +aki
fiber.mat +INpl dried.corn +ANpl
```

and fiber mats and dried corn(P).

* * *

B ke·htena=wi·na=meko kenwe·ši·me·hi nemenwi‿to·ta·kwa wi·čawiwaka.

```
ke·htena =wi·na =meko kenwe·ši·me·hi ne+ menwi    to·taw      +ekwa
truly    =but   =EMPH long.time/DIM  1+  well/PV treat.{so} +3s-1s/IND

IC+ wi·čawiw +aka
xx+ be.with  +1s-3/PPL(ANsg)
```

For quite a long time my husband(P) really did treat me well.

C nekya=na·hka pe·hki=meko‿neneškimekwa wi·h=ayi·ši‿kakano·neti·hemaki kotakani.

```
ne+ -ky    +a    na·hka       pe·hki  =meko ne+ neškim            +ekwa
1+  mother +ANsg also,again really =EMPH 1+  forbid,admonish +3s-1s/IND

wi·h= ayi·ši          kakano·neti·h  +emaki     kotak +ani
FUT+  continue.to/PV converse.with +1s-3′/AOR other +OBVsg
```

Also, my mother(P) completely forbade me to continue talking to the other one(O).

D netahkawa·pamekwa=meko.
ne+ ahkawa·pam +ekwa =meko
1+ guard +3s-1s/IND =EMPH
She[P] watched me very closely.

95
A šewe·na a·kwi=meko‿kaški‿po·ni‿nenehke·nemakini ni·na·=’na.
šewe·na a·kwi =meko kaški po·ni nenehke·nem +akini ni·na i·na
but not =EMPH able.to/PV cease/PV think.about +1s-3/NEG 1s/EMPH that/ANsg
But I just couldn’t stop thinking about him[P].

B ta·ni!?
ta·ni !?
how EN
How could I?

C i·na=ni·na‿me·nwe·nemaka,
i·na ni·na IC+ menwe·nem +aka
that/ANsg 1s/EMPH xx+ like +1s-3/PPL(ANsg)
He[P] was the one[P] I liked,

D wi·čawiwaka=ke·h a·kwi=ni·na‿menwe·nemakini.
IC+ wi·čawiw +aka =ke·hi a·kwi ni·na menwe·nem +akini
xx+ be.with +1s-3/PPL(ANsg) =moreover not 1s/EMPH like +1s-3/NEG
while my husband[P] I didn’t like.

E i·ni=ča·hi·=’na=kotaka‿we·či-a·hpeči‿nenehke·nemaki.
i·ni =ča·hi i·na kotak +a
that/INsg =so that/ANsg other +ANsg

IC+ oči a·hpeči nenehke·nem +aki
xx+ from.{smth}/PV permanently/PV think.about +1s-3/PPL(obl)
So that’s why I was forever thinking about the other one[P].

F ke·ko·h=e·nahkiwikini, nekya=meko| neki·wi·‿’te·ma·wa,|
ke·ko·h +i IC+ inahkiwi +kini
something +INsg xx+ be.{such}.event +0/ITER

ne+ -ky +a =meko ne+ ki·wi wi·te·m +a·wa
1+ mother +ANsg =EMPH 1+ around/PV accompany +1s-3s/IND
Whenever any activity was going on, I had to go around with my mother[P],

G e·h=ahkawa·pamiči wi·h=pwa·wi-‿kotakah=na·hka‿-kakano·neti·hemaki.
e·h= ahkawa·pam +iči
AOR+ guard +3s-1s/AOR

wi·h= pwa·wi kotak +ahi na·hka kakano·neti·h +emaki
FUT+ NEG/PV other +OBVpl also,again converse.with +1s-3′/AOR
as she[P] was watching me so I wouldn’t have conversations with any others[O].

96

A na·hka nešihka nekotah=wi·h=a·ya·ni neneškimekwa.
na·hka nešihka nekotahi wi·h= iha· +ya·ni ne+ neškim +ekwa
also,again alone somewhere FUT+ go.{smwh} +1s/AOR 1+ forbid,admonish +3s-1s/IND
And she(P) also forbade me to go anyplace by myself.

B "wi·te·mi wi·čawiwata‿nekotah=e·ya·yanini.
wi·te·m +i IC+ wi·čawiw +ata nekotahi IC+ iha· +yanini
accompany +2s-3/IMP xx+ be.with +2s-3/PPL(ANsg) somewhere xx+ go.{smwh} +2s/ITER
"Go along with your husband(P) whenever you go anyplace.

C ke·ko·h‿ina·čimenaki·ke.|
ke·ko·h +i ina·čim +enaki·ke
something +INsg tell.about.{so} +X-2s/PROH
Something might be said about you.

D 'taši·hka·ti·wa kotakani neniwani,'| inenakiče owiye·ha.
taši·hka·ti· +wa kotak +ani neniw +ani
be.dealing.with.each.other +3s/IND other +OBVsg man +OBVsg

iN +enakiče owiye·h +a
say.{so}.to +3-2s/PROH someone +ANsg
Someone(P) might say about you, 'She(P)'s involved with another man(O).'

E nahi·wesiwaki=ma·h ne·tawi|-memye·škiha·čiki we·wi·weti·ničihi," neteko·p=a·pehe. ‖
nahi·wesi +waki =ma·hi IC+ natawi memye·ških +a·čiki
be.clever +3p/IND =you.see xx+ seek/PV mess.up +3-3′/PPL(ANpl)

IC+ owi·weti· +ničihi ne+ iN +eko·pi =a·pehe
xx+ marry.each.other +3′/PPL(OBVpl) 1+ say.{so}.to +X-1s/IND =usually
You see, people(P) who try to break up married couples(O) are clever," I would be told.

97

A kaho·ni e·taswi‿=meko‿-pehkote·kini netaši·hka·kwa‿wi·čawiwaka ke·ko·h wi·h=išawiya·ke.
kaho·ni IC+ taswi =meko pehkote· +kini
so.then xx+ {so.much,many}/PV =EMPH be.night +0/ITER

ne+ taši·hkaw +ekwa IC+ wi·čawiw +aka
1+ be.dealing.with +3s-1s/IND xx+ be.with +1s-3/PPL(ANsg)

ke·ko·h +i wi·h= išawi +ya·ke
something +INsg FUT+ do.{so} +1p/AOR
And then, every night(P) my husband(P) was after me for us to make love.

B nekotenwi=meko ahpene·či‿ke·ko·h‿netešawipena.
nekotenwi =meko ahpene·či ke·ko·h +i ne+ išawi +pena
once =EMPH every.time something +INsg 1+ do.{so} +1p/IND
We always had to make love once.

C čačawi·h=wi·n=a·peh neša·kwe·nemo.
```
čačawi·hi =wi·na =a·pehe   ne+ ša·kwe·nemo  +Ø
sometimes =but   =usually 1+  be.unwilling +1s/IND
```
Sometimes I wouldn't want to.

D a·kwi=ni·na me·meta·te·netama·nini.
```
a·kwi ni·na   CV+   meta·te·net       +ama·nini
not   1s/EMPH RED1+ get.pleasure.from +1s-0/NEG
```
I got no pleasure from it, myself.

E "kaši=ye·tok=e·h=teki wi·na mana| e·h=mata·kwe·netaki i·n=e·h=išawiči," netešite·h=a·pehe.
```
kaši  =ye·toke  e·h= t(o)    +ki    wi·na   mana      e·h= mata·kwe·net +aki
what? =it.seems AOR+ be.{so} +0/AOR 3s/EMPH this/ANsg AOR+ enjoy        +3s-0/AOR

i·ni      e·h= išawi   +či     ne+ išite·he· +Ø      =a·pehe
that/INsg AOR+ do.{so} +3s/AOR 1+  think.{so} +1s/IND =usually
```
"I wonder how come he[P] likes to do that?" I would think.

F a·kwi_kehke·nemakini|| e·hpi·hči-me·meta·ča·hikwe·ni i·n=e·h=išawiči.
```
a·kwi kehke·nem +akini    IC+ ahpi·hči
not   know      +1s-3/NEG xx+ to.{such}.degree/PV

CV+   meta·ča·hi     +kwe·ni               i·ni      e·h= išawi   +či
RED1+ have.good.time +3s,0/INT.PPL(obl) that/INsg AOR+ do.{so} +3s/AOR
```
I didn't know how great a time he[P] had doing it.

* * *

98

A o·ni a·pehtawawahi·ne ki·ši·_'čawiwaki,
```
o·ni      a·pehtawawahi·ne IC+ ki·ši   wi·čawiw +aki
and,then  for.a.half.year  xx+ PERF/PV be.with  +1s-3/CC
```
And then, after I had been married to him[P] for half a year,

B kapo·twe_nepo·ni_mya·no·te.
```
kapo·twe      ne+ po·ni    mya·no·te· +Ø
at.some.point 1+  cease/PV menstruate +1s/IND
```
I suddenly stopped menstruating.

C kaho·ni na·hka e·h=a·čimohiki.
```
kaho·ni na·hka       e·h= a·čimoh +iki
so.then also,again AOR+ inform  +X-1s/AOR
```
So then I was again given instructions.

D "nahi', mani=yá·pi e·šawiki.
```
nahi' mani      =ya·pi          '    IC+ išawi   +eki
Well! this/INsg =here.I,we.go EMPH xx+ do.{so} +X/PPL(obl)
```
"Alright now, here's what we do.

E i·ni=’yo=me·kwe·h wi·h=oni·ča·nesiye·kwe.
i·ni =iyo me·kwe·he wi·h= oni·ča·nesi +ye·kwe
then =for I.believe FUT+ have.child +2p/AOR
(Since I believe you and [your husband] are now going to have a child.)

F ke·ko·h| e·h=wača·hoki e·h=ahkate·ki,
ke·ko·h +i e·h= wača·ho +eki e·h= ahkate· +ki
something +INsg AOR+ cook.02 +X/AOR AOR+ burn.(up) +0/AOR
When we’re cooking something and it burns,

G a·kwi nahi‿mi·čikini,
a·kwi nahi mi·či +ekini
not given.to/PV eat +X-0/NEG
we never eat it,

H wi·h=pwa·wi-akote·ki apeno·haki otahpitiye·pi·nwa·wani.||
wi·h= pwa·wi akote· +ki apeno·h +aki o+ ahpitiye·pi·n +wa·wani
FUT+ NEG/PV stick.from.heat +0/AOR child +ANpl 3+ afterbirth +3p(INpl)
so that the babies’[(P)] afterbirths won’t stick.

99
A na·hka paka·nani a·kwi‿nahi‿mi·čikini,
na·hka paka·n +ani a·kwi nahi mi·či +ekini
also,again nut +INpl not given.to/PV eat +X-0/NEG
And also we never eat nuts,

B wi·h=pwa·wi‿=’pi -a·nwi‿po·hkepye·ki·wa·či apeno·haki.
wi·h= pwa·wi =ipi a·nwi po·hkepye·ki· +wa·či apeno·h +aki
FUT+ NEG/PV =HRSY fail.to/PV make.hole.through.water +3p/AOR child +ANpl
so that the babies[(P)] won’t be unable to break the waters, they say.

C na·hka e·h=pepo·ki a·kwi nahi-apika·sokini,
na·hka e·h= pepo· +ki a·kwi nahi apika·so +ekini
also,again AOR+ be.winter +0/AOR not given.to/PV warm.feet.by.heat +X/NEG
And also in winter[(P)] we never warm our feet by the fire,

D wi·h=pwa·wi-akosoči apeno·haki.
wi·h= pwa·wi akosw +eči apeno·h +aki
FUT+ NEG/PV make.stick.by.heat +X-3/AOR child +ANpl
so that we won’t make the babies[(P)] stick to the caul.

E na·hka a·kwi‿nahi‿wa·wa·čika·šinekini wi·čawiwočiki,
na·hka a·kwi nahi wa·wa·čika·šin +ekini
also,again not given.to/PV lie.with.feet.facing.each.other +X/NEG

IC+ wi·čawiw +ečiki
xx+ be.with +X-3/PPL(ANpl)
And also we never lie with our feet and those of our husbands[(P)] facing each other,

F wi·h=pwa·wi- ohka·twa·ki -oči‿ni·kiwa·či.‿
```
wi·h= pwa·wi o+ -hka·t +wa·ki   oči              ni·ki    +wa·či
FUT+  NEG/PV 3+  feet  +3p(LOC) from.{smth}/PV be.born +3p/AOR
```
so that they(P) won't be born feet-first.

G na·hka owiye·he·haki ohka·twa·wani‖ a·kwi nahi‿mi·čikini.
```
na·hka     owiye·he·h +aki  o+ -hka·t +wa·wani  a·kwi nahi          mi·či +ekini
also,again animal/DIM +ANpl 3+  feet  +3p(INpl) not   given.to/PV eat   +X-0/NEG
```
And also we never eat animals'(P) feet.

100

A aša·hki·waki=na·hka‿wi·ke·sipi wi·h=pwa·wi‿me·šehkawoči.
```
aša·hki·w +aki  na·hka     wi·ke·si     +pi    wi·h= pwa·wi me·šehkaw      +eči
crawfish  +ANpl also,again be.careful +X/IND FUT+  NEG/PV touch.by.body +X-3/AOR
```
And we're also careful not to come in contact with crawfish(P).

B e·yi·ki='pi·='niki e·h=me·šeneči·='n=e·h=iš‿ačihkwiki,|
```
e·yi·ki =ipi  i·niki    e·h= me·šen +eči
as.well =HRSY that/ANpl AOR+ touch  +X-3/AOR

i·ni      e·h= iši     ačihkwi     +eki
that/INsg AOR+ {so}/PV be.pregnant +X/AOR
```
They say that likewise if we touch those(P) when we're pregnant, like you,

C ohka·twa·ki oči‿ni·kiwaki apeno·haki.
```
o+ -hka·t +wa·ki   oči              ni·ki   +waki   apeno·h +aki
3+  feet  +3p(LOC) from.{smth}/PV be.born +3p/IND child   +ANpl
```
the babies(P) are born feet-first.

D sanakesiwaki=ke·hi='pi i·nah=e·h=oči‿ni·kiwa·či.
```
sanakesi      +waki   =ke·hi     =ipi  i·nahi    e·h= oči              ni·ki   +wa·či
be.difficult +3p/IND =moreover =HRSY that/LOC AOR+ from.{smth}/PV be.born +3p/AOR
```
And the thing is, they say they(P)'re hard to deal with when they(P)'re born that way.

E "we·či‿te·pwe·še·ki| e·h=se·kiti·ki.
```
IC+ oči             te·pwe·še·     +eki
xx+ from.{smth}/PV believe,obey +X/PPL(obl)

e·h= se·kiti·                          +eki
AOR+ frighten.each.other.by.speech +X/AOR
```
"The reason we listen to what we're told is that we're frightened by it.

F wi·h=pwa·wi- kenwe·ši‿-taši|-kotakihto·ki‿na·hina·h no·še·ke,
```
wi·h= pwa·wi kenwe·ši  taši                 kotakiht +o·ki
FUT+  NEG/PV long.time be.engaged.in/PV suffer    +X(-0)/AOR

na·hina·hi    no·še·     +eke
time,distance give.birth +X/SUBJ
```
In order not to be suffering for a long time when we give birth,

G e·šiti·kini=meko·=’ni e·šawiki.
IC+ išiti· +ekini =meko i·ni IC+ išawi +eki
xx+ speak.{so}.to.each.other +X/PPL(obl.pl) =EMPH that/INsg xx+ do.{so} +X/PPL(obl)
we need to do the things we’re told to do.

101
A “na·hka owiye·ha ne·peka wi·h=pwa·wi-me·šeneči.
na·hka owiye·h +a IC+ nep +ka wi·h= pwa·wi me·šen +eči
also,again someone +ANsg xx+ die +3/PPL(ANsg) FUT+ NEG/PV touch +X-3/AOR
“And also not to touch a dead person[P].

B me·šenete=ke·hi=’pi‿nepo·hiwa·sa apeno·haki‿ki·ši‿ni·kiwa·te,
me·šen +ete =ke·hi =ipi nepo·hi +wa·sa apeno·h +aki
touch +X-3/SUBJ =moreover =HRSY die/DIM +3p/POT child +ANpl

ki·ši ni·ki +wa·te
PERF/PV be.born +3p/SUBJ
The thing is, they say, if we touched one[P]*, the babies*[P] *would die after they*[P]*’re born,*

C mehpo·še·ke.
mehpo·še· +eke
pass.on.effect.of.violating.pregnancy.taboo +X/SUBJ
if we passed it on to them in the womb.

D o=še·ški=ke·h e·h=wa·pameči ne·pekiki,| maya·wa·pama·pi=meko.
o še·ški =ke·hi e·h= wa·pam +eči IC+ nep +kiki
or only =moreover AOR+ look.at +X-3/AOR xx+ die +3/PPL(ANpl)

maya·wa·pam +a·pi =meko
look.straight.at +X-3/IND =EMPH
And another thing, when we look at dead people[P] *we must only look straight at them*[P].

E e·yi·ki=’pi·=’ni e·h=sakakwa·piki e·h=wa·pameči,
e·yi·ki =ipi i·ni e·h= sakakwa·pi +eki e·h= wa·pam +eči
as.well =HRSY then AOR+ look.aslant +X/AOR AOR+ look.at +X-3/AOR
Likewise in that case, they say, when we look at an angle in looking at them[P],

F pye·miškwa·naki·kwe·waki apeno·haki.‿
pye·miškwa·naki·kwe· +waki apeno·h +aki
be.wall-eyed +3p/IND child +ANpl
the babies[P] *are wall-eyed.*

G “kaho·ni=na·hka‿ki·šekwi‿wa·pata·haki e·h=me·šehkawoči,
kaho·ni na·hka ki·šekwi-wa·pata·h +aki e·h= me·šehkaw +eči
so.then also,again least.bittern +ANpl AOR+ touch.by.body +X-3/AOR
“And then, also, when we come into contact with least bitterns[P],

102

A ahpemeki=ʼpi a·hpeči‿ʼna·piwaki.
ahpemeki =ipi a·hpeči ina·pi +waki
up.above =HRSY permanently/PV look.{smwh} +3p/IND
they say the babies(P) always look up.

B a·kwi=ʼpi ahkiki kaški‿ʼna·piwa·čini apeno·haki.
a·kwi =ipi ahkiki kaški ina·pi +wa·čini apeno·h +aki
not =HRSY down.below able.to/PV look.{smwh} +3p/NEG child +ANpl
They say they(P) can't look down.

C na·hka owiye·he·ha e·škepya·ta e·h=me·šeneči,
na·hka owiye·he·h +a IC+ aškepye· +ta e·h= me·šen +eči
also,again animal/DIM +ANsg xx+ drown +3/PPL(ANsg) AOR+ touch +X-3/AOR
And also when we touch a drowned animal(P),

D nepo·hiwaki apeno·haki.
nepo·hi +waki apeno·h +aki
die/DIM +3p/IND child +ANpl
the babies(P) die.

E i·ni taswayaki| ne·škiti·ki=ke·ko·hi.
i·ni taswayaki IC+ neškiti· +eki ke·ko·h +i
that/INsg {so.many}.kinds xx+ admonish.each.other +X/PPL(obl) thing +INsg
That's all the kinds of things we're warned against.

F "o·ni ahpene·či=meko wi·h=na·to·tameki mese·hani, wi·h=owi·wašiki=meko, išiti·pi,
o·ni ahpene·či =meko wi·h= na·to·t +ameki
and,then every.time =EMPH FUT+ go.to.carry.on.back +X-0/AOR

mese·h +ani wi·h= owi·waši +eki =meko
piece.of.firewood +INpl FUT+ carry.pack +X/AOR =EMPH

išiti· +pi
speak.{so}.to.each.other +X/IND
"And we're told to take every opportunity to go after firewood, in order to carry back-loads,

103

A wi·h=ke·šawahokowa·či apeno·haki.
wi·h= ke·šawahoko +wa·či apeno·h +aki
FUT+ be.loosened.by.weight +3p/AOR child +ANpl
so that the babies(P) will be loosened up by the weight.

B na·hka‿ki·ši‿kehke·netisokini e·h=ačihkwiki,
na·hka IC+ ki·ši kehke·netiso +ekini e·h= ačihkwi +eki
also,again xx+ PERF/PV know.about.self +X/ITER AOR+ be.pregnant +X/AOR
And also, after we learn that we're pregnant,

C i·n=e·h=po·ni‿ke·ko·h‿išawiki ona·pe·minawaki.
i·ni e·h= po·ni ke·ko·h +i išawi +eki o+ -na·pe·m +inawaki
then AOR+ cease/PV something +INsg do.{so} +X/AOR 3+ husband +X(ANpl)
then we stop making love with our husbands[P].

D wi·nesiwaki=’pi e·h=ni·kiwa·či apeno·haki,
wi·nesi +waki =ipi e·h= ni·ki +wa·či apeno·h +aki
be.dirty +3p/IND =HRSY AOR+ be.born +3p/AOR child +ANpl
They say babies[P] are filthy when they’re born,

E ki·ši‿we·pi|-mama·či·wa·čini pa·ši‿ke·ko·h=e·h=išahišawiniči omeso·ta·nwa·wahi.
IC+ ki·ši we·pi Ca+ ma·či· +wa·čini pa·ši ke·ko·h +i
xx+ PERF/PV begin/PV RED1+ move +3p/ITER continuing.(until) something +INsg

e·h= CVCV+ išawi +niči o+ meso·ta·n +wa·wahi
AOR+ RED2+ do.{so} +3′/AOR 3+ parent +3p(OBVpl)
when their[P] parents[O] keep on making love after they[P]’ve started to move.

F i·ni e·šikeki i·n=e·h=išawiki.
i·ni IC+ išiken +ki i·ni e·h= išawi +eki
that/INsg xx+ be.{so} +0/PPL(obl) that/INsg AOR+ do.{so} +X/AOR
That’s what happens when we do that.

104

A “sanakatwi=koči=wi·na=meko pe·hki| e·h=ihkwe·wiyakwe no·še·yakwini.
sanakat +wi =koči =wi·na =meko pe·hki e·h= ihkwe·wi +yakwe
be.difficult +0s/IND =you.know =but =EMPH really AOR+ be.woman +12/AOR

IC+ no·še· +yakwini
xx+ give.birth +12/ITER
“But of course, it[P]’s really hard for us women whenever we give birth.

B kekotakihto·pena.
ke+ kotakiht +o·pena
2+ suffer +12(-0)/IND
We suffer.

C a·neta neseko·ki apeno·hahi.
a·neta neS +eko·ki apeno·h +ahi
some kill +3′-3p/IND child +OBVpl
Some[P] are killed by babies[O].

D šewe·na a·kwi kohtamakwini.
šewe·na a·kwi koht +amakwini
but not fear +12-0/NEG
Still, we aren’t afraid of it.

E iše=koči i·n=e·šikihenakwe wi·h=išahišawiyakwe.
```
išе  =koči       i·ni         IC+ išikih        +enakwe
just =you.know that/INsg xx+ be.made.{so} +3,X-12/PPL(obl)

wi·h= CVCV+ išawi    +yakwe
FUT+  RED2+ do.{so} +12/AOR
```
It's just that that's what we're made to keep on doing, you know.

F i·ni=ča·h=ye·toke we·či-pwa·wi‿kohtamakwe.
```
i·ni        =ča·hi =ye·toke    IC+ oči             pwa·wi koht +amakwe
that/INsg =so     =it.seems xx+ from.{smth}/PV NEG/PV fear +12-0/PPL(obl)
```
So that's probably why we aren't afraid of it.

G o=ča·ki‿=ke·h‿-kohtamakwe,
```
o  ča·ki   =ke·hi      koht +amakwe
or all/PV =moreover fear +12-0/SUBJ
```
And besides, if we were all afraid of it,

H na·hina·h=meko=ye·toke e·h=ča·ki-kehkya·wakwe·ni,| i·ni=meko a·m‿ahkwi·yakwe.
```
na·hina·hi      =meko =ye·toke   e·h= ča·ki   kehkya· +wakwe·ni
time,distance =EMPH =it.seems AOR+ all/PV be.old  +12/AOR.INT

i·ni        =meko IC+ a·mi    ahkwi·        +yakwe
that/INsg =EMPH xx+ POT/PV go.{so}.far +12/PPL(obl)
```
right at whatever time we all reached old age, that's probably just as far as we would go.

105

A awita‿kaški-a·nehkwikihkakoha.
```
awita    kaški         a·nehkwiki                    +hkakoha
not/POT able.to/PV grow.to.next.generation +12/POT
```
We wouldn't be able to go on to the next generation.

B še·ški=ča·h e·šiti·kini=meko išawipi na·hina·h‿no·še·kini.
```
še·ški =ča·hi IC+ išiti·                        +ekini             =meko išawi    +pi
only   =so      xx+ speak.{so}.to.each.other +X/PPL(obl.pl) =EMPH do.{so} +X/IND

na·hina·hi      IC+ no·še·      +ekini
time,distance xx+ give.birth +X/ITER
```
So anytime we have a baby, we only do exactly what we're told to do.

C pwa·wi‿=ke·h e·šimečini -išawičiki i·niki ma·mya·hkeška·kočiki oni·ča·neswa·wahi.
```
IC+ pwa·wi =ke·hi      IC+ išim            +ečini               išawi    +čiki
xx+ NEG/PV =moreover xx+ speak.{so}.to +X-3/PPL(obl.pl) do.{so} +3/PPL(ANpl)

i·niki      IC+ CV+    mya·hkeškaw      +ekočiki             o+ -ni·ča·nes +wa·wahi
that/ANpl xx+ RED1+ injure.by.body +3′-3/PPL(ANpl) 3+  child        +3p(OBVpl)
```
And those[P] who don't do the things they[P]'re told to do are the ones[P] who are injured by their[P] children[O].

D “i·ni e·h=ki·ši‿ča·ki-a·čimohena·ni e·šawiki,
i·ni e·h= ki·ši ča·ki a·čimoh +ena·ni IC+ išawi +eki
then AOR+ PERF/PV all/PV inform +1s-2s/AOR xx+ do.{so} +X/PPL(obl)
“Now I’ve instructed you about everything that we do,

E e·h=pwa·wi‿ki·ši|-kehke·netamani e·hpi·hči‿sanakahki e·h=no·še·ki.
e·h= pwa·wi ki·ši kehke·net +amani
AOR+ NEG/PV PERF/PV know +2s-0/AOR

IC+ ahpi·hči sanakat +ki e·h= no·še· +eki
xx+ to.{such}.degree/PV be.difficult +0/PPL(obl) AOR+ give.birth +X/AOR
as you haven’t yet learned how hard having a baby is[p].

106
A a·kwi=mo·hči=meko e·yi·ki i·noki wi·h=kaški-kehke·netamanini.
a·kwi mo·hči =meko e·yi·ki i·noki wi·h= kaški kehke·net +amanini
not even =EMPH as.well now FUT+ able.to/PV know +2s-0/NEG
You won’t even be able to learn it today, either.

B pa·no·h=meko‿ki·ši‿no·še·yane na·hina·hi, i·ni‿wi·h=kehke·netamani e·hpi·hči‿sanakahki.”‿
pa·no·hi =meko ki·ši no·še· +yane na·hina·hi
not.until.(then) =EMPH PERF/PV give.birth +2s/SUBJ time,distance

i·ni wi·h= kehke·net +amani IC+ ahpi·hči sanakat +ki
then FUT+ know +2s-0/AOR xx+ to.{such}.degree/PV be.difficult +0/PPL(obl)
Not until you’ve given birth will you know how hard it[p] *is.”*

C kapo·twe ke·htena‿netanemi-opiškwe·če.|
kapo·twe ke·htena ne+ anemi opiškwe·če· +Ø
at.some.point truly 1+ go.on/PV have.distended.belly +1s/IND
In time my belly did in fact swell up.

D neme·nešite·he.
ne+ me·nešite·he· +Ø
1+ be.bashful +1s/IND
I was embarrassed.

E a·kwi=meko ni·miheti·kini i·tepi iha·ya·nini, e·h=me·nešite·he·ya·ni. ‖
a·kwi =meko ni·miheti· +ekini i·tepi iha· +ya·nini
not =EMPH dance.together +X/ITER to.there go.{smwh} +1s/NEG

e·h= me·nešite·he· +ya·ni
AOR+ be.bashful +1s/AOR
When dances were held I didn’t go, because of my embarrassment.

* * *

107

A kapo·twe·=’ni_šwa·šika_taswi_ki·šeswe| e·h=pye·čisa·ki,

```
kapo·twe      i·ni šwa·šika taswi              ki·šeswe  e·h= pye·čisa·  +ki
at.some.point then eight    {so.much,many}/PP month/ECM AOR+ time.comes +0/AOR
```

In time, then, eight months(P) went by,

B no·hkoma e·h=pya·či, nekye·ni e·h=pye·či_kakano·neti·ha·či.

```
ne+ -o·hkom        +a     e·h= pya· +či      ne+ -ky      +ani
1+   mother-in-law +ANsg AOR+ come +3s/AOR 1+   mother +OBVsg
```

```
e·h= pye·či     kakano·neti·h +a·či
AOR+ coming/PV converse.with +3s-3′/AOR
```

and my mother-in-law(P) came over to have a talk with my mother(O).

C “i·ni=ma·h=me·kwe·he e·h=katawi_no·še·či.

```
i·ni =ma·hi    me·kwe·he e·h= katawi     no·še·     +či
then =you.see I.believe AOR+ almost/PV give.birth +3s/AOR
```

“I believe it’s almost time for her(P) to give birth, as I don’t have to tell you.

D wi·h=pako·ši_=ča·h=_ašikawakwe wi·h=tano·še·či we·či_wa·wotami|-pya·ya·ni.

```
wi·h= pako·ši            =ča·hi ašikaw                 +akwe
FUT+  ahead.of.time/PV =so     make.O2.as.house.for +12-3/AOR
```

```
IC+ wi·h= tano·še·            +či
xx+ FUT+  give.birth.{smwh} +3s/PPL(loc.obl)
```

```
IC+ oči                CV+   otami               pya· +ya·ni
xx+ from.{smth}/PV RED1+ taking.time/PV come +1s/PPL(obl)
```

So the reason I’m taking the time to come is so we might build a place to be ready for her(P) to give birth in.

E tepehki a·hkwamatakiče,” ine·wa=nekye·ni.

```
tepehki  a·hkwamat +akiče       iN            +e·wa       ne+ -ky     +ani
at.night be.sick   +3s(-0)/PROH say.{so}.to +3s-3′/IND 1+   mother +OBVsg
```

She(P) might get sick at night, I thought,” she(P) said to my mother(O).

F e·h=ašike·wa·či.

```
e·h= ašike·      +wa·či
AOR+ build.house +3p/AOR
```

And they(P) built it.

G ki·šike·wa·či·=’ni,

```
IC+ ki·šike·                  +wa·či i·ni
xx+ finish.building.house +3p/CC then
```

After they(P) had finished building it,

H “na·pi=we·=ki·h=natomi na·hina·h=a·hkwamatamokwe·ni,” e·h=ina·či nekye·ni.

```
na·pi           =we·na   ke+ wi·h= natom        +i
for.the.better  =in.fact 2+  FUT+  ask.to.come  +2s-1s/IND

na·hina·hi     IC+ a·hkwamat  +amokwe·ni
time,distance  xx+ be.sick    +3s(-0)/CH.INT

e·h= iN           +a·či       ne+ -ky     +ani
AOR+ say.{so}.to  +3s-3′/AOR  1+  mother  +OBVsg
```

she[P] said to my mother[O], “Now, make sure you call me over anytime she[P] has her pains.”

108

A kapo·twe·=’ni e·h=a·hkwamatama·ni neši·kani.

```
kapo·twe       i·ni e·h= a·hkwamat +ama·ni      ne+ -ši·kan +i
at.some.point  then AOR+ be.sick   +1s(-0)/AOR  1+  hips    +INsg
```

The time soon came when I had pains across my lower back.

B ana·kwiwi=’yo=ke·hi, nešekišekišine.

```
ana·kwi     +wi      =iyo  =ke·hi     ne+ CVCV+ šekišin  +Ø
be.evening  +0s/IND  =for  =moreover  1+  RED2+ lie.down +1s/IND
```

(By the way, it[P] was evening, and I was lying down.)

C a·kwi=ke·h=a·čimoya·nini.

```
a·kwi =ke·hi     a·čimo  +ya·nini
not   =moreover  narrate +1s/NEG
```

But I didn’t tell.

D kapo·twe·=’ni, “ši·´, a·hkwamatakani=wi·na=ne·hi,”| e·h=išiki.

```
kapo·twe       i·ni ši·´ a·hkwamat +akani        =wi·na =ne·hi
at.some.point  then Say! be.sick   +2s(-0)/PROH  =but   =too

e·h= iN           +iki
AOR+ say.{so}.to  +X-1s/AOR
```

Then at some point I was asked, “Say, might you be having pains.”

E “ehę·he,” nesi.

```
ehę·he ne+ i         +Ø
yes    1+  say.{so}  +1s/IND
```

“Yes,” I said.

F “neši·kani=koh| taka·wi neta·hkwamata,” netena·wa=nekya.

```
ne+ -ši·kan +i     =kohi       taka·wi     ne+ a·hkwamat +a
1+  hips    +INsg  =certainly  little.bit  1+  be.sick   +1s(-0)/IND

ne+ iN           +a·wa       ne+ -ky     +a
1+  say.{so}.to  +1s-3s/IND  1+  mother  +ANsg
```

“Actually, my lower back is hurting a little,” I told my mother[P].

G “ǫ·hǫ·´,” iwa.
ǫ·hǫ·´ i +wa
so.that's.it say.{so} +3s/IND
“So that's it,” she[P] said.

H “i·ni=ma·h=ye·toke wi·h=oni·ča·nesiyani.
i·ni =ma·hi =ye·toke wi·h= oni·ča·nesi +yani
then =you.see =it.seems FUT+ have.child +2s/AOR
“In that case you must be going to have your baby now.

I ni·h=natoma·wa i·niya.|
ne+ wi·h= natom +a·wa i·niya
1+ FUT+ ask.to.come +1s-3s/IND that/ABS(ANsg)
I'll ask your mother-in-law[P] to come.

109

A ‘ki·h=natomi,’ iwa=koči=’yo·we.”
ke+ wi·h= natom +i i +wa =koči =iyo·we
2+ FUT+ ask.to.come +2s-1s/IND say.{so} +3s/IND =you.know =PAST
She[P] did say I should ask her to come.”

B no·make=meko e·h=ki·ši_pya·či.|
no·make =meko e·h= ki·ši pya· +či
in,for.short.time =EMPH AOR+ PERF/PV come +3s/AOR
And in no time she[P] was there.

C “nahi´, i·tepi·=’nahi=’ha·no| wi·kiya·pe·heki,” netekwa.
nahi´ i·tepi =i·nahi iha· +no wi·kiya·pe·h +eki
Well! to.there =with.that go.{smwh} +2s/IMP house/DIM +LOC

ne+ iN +ekwa
1+ say.{so}.to +3s-1s/IND
“Alright, go over to the little house now,” she[P] told me.

D e·h=ana·hkahamawiki,
e·h= ana·hkahamaw +iki
AOR+ spread.02.as.mat.for +X-1s/AOR
And something was spread on the ground for me,

E e·h=nana·hapiya·ni·=’nahi,
e·h= nana·hapi +ya·ni i·nahi
AOR+ sit.down.{smwh} +1s/AOR that/LOC
and I sat down on it,

F apihka·ni ahpemeki e·h=ota·pihka·tawiki._
apihka·n +i ahpemeki e·h= ota·pihka·taw +iki
tumpline +INsg up.above AOR+ string.02.from.{smth}.for +X-1s/AOR
and a tumpline was strung from the top for me.

G “mani‿ki·h=ata·hpenama·hkwi na·hina·hi pe·hki| we·pamatamanini,” neteko·pi.
mani ke+ wi·h= ata·hpenama·hkwi· +Ø
this/INsg 2+ FUT+ pull.on.O2.for.support +2s/IND

na·hina·hi pe·hki IC+ we·pamat +amanini ne+ iN +eko·pi
time,distance really xx+ have.pain.set.in +2s(-0)/ITER 1+ say.{so}.to +X-1s/IND
“You must pull yourself up on this whenever you have a hard pain,” I was told.

H e·škami=či·h=meko pe·hki netanemi-ahpihahpi·htamata. ||
e·škami =či·hi =meko pe·hki
increasingly =it.was.discovered =EMPH really

ne+ anemi CVCV+ ahpi·htamat +a
1+ go.on/PV RED2+ have.pain.to.{such}.degree +1s(-0)/IND
I found my pains becoming more and more intense each time.

110

A ke·keya·hi·=’ni, “šekišineno.
ke·keya·hi i·ni šekišin +no
eventually then lie.down +2s/IMP
Then eventually I was told, “Lie down.

B pe·hki=ča·h‿we·pamatamanini,| ki·h=kotapi.
pe·hki =ča·hi IC+ we·pamat +amanini ke+ wi·h= kotapi +Ø
really =so xx+ have.pain.set.in +2s(-0)/ITER 2+ FUT+ try.to.sit +2s/IND
And whenever you feel a hard pain, you must try and sit up.

C ki·h=oči·kwanapi=koči.
ke+ wi·h= oči·kwanapi +Ø =koči
2+ FUT+ kneel +2s/IND =you.know
You must be on your knees, of course.

D tepina·h=meko ki·h=iši‿pešikwapi,” e·h=išiki.
tepina·hi =meko ke+ wi·h= iši pešikwapi +Ø
in.straight.direction =EMPH 2+ FUT+ {so}/PV sit.straight +2s/IND

e·h= iN +iki
AOR+ say.{so}.to +X-1s/AOR
You must kneel straight up on your knees.”

E i·ni·=’ni e·h=išawiya·ni,
i·ni i·ni e·h= išawi +ya·ni
then that/INsg AOR+ do.{so} +1s/AOR
Then I did that,

F e·h=ata·hpenama·hkwi·ya·n=a·peh‿apihka·ni.|
e·h= ata·hpenama·hkwi· +ya·ni =a·pehe apihka·n +i
AOR+ pull.on.O2.for.support +1s/AOR =usually tumpline +INsg
and I would pull myself up on the tumpline.

G a·kwi=me·h‿kaški‿ni·kičini.
a·kwi me·hi kaški ni·ki +čini
not yet/PV able.to/PV be.born +3s/NEG
It[P] wasn't able be born yet.

H ki·ši‿na·witepehki·ki·=’ni e·h=katawi-a·nawihto·ya·ni wi·h=wana·ki·ya·ni,|
IC+ ki·ši na·witepehki· +ki i·ni e·h= katawi a·nawiht +o·ya·ni
xx+ PERF/PV be.midnight +0/CC then AOR+ almost/PV fail +1s(-0)/AOR

wi·h= wana·ki· +ya·ni
FUT+ get.up.from.lying +1s/AOR
After midnight I was almost unable to get up,

I e·h=se·kesiwa·či e·taši‿nana·hi·hkawičiki ihkwe·waki.
e·h= se·kesi +wa·či IC+ taši nana·hi·hkaw +ičiki
AOR+ be.frightened +3p/AOR xx+ be.engaged.in/PV attend.to +3-1s/PPL(ANpl)

ihkwe·w +aki
woman +ANpl
and the women[P] who were attending to me became frightened.

111

A “ki·h=mama·tomopena,” i·n=e·h=iyowa·či.
ke+ wi·h= mama·tomo +pena i·ni e·h= i +wa·či
2+ FUT+ pray,request.medical.aid +12/IND then AOR+ say.{so} +3p/AOR
Then they[P] said, “We must ask for help.”

B nese·ma·wani·=’ni, a·hkone·wani, e·h=awana·či| no·hkoma,
nese·ma·w +ani i·ni a·hkone·w +ani
tobacco +OBVsg then Indian.tobacco +OBVsg

e·h= awaN +a·či ne+ -o·hkom +a
AOR+ take.away +3s-3′/AOR 1+ mother-in-law +ANsg
Then my mother-in-law[P] took some tobacco[O], Indian tobacco[O],

C e·h=mawi|-mama·toma·či| ihkwe·wani ne·hi‿no·še·hčika·ničini.|
e·h= mawi mama·tom +a·či ihkwe·w +ani
AOR+ go.and/PV pray.to,request.medical.aid.from +3s-3′/AOR woman +OBVsg

IC+ nahi no·še·hčike· +ničini
xx+ given.to/PV serve.as.midwife +3′/PPL(OBVsg)
and went to request help from a woman[O] who was skilled as a midwife.

D o·ni e·h=pya·či i·na ihkwe·wa.
o·ni e·h= pya· +či i·na ihkwe·w +a
and,then AOR+ come +3s/AOR that/ANsg woman +ANsg
And then that other woman[P] came.

E sese·si=meko·=’ni e·h=ana·po·hke·či na·tawino·ni.|
sese·si =meko i·ni e·h= ana·po·hke· +či na·tawino·n +i
hurriedly =EMPH then AOR+ boil.02.as.liquid +3s/AOR medicine +INsg
And right away she[P] hurriedly boiled up some medicine.

F ki·ša·po·hke·či·=’ni,
IC+ ki·ša·po·hke· +či i·ni
xx+ finish.boiling.(liquid) +3s/CC then
After she[P] had boiled it, then she[P] said,

G “nahi´, ki·hki·hki=meko nawači‿či·tapiče.‖
nahi´ ki·hki·hki =meko nawači či·tapi +če
Well! contrarily =EMPH first,stop.to/PV sit.up +3s,0/IMP
“Alright, let her[P], nevertheless, first sit up.

112

A ki·h=kekye·nena·pwa| wi·h=pwa·wi-ki·pisa·či,” e·h=iči.‿
ke+ wi·h= kekye·nen +a·pwa wi·h= pwa·wi ki·pisa· +či
2+ FUT+ hold.firmly +2p-3/IND FUT+ NEG/PV fall.over +3s/AOR

e·h= i +či
AOR+ say.{so} +3s/AOR
You two must hold her so she[P] doesn’t fall over.”

B ki·ši‿či·tapihiki·=’ni newi·šemeki e·h=seswamiči.
IC+ ki·ši či·tapih +iki
xx+ PERF/PV to.sit.up].cause +X-1s/CC

i·ni ne+ -wi·š +emeki e·h= seswam +iči
then 1+ head +1s(LOC) AOR+ spray.on.by.mouth +3s-1s/AOR
After I had been made to sit up, she[P] sprayed it on my head with her mouth.

C o·ni e·h=menahiči.
o·ni e·h= menah +iči
and,then AOR+ to.drink.02].cause +3s-1s/AOR
And then she[P] had me drink it.

D ki·ši‿menahiči·=’ni, e·h=we·pina·ke·či.
IC+ ki·ši menah +iči i·ni e·h= we·pina·ke· +či
xx+ PERF/PV to.drink.02].cause +3s-1s/CC then AOR+ begin.singing +3s/AOR
After she[P] had me drink it, she[P] began to sing.

E e·h=pemi-nowina·ke·či,
e·h= pemi nowina·ke· +či
AOR+ along/PV go.out.singing +3s/AOR
And she[P] went out singing

F e·h=tetepina·ke·či i·ni| wi·kiya·pe·hi.

```
e·h= tetepina·ke·   +či      i·ni       wi·kiya·pe·h +i
AOR+ circle.singing +3s/AOR that/INsg house/DIM    +INsg
```

and continued singing as she[P] circled around that little house.

G e·h=awiya·ni_tepina·h_pe·mehka·čini, pakapahkwe·hamwa.

```
e·h= awi        +ya·ni          tepina·hi               IC+ pemehka· +čini
AOR+ be.{smwh} +1s/PPL(loc.obl) in.straight.direction xx+ go.past  +3s/ITER

pakapahkwe·h            +amwa
strike.wall.of.by.tool +3s-0/IND
```

Each time she[P] passed by opposite the place where I was, she[P] knocked on the side of the house.

H "nowi·no, kwi·yese·hiwane·ni," iw=a·pehe.

```
nowi·  +no     IC+ kwi·yese·hi +wane·ni    i          +wa      =a·pehe
go.out +2s/IMP xx+ be.boy      +2s/CH.INT say.{so} +3s/IND =usually
```

"Come out, if you're a boy," she[P] would say.

I na·hk=a·peh e·h=we·pina·ke·či.|

```
na·hka      =a·pehe  e·h= we·pina·ke·   +či
also,again =usually AOR+ begin.singing +3s/AOR
```

And she[P] would start singing again.

113

A pe·mehka·čini,_na·hka=meko_pakapahkwe·hike·wa.

```
IC+ pemehka· +čini    na·hka      =meko pakapahkwe·hike·     +wa
xx+ go.past  +3s/ITER also,again =EMPH strike.wall.by.tool +3s/IND
```

And each time she[P] went by, she[P] again knocked on the side.

B "nowi·no, e·škwe·se·hiwane·ni," i·ni=na·hk=a·peh| e·h=iči.

```
nowi·  +no      IC+ iškwe·se·hi +wane·ni
go.out +2s/IMP xx+ be.girl     +2s/CH.INT

i·ni na·hka      =a·pehe  e·h= i          +či
then also,again =usually AOR+ say.{so} +3s/AOR
```

And then this time she[P] would say, "Come out, if you're a girl."

C nye·wenwi| ki·ši-tetepina·ke·či, e·h=pi·tike·či.|

```
nye·wenwi  IC+ ki·ši    tetepina·ke·    +či     e·h= pi·tike· +či
four.times xx+ PERF/PV circle.singing +3s/CC AOR+ go.in    +3s/AOR
```

After she[P] had gone around it singing four times, she[P] came in.

D na·hka e·h=menahiči.

```
na·hka      e·h= menah                 +iči
also,again AOR+ to.drink.02].cause +3s-1s/AOR
```

And she[P] gave me another drink of it.

E "i·ni=koči‿wi·h=ni·kiniči.
i·ni =koči wi·h= ni·ki +niči
then =you.know FUT+ be.born +3′/AOR
"It[(O)]'s going to be born now.

F meše·='nah wi·h=šekišinwa.‿
meše·='nahi wi·h= šekišin +wa
as.may.be FUT+ lie.down +3s/IND
She[(P)] can lie down now.

G še·ški wi·ke·čišimehko.
še·ški wi·ke·čišim +ehko
only lay.carefully +2p-3/IMP
Only, lie her down carefully.

H ki·h=kekye·niči·kwane·na·pwa‿tepina·hi='ši še·ški,"‖ iwa.
ke+ wi·h= kekye·niči·kwane·n +a·pwa tepina·hi iši še·ški
2+ FUT+ hold.knees.of +2p-3/IND in.straight.direction {so} only

i +wa
say.{so} +3s/IND
You must hold her knees straight up, that's all," she[(P)] said.

114

A ke·htena=či·h=meko i·n=e·h=ni·kiči‿kwi·yese·he·ha.
ke·htena =či·hi =meko i·ni e·h= ni·ki +či kwi·yese·he·h +a
truly =it.was.discovered =EMPH then AOR+ be.born +3s/AOR boy/DIM +ANsg
Sure enough then, the next thing I knew a little boy[(P)] was born.

B i·ni e·h=ki·ši‿kehke·netama·ni e·hpi·htamatameki e·h=no·še·ki.
i·ni e·h= ki·ši kehke·net +ama·ni
then AOR+ PERF/PV know +1s-0/AOR

IC+ ahpi·htamat +ameki e·h= no·še· +eki
xx+ have.pain.to.{such}.degree +X(-0)/PPL(obl) AOR+ give.birth +X/AOR
Then I had learned how much pain one feels in giving birth.

C ki·ši‿no·še·ya·ni=na·hka, a·kwi=či·h=meko=na·hka paši‿nekotah‿tanamatama·nini.
IC+ ki·ši no·še· +ya·ni na·hka a·kwi =či·hi =meko
xx+ PERF/PV give.birth +1s/CC also,again not =it.was.discovered =EMPH

na·hka paši nekotahi tanamat +ama·nini
also,again (at.all)/PV somewhere have.pain.{smwh} +1s(-0)/NEG
Also, after I had given birth, I realized that I didn't feel any more pain anywhere at all.

D nemenwi‿pema·tesi.
ne+ menwi pema·tesi +Ø
1+ well/PV live,be.healthy +1s/IND
I felt fine.

E apeno·he·ha·=’ni e·h=pahkešamawoči owi·nwi.
apeno·he·h +a i·ni e·h= pahkešamaw +eči o+ -i·nwiy +i
child/DIM +ANsg then AOR+ cut.stringlike.02.for +X-3/AOR 3+ navel +INsg
Then the baby[P]’s umbilical cord was cut.

F nekoti·čiše ahkošamawa·pi.
nekoti·čiše ahkošamaw +a·pi
one.inch cut.02.{so}.long.for +X-3/IND
It was cut to a length of one inch on him[P].

115

A e·škikeniki=ke·h=meko ayo·pi| mo·šowa·kani.|
IC+ aškiken +niki =ke·hi =meko ayo· +pi mo·šowa·kan +i
xx+ be.new +0′/PPL(INsg) =moreover =EMPH use +X-0/IND scissors +INsg
What’s more, a brand-new pair of scissors[O] was used for him[P].

B e·h=so·kihtawoči| we·či-pahkešamawoči,
e·h= so·kihtaw +eči IC+ oči pahkešamaw +eči
AOR+ tie.02.for +X-3/AOR xx+ from.{smth}/PV cut.stringlike.02.for +X-3/PPL(obl)
And the place where it was cut from him[P] was tied off,

C e·h=ko·keče·neči.
e·h= ko·keče·n +eči
AOR+ wash.belly.of +X-3/AOR
and his[P] belly was washed.

D wa·paniki·=’ni e·h=tehkineči tehkina·kaneki.
wa·pan +niki i·ni e·h= tehkiN +eči tehkina·kan +eki
be.morning +0′/CC then AOR+ put.on.cradle-board +X-3/AOR cradle-board +LOC
Then the next day[O] he[P] was placed on a cradleboard.

E o·ni owi·nwi·ki owi·ya·se·hi| e·h=tetepa·hkwisetawoči.
o·ni o+ -i·nwiy +eki owi·ya·se·h +i
and,then 3+ navel +LOC flesh,meat/DIM +INsg

e·h= tetepa·hkwisetaw +eči
AOR+ place.{smwh}.02.encircling.for +X-3/AOR
And then a small piece of meat was wrapped around his[P] navel.

F papakiwaya·he·hi ošehkeki apa·hkwisetawa·pi.
papakiwaya·he·h +i o+ -šehk +eki apa·hkwisetaw +a·pi
cotton.cloth/DIM +INsg 3+ belly +LOC place.02.as.padding.for +X-3/IND
A small piece of cloth was placed on his[P] belly as padding.

G “ki·h=ši·hkaši·hkawisetawa·wa a·yahpi·hčina·hi,
ke+ wi·h= CVCV+ ši·hkawisetaw +a·wa a·yahpi·hčina·hi
2+ FUT+ RED2+ moisten.02.for +2s-3s/IND every.now.and.then
“You must keep wetting it every now and then,

116

A wi·h=kekeni_pahkinwiye·či," neteko·pi.
```
wi·h= kekeni      pahkinwiye·                         +či      ne+ iN           +eko·pi
FUT+  quickly/PV have.umbilical.cord.fall.off +3s/AOR 1+  say.{so}.to +X-1s/IND
```
so that his(P) umbilical cord will fall off quickly," I was told.

B i·n=e·h=to·tawaki.
```
i·ni       e·h= to·taw     +aki
that/INsg AOR+ treat.{so} +1s-3/AOR
```
And I did that with him(P).

C a·kwi=wi·na=ni·na nahi_ko·kenakini.|
```
a·kwi =wi·na ni·na    nahi          ko·ken +akini
not   =but   1s/EMPH given.to/PV wash    +1s-3/NEG
```
But it wasn't me that washed him.

D nekya_nenana·hi·hkama·kwa.
```
ne+ -ky      +a     ne+ nana·hi·hkamaw    +ekwa
1+   mother +ANsg 1+  attend.to.02.for +3s-1s/IND
```
My mother(P) attended to him for me.

E ne·sokonakesiči e·h=pahkinwiye·či.
```
IC+ nesokonakesi        +či    e·h= pahkinwiye·                         +či
xx+ be.three.days.old +3s/CC AOR+ have.umbilical.cord.fall.off +3s/AOR
```
And when he(P) was three days old his(P) umbilical cord fell off.

F a·kwi=ke·h=e·yi·ki ka·hkami otatakini e·h=no·taki,
```
a·kwi =ke·hi     e·yi·ki ka·hkami       otat                 +akini
not   =moreover as.well from.the.start draw.out.by.mouth +3s-0/NEG

e·h= no·t          +aki
AOR+ breast-feed +1s-3/AOR
```
And another thing, he(P) didn't draw milk right away when I nursed him(P),

G ni·šokoni=meko.
```
ni·šokoni     =meko
for.two.days =EMPH
```
not for two whole days.

H o·ni, "ki·h=a·hpeči_=meko -tehkina·wa.
```
o·ni      ke+ wi·h= a·hpeči          =meko tehkiN                    +a·wa
and,then 2+  FUT+  permanently/PV =EMPH put.on.cradle-board +2s-3s/IND
```
And then I was told, "You must keep him(P) on the cradleboard all the time.

117

A čiˑkihtaˑhpeˑhkiče, waˑkisikiweˑhkiče,| waˑwaˑkapayeˑhkiče.
čiˑkihtaˑhpeˑ +hkiče waˑkisikiweˑ +hkiče CV+ waˑkapayeˑ +hkiče
have.nape.protrude +3s/PROH have.bent.spine +3s/PROH RED1+ have.bent.femur +3s/PROH
The nape of his[P] neck might stick out, or he[P] might be hunchbacked, or he[P] might be bow-legged.

B iˑni=maˑh‿weˑči|-wiˑkeˑtapineči, wiˑh=išikiwaˑči| eˑh=inapineči,
iˑni =maˑhi IC+ oči wiˑkeˑtapiN +eči
that/INsg =you.see xx+ from.{smth}/PV tie.carefully +X-3/PPL(obl)

wiˑh= išiki +waˑči eˑh= inapiN +eči
FUT+ be,grow.{so} +3p/PPL(obl) AOR+ tie.{so} +X-3/AOR
See, that's why we tie them[P] carefully the way they[P]'re supposed to grow,

C wiˑh=šoˑškaˑhkwikiwaˑči.
wiˑh= šoˑškaˑhkwiki +waˑči
FUT+ grow.straight +3p/AOR
so that they[P]'ll grow straight.

D katawi=keˑh=meko nekotawahiˑne tehkinaˑpi.
katawi =keˑhi =meko nekotawahiˑne tehkiN +aˑpi
almost =moreover =EMPH one.year put.on.cradle-board +X-3/IND
Furthermore, we keep them[P] on cradleboards for pretty nearly a year.

E naˑhka aˑkwi aˑhpeči‿soˑkenečini.
naˑhka aˑkwi aˑhpeči soˑken +ečini
also,again not permanently/PV hold +X-3/NEG
And we also don't hold them[P] all the time.

F weˑweˑpisoˑneki asaˑpi‿kiˑši‿noˑnowaˑčini,|
weˑweˑpisoˑn +eki aS +aˑpi IC+ kiˑši noˑN +waˑčini
baby.hammock +LOC put,have +X-3/IND xx+ PERF/PV suck.at.breast +3p/ITER
We put them[P] in baby swings after they[P] nurse,

G wiˑh=pwaˑwi-otamihiweˑwaˑči.
wiˑh= pwaˑwi otamihiweˑ +waˑči
FUT+ NEG/PV bother.people +3p/AOR
so they[P] won't be a nuisance.

118

A kwayeˑši=čaˑh=mešeˑ=ʼnah neˑnesapiˑhiwaki nekotah=eˑyaˑkini,
kwayeˑši =čaˑhi mešeˑ=ʼnahi CV+ nesapiˑhi +waki
that.way =so as.may.be RED1+ stay.at.home/DIM +3p/IND

nekotahi IC+ ihaˑ +ekini
somewhere xx+ go.{smwh} +X/ITER
So that way, they[P] can be left at home for a bit whenever we go someplace,

B e·h=pwa·wi-ki·hki·twe·wa·či.
e·h= pwa·wi ki·hki·twe· +wa·či
AOR+ NEG/PV be.cry-baby +3p/AOR
since they[P]'re not cry-babies.

C i·ni=ke·h e·h=sa·so·kena·wa·či a·neta,
i·ni =ke·hi e·h= CV+ so·ken +a·wa·či a·neta
that/INsg =moreover AOR+ RED1+ hold +3p-3′/AOR some
On the other hand, when some people[P] constantly hold them[O],

D pe·kisena·wa·čini=meko·='ni e·h=mayo·niči.
IC+ pakisen +a·wa·čini =meko i·ni e·h= mayo· +niči
xx+ set.down,let.go +3p-3′/ITER =EMPH then AOR+ cry +3′/AOR
they[O] cry just as soon as they[P] let go of them[O].

E otamiheko·ki e·h=a·šiha·wa·či e·h=sa·so·kena·wa·či," neteko·pi.
otamih +eko·ki e·h= a·ših +a·wa·či
hinder,bother +3′-3p/IND AOR+ get.into.bad.habits +3p-3′/AOR

e·h= CV+ so·ken +a·wa·či ne+ iN +eko·pi
AOR+ RED1+ hold +3p-3′/AOR 1+ say.{so}.to +X-1s/IND
They[O]'re a nuisance to them[P] when they[P] get them[O] into the habit of constantly being held by them[P]."

F neswa·pitaki neswi tasokoni sa·kiči| netawi.
neswa·pitaki neswi tasokoni sa·kiči ne+ awi +Ø
thirty three for.{so.many}.days outside 1+ be.{smwh} +1s/IND
I stayed outside for thirty-three days.

G i·ni=meko tasokoni pwa·wi-_ke·ko·h_-išawiya·ke wi·čawiwaka.|
i·ni =meko tasokoni IC+ pwa·wi ke·ko·h +i išawi +ya·ke
that/INsg =EMPH for.{so.many}.days xx+ NEG/PV something +INsg do.{so} +1p/PPL(obl)

IC+ wi·čawiw +aka
xx+ be.with +1s-3/PPL(ANsg)
And for the same number of days my husband[P] and I didn't make love.

* * *

119

A o·ni=kapo·twe e·h=we·pi-pehki·nawiči wi·čawiwaka.
o·ni kapo·twe e·h= we·pi pehki·nawi +či
and,then at.some.point AOR+ begin/PV act.different +3s/AOR

IC+ wi·čawiw +aka
xx+ be.with +1s-3/PPL(ANsg)
And then at some point my husband[P] started acting different.

B a·kwi=meko meči-kwi·yena,| pye·či-iši-menwawitehe, išawičini.

```
a·kwi =meko meči  kwi·yena IC+ pye·či    iši     menwawi +tehe
not   =EMPH quite exactly  xx+ coming/PV {so}/PV do.well +3s/PRET.PPL(obl)

išawi   +čini
do.{so} +3s/NEG
```

He[P] didn't act quite right, not the nice way he[P] had been acting earlier.

C keye·hapa=ke·h i·niya| ihkwe·he·ha='yo·we e·ye·h-pwa·wi-ona·pe·miya·ni ka·ki·wi·-'te·maka ke·ko·h_e·nahina·čimoha·tehe.|

```
keye·hapa      =ke·hi     i·niya           ihkwe·he·h +a    =iyo·we
it.turned.out =moreover that/ABS(ANsg) woman/DIM  +ANsg =PAST

IC+ aye·hi          pwa·wi ona·pe·mi     +ya·ni IC+ CV+   ki·wi
xx+ continue.to/PV NEG/PV have.husband +1s/CC xx+ RED1+ around/PV

wi·te·m   +aka               ke·ko·h   +i     IC+ CVCV+ ina·čimoh    +a·tehe
accompany +1s-3/PPL(ANsg) something +INsg xx+ RED2+ inform.{so} +3s-3′/CH.PRET
```

I later found out that that young woman[P] I had gone around with before I got married had been telling him[O] tales.

D "pe·hki=meko ki·na·='na ketaši-menwi-to·tawa·wa. ‖

```
pe·hki =meko ki·na    i·na      ke+ taši                  menwi    to·taw      +a·wa
really =EMPH 2s/EMPH that/ANsg 2+  be.engaged.in/PV well/PV treat.{so} +2s-3s/IND
```

"You're treating her[P] very well.

120

A pe·hki=ke·h=wi·na='yo·we i·na ki·wa kotakani neniwani mehto·či=meko ona·pe·miwa,|

```
pe·hki =ke·hi     =wi·na =iyo·we i·na      ke+ -i·w  +a
really =moreover =but   =PAST   that/ANsg 2+   wife +ANsg

kotak +ani   neniw +ani   mehto·či    =meko ona·pe·mi                 +wa
other +OBVsg man   +OBVsg as.though =EMPH have.O2.as.husband +3s/IND
```

And yet formerly your wife[P] was really acting like she was married to another man[O],

B ni·na e·ši-kehke·nemaki.

```
ni·na    IC+ iši      kehke·nem +aki
1s/EMPH xx+ {so}/PV know       +1s-3/PPL(obl)
```

according to what I know about her[P].

C 'a·kwi=nana·ši wi·h=po·ni·hka·ti·yakwini, mo·hči=meko kotakaki wi·čawiwakwe,' iti·waki=ke·hi,"

```
a·kwi nana·ši wi·h= po·ni·hka·ti·                      +yakwini mo·hči =meko
not   (ever)  FUT+  stop.dealing.with.each.other +12/NEG  even   =EMPH

kotak +aki  wi·čawiw +akwe       iti·                          +waki    =ke·hi
other +ANpl be.with  +12-3/SUBJ say.{so}.to.each.other +3p/IND =moreover
```

What's more, they[P] told each other, 'We'll never stop being with each other, even if we marry other people[P].' "

D e·h=ina·čimoha·tehe.|

```
e·h= ina·čimoh   +a·tehe
AOR+ inform.{so} +3s-3′/AOR.PRET
```

So she[P] had told him[O].

E ke·keya·h=meko·=’ni ke·htena e·h=te·pwe·htawa·tehe=ye·toke.

```
ke·keya·hi  =meko i·ni ke·htena e·h= te·pwe·htaw +a·tehe         =ye·toke
eventually  =EMPH then truly    AOR+ believe     +3s-3′/AOR.PRET =it.seems
```

Eventually, then, he[P] actually seems to have believed her[O].

F i·nina·h=meko·=’ni ‖ očiwe·pi e·h=we·pi-anemi-mya·ši-to·tawiči.

```
i·nina·hi    =meko i·ni očiwe·pi
at.that.time =EMPH then from.{smth}.on

e·h= we·pi    anemi     mya·ši              to·taw      +iči
AOR+ begin/PV go.on/PV  badly,sort.of/PV    treat.{so}  +3s-1s/AOR
```

And then from that point on he[P] began to treat me badly.

121

A iše=ke·h=wi·na=meko i·na ihkwe·he·ha e·h=kekye·škatawe·nemiči e·h=menwi-to·tawiniči we·či-inahina·čimoha·či.

```
iše  =ke·hi      =wi·na =meko i·na       ihkwe·he·h  +a
just =moreover   =but   =EMPH that/ANsg  woman/DIM   +ANsg

e·h= kekye·škatawe·nem  +iči         e·h= menwi    to·taw      +iniči
AOR+ resent,begrudge    +3s-1s/AOR   AOR+ well/PV  treat.{so}  +3′-1s/AOR

IC+ oči              CVCV+ ina·čimoh    +a·či
xx+ from.{smth}/PV   RED2+ inform.{so}  +3s-3′/PPL(obl)
```

And it was just because that young woman[P] resented me being treated well by him[O] that she[P] kept telling him[O] things.

B (wi·na=’yo=ke·h_a·kwi owi·wemekočini neniwahi e·h=wa·waneška·hiči.)

```
wi·na     =iyo  =ke·hi     a·kwi  owi·wem  +ekočini       neniw  +ahi
3s/EMPH   =for  =moreover  not    marry    +3′-3s/NEG     man    +OBVpl

e·h= wa·waneška·hi  +či
AOR+ be.bad         +3s/AOR
```

(Now, as for her[P], men[O] wouldn’t marry her[P] because of her[P] wanton behavior.)

C ke·keya·h=meko newe·pi-ne·neseko·pi.

```
ke·keya·hi =meko ne+ we·pi     CV+    neS   +eko·pi
eventually =EMPH 1+  begin/PV  RED1+  kill  +X-1s/IND
```

Eventually I began to get beatings.

D "i·ni•kohi•'yo·we we·či‿neškimena·ni| meše•meko·•'nah|| wi·h•kano·neti·hači neniwaki,
i·ni =kohi =iyo·we IC+ oči neškim +ena·ni
that/INsg =certainly =PAST xx+ from.{smth}/PV forbid,admonish +1s-2s/PPL(obl)

meše=meko·='nahi wi·h= kano·neti·h +ači neniw +aki
any FUT+ converse.with +2s-3/AOR man +ANpl
"That's certainly why I forbade you to talk with just any men[P],

122
A 'mehteno·h•meko‿wi·h•ona·pe·miwane·na| ki·h•kakano·neti·ha·wa,' we·či‿'nena·nehe,"
mehteno·hi =meko IC+ wi·h= ona·pe·mi +wane·na
only =EMPH xx+ FUT+ have.O2.as.husband +2s/INT.PPL(ANsg)

ke+ wi·h= kakano·neti·h +a·wa
2+ FUT+ converse.with +2s-3s/IND

IC+ oči iN +ena·nehe
xx+ from.{smth}/PV say.{so}.to +1s-2s/PRET.PPL(obl)
why I told you, 'You should have conversations only with whoever[P] you're going to marry,' "

B netekwa•nekya.
ne+ iN +ekwa ne+ -ky +a
1+ say.{so}.to +3s-1s/IND 1+ mother +ANsg
my mother[P] told me.

C "ke·keya·h•ma·h‿ki·h•a·hkwe·ha·pwa kekwiswa·wa e·h•a·hpeči-pekiški·hka·ti·ye·kwe.
ke·keya·hi =ma·hi ke+ wi·h= a·hkwe·h +a·pwa ke+ -kwis +wa·wa
eventually =you.see 2+ FUT+ to.be.angry].cause +2p-3/IND 2+ son +2p(ANsg)

e·h= a·hpeči pekiški·hka·ti· +ye·kwe
AOR+ permanently/PV be.at.odds.with.each.other +2p/AOR
"Mind you, eventually you two will make your son[P] angry by constantly being at sixes and sevens with each other.

D nepo·hiwaki•ma·h‿apeno·haki e·h•a·hkwe·wa·či,"| neteko·pi.
nepo·hi +waki =ma·hi apeno·h +aki e·h= a·hkwe· +wa·či
die/DIM +3p/IND =you.see child +ANpl AOR+ be.angry +3p/AOR

ne+ iN +eko·pi
1+ say.{so}.to +X-1s/IND
And mind you, babies[P] die when they get angry," I was told.

E kapo·twe·•'ni ke·tawi‿nahetone·mo·hiči nekwi·yese·hemena·na|| e·h•a·hkwamataki.
kapo·twe i·ni IC+ katawi nahetone·mo·hi +či
at.some.point then xx+ almost know.how.to.talk/DIM +3s/CC

ne+ kwi·yese·h +emena·na e·h= a·hkwamat +aki
1+ boy +1p(ANsg) AOR+ be.sick +3s(-0)/AOR
Some time after that, when our boy[P] had almost learned to talk, he[P] fell sick.

123

A pe·hki▪meko‿nekwi·natawi‿'šite·he.‿
pe·hki =meko ne+ kwi·natawi išite·he· +Ø
really =EMPH 1+ at.a.loss/PV think.{so} +1s/IND
I was completely at a loss what to think.

B ke·keya·h▪meko·▪'ni e·h▪nepo·hiči.
ke·keya·hi =meko i·ni e·h= nepo·hi +či
eventually =EMPH then AOR+ die/DIM +3s/AOR
And in time then he[P] died.

C kaši', pe·hki▪či·h▪meko‿ki·ša·koči‿sanakatwi‿e·h▪nepo·hke·ki.‿
kaši' pe·hki =či·hi =meko ki·ša·koči sanakat +wi
Why! really =it.was.discovered =EMPH extremely/PV be.difficult +0s/IND

e·h= nepo·hke· +eki
AOR+ have.death.in.family +X/AOR
Let me tell you, I then learned that it[P]'s really just the hardest thing there is to have a death in the family.

D kana·kwa▪meko wi·h▪pwa·wi-mya·šite·he·ki.
kana·kwa =meko wi·h= pwa·wi mya·šite·he· +eki
impossible =EMPH FUT+ NEG/PV feel.bad +X/AOR
It's just impossible not to feel bad.

E "i·ni▪koči▪'yo·we‿we·či-a·čimohena·ni,|
i·ni =koči =iyo·we IC+ oči a·čimoh +ena·ni
that/INsg =you.know =PAST xx+ from.{smth}/PV inform +1s-2s/PPL(obl)
"That was why I lectured you, of course,

F mi·škota e·h▪taši‿se·se·kihe·kwe▪'yo·we,"| neteko·pi.‿
mi·škota e·h= taši CV+ se·kih +e·kwe =iyo·we
what's.more AOR+ be.engaged.in/PV RED1+ frighten +2p-3/AOR =PAST

ne+ iN +eko·pi
1+ say.{so}.to +X-1s/IND
since, on top of everything else, you two were frightening him[P]," I was told.

G "i·ni▪ma·h| we·či-pwa·wi‿nahi‿pakameči oni·ča·nesinawaki.‿
i·ni =ma·hi IC+ oči pwa·wi nahi pakam +eči
that/INsg =you.see xx+ from.{smth}/PV NEG/PV given.to/PV hit +X-3/PPL(obl)

o+ -ni·ča·nes +inawaki
3+ child +X(ANpl)
"See, that's why we never hit our children[P].

124

A a·wasi=meko iši‿ki·ša·kočite·he·ne·ha ne·nesete," neteko·pi.|

```
a·wasi =meko iši     ki·ša·kočite·he· +ene·ha CV+   neS  +ete
more   =EMPH {so}/PV feel.terrible    +X/POT  RED1+ kill +X-3/SUBJ

ne+ iN           +eko·pi
1+  say.{so}.to +X-1s/IND
```

We would feel even more terrible if we gave them[P] *beatings," I was told.*

B ki·ši‿pi·tahoči‿a·wasi=meko·='ni e·h=mya·šite·he·ya·ni.|

```
IC+ ki·ši    pi·tahw +eči     a·wasi =meko i·ni e·h= mya·šite·he· +ya·ni
xx+ PERF/PV bury    +X-3/CC more   =EMPH then AOR+ feel.bad      +1s/AOR
```

After he[P] *was buried I felt even worse.*

C nye·wokoni e·na·kwiki·='ni e·h=ašamakeči pi·tahwa·čiki.

```
nye·wokoni    IC+ ana·kwi    +ki     i·ni e·h= ašam            +akeči
for.four.days xx+ be.evening +0/CC then AOR+ give.to.eat.to +1p-3/AOR

IC+ pi·tahw +a·čiki
xx+ bury    +3-3´/PPL(ANpl)
```

Four days later in the evening[P] *we prepared food for those*[P] *who buried him*[O]*.*

D e·h=we·pi-ašihto·ya·ke mi·ša·tesiweni, e·škikeki=meko.

```
e·h= we·pi    ašiht +o·ya·ke  mi·ša·tesiwen +i     IC+ aškiken +ki            =meko
AOR+ begin/PV make  +1p-0/AOR finery        +INsg xx+ be.new  +0/PPL(INsg) =EMPH
```

And we began to make fancy clothes, all brand-new[P]*.*

E ki·šihto·ya·ke, e·h=natawe·nemaki wi·h=ošehki·haketa.

```
IC+ ki·šiht +o·ya·ke e·h= natawe·nem +aki
xx+ make    +1p-0/CC AOR+ seek       +1s-3/AOR

IC+ wi·h= ošehki·h      +aketa
xx+ FUT+  clothe,adopt +1p-3/PPL(ANsg)
```

When we had finished making them, I tried to think of who[P] *we would adopt.*

F neča·ki‿=meko -nenehke·nema·waki apeno·haki.|

```
ne+ ča·ki  =meko nenehke·nem  +a·waki     apeno·h +aki
1+  all/PV =EMPH think.about +1s-3p/IND child   +ANpl
```

I thought about all the babies[P]*.*

125

A nekoti·='ni e·h=mehkawaki=mehto·či.

```
nekoti i·ni e·h= mehkaw +aki      mehto·či
one    then AOR+ find   +1s-3/AOR as.though
```

And then it seemed to me that I had found the one[P]*.*

B “mana=me·kwe·he e·hpi·hči|-tepa·nakehe netapeno·hema e·hpi·hči‿tepa·na·sota,”‿netešite·he.
mana me·kwe·he IC+ ahpi·hči tepa·N +akehe
this/ANsg I.believe xx+ to.{such}.degree/PV love +1s-3/PRET.PPL(obl)

ne+ apeno·h +ema IC+ ahpi·hči tepa·na·so +ta
1+ child +1s(ANsg) xx+ to.{such}.degree/PV be.loved +3/PPL(ANsg)

ne+ išite·he· +Ø
1+ think.{so} +1s/IND
I thought, “I believe this[P] is one[P] who’s loved as much as I loved my baby[P].”

C o·ni·=’na| e·h=ošehki·hakeči‿wi·h=okwisiya·ke=ta·taki.
o·ni i·na e·h= ošehki·h +akeči wi·h= okwisi +ya·ke
and,then that/ANsg AOR+ clothe,adopt +1p-3/AOR FUT+ have.O2.as.son +1p/AOR

ta·taki
in.a.way
And then we adopted him[P] to be, in effect, our son.

D o·ni aškači·me·hi a·wasi·me·h=meko| e·h=anemi‿’ši‿mya·šawiči wi·čawiwaka.
o·ni aškači·me·hi a·wasi·me·hi =meko e·h= anemi iši mya·šawi +či
and,then later/DIM more/DIM =EMPH AOR+ go.on/PV {so}/PV be.bad +3s/AOR

IC+ wi·čawiw +aka
xx+ be.with +1s-3/PPL(ANsg)
And then a little later on my husband[P] got even worse.

E na·ni·kihto·hiwa.
na·ni·kihto·hi +wa
be.lazy +3s/IND
He[P] was lazy.

F šewe·na neneškimekwa nekya wi·h=pešekwa·hiya·ni.
šewe·na ne+ neškim +ekwa ne+ -ky +a wi·h= pešekwa·hi +ya·ni
but 1+ forbid,admonish +3s-1s/IND 1+ mother +ANsg FUT+ get.divorced +1s/AOR
Still, my mother[P] forbade me to be divorced.

* * *

126

A o·ni=na·hka=kapo·twe‿nekya e·h=nepeki,
o·ni na·hka kapo·twe ne+ -ky +a e·h= nep +ki
and,then also,again at.some.point 1+ mother +ANsg AOR+ die +3s/AOR
And then next, at some point my mother[P] died.

B ni·šwa·pitaki‿nya·nanwi e·h=taswipepo·nwe·ya·ni.
ni·šwa·pitaki nya·nanwi e·h= taswipepo·nwe· +ya·ni
twenty five AOR+ be.{so.many}.years.old +1s/AOR
I was twenty-five.

C pe·hki▪meko‿neki·ša·kočite·he.
pe·hki ▪meko ne+ ki·ša·kočite·he· +Ø
really ▪EMPH 1+ feel.terrible +1s/IND
I really felt just terrible.

D ča·ki▪meko nemehkwe·neta e·nahina·čimohitehe.
ča·ki ▪meko ne+ mehkwe·net +a IC+ CVCV+ ina·čimoh +itehe
all ▪EMPH 1+ remember +1s-0/IND xx+ RED2+ inform.{so} +3s-1s/PRET.PPL(obl)
I remembered everything she(P) had ever told me.

E o·ni očiwe·pi‿e·h▪we·pi- ke·htena -neši|-pemenama·ni| ni·yawi.
o·ni očiwe·pi e·h= we·pi ke·htena
and,then from.{smth}.on AOR+ begin/PV truly

neši pemen +ama·ni ne+ -i·yaw +i
alone/PV take.care.of +1s-0/AOR 1+ body,self +INsg
From then on I really did have to take care of myself on my own.

F pe·hki▪či·h=meko‿sanakatwi.|
pe·hki ▪či·hi ▪meko sanakat +wi
really ▪it.was.discovered ▪EMPH be.difficult +0s/IND
I learned then that it(p) was really hard.

G a·kwi nana·ši ašenokini mi·hkeče·wi·weni.
a·kwi nana·ši ašeno +kini mi·hkeče·wi·wen +i
not (ever) be.absent +0/NEG work +INsg
The work(p) was never done.

127

A kana·kwa▪meko‿še·ški‿wi·h▪ki·wita·ki.‿
kana·kwa ▪meko še·ški wi·h= ki·wita· +eki
impossible ▪EMPH only FUT+ stay.around +X/AOR
It was simply impossible to loaf around doing nothing.

B "we·nahi▪ke·htena menwi‿to·tawikwe·ni nekya ke·ko·h‿wi·h=nahihto·ya·ni e·h=taši·hkawiči.
we·nahi ke·htena menwi to·taw +ikwe·ni ne+ -ky +a
I.see.now truly well/PV treat.{so} +3s-1s/INT 1+ mother +ANsg

ke·ko·h +i wi·h= nahiht +o·ya·ni e·h= taši·hkaw +iči
thing +INsg FUT+ know.how.to.make +1s-0/AOR AOR+ be.dealing.with +3s-1s/AOR
"Well, I can see now that my mother(P) really did treat me well in keeping after me to learn how to make things.

C a·mi‿'šawiwa·ne·ni·='nah=mani| pwa·wi-kehke·netama·nehe iši‿mi·hkeče·wi·weni ihkwe·wiweni.

```
IC+ a·mi   išawi   +wa·ne·ni         =i·nahi      =mani          pwa·wi
xx+ POT/PV do.{so} +1s/INT.PPL(obl) =with.that =as.it.is.now NEG/PV

kehke·net +ama·nehe       iši     mi·hkeče·wi·wen +i     ihkwe·wiwen +i
know      +1s/PRET.SUBJ {so}/PN work              +INsg womanhood   +INsg
```

I wonder what would have become of me now if I hadn't learned the work of a woman.

D a·wasi=meko iši-ketema·kesihka·ha pwa·wi‿ki·ši‿kekye·hkimitehe nekya,"

```
a·wasi =meko iši      ketema·kesi          +hka·ha
more   =EMPH {so}/PV be.miserable,poor +1s/POT

pwa·wi ki·ši    kekye·hkim +itehe             ne+ -ky     +a
NEG/PV PERF/PV teach       +3s-1s/SUBJ.PRET 1+   mother +ANsg
```

I would be even more poorly off if my mother[P] hadn't taught me."

128

A netešite·he=meko ahpene·či,

```
ne+ išite·he·   +Ø       =meko ahpene·či
1+  think.{so} +1s/IND =EMPH every.time
```

So I always thought with conviction,

B e·h=ašihašihto·ya·ni=meko‿ke·ko·hi.

```
e·h= CVCV+ ašiht +o·ya·ni   =meko ke·ko·h +i
AOR+ RED2+ make  +1s-0/AOR =EMPH thing    +INsg
```

as I <u>was</u> making things.

C ke·htena=meko nenahi‿mi·neko·pi| wi·h=ošehki·tamo·hiya·ni,

```
ke·htena =meko ne+ nahi          mi·N          +eko·pi
truly    =EMPH 1+  given.to/PV give.02.to +X-1s/IND

IC+ wi·h= ošehki·t             +amo·hiya·ni
xx+ FUT+  wear.(as).clothing +1s-0/DIM/PPL(INsg)
```

And I really did get things to wear given to me all the time,

D o·ni=ni·na ki·šihto·ya·ni e·h=mi·šiwe·ya·ni.

```
o·ni       ni·na    IC+ ki·šiht +o·ya·ni           e·h= mi·šiwe·                 +ya·ni
and,then 1s/EMPH xx+ make     +1s-0/PPL(INsg) AOR+ give.02.to.people +1s/AOR
```

and also I gave away what <u>I</u> had made.

E me·no·hkami·kini e·h=ahčike·ya·ni ke·ko·hi, e·h=wi·ke·či·hkama·ni.

```
IC+ meno·hkami· +kini     e·h= ahčike·    +ya·ni   ke·ko·h +i
xx+ be.spring     +0/ITER AOR+ plant.02 +1s/AOR thing     +INsg

e·h= wi·ke·či·hk              +ama·ni
AOR+ deal.with.carefully +1s-0/AOR
```

In the springtime[P] I planted things and tended them carefully.

F ke·htena ki·na·kwi ki·šikekini newačawača·ho.
```
ke·htena ki·na·kwi   IC+ ki·šiken    +kini    ne+ CVCV+ wača·ho +Ø
truly    confidently xx+ be.mature +0/ITER 1+  RED2+ cook.02 +1s/IND
```
I really did have the confidence to cook them as they[P] became ripe.

G pe·po·kini=ke·h‖ a·kwi kwi·natawi‿wača·hoya·nini‿
```
IC+ pepo·      +kini   =ke·hi     a·kwi kwi·natawi    wača·ho +ya·nini
xx+ be.winter +0/ITER =moreover not   at.a.loss/PV cook    +1s/NEG
```
And likewise in wintertime[P] I didn't lack for things to cook.

129

A o·ni| wi·čawiwaka, še·ški=meko e·h=taši‿mya·šawiči.
```
o·ni      IC+ wi·čawiw +aka
and,then xx+ be.with  +1s-3/PPL(ANsg)

še·ški =meko e·h= taši              mya·šawi +či
only   =EMPH AOR+ be.engaged.in/PV be.bad   +3s/AOR
```
And as for my husband[P], he[P] did nothing but just be mean.

B ni·miheti·kini, a·kwi| wi·to·hkawičini| wi·h=mawi-wa·pake·ya·ni.
```
IC+ ni·miheti·      +ekini  a·kwi wi·to·hkaw +ičini
xx+ dance.together +X/ITER not   allow       +3s-1s/NEG

wi·h= mawi      wa·pake·         +ya·ni
FUT+  go.and/PV look.at.people +1s/AOR
```
When there was a dance he[P] wouldn't permit me to go and look on.

C kapo·twe·=ni, "nahi′, a·wa·či nekya e·h=ki·ši-ašenoči netaši‿=mana| -ketema·kihekwa.
```
kapo·twe      i·ni nahi′ a·wa·či ne+ -ky    +a    e·h= ki·ši    ašeno      +či
at.some.point then Well! even    1+  mother +ANsg AOR+ PERF/PV be.absent +3s/AOR

ne+ taši              mana      ketema·kih +ekwa
1+  be.engaged.in/PV this/ANsg ill-treat  +3s-1s/IND
```
Then at some point I thought, "Alright now, even with my mother[P] now gone, here I am being treated cruelly by this guy[P].

D iše=ke·h=wi·na=’yo·we nekya e·h=ne·neškimiči| wi·h=pešekwa·hiya·ni we·či‿=mana‿-taši‿ketema·kihiči.
```
iše  =ke·hi     =wi·na =iyo·we ne+ -ky    +a
just =moreover =but   =PAST   1+  mother +ANsg

e·h= CV+   neškim              +iči        wi·h= pešekwa·hi     +ya·ni
AOR+ RED1+ forbid,admonish +3s-1s/AOR FUT+  get.divorced +1s/AOR

IC+ oči                 mana      taši              ketema·kih +iči
xx+ from.{smth}/PV this/ANsg be.engaged.in/PV ill-treat  +3s-1s/PPL(obl)
```
And I'm here being cruelly treated by him[P] just because my mother[P] forbade me to get divorced.

130

A a·kwi=ke·h=wi·na ni·na menwe·nemakini.
a·kwi =ke·hi =wi·na ni·na menwe·nem +akini
not =moreover =but 1s/EMPH like,desire +1s-3/NEG
And besides, I don't like him[P].

B i·noki=ke·h=wi·na awita owiye·ha‿neškimisa.|
i·noki =ke·hi =wi·na awita owiye·h +a neškim +isa
now =moreover =but not/POT someone +ANsg forbid,admonish +3s-1s/POT
And now no one[P] would forbid me.

C kotaka='yo=ke·h=ni·na| me·nwe·nemaka.|
kotak +a =iyo =ke·hi ni·na IC+ menwe·nem +aka
other +ANsg =for =moreover 1s/EMPH xx+ like,desire +1s-3/PPL(ANsg)
After all, it's the other one[P] I like.

D wi·na=ke·h neneškinawa·wa,"
wi·na =ke·hi ne+ neškinaw +a·wa
3s/EMPH =moreover 1+ hate +1s-3s/IND
But him[P] I hate."

E netešite·he.|
ne+ išite·he· +Ø
1+ think.{so} +1s/IND
Such were my thoughts.

F ki·hki·hki=meko·='ni e·h=we·pi‿wa·pake·ya·ni| ni·miheti·kini.‿
ki·hki·hki =meko i·ni e·h= we·pi wa·pake· +ya·ni
contrarily =EMPH then AOR+ begin/PV look.at.people +1s/AOR

IC+ ni·miheti· +ekini
xx+ dance.together +X/ITER
Then I went ahead anyway and began to look on when there were dances.

G pe·hki=meko·='ni e·h=kehč‿a·hkwe·či,|
pe·hki =meko i·ni e·h= kehči a·hkwe· +či
really =EMPH then AOR+ greatly/PV be.angry +3s/AOR
Then he[P] got really furious,

H “i·na=ke·h=ye·toke_wi·h=ne·wači_we·či_ki·hki·hkesiyani i·tepi_wi·h=a·yani,” e·h=isiči.‖

```
i·na         =ke·hi      =ye·toke   wi·h=  ne·w  +ači
that/ANsg    =moreover   =it.seems  FUT+   see   +2s-3/AOR

IC+ oči                  ki·hki·hkesi  +yani          i·tepi     wi·h=  iha·          +yani
xx+ from.{smth}/PV       be.contrary   +2s/PPL(obl)   to.there   FUT+   go.{smwh}     +2s/AOR

e·h=  iN              +iči
AOR+  say.{so}.to     +3s-1s/AOR
```

and he[P] said to me, “It was probably so you could see that guy[P] that you were obstinate and went there.”

131

A “netaka·wa·na·wa=koh| wi·h=ne·waki,” netena·w=a·peh,

```
ne+  aka·wa·N  +a·wa        =kohi         wi·h=  ne·w  +aki
1+   desire    +1s-3s/IND   =certainly    FUT+   see   +1s-3/AOR

ne+  iN             +a·wa        =a·pehe
1+   say.{so}.to    +1s-3s/IND   =usually
```

“I definitely do want to see him[P],” I kept telling him[P],

B natawa·či e·h=we·pi_ma·mi·wešihwaki.

```
natawa·či                e·h=  we·pi      CV+    mi·wešihw    +aki
resolving.accordingly    AOR+  begin/PV   RED1+  order.away   +1s-3/AOR
```

deciding there was nothing else to be done but to broach telling him[P] to leave.

C “kotakaki natawi-owi·wino me·hkwa·tesičiki.

```
kotak  +aki    natawi     owi·wi               +no       IC+  mahkwa·tesi            +čiki
other  +ANpl   seek/PV    have.O2.as.wife      +2s/IMP   xx+  be.quiet,reserved      +3/PPL(ANpl)
```

“Try and marry other women[P], of the quiet type.

D a·kwi=ma·h=mani=nana·ši wi·h=kaški_menwi-wi·čawi·ti·yakwini.

```
a·kwi  =ma·hi      =mani            nana·ši
not    =you.see    =as.it.is.now    (ever)

wi·h=  kaški       menwi     wi·čawi·ti·            +yakwini
FUT+   able.to/PV  well/PV   be.with.each.other     +12/NEG
```

We obviously will never be able to live together nicely now.

E e·ye·ši_=koči mahkwa·či_-taši_wi·čawi·na·ni, kewe·pi_mya·šawi.|

```
IC+  aye·ši            =koči        mahkwa·či           taši
xx+  continue.to/PV    =you.know    quietly,calmly      be.engaged.in/PV

wi·čawiw  +ena·ni      ke+  we·pi      mya·šawi  +Ø
be.with   +1s-2s/CC    2+   begin/PV   be.bad    +2s/IND
```

While I was living quietly with you, let’s remember, you began to be cruel.

F meči=’h=we·=ke·h=ni·na_netešite·he!?_wi·h=wi·čawi·na·ni!?
meči =ihi =we·na =ke·hi ni·na ne+ išite·he· +Ø
quite =NEG =in.fact =moreover 1s/EMPH 1+ think.{so} +1s/IND

wi·h= wi·čawiw +ena·ni !?
FUT+ be.with +1s-2s/AOR EN
And anyway, you don’t seriously believe it was my idea to marry you, do you?

G iše=ma·h| neta·šimeko·pi=ki·yawi.
iše =ma·hi ne+ a·šim +eko·pi ke+ -i·yaw +i
just =you.see 1+ urge.02.on +X-1s/IND 2+ body,self +INsg
Mind you, it was just that you were urged on me.

132
A wi·h=menwi-to·tawiyani=ke·h=ye·toke_we·či-a·šimiki,|
wi·h= menwi to·taw +iyani =ke·hi =ye·toke
FUT+ well/PV treat.{so} +2s-1s/AOR =moreover =it.seems

IC+ oči a·šim +iki
xx+ from.{smth}/PV urge.02.on +X-1s/PPL(obl)
And I imagine the reason you were urged on me was that they thought you would treat me nicely,

B a·kwi=ke·h_wi·h=ketema·kihiyani.
a·kwi =ke·hi wi·h= ketema·kih +iyani
not =moreover FUT+ ill-treat +2s-1s/AOR
not that you would be cruel to me.

C i·ni=ča·h_wi·h=oči-pešekwa·hiyakwe.
i·ni =ča·hi IC+ wi·h= oči pešekwa·hi +yakwe
that/INsg =so xx+ FUT+ from.{smth}/PV get.divorced +12/PPL(obl)
So that’s the reason why we have to be divorced.

D ki·h=na·kwa=ča·h=meko.
ke+ wi·h= na·kwa· +Ø =ča·hi =meko
2+ FUT+ leave +2s/IND =so =EMPH
And so you really have to leave.

E menwawihkapa_koči, wi·h=a·hpeči-wi·čawi·ti·yakwe išite·he·yane.
menwawi +hkapa koči wi·h= a·hpeči wi·čawi·ti· +yakwe
do.well +2s/POT try.to/(PV) FUT+ permanently/PV be.with.each.other +12/AOR

išite·he· +yane
think.{so} +2s/SUBJ
If you wanted to stay together permanently, you’d make an attempt to be good.

F mahkwa·či=ma·h‿mi·hkeče·wi·hkapa‿wi·h=pwa·wi‿ketema·kesiyakwe.
mahkwa·či =ma·hi mi·hkeče·wi· +hkapa
quietly,calmly =you.see work +2s/POT

wi·h= pwa·wi ketema·kesi +yakwe
FUT+ NEG/PV be.miserable,poor +12/AOR
I mean, you'd peacefully work so that we wouldn't be poor.

G ni·na=’yo i·ni pye·či‿’šawiya·ni.
ni·na =iyo i·ni IC+ pye·či išawi +ya·ni
1s/EMPH =for that/INsg xx+ coming/PV do.{so} +1s/PPL(obl)
Like me, that's what I've been doing.

H kekehke·nemi.
ke+ kehke·nem +i
2+ know +2s–1s/IND
You know that I have.

I mahkwa·či nema·mi·hkeče·wi.‖
mahkwa·či ne+ CV+ mi·hkeče·wi· +Ø
quietly,calmly 1+ RED1+ work +1s/IND
I've been peacefully working away.

133

A “kaho·ni=ki·na pi·neši=meko e·h=we·pi-kya·we·yani.
kaho·ni ki·na pi·neši =meko e·h= we·pi kya·we· +yani
so.then 2s/EMPH of.own.accord =EMPH AOR+ begin/PV be.jealous +2s/AOR
“And then you, without any provocation, began to be jealous.

B a·kwi=ke·h=ni·na| owiye·ha kakano·neti·ya·nini nehki ki·ši‿wi·čawi·ti·yakwe.|
a·kwi =ke·hi ni·na owiye·h +a kakano·neti· +ya·nini
not =moreover 1s/EMPH someone +ANsg converse.with.O2 +1s/NEG

nehki IC+ ki·ši wi·čawi·ti· +yakwe
for.{so}.long xx+ PERF/PV be.with.each.other +12/PPL(obl)
And here I haven't had conversations with anyone else(P) for as long as we've been married.

C i·noki=ča·h=mani ma·mahka·či=meko ki·h=pešekwa·hipena,” netena·wa.
i·noki =ča·hi =mani ma·mahka·či =meko ke+ wi·h= pešekwa·hi +pena
now =so =as.it.is.now necessarily =EMPH 2+ FUT+ get.divorced +12/IND

ne+ iN +a·wa
1+ say.{so}.to +1s–3s/IND
So the way it is now, we've got to be divorced,” I said to him(P).

D “ke·htena.
ke·htena
truly
“It's true.

E i·ni.‿
i·ni
that/INsg
That's so.

F ni·h=po·ni‿=ča·hi·='ni=‿'šawi.
ne+ wi·h= po·ni =ča·hi i·ni išawi +Ø
1+ FUT+ cease/PV =so that/INsg do.{so} +1s/IND
Well, I'm going to stop being like that.

G ki·h=we·pi‿menwi‿to·to·ne.
ke+ wi·h= we·pi menwi to·taw +ene
2+ FUT+ begin/PV well/PV treat.{so} +1s-2s/IND
I'm going to start being nice to you.

H na·hka‿ni·h=ma·mi·hkeče·wi.
na·hka ne+ wi·h= CV+ mi·hkeče·wi· +Ø
also,again 1+ FUT+ REDl+ work +1s/IND
And I'm also going to be working.

I a·kwi wi·h=nahi-a·nomiyanini ke·ko·h| e·šiyanini.
a·kwi wi·h= nahi a·nom +iyanini
not FUT+ given.to/PV fail.to.persuade +2s-1s/NEG

ke·ko·h +i IC+ iN +iyanini
something +INsg xx+ say.{so}.to +2s-1s/ITER
I'll never refuse you when you ask me to do something.

J ayo·h=očiwe·pi ki·na=meko|| ki·h=we·we·ne·neta‿wi·h=anemi‿'šawiyakwe," netekwa.
ayo·hi očiwe·pi ki·na =meko ke+ wi·h= we·we·ne·net +a
this/LOC from.{smth}.on 2s/EMPH =EMPH 2+ FUT+ have.control.over +2s-0/IND

IC+ wi·h= anemi išawi +yakwe ne+ iN +ekwa
xx+ FUT+ go.on/PV do.{so} +12/PPL(obl) 1+ say.{so}.to +3s-1s/IND
From now on <u>*you'll*</u> *have the say over what we do," he[(P)] said to me.*

134

A "kana·kwa=meko.
kana·kwa =meko
impossible =EMPH
"No, I just can't.

B a·kwi=meko wi·h=paši‿te·pwe·hto·na·nini,|
a·kwi =meko wi·h= paši te·pwe·htaw +ena·nini
not =EMPH FUT+ (at.all)/PV believe +1s-2s/NEG
I'm just not going to believe you at all,

C ayi·kwa·mi‿taši‿me·menwa·čimoyane.
ayi·kwa·mi taši CV+ menwa·čimo +yane
with.best.effort/PV be.engaged.in/PV RED1+ speak.well +2s/SUBJ
even if you do your best to keep talking nicely.

D asa·mi-kenwe·ši‿kepye·či‿ketema·kihi," netena·wa.
asa·mi kenwe·ši ke+ pye·či ketema·kih +i
too.much/PP long.time 2+ coming/PV ill-treat +2s-1s/IND

ne+ iN +a·wa
1+ say.{so}.to +1s-3s/IND
You've been cruel to me for too long a time now," I said to him[P].

E a·kwi=meko‿kaškešihwakini,
a·kwi =meko kaškešihw +akini
not =EMPH be.able.to.chase.away +1s-3/NEG
I just wasn't able to chase him[P] away,

F e·h=na·kwa·ya·ni e·h=pye·či‿mešeniči.
e·h= na·kwa· +ya·ni e·h= pye·či mešen +iči
AOR+ leave +1s/AOR AOR+ coming/PV catch +3s-1s/AOR
and as I was leaving he[P] came and grabbed me.

G "te·pwe·htawino," netekwa.
te·pwe·htaw +ino ne+ iN +ekwa
believe +2s-1s/IMP 1+ say.{so}.to +3s-1s/IND
"Believe me," he[P] said to me.

H "a·kwi=ča·h=meko," netena·wa.|
a·kwi =ča·hi =meko ne+ iN +a·wa
not =so =EMPH 1+ say.{so}.to +1s-3s/IND
"No, I just can't," I said to him[P].

I netaši‿kehtenekwa=meko.
ne+ taši kehten +ekwa =meko
1+ be.engaged.in/PV hold.firmly +3s-1s/IND =EMPH
He[P] was really holding me firmly.

J "a·kwi nekotah‿wi·h=a·yanini," netekwa,|
a·kwi nekotahi wi·h= iha· +yanini ne+ iN +ekwa
not somewhere FUT+ go.{smwh} +2s/NEG 1+ say.{so}.to +3s-1s/IND
"You're not going anywhere," he[P] said to me,

135

A e·h=kehči‿mayo·ya·ni.
e·h= kehči mayo· +ya·ni
AOR+ greatly/PV cry +1s/AOR
and I cried hard.

B o·ni e·h=pakiseniči,|
o·ni e·h= pakisen +iči
and,then AOR+ set.down,let.go +3s-1s/AOR
And then he$^{(P)}$ let go of me,

C nešise·ha e·h=owi·kiwa·či e·h=a·ya·ni.
ne+ -šise·h +a e·h= owi·ki +wa·či e·h= iha· +ya·ni
1+ cross-uncle +ANsg AOR+ dwell.{smwh} +3p/PPL(loc.obl) AOR+ go.{smwh} +1s/AOR
and I went to my uncle's house – where my mother's brother$^{(P)}$ and his family lived.

D i·ya·hi·=’ni e·h=nepa·ya·ni.
i·ya·hi i·ni e·h= nepa· +ya·ni
yonder then AOR+ sleep.{smwh} +1s/AOR
And I slept over there that night.

E wa·paki·=’ni‿nešise·ha,
IC+ wa·pan +ki i·ni ne+ -šise·h +a
xx+ be.morning +0/CC then 1+ cross-uncle +ANsg
Then the next morning my uncle$^{(P)}$ said to me,

F “nama·nike kepye·či‿nepe·wipena.
nama·nike ke+ pye·či nepe·w +ipena
unprecedentedly 2+ coming/PV sleep.at.house.of +2-1p/IND
“This is the first time you've ever come over and spent the night with us.

G ke·ko·h=meko ketešawi,” netekwa.
ke·ko·h +i =meko ke+ išawi +Ø ne+ iN +ekwa
something +INsg =EMPH 2+ do.{so} +2s/IND 1+ say.{so}.to +3s-1s/IND
Something is up with you.”

H “pe·hki=koh‿nemya·ši‿to·ta·kwa‿wi·čawiwaka.
pe·hki =kohi ne+ mya·ši to·taw +ekwa
really =certainly 1+ badly,sort.of/PV treat.{so} +3s-1s/IND

IC+ wi·čawiw +aka
xx+ be.with +1s-3/PPL(ANsg)
“My husband$^{(P)}$ really treats me badly, as you must know.

I i·ni=ča·h e·h=ša·kwe·nemoya·ni,” netena·wa.
i·ni =ča·hi e·h= ša·kwe·nemo +ya·ni ne+ iN +a·wa
then =so AOR+ be.unwilling +1s/AOR 1+ say.{so}.to +1s-3s/IND
Well, now I don't want any more of it,” I told him$^{(P)}$.

J “meso·te·wi=ma·h| kekehke·nemeko·pi| e·h=ketema·kihehki.||
meso·te·wi =ma·hi ke+ kehke·nem +eko·pi e·h= ketema·kih +ehki
universally =you.see 2+ know +X-2s/IND AOR+ ill-treat +3-2s/AOR
“Obviously it's known all over that you're treated cruelly by him.

136

A a·kwi=ča·h‿owiye·ha‿wi·h=a·nwe·nemehkini| wi·h=pešekwa·hiyani| e·šite·he·wane·ni.

```
a·kwi =ča·hi owiye·h +a    wi·h= a·nwe·nem            +ehkini
not   =so    someone +ANsg FUT+  consider.inadequate +3-2s/NEG

wi·h= pešekwa·hi    +yani   IC+ išite·he·  +wane·ni
FUT+  get.divorced +2s/AOR xx+ think.{so} +2s/CH.INT
```

So no one(P) will think you're falling short should you want to be divorced.

B ni·na=’yo=wi·na a·kwi‿wi·h=neškimena·nini.‿

```
ni·na    =iyo =wi·na a·kwi wi·h= neškim           +ena·nini
1s/EMPH =for =but   not   FUT+  forbid,admonish +1s-2s/NEG
```

Like me, for instance, I won't scold you.

C wi·h=če·w-ahpi·hči-=koči=meko -menwi-to·ta·ti·ki išikenwi| e·h=wi·čawi·ti·kini.

```
wi·h= če·wi       ahpi·hči              =koči      =meko
FUT+  equally/PV to.{such}.degree/PV =you.know =EMPH

menwi    to·ta·ti·                +eki    išiken   +wi
well/PV treat.each.other.{so} +X/AOR be.{so} +0s/IND

e·h= wi·čawi·ti·         +ekini
AOR+ be.with.each.other +X/PPL(loc.obl.pl)
```

It(P) is the rule, after all, that in marriages each person should treat the other equally well.

D ni·na=’yo=mana wi·čawiwaka nemenwi-to·tawa·wa,|

```
ni·na    =iyo mana       IC+ wi·čawiw +aka
1s/EMPH =for this/ANsg xx+ be.with  +1s-3/PPL(ANsg)

ne+ menwi    to·taw       +a·wa
1+  well/PV treat.{so} +1s-3s/IND
```

For instance, I treat my wife(P) here well,

E wi·na na·hka nemenwi-to·ta·kwa.

```
wi·na    na·hka       ne+ menwi    to·taw      +ekwa
3s/EMPH also,again 1+  well/PV treat.{so} +3s-1s/IND
```

and she(P), in turn, treats me well.

F ahpene·či=meko‿newača·hekwa mi·hkeče·wi·ya·nini.

```
ahpene·či   =meko ne+ wača·h    +ekwa       IC+ mi·hkeče·wi· +ya·nini
every.time =EMPH 1+  cook.for +3s-1s/IND xx+ work            +1s/ITER
```

She(P) always cooks for me when I work.

137

A o=kapo·twe we·pi-mya·ši-to·tawake,

```
o  kapo·twe        we·pi      mya·ši                to·taw      +ake
or at.some.point begin/PV badly,sort.of/PV treat.{so} +1s-3/SUBJ
```

And if, on the other hand, I began at some point to treat her(P) badly,

B e·ye·ši-taši‿menwi‿to·tawiči na·hka e·ye·ši‿mahkwa·či-ki·wita·či,
IC+ aye·ši taši menwi to·taw +iči
xx+ continue.to/PV be.engaged.in/PV well/PV treat.{so} +3s-1s/CC

na·hka IC+ aye·ši mahkwa·či ki·wita· +či
also,again xx+ continue.to/PV quietly,calmly stay.around +3s/CC
while she[P] was still treating me well and also still staying quietly at home,

C ke·ko·h‿iši‿we·pi‿nano·či-kya·we·ya·ne,
ke·ko·h +i iši we·pi nano·či kya·we· +ya·ne
something +INsg {so}/PV begin/PV persisting.to.end/PV be.jealous +1s/SUBJ
and if I began to persist for no apparent reason in being somehow jealous,

D awita‿menwe·netamowa·sa| či·nawe·ma·čiki.|
awita menwe·net +amowa·sa IC+ či·nawe·m +a·čiki
not/POT like +3p-0/POT xx+ be.related.to +3-3′/PPL(ANpl)
her[O] relatives[P] wouldn't like it.

E ke·htena=ʼyo=ke·h=ni·na| mya·šawihka·ha.
ke·htena =iyo =ke·hi ni·na mya·šawi +hka·ha
truly =for =moreover 1s/EMPH be.bad +1s/POT
Remember, it would truly be me that wasn't doing right.

F pakišite, awita=meko owiye·hani‿neškimekosa‿či·nawe·ma·čihi.
pakiN +ite awita =meko owiye·h +ani
discard,release +3s-1s/SUBJ not/POT =EMPH someone +OBVsg

neškim +ekosa IC+ či·nawe·m +a·čihi
forbid,admonish +3′-3s/POT xx+ be.related.to +3s-3′/PPL(OBVpl)
If she[P] divorced me, none[O] of her[P] relatives[O] would scold her[P],

G ni·na=ke·h‿waninawe‿taši‿te·pe·nemine·ha.
ni·na =ke·hi waninawe taši te·pe·nem +ine·ha
1s/EMPH =moreover on.all.sides {smwh}/PV be.content.about +X-1s/POT
while as for me, it would be the opinion on all sides that I'd gotten what I deserved.

138
A me·mešihka=ʼyo=meko awita=na·hka mehkawiye·ka·ha i·ni| a·mi‿ʼši‿menwawikwe·na.
me·mešihka =iyo =meko awita na·hka mehkaw +iye·ka·ha
perhaps =for =EMPH not/POT also,again find +1s-3/POT

i·ni IC+ a·mi iši menwawi +kwe·na
that/INsg xx+ POT/PV {so}/PV do.well +3s/INT.PPL(ANsg)
Since after all, I wouldn't be likely to ever find anyone else[P] as good as she is.

B ke·htena i·n=a·mihtahi peteki=meko a·hpeči‿natawe·nemaki i·niya me·nwawita.‿
ke·htena i·ni a·mihtahi peteki =meko
truly then POT back =EMPH

a·hpeči natawe·nem +aki i·niya IC+ menwawi +ta
permanently/PV seek +1s-3/CONJ that/ABS(ANsg) xx+ do.well +3/PPL(ANsg)
Sure enough, I would then always want back the good one[P] I had lost.

C kwaya·ši=’yo=ke·h ki·ši‿neškinawe·hiye·ka·ha.‿
kwaya·ši =iyo =ke·hi ki·ši neškinawe·h +iye·ka·ha
irreversibly =for =moreover PERF/PV make.angry +1s-3/POT
But, understand, it would be too late, as I would already have gotten her angry.

D ni·na=ča·h=meko‿nešihka‿taši|-nenehke·nemiye·ka·ha‿kete·=’nahi.
ni·na =ča·hi =meko nešihka taši nenehke·nem +iye·ka·ha kete·=’nahi
1s/EMPH =so =EMPH alone be.engaged.in/PV think.about +1s-3/POT by.reversal
So it would just be me remorsefully thinking of her.

E wi·na=ke·h‿awita‿taši‿nenehke·nemisa.‖
wi·na =ke·hi awita taši nenehke·nem +isa
3s/EMPH =moreover not/POT be.engaged.in/PV think.about +3s-1s/POT
She[P] would not be thinking of me.

139
A ki·ša·koči‿=meko| -neškinawisa,”‿netekwa‿nešise·ha.
ki·ša·koči =meko neškinaw +isa ne+ iN +ekwa
extremely/PV =EMPH hate +3s-1s/POT 1+ say.{so}.to +3s-1s/IND

ne+ -šise·h +a
1+ cross-uncle +ANsg
She[P] would hate me as much as she possibly could,” my uncle[P] said to me.

B “nahi′‚‿nešemi, pe·hki=meko=mani·=’ni e·hkwi‿mi·na·wi‿peseše·yani e·h=ki·ši-ahpi·hčikiyani,” i·n=e·h=išiči.|
nahi′ ne+ -šemi·h +Ø pe·hki =meko =mani
Well! 1+ cross-niece +1s/IND really =EMPH =as.it.is.now

i·ni IC+ ahkwi mi·na·wi peseše· +yani
that/INsg xx+ {so.far}/PV in.detail/PV listen +2s/PPL(obl)

e·h= ki·ši ahpi·hčiki +yani i·ni e·h= iN +iči
AOR+ PERF/PV be.{so}.old +2s/AOR then AOR+ say.{so}.to +3s-1s/AOR
“Well now, niece, by now you’re fully old enough to pay close attention,” he[P] then said to me.

C “ke·waki=koči kenenehke·neta·petoke kekya e·nahina·čimohenokwe·ni.

```
ke·waki       =koči       ke+ nenehke·net +a·petoke
as.yet,still  =you.know 2+   think.about  +2s-0/DUB

ke+ -ky      +a     IC+ CVCV+ ina·čimoh    +enokwe·ni
2+  mother +ANsg xx+ RED2+ inform.{so} +3s-2s/INT.PPL(obl)
```

“I suppose you must, of course, still remember the things your mother(P) used to tell you.

D wa·wosa·hi·’=ča·hi ki·h=we·pi‿wa·waneška·hi.

```
wa·wosa·hi              =ihi =ča·hi ke+ wi·h= we·pi    wa·waneška·hi +Ø
it’s.(not).expected =NEG =so     2+  FUT+  begin/PV be.bad          +2s/IND
```

So it wouldn’t be expected that you would start being badly behaved.

E mahkwa·či=ča·h=meko wa·pamiye·kapa neniwaki.

```
mahkwa·či       =ča·hi =meko wa·pam  +iye·kapa neniw +aki
quietly,calmly =so     =EMPH look.at +2s-3/POT man    +ANpl
```

By the same token, you should take care in considering men(P).

140

A ‘mana; mana=we·=me·kwe·he a·mi|-menwi-to·tawita,’ e·ne·nema·wate·na=ča·h i·na=na·hka a·mi-ona·pe·miyana.

```
mana       mana       =we·na    me·kwe·he IC+ a·mi    menwi
this/ANsg this/ANsg =in.fact I.believe xx+ POT/PV well/PV

to·taw      +ita              IC+ ine·nem            +a·wate·na              =ča·hi
treat.{so} +3-1s/PPL(ANsg) xx+ think.about.{so} +2s-3/INT.PPL(ANsg) =so

i·na       na·hka        IC+ a·mi    ona·pe·mi              +yana
that/ANsg also,again xx+ POT/PV have.O2.as.husband +2s/PPL(ANsg)
```

And whoever(P) you may think of as: ‘This is him(P); I believe this one(P) would be nice to me,’ that should be the one(P) you marry the next time.

B wanimo·či·=’na‿menwi‿to·to·hke,‿

```
wanimo·či i·na       menwi    to·taw      +ehke
perchance that/ANsg well/PV treat.{so} +3-2s/SUBJ
```

And should it happen that he(P)’s nice to you,

C mahkwa·či=meko| ki·h=taši-wi·čawiwa·wa.

```
mahkwa·či       =meko ke+ wi·h= taši                   wi·čawiw +a·wa
quietly,calmly =EMPH 2+  FUT+  be.engaged.in/PV be.with  +2s-3s/IND
```

you ought to keep living with him(P) quietly.

D ka·ta=na·hka=kotaka natawe·nemiye·kani.

```
ka·ta na·hka       kotak +a      natawe·nem +iye·kani
don’t also,again other +ANsg seek         +2s-3/PROH
```

Don’t wish for anyone else(P) after that.

E a·kwi=koh=e·yi·ki menwikekini ma·nenwi wi·h=ona·pe·miye·kwe e·h=ihkwe·wiye·kwe.
a·kwi =kohi e·yi·ki menwiken +kini
not =certainly as.well be.good +0/NEG

ma·nenwi wi·h= ona·pe·mi +ye·kwe e·h= ihkwe·wi +ye·kwe
many.times FUT+ have.husband +2p/AOR AOR+ be.woman +2p/PPL(loc.obl)
You must realize that it[P]'s not a good thing, either, for you women to marry many times.

141

A ta·tašima·pi ihkwe·wa i·n=e·h=išawiči.|
CV+ tašim +a·pi ihkwe·w +a i·ni e·h= išawi +či
RED1+ talk.about +X-3/IND woman +ANsg that/INsg AOR+ do.{so} +3s/AOR
A woman[P] is the topic of gossip when she does that.

B mehto·či e·h=pemešito·či neniwah.‿
mehto·či e·h= pemešit +o·či neniw +ahi
as.though AOR+ go.down.the.line +3s(-0)/AOR man +OBVpl
It's as if she[P] passes from man to man[O].

C "i·ni,| nešemi, e·ne·nemena·ni wi·h=išawiyani.
i·ni ne+ -šemi·h +Ø IC+ ine·nem +ena·ni
that/INsg 1+ cross-niece +VOCsg xx+ think.about.{so} +1s-2s/PPL(obl)

wi·h= išawi +yani
FUT+ do.{so} +2s/AOR
"That, niece, is what I think you ought to do.

D e·h=ki·ši-ašenoči=kekya we·či-a·ya·čimohena·ni ni·na‿ta·taki e·ši‿kehke·netamo·hiya·ni.
e·h= ki·ši ašeno +či ke+ -ky +a
AOR+ PERF/PV be.absent +3s/AOR 2+ mother +ANsg

IC+ oči CV+ a·čimoh +ena·ni ni·na ta·taki
xx+ from.{smth}/PV RED1+ inform +1s-2s/PPL(obl) 1s/EMPH in.a.way

IC+ iši kehke·net +amo·hiya·ni
xx+ {so}/PV know +1s-0/DIM/PPL(obl)
It's because your mother[P] is gone that I'm telling you how I understand things to be, to the extent I do.

E "na·hka=mani·=’noki| pešekwa·hiyane,
na·hka =mani i·noki pešekwa·hi +yane
also,again =as.it.is.now now get.divorced +2s/SUBJ
"And also, if you're divorced now,

F kana·h nekotawahi·ne,| ni·šwawahi·ne=ke·h, še·ški‿ki·ki·wita·hkapa.
kana·hi nekotawahi·ne ni·šwawahi·ne =ke·hi še·ški Ci·+ ki·wita· +hkapa
at.least one.year two.years =moreover only RED1+ stay.around +2s/POT
for at least one year, if not two, you should just stay single.

G še·ški_taši-‖ma·mi·hkeče·wi·hkapa.
še·ški taši CV+ mi·hkeče·wi· +hkapa
only be.engaged.in/PV RED1+ work +2s/POT
You should just be working along.

142
A meše·='nah=ča·hi·='nina·h ona·pe·mihkapa," netekwa_nešise·ha.
meše·='nahi =ča·hi i·nina·hi ona·pe·mi +hkapa
as.may.be =so at.that.time have.husband +2s/POT

ne+ iN +ekwa ne+ -šise·h +a
1+ say.{so}.to +3s-1s/IND 1+ cross-uncle +ANsg
And then at that time you could get married," my uncle[P] said to me.

B i·ni=ča·h=meko e·h=pešekwa·hiya·ni.
i·ni =ča·hi =meko e·h= pešekwa·hi +ya·ni
then =so =EMPH AOR+ get.divorced +1s/AOR
And so, right then I got divorced.

C koči·h| ahpene·či=meko_nekoči·hka·kwa,
koči·hi ahpene·či =meko ne+ koči·hkaw +ekwa
although every.time =EMPH 1+ try.to.persuade +3s-1s/IND
Even though he[P] was always trying with me,

D šewe·na a·kwi=meko_paši-we·te·we wi·h=ne·ya·pi-keša·čihaki.|
šewe·na a·kwi =meko paši we·te·we
but not =EMPH (at.all)/PP (the.least.bit)

wi·h= ne·ya·pi keša·čih +aki
FUT+ same.as.before/PV be.kind.to +1s-3/AOR
still there was absolutely no way that I would go back to being friendly to him[P].

E pe·hki=meko_neneškinawa·wa.
pe·hki =meko ne+ neškinaw +a·wa
really =EMPH 1+ hate +1s-3s/IND
I really hated him[P] a lot.

* * *

F o·ni·='niya e·ye·h-še·škesi·hiya·ni ke·kano·neti·ya·na kapo·twe owi·wani e·h=nepeniči.
o·ni i·niya IC+ aye·hi še·škesi·hi +ya·ni
and,then that/ABS(ANsg) xx+ continue.to/PV be.teenage.girl +1s/CC

IC+ kakano·neti· +ya·na
xx+ converse.with.O2 +1s/PPL(ANsg)

kapo·twe o+ -i·w +ani e·h= nep +niči
at.some.point 3+ wife +OBVsg AOR+ die +3′/AOR
And then sometime later the wife[O] of the one[P] I used to go with when I was still a young girl died.

143

A nekotawahi·ne ki·ši‿pešekwa·hiya·ni, ki·ši‿pa·ni·či,‿
nekotawahi·ne IC+ ki·ši pešekwa·hi +ya·ni
one.year xx+ PERF/PV get.divorced +1s/CC

IC+ ki·ši pa·ni· +či
xx+ PERF/PV be.widow(er).no.longer.in.strict.mourning +3s/CC
And after I had been divorced for a year and he(P) had been formally released from his mourning,

B na·hka·▪'ni e·h▪we·pi·hkawiči.
na·hka i·ni e·h= we·pi·hkaw +iči
also,again then AOR+ begin.dealing.with +3s-1s/AOR
then he(P) took up with me again.

C kotakaki▪wi·na‿ma·ne▪meko netaši·hka·ko·ki,
kotak +aki =wi·na ma·ne =meko ne+ taši·hkaw +eko·ki
other +ANpl =but much,many =EMPH 1+ be.dealing.with +3p-1s/IND
Meanwhile, there were others(P) after me, quite a few of them,

D šewe·na| a·kwi kakano·neti·hakini.
šewe·na a·kwi kakano·neti·h +akini
but not converse.with +1s-3/NEG
but I didn't talk with them(P).

E kaho·ni·▪'na| kapo·twe e·h▪we·pi‿▪na·hka‿-kakano·neti·haki.
kaho·ni i·na kapo·twe e·h= we·pi na·hka kakano·neti·h +aki
so.then that/ANsg at.some.point AOR+ begin/PV also,again converse.with +1s-3/AOR
So then, at some point I began talking with him(P) again.

F neki·ši‿▪'yo▪ke·h| -anehka·ti·pena e·ye·h‿aškikiya·ke.|
ne+ ki·ši =iyo =ke·hi anehka·ti· +pena
1+ PERF/PV =for =moreover be.acquainted.with.each.other +1p/IND

IC+ aye·hi aškiki +ya·ke
xx+ continue.to/PV be.young +1p/CC
Of course, we had already become acquainted while we were young.

G o·ni kapo·twe e·h▪nana·tohtawiči we·či‿pešekwa·hiwa·ne·ni.
o·ni kapo·twe e·h= nana·tohtaw +iči
and,then at.some.point AOR+ ask.question.of +3s-1s/AOR

IC+ oči pešekwa·hi +wa·ne·ni
xx+ from.{smth}/PV get.divorced +1s/INT.PPL(obl)
And then at some point he(P) asked me why I had become divorced.

144

A e·h=a·čimohaki| na·na·kači=meko e·šawiya·ni we·či͜pešekwa·hiya·ni.
e·h= a·čimoh +aki na·na·kači =meko IC+ išawi +ya·ni
AOR+ inform +1s-3/AOR exactly =EMPH xx+ do.{so} +1s/PPL(obl)

IC+ oči pešekwa·hi +ya·ni
xx+ from.{smth}/PV get.divorced +1s/PPL(obl)
And I told him[P] exactly what happened to me that was the reason why I got divorced.

B "pe·hki=ní·hka, nano·te·nemenowakwe·ni.
pe·hki =ni·hka ´ nano·te·nem +enowakwe·ni
really =MAN'S.EXPL EMPH persist.in.thinking.wrongly.of +3,X-12/INT
"Golly, he[P] had it all wrong about us.

C apina=ke·h=mo·hči͜me·h͜ona·pe·miwane=meko kepo·ni͜ne·wone.͜
apina =ke·hi mo·hči IC+ me·hi ona·pe·mi +wane =meko
even =moreover even xx+ yet/PV have.husband +2s/CH.PRI =EMPH

ke+ po·ni ne·w +ene
2+ cease/PV see +1s-2s/IND
Actually, I even stopped seeing you before you got married.

D ne·wona·neh=ke·h=mo·hči,| awita kaški͜mačino·naka·ha ke·ko·h͜wi·h=inena·ni.
ne·w +ena·nehe =ke·hi mo·hči awita kaški
see +1s-2s/SUBJ.PRET =moreover even not/POT able.to/PV

mačinaw +enaka·ha ke·ko·h +i wi·h= iN +ena·ni
dare.with.regard.to +1s-2s/POT something +INsg FUT+ say.{so}.to +1s-2s/AOR
And what's more, even if I had seen you, I wouldn't have had the nerve to say anything to you.

E me·me·čiki='yo=meko a·čimihkapa,||
me·me·čiki =iyo =meko a·čim +ihkapa
being.sure =for =EMPH tell.of +2s-1s/POT
Since I'm sure you would've told on me,

145

A ketešawi=ta·taki e·h=ona·pe·miyani.
ke+ išawi +Ø ta·taki e·h= ona·pe·mi +yani
2+ do.{so} +2s/IND in.a.way AOR+ have.husband +2s/AOR
the way you acted when you were married.

B na·pi͜ni·na='yo·we| kaškimena·nehe awita͜nahi͜nesenaka·ha.
na·pi ni·na =iyo·we kaškim +ena·nehe
for.the.better 1s/EMPH =PAST persuade +1s-2s/SUBJ.PRET

awita nahi neS +enaka·ha
not/POT given.to/PV kill +1s-2s/POT
Better would have been if I'd been able to persuade you to marry me, and I would never have beaten you.

C i·noki=wi·na·=ʼni wi·h=anwa·či·yani ki·na·na i·ni‿wi·h=išawiyakwe,"| netekwa.
```
i·noki =wi·na i·ni wi·h= anwa·či· +yani   ki·na·na i·ni      wi·h= išawi   +yakwe
now    =but   then FUT+  consent  +2s/AOR 12/EMPH  that/INsg FUT+  do.{so} +12/AOR

ne+ iN          +ekwa
1+  say.{so}.to +3s-1s/IND
```
But now this time you must consent for us to do that," he[(P)] *said to me.*

D "iše=ye·toke=na·hka=ki·na‿wi·h=ne·nešiyani we·či‿taši·hkawiyani," netena·wa.
```
iše  =ye·toke  na·hka       ki·na    wi·h= CV+    neS  +iyani
just =it.seems also,again 2s/EMPH FUT+  RED1+ kill +2s-1s/AOR

IC+ oči            taši·hkaw         +iyani          ne+ iN          +a·wa
xx+ from.{smth}/PV be.dealing.with +2s-1s/PPL(obl) 1+  say.{so}.to +1s-3s/IND
```
"You're probably just after me so you can beat me also," I said to him[(P)].

E "kašina·kwa, ke·senwi=yá·pi keno·ta·ke| i·niya wi·čawiwaka e·h=pakamaki.|
```
kašina·kwa ke·senwi        =ya·pi        ʹ    ke+ no·ta·ke·              +Ø
Well!      how.many.times =here.I,we.go EMPH 2+  hear.what.people.say +2s/IND

i·niya         IC+ wi·čawiw +aka            e·h= pakam +aki
that/ABS(ANsg) xx+ be.with  +1s-3/PPL(ANsg) AOR+ hit    +1s-3/AOR
```
"Well, now tell me, how many times did you hear that I hit my late wife[(P)]*?*

146
A a·kwi=mo·hči‿nekotenwi| pakamakini.
```
a·kwi mo·hči nekotenwi pakam +akini
not   even   once      hit   +1s-3/NEG
```
I didn't hit her[(P)] *even once.*

B a·kwi| nahi‿neškimakini.
```
a·kwi nahi        neškim           +akini
not   given.to/PV forbid,admonish +1s-3/NEG
```
And I never scolded her[(P)].

C na·ni·miwa=na·hka ni·mihete·nikini e·ye·h‿pwa·wi-we·pi-ki·w‿a·hkwamataki.
```
CV+   ni·mi +wa     na·hka      IC+ ni·mihete· +nikini
RED1+ dance +3s/IND also,again xx+ be.dancing +0ʹ/ITER

IC+ aye·hi           pwa·wi we·pi    ki·wi       a·hkwamat +aki
xx+ continue.to/PV NEG/PV begin/PV around/PV be.sick    +3s(-0)/CC
```
And also, she[(P)] *danced at dances*[(i)] *before she*[(P)] *started getting sick.*

D i·ni=ča·h=meko=ki·na na·hka a·mi‿to·to·na·ni.
```
i·ni      =ča·hi =meko ki·na   na·hka      IC+ a·mi   to·taw      +ena·ni
that/INsg =so    =EMPH 2s/EMPH also,again xx+ POT/PV treat.{so} +1s-2s/PPL(obl)
```
So that's exactly how I would be with you also.

E wi·h=na·ni·miyani=ke·h‿išite·he·yane,‿na·ni·mihkapa.

```
wi·h= CV+   ni·mi +yani    =ke·hi     išite·he·  +yane     CV+   ni·mi +hkapa
FUT+  RED1+ dance +2s/AOR =moreover think.{so} +2s/SUBJ RED1+ dance +2s/POT
```

If you want to dance, for instance, you should dance.

F iše=ma·h‿išikiheti·pi‿wi·h=na·ni·miki.

```
iše  =ma·hi    išikiheti·                      +pi     wi·h= CV+   ni·mi +eki
just =you.see to.be.{so}].cause.each.other +X/IND FUT+  RED1+ dance +X/AOR
```

I mean, for us to dance is just the way we're made.

G a·kwi=ke·hi·=’nah me·h‿kehke·nemakini‖ owiye·ha‿wi·h=taši˛owi·weti·či.

```
a·kwi =ke·hi     i·nahi   me·hi  kehke·nem +akini     owiye·h +a
not   =moreover that/LOC yet/PV know      +1s-3/NEG someone +ANsg

wi·h= taši       owi·weti·        +či
FUT+  {smwh}/PV marry.each.other +3s/AOR
```

Besides, I've never yet known anyone[P] to get married there.

147

A ta·ni=ye·toke a·mi˛’šawiči| wi·h=mi·hketi·či=ke·h.|

```
ta·ni =ye·toke  IC+ a·mi   išawi     +či             wi·h= mi·hketi· +či     =ke·hi
how   =it.seems xx+ POT/PV do.{so} +3s/PPL(obl) FUT+  court      +3s/AOR =moreover
```

How could they[P] possibly manage to make out, of all things?

B ma·ne·waki=’yo=ke·h| mehtose·neniwaki.

```
ma·ne·          +waki   =iyo =ke·hi     mehtose·neniw +aki
be.much,many +3p/IND =for =moreover person          +ANpl
```

Remember, there are lots of people[P].

C awita=ča·h=meko pana·pamene·ha| owiye·ha i·nah‿taši˛mi·hketi·te.

```
awita   =ča·hi =meko pana·pam       +ene·ha  owiye·h +a
not/POT =so    =EMPH lose.sight.of +X-3/POT someone +ANsg

i·nahi   taši       mi·hketi· +te
that/LOC {smwh}/PV court      +3s/SUBJ
```

So no one[P] would avoid being seen if they[P] were making out there.

D ni·na=we·n=a·pehe e·šite·he·ya·ni.

```
ni·na   =we·na    =a·pehe   IC+ išite·he·  +ya·ni
1s/EMPH =in.fact =usually xx+ think.{so} +1s/PPL(obl)
```

At least it's what I always think.

E “anwa·či·yane=ča·hi, i·ni=meko| ki·h=išawipena.|

```
anwa·či· +yane     =ča·hi i·ni       =meko ke+ wi·h= išawi    +pena
consent  +2s/SUBJ =so     that/INsg =EMPH 2+  FUT+  do.{so} +12/IND
```

“So if you're willing, that's what we'll do.

F ketaka·wa·nene‿wi·h=anwa·či·yani‿pe·hki=meko.
ke+ aka·wa·N +ene wi·h= anwa·či· +yani pe·hki =meko
2+ desire +1s-2s/IND FUT+ consent +2s/AOR really =EMPH
I want you to consent, very much.

G ahpene·či, 'ta·ni·='nahi‿wi·čawiwake,' netešite·h,"| netekwa.
ahpene·či ta·ni =i·nahi wi·čawiw +ake ne+ išite·he· +Ø
every.time how =with.that be.with +1s-3/SUBJ 1+ think.{so} +1s/IND

ne+ iN +ekwa
1+ say.{so}.to +3s-1s/IND
I have always wished I could be with you," he[P] said to me.

148

A "o·ˊ‿meše=wi·na‿nekotawahi·nakahke ayo·h=oči anwa·či·hka·ha,
o·ˊ meše =wi·na nekotawahi·nakat +ke ayo·hi oči anwa·či· +hka·ha
Oh freely =but be.one.year +0/SUBJ this/LOC from.{smth} consent +1s/POT
"Oh, maybe a year[P] from now I would consent,

B i·noki=wi·na a·kwi," i·n=e·h=inaki.
i·noki =wi·na a·kwi i·ni e·h= iN +aki
now =but not then AOR+ say.{so}.to +1s-3/AOR
but not now," I then said to him[P].

C še·ški·='ni a·yaškači e·h=kakano·neti·ya·ke.
še·ški i·ni CV+ aškači e·h= kakano·neti· +ya·ke
only then RED1+ later AOR+ converse +1p/AOR
And then all we did was, once in a while we talked together.

D i·niya=ke·h‿ke·hta‿wi·čawiwaka a·kwi=meko| pe·we·nemočini.
i·niya =ke·hi ke·hta IC+ wi·čawiw +aka
that/ABS(ANsg) =moreover former/PN xx+ be.with +1s-3/PPL(ANsg)

a·kwi =meko pe·we·nemo +čini
not =EMPH give.up.trying +3s/NEG
But that former husband[P] of mine just wouldn't give it up.

E ahpene·či=meko| nekoči·hka·kwa.
ahpene·či =meko ne+ koči·hkaw +ekwa
every.time =EMPH 1+ try.to.persuade +3s-1s/IND
He[P] was always trying with me.

F šewe·na a·kwi=meko‿paši‿we·te·wi|| wi·h=ne·ya·pi‿keša·te·nemaki.
šewe·na a·kwi =meko paši we·te·wi
but not =EMPH (at.all)/PP (the.least.bit)

wi·h= ne·ya·pi keša·te·nem +aki
FUT+ same.as.before/PV think.kindly.of +1s-3/AOR
But there was absolutely no way that I would go back to thinking kindly of him[P].

149

A kaši′, neneškinawe·hekwa=koči kwaya·ši e·h=mya·ši‿to·tawiči.|

kaši′ ne+ neškinawe·h +ekwa =koči kwaya·ši
Why! 1+ make.angry +3s–1s/IND =you.know irreversibly

e·h= mya·ši to·taw +iči
AOR+ badly,sort.of/PV treat.{so} +3s–1s/AOR

Well, of course, he[P] had made me angry for good by treating me badly.

B pe·hki=ča·h=meko neneškinawa·wa.|

pe·hki =ča·hi =meko ne+ neškinaw +a·wa
really =so =EMPH 1+ hate +1s–3s/IND

So I really hated him[P] a lot.

C i·ni=kapo·twe e·h=pye·čisa·ki na·hina·h| e·h=kehkahamawaki| wi·h=wi·čawi·ti·ya·ke.

i·ni kapo·twe e·h= pye·čisa· +ki
then at.some.point AOR+ time.comes +0/AOR

na·hina·hi e·h= kehkahamaw +aki wi·h= wi·čawi·ti· +ya·ke
time,distance AOR+ designate.02.for +1s–3/AOR FUT+ be.with.each.other +1p/AOR

Then eventually the time[P] came that I had set with him[P] for us to be married.

D e·h=ne·woti·ya·ke,

e·h= ne·woti· +ya·ke
AOR+ see.each.other +1p/AOR

When we saw each other, he[P] said to me,

E "kaši·='ni=yá·pi na·hina·hi='yo·we‿ke·hkahamawiyani wi·h=anwa·či·yani.

kaši′ i·ni =ya·pi ′
Why! then =here.I,we.go EMPH

na·hina·hi =iyo·we IC+ kehkahamaw +iyani wi·h= anwa·či· +yani
time,distance =PAST xx+ designate.02.for +2s–1s/PPL(INsg) FUT+ consent +2s/AOR

"Well, alright now, this is the time you set with me that you would consent.

F i·noki=ča·h‿pehkote·ke ka·ta wi·šika·hkohakani ketaškwa·te·mwa·wi.

i·noki =ča·hi pehkote· +ke ka·ta wi·šika·hkoh +akani
now =so be.night +0/SUBJ don't fasten.firmly +2s–0/PROH

ke+ aškwa·te·m +wa·wi
2+ door +2p(INsg)

So, tonight, don't secure the door tightly where you people live.

150

A i·tepi·='ni‿wi·h=pye·noto·na·ni," netekwa.|

i·tepi i·ni wi·h= pye·notaw +ena·ni ne+ iN +ekwa
to.there then FUT+ come.to +1s–2s/AOR 1+ say.{so}.to +3s–1s/IND

I'll come to you there then."

B i·ni·=’ni e·h=išawiya·ni,
i·ni i·ni e·h= išawi +ya·ni
then that/INsg AOR+ do.{so} +1s/AOR
Then I did that,

C e·h=pya·či.
e·h= pya· +či
AOR+ come +3s/AOR
and he[P] came.

D ke·htena| e·h=wi·hpe·ti·ya·ke.
ke·htena e·h= wi·hpe·ti· +ya·ke
truly AOR+ sleep.with.each.other +1p/AOR
And we really did sleep together.

E i·ni=meko no·te·tepehkwe·=’ni| ke·ko·h_e·h=išawiya·ke.
i·ni =meko no·te·tepehkwe i·ni ke·ko·h +i e·h= išawi +ya·ke
then =EMPH before.night’s.end then something +INsg AOR+ do.{so} +1p/AOR
Right away, before that night was out, we made love.

F šewe·na a·kwi i·na_kenwe·ši_pe·hki_pemi_mata·kwe·netakini ke·ko·h_e·h=išawiya·ke.
šewe·na a·kwi i·na kenwe·ši pe·hki pemi mata·kwe·net +akini
but not that/ANsg long.time really along/PV enjoy +3s-0/NEG

ke·ko·h +i e·h= išawi +ya·ke
something +INsg AOR+ do.{so} +1p/AOR
But he didn’t really like for us to make love for long.

G no·make=meko e·taswi|-pehkote·kini i·ni_netešawipena.
no·make =meko IC+ taswi pehkote· +kini
in,for.short.time =EMPH xx+ {so.much,many}/PV be.night +0/ITER

i·ni ne+ išawi +pena
that/INsg 1+ do.{so} +1p/IND
We did that just for a short time every night[P].

151
A kapo·twe=meko·=’ni a·yaškači i·n=e·h=išite·he·či.
kapo·twe =meko i·ni CV+ aškači i·ni e·h= išite·he· +či
at.some.point =EMPH then RED1+ later that/INsg AOR+ think.{so} +3s/AOR
Then at some point he[P] wanted to do that only once in a while.

B meše=meko_nene·nepa·pena.
meše =meko ne+ CV+ nepa· +pena
freely =EMPH 1+ RED1+ sleep +1p/IND
We would just contentedly go ahead and sleep.

C a·kwi‿nekotenwi| taši‿meškwi·kite·wi‿wi·kawihičini.
```
a·kwi nekotenwi taši             meškwi·kite·wi    wi·kawih +ičini
not   once      be.engaged.in/PV exasperatingly/PV bother   +3s-1s/NEG
```
Not once did he(P) keep on bothering me to the point of making me irritated.

D na·hka‿ke·ko·h‿wi·h=išawiya·ke e·šičini, e·h=a·nomiči,
```
na·hka       ke·ko·h   +i     wi·h= išawi    +ya·ke  IC+ iN             +ičini
also,again something +INsg FUT+  do.{so} +1p/AOR xx+ say.{so}.to +3s-1s/NEG

e·h= a·nom             +iči
AOR+ fail.to.persuade +3s-1s/AOR
```
And also, whenever he(P) asked me to make love and I refused him(P),

E a·kwi‿taši‿ki·hki·hkihičini.
```
a·kwi taši             ki·hki·hkih        +ičini
not   be.engaged.in/PV force.against.will +3s-1s/NEG
```
he(P) wouldn't keep on trying to force me to anyway.

F na·hka meše·=’nah=meko čačawi·hi nekotah‿nepe·wa atehči,
```
na·hka      meše·=’nahi =meko čačawi·hi nekotahi  nepa· +wa     atehči
also,again as.may.be   =EMPH sometimes somewhere sleep +3s/IND away
```
And also, he(P) might sometimes sleep away someplace,

G wi·kiya·peki‿či·nawe·ma·čihi e·h=awiniči.
```
wi·kiya·p +eki IC+ či·nawe·m     +a·čihi              e·h= awi        +niči
house     +LOC xx+ be.related.to +3s-3′/PPL(OBVpl) AOR+ be.{smwh} +3′/PPL(loc.obl)
```
at houses where his(P) relatives(O) lived.

152

A ni·na=na·hka| meše=meko·=’nahi| či·nawe·makiki‿neka·ki·wi‿pi·tikawa·waki.
```
ni·na    na·hka     meše=meko·=’nahi IC+ či·nawe·m     +akiki
1s/EMPH also,again any              xx+ be.related.to +1s-3/PPL(ANpl)

ne+ CV+   ki·wi      pi·tikaw +a·waki
1+  RED1+ around/PV go.in.to +1s-3p/IND
```
And I <u>also</u> went around visiting any of <u>my</u> relatives(P).

B a·kwi=meko nahi‿mya·šimičini.
```
a·kwi =meko nahi        mya·šim     +ičini
not   =EMPH given.to/PV complain.to +3s-1s/NEG
```
He(P) never complained to me.

C pe·hki=ča·h=meko‿neki·ša·koči|-tepa·na·wa.
```
pe·hki =ča·hi =meko ne+ ki·ša·koči   tepa·N +a·wa
really =so    =EMPH 1+  extremely/PV love   +1s-3s/IND
```
So I really loved him(P) very much.

D i·niya=ke·h_menehta_wi·čawiwaka_pe·hki=meko meme·satesiwa.

```
i·niya         =ke·hi     menehta IC+ wi·čawiw +aka
that/ABS(ANsg) =moreover first    xx+ be.with  +1s-3/PPL(ANsg)

pe·hki =meko meme·satesi +wa
really =EMPH be.lustful  +3s/IND
```

But that first husband[P] *of mine, on the other hand, was just terribly oversexed.*

E ša·kwe·nemoya·nini ke·ko·h_wi·h=to·tawiči,

```
IC+ ša·kwe·nemo   +ya·nini ke·ko·h   +i    wi·h= to·taw       +iči
xx+ be.unwilling +1s/ITER something +INsg FUT+  treat.{so} +3s-1s/AOR
```

Whenever I didn't want him[P] *to make love to me,*

F o·n=e·h=a·hkwe·či.

```
o·ni      e·h= a·hkwe·   +či
and,then AOR+ be.angry +3s/AOR
```

then he[P] *got mad.*

G na·hka_wi·h=a·hpeči_=meko_-taši·hkawiči išite·he·wa.

```
na·hka      wi·h= a·hpeči          =meko taši·hkaw       +iči       išite·he·   +wa
also,again FUT+  permanently/PV =EMPH be.dealing.with +3s-1s/AOR think.{so} +3s/IND
```

And also he[P] *wanted to be after me just incessantly.*

153

A newa·wi·kawihekwa.

```
ne+ CV+   wi·kawih +ekwa
1+  RED1+ bother   +3s-1s/IND
```

He[P] *bothered me constantly.*

B a·kwi=meko nahi_menwi_nepa·ya·nini e·ye·h_wi·čawiwaki.

```
a·kwi =meko nahi          menwi   nepa· +ya·nini
not   =EMPH given.to/PV well/PV sleep +1s/NEG

IC+ aye·hi          wi·čawiw +aki
xx+ continue.to/PV be.with  +1s-3/CC
```

I never slept well while I was married to him[P]*.*

C i·ni=ča·h_we·či_neškinawaki.

```
i·ni      =ča·hi IC+ oči              neškinaw +aki
that/INsg =so    xx+ from.{smth}/PV hate     +1s-3/PPL(obl)
```

So that's why I hated him[P]*.*

D o·ni=kotaka ki·ši·_'čawiwaki, pe·hki=meko_nemenwi_pema·tesi.

```
o·ni      kotak +a    IC+ ki·ši   wi·čawiw +aki
and,then other +ANsg xx+ PERF/PV be.with  +1s-3/CC

pe·hki =meko ne+ menwi   pema·tesi          +Ø
really =EMPH 1+  well/PV live,be.healthy +1s/IND
```

And then, after I was married to the other one[P]*, I really felt good.*

E ni·miheti·kini, "mawi‿ni·mino′. me·me·nešimihki·ke| pwa·wi- i·ya·h‿-na·kosiyane e·h=tanahki·ki,"
netekwa=meko.

```
IC+ ni·miheti·     +ekini  mawi       ni·mi +no        ′
xx+ dance.together +X/ITER go.and/PV dance +2s/IMP INTERJ

CV+   me·nešim          +ihki·ke   pwa·wi i·ya·hi na·kosi +yane
RED1+ shame.by.speech +X-1s/PROH NEG/PV yonder  show.up +2s/SUBJ

e·h= tanahki·                +ki               ne+ iN           +ekwa      =meko
AOR+ be.social.event.{smwh} +0/PPL(loc.obl) 1+  say.{so}.to +3s-1s/IND =EMPH
```

Whenever there was a dance, he[(P)] would tell me outright, "Go and dance! People might say embarrassing things about me if you don't show up over at the doings[(P)].

F " 'kya·we·toke,' išihki·ke.

```
kya·we·     +wetoke iN          +ihki·ke
be.jealous +3s/DUB say.{so}.to +X-1s/PROH
```

People might say that I must be jealous.

154

A neme·nešite·h‿i·ni‿wi·h=išiki,"| netekw=a·pehe.

```
ne+ me·nešite·he· +Ø      i·ni      wi·h= iN          +iki
1+  be.bashful    +1s/IND that/INsg FUT+  say.{so}.to +X-1s/AOR

ne+ iN          +ekwa      =a·pehe
1+  say.{so}.to +3s-1s/IND =usually
```

I'm embarrassed to have people say that about me," he[(P)] would say to me.

B "mi·ša·tesino′," netekwa=na·hk=a·pehe.

```
mi·ša·tesi +no       ′       ne+ iN          +ekwa      na·hka       =a·pehe
dress.up   +2s/IMP INTERJ 1+  say.{so}.to +3s-1s/IND also,again =usually
```

And he[(P)] would also tell me, "Get dressed up!"

C kapo·tw=a·pehe še·ški e·h=taši-ka·kakano·neti·ya·ke,

```
kapo·twe       =a·pehe  še·ški e·h= taši                  CV+   kakano·neti· +ya·ke
at.some.point =usually only   AOR+ be.engaged.in/PV RED1+ converse      +1p/AOR
```

At times, when we would just be talking,

D "iši‿pwa·wi‿=ni·hka=’yo·we ni·na‿-kaškimenowa·ne·ni.

```
iši      pwa·wi =ni·hka      =iyo·we ni·na    kaškim   +enowa·ne·ni
{so}/PV NEG/PV =MAN'S.EXPL =PAST   1s/EMPH persuade +1s-2s/INT
```

he[(P)] asked me, "Darn it, how come I couldn't win your consent, before?

E menehta=ke·h=wi·na=’yo·we ki·na·na kekakano·neti·pena," netekwa.

```
menehta =ke·hi      =wi·na =iyo·we ki·na·na ke+ kakano·neti· +pena
first   =moreover =but   =PAST   12/EMPH  2+  converse     +12/IND

ne+ iN          +ekwa
1+  say.{so}.to +3s-1s/IND
```

After all, we had talks together first."

F "kašina·kwa," i·n=e·h=inaki,
```
kašina·kwa i·ni e·h= iN           +aki
Well!      then AOR+ say.{so}.to +1s-3/AOR
```
"Well now," I then said to him[P],

G "a·kwi=koči we·we·ne·netisoya·nini nekya| e·ye·h‿pema·tesiči.|
```
a·kwi =koči     we·we·ne·netiso        +ya·nini ne+ -ky     +a
not   =you.know have.control.over.self +1s/NEG  1+  mother +ANsg

IC+ aye·hi          pema·tesi         +či
xx+ continue.to/PV live,be.healthy +3s/CC
```
"I didn't, of course, have my own say over myself while my mother[P] was alive.

155

A kapo·twe=koči='yo·we| nekehke·nemeko·pi| e·h=kakano·neti·hena·ni,
```
kapo·twe      =koči      =iyo·we ne+ kehke·nem +eko·pi
at.some.point =you.know =PAST    1+  know      +X-1s/IND

e·h= kakano·neti·h +ena·ni
AOR+ converse.with +1s-2s/AOR
```
And, of course, at some point it was found out that I was talking with you,

B e·h=tanwe·we·miki, e·h=neškimiki.
```
e·h= tanwe·we·m   +iki      e·h= neškim           +iki
AOR+ quarrel.with +X-1s/AOR AOR+ forbid,admonish +X-1s/AOR
```
and I got a tongue-lashing and a lecture.

C kotaka·='ni,‿'ki·h=ona·pe·mi,' e·h=išiki.
```
kotak +a    i·ni ke+ wi·h= ona·pe·mi              +Ø      e·h= iN           +iki
other +ANsg then 2+  FUT+  have.O2.as.husband +2s/IND AOR+ say.{so}.to +X-1s/AOR
```
I was then told there was another guy[P] that I was to marry.

D i·na=ča·h mačawahi·na keye·hapa.|
```
i·na      =ča·hi mačawahi·n                +a    keye·hapa
that/ANsg =so    rascal,good.for.nothing +ANsg it.turned.out
```
Well, it was that old meanie[P], as it turned out.

E ni·na=ke·h,‿we·we·ne·netisoya·neh, awita i·na‿kaški-ona·pe·mihka·ha.
```
ni·na   =ke·hi     we·we·ne·netiso        +ya·nehe
1s/EMPH =moreover have.control.over.self +1s/SUBJ.PRET

awita   i·na      kaški       ona·pe·mi              +hka·ha
not/POT that/ANsg able.to/PV have.O2.as.husband +1s/POT
```
As far as I was concerned, if I had had my own say over myself, I couldn't have married that other guy[P].

F wi·ša·wi=meko=ki·na| kaškimihkapa.‖
wi·ša·wi =meko ki·na kaškim +ihkapa
maybe,perhaps =EMPH 2s/EMPH persuade +2s-1s/POT
Quite possibly you would have won my consent.

156
A keki·ši̲=koči=meko=’yo·we -anehko·ne.|
ke+ ki·ši =koči =meko =iyo·we anehkaw +ene
2+ PERF/PV =you.know =EMPH =PAST get.acquainted.with +1s-2s/IND
I had already become acquainted with you, after all.

B ahpene·či=koči=wi·na=meko kenenehke·nemene, ahkwiya·h| aškiča·h.
ahpene·či =koči =wi·na =meko ke+ nenehke·nem +ene ahkwiya·hi aškiča·hi
every.time =you.know =but =EMPH 2+ think.about +1s-2s/IND especially at.first
But I thought about you all the time, you know, especially at first.

C e·ški̲po·ni̲kakano·neti·hena·ni neki·wa·tesi,” netena·wa.
IC+ aški po·ni kakano·neti·h +ena·ni ne+ ki·wa·tesi +Ø
xx+ first/PV cease/PV converse.with +1s-2s/CC 1+ be.lonely +1s/IND

ne+ iN +a·wa
1+ say.{so}.to +1s-3s/IND
When I first stopped talking with you, I was lonely," I said to him[(P)].

D “nahi´, meše·=’nahi.
nahi´ meše·=’nahi
Well! as.may.be
“Well, let it go," he[(P)] then said to me.

E keki·ši̲=koči mani| -menwi-otehteneti·pena,” i·n=e·h=išiči.
ke+ ki·ši =koči mani menwi otehteneti· +pena
2+ PERF/PV =you.know as.it.is.now well/PV get.each.other +12/IND

i·ni e·h= iN +iči
then AOR+ say.{so}.to +3s-1s/AOR
“After all, we've now come by each other in fine fettle."

F kaši´, pe·hki=meko| me·menowe·wa.|
kaši´ pe·hki =meko CV+ menowe· +wa
Why! really =EMPH RED1+ say.something.good.to.people +3s/IND
My, but he[(P)] really said nice things.

G meše·=’nah=meko ni·šwawahi·ne‿nepye·či̲wi·čawiwa·wa.|
meše·=’nahi =meko ni·šwawahi·ne ne+ pye·či wi·čawiw +a·wa
as.may.be =EMPH two.years 1+ coming/PV be.with +1s-3s/IND
By then I'd been married to him[(P)] for maybe two years.

157
A ni·na=ke·h‿e·škami=meko‿netanemi-ahpi·hči‿tepa·na·wa e·h=menwi‿to·tawiči.|
ni·na =ke·hi e·škami =meko ne+ anemi ahpi·hči
1s/EMPH =moreover increasingly =EMPH 1+ go.on/PV to.{such}.degree/PV

tepa·N +a·wa e·h= menwi to·taw +iči
love +1s-3s/IND AOR+ well/PV treat.{so} +3s-1s/AOR
And as far as I was concerned, I came to love him[P] *more and more, since he*[P] *was nice to me.*

B kapo·twe=na·hka‿netoni·ča·nese·hipena, iškwe·se·he·ha.
kapo·twe na·hka ne+ oni·ča·nese·hi +pena iškwe·se·he·h +a
at.some.point also,again 1+ have.O2.as.child/DIM +1p/IND girl/DIM +ANsg
At some point [my husband] and I had a baby, my second, a little girl[P].

C šewe·na nye·wiki·šeswakesiči nepo·hiwa.
šewe·na IC+ nye·wiki·šeswakesi +či nepo·hi +wa
but xx+ be.four.months.old +3s/CC die/DIM +3s/IND
But when she[P] *was four months old she*[P] *died.*

D natawa·či·=’ni| e·h=menahiki na·tawino·ni wi·h=pwa·wi‿=na·hka -oni·ča·nesiya·ni,
natawa·či i·ni e·h= menah +iki na·tawino·n +i
resolving.accordingly then AOR+ to.drink.O2].cause +X-1s/AOR medicine +INsg

wi·h= pwa·wi na·hka oni·ča·nesi +ya·ni
FUT+ NEG/PV also,again have.child +1s/AOR
Then I resigned myself to being given some medicine so that I wouldn't have another child,

E e·h=a·hkowi‿nepo·hiwa·či we·ni·ča·nesiya·nini.||
e·h= a·hkowi nepo·hi +wa·či IC+ oni·ča·nesi +ya·nini
AOR+ every.time die/DIM +3p/AOR xx+ have.child +1s/ITER
since whenever I had children they[P] *died each time.*

158
A a·kwi=meko=nana·ši| no·tawakini wi·čawiwaka wi·h=mya·nowe·či.
a·kwi =meko nana·ši no·taw +akini IC+ wi·čawiw +aka
not =EMPH (ever) hear.talk.of +1s-3/NEG xx+ be.with +1s-3/PPL(ANsg)

wi·h= mya·nowe· +či
FUT+ complain.to.people +3s/AOR
I never heard my husband[P] *to make critical remarks.*

B mo·hči=meko| tepehki e·h=ša·waša·wano·winiči,
mo·hči =meko tepehki e·h= CVCV+ ša·wano·wi +niči
even =EMPH at.night AOR+ RED2+ do.Shawnee.dance +3′/AOR
Even when other people[O] *had Shawnee dances at night,*

C “na·ni·mino´,”‿netekwa=meko.
CV+ ni·mi +no ´ ne+ iN +ekwa =meko
RED1+ dance +2s/IMP INTERJ 1+ say.{so}.to +3s-1s/IND =EMPH
he[P] readily said to me, “Go and dance!”

D “kaši´‿pe·hki=meko‿nemehkawa·wa neniwa,” netešite·he.
kaši´ pe·hki =meko ne+ mehkaw +a·wa neniw +a ne+ išite·he· +Ø
Why! really =EMPH 1+ find +1s-3s/IND man +ANsg 1+ think.{so} +1s/IND
“Well now, I’ve really found a man[P]!” I thought.

E “aniwe·wi=meko, mana·=’noki=kapo·twe‿pakišite, ki·wi·hkawiye·ka·ha=meko,” netešite·h.
aniwe·wi =meko mana i·noki kapo·twe pakiN +ite
contrariwise =EMPH this/ANsg now at.some.point discard,release +3s-1s/SUBJ

ki·wi·hkaw +iye·ka·ha =meko ne+ išite·he· +Ø
go.around.dealing.with +1s-3/POT =EMPH 1+ think.{so} +1s/IND
“If this man[P] up and divorced me now, I <u>would</u> go chasing around after <u>him</u>,” I thought.

F kenwe·ši nekotah‿e·ya·čini, nekwi·noma·wa.|
kenwe·ši nekotahi IC+ iha· +čini ne+ kwi·nom +a·wa
long.time somewhere xx+ go.{smwh} +3s/ITER 1+ long.for +1s-3s/IND
Whenever he[P] went anywhere for a long time, I missed him[P].

159

A o·ni, “nahi´, nete·pihekwa mana e·h=menwi‿to·tawiči,”‿netešite·he,
o·ni nahi´ ne+ te·pih +ekwa mana
and,then Well! 1+ please.by.act +3s-1s/IND this/ANsg

e·h= menwi to·taw +iči ne+ išite·he· +Ø
AOR+ well/PV treat.{so} +3s-1s/AOR 1+ think.{so} +1s/IND
And I thought, “Alright, this man[P] makes me happy by being nice to me,”

B e·h=we·pi-ašihašihtawaki omi·ša·tesiweni –
e·h= we·pi CVCV+ ašihtaw +aki o+ mi·ša·tesiwen +i
AOR+ begin/PV RED2+ make.02.for +1s-3/AOR 3+ finery +INsg
and I set about making him[P] his fancy clothes –

C omahkese·hani, omatete·hani, opi·sehka·hi, okahkika·pi·hahi, ota·šowa·nekwaha·te·hi.|
o+ mahkese·h +ani o+ matete·h +ani o+ pi·sehka·h +i o+ kahkika·pi·h +ahi
3+ moccasin +INpl 3+ leggings +INpl 3+ shirt +INsg 3+ garter +OBVpl

o+ a·šowa·nekwaha·te·h +i
3+ cross-belt +INsg
his moccasins, his leggins, his shirt, his[P] garters[O], and his crossbelt.

D ča·ki‿=meko‿-ke·ko·hi mi·ša·tesiweni| ki·šihtawaki·=’ni,
ča·ki =meko ke·ko·h +i mi·ša·tesiwen +i IC+ ki·šihtaw +aki i·ni
all =EMPH thing +INsg finery +INsg xx+ complete.02.for +1s-3/CC then
After I had made for him[P] every part of the fancy clothes, [I said to him],

E “ma·hani ki·šihto·na·nini
ma·hani IC+ ki·šihtaw +ena·nini
this/INpl xx+ complete.O2.for +1s-2s/PPL(INpl)
“These are what I’ve made for you,

F e·hpi·hči_te·pihiyani nehki_wi·čawi·na·ni,
IC+ ahpi·hči te·pih +iyani
xx+ to.{such}.degree/PV please.by.act +2s-1s/PPL(obl)

nehki IC+ wi·čawiw +ena·ni
for.{so}.long xx+ be.with +1s-2s/PPL(obl)
since you’ve made me so happy for as long as I’ve been with you,

160
A e·h=pwa·wi_=nana·ši_ke·ko·h_iši_mya·šinawe·hiyani.
e·h= pwa·wi nana·ši ke·ko·h +i iši mya·šinawe·h +iyani
AOR+ NEG/PV (ever) something +INsg {so}/PV make.feel.bad +2s-1s/AOR
and since you’ve never done anything to make me feel out of sorts.

B ki·na=ke·h wi·h=na·ni·miyani e·h=ine·nemena·ni we·či-ašihto·na·ni.”
ki·na =ke·hi wi·h= CV+ ni·mi +yani e·h= ine·nem +ena·ni
2s/EMPH =moreover FUT+ RED1+ dance +2s/AOR AOR+ think.about.{so} +1s-2s/AOR

IC+ oči ašihtaw +ena·ni
xx+ from.{smth}/PV make.O2.for +1s-2s/PPL(obl)
I made them for you because I also want you to go and dance.”

C “pe·hki=meko_kete·pihi.
pe·hki =meko ke+ te·pih +i
really =EMPH 2+ please.by.act +2s-1s/IND
He[P] said to me, “You really make me happy by what you’ve done.

D i·ni=meko e·šimiki e·h=a·ya·čimohiki.
i·ni =meko IC+ išim +iki e·h= CV+ a·čimoh +iki
that/INsg =EMPH xx+ speak.{so}.to +X-1s/PPL(obl) AOR+ RED1+ inform +X-1s/AOR
I’m only doing what I was told to do when I was instructed.

E ‘wi·čawiwate ihkwe·wa,
wi·čawiw +ate ihkwe·w +a
be.with +2s-3/SUBJ woman +ANsg
‘When you’re married to a woman[P],’ I was told,

F menwa·ko·mehke, menwi_to·tawate,
menwa·ko·m +ehke menwi to·taw +ate
like.the.ways.of +3-2s/SUBJ well/PV treat.{so} +2s-3/SUBJ
‘if she likes your ways, and if you treat her[P] well,

G ki·na=koh_e·yi·ki_ki·h=nana·hi·hka·kwa,
ki·na =kohi e·yi·ki ke+ wi·h= nana·hi·hkaw +ekwa
2s/EMPH =certainly as.well 2+ FUT+ attend.to +3s-2s/IND
you can be sure she[P]'ll attend to your needs as well,

H nepwa·hka·te.
nepwa·hka· +te
be.smart +3s/SUBJ
if she[P] has good sense.

I wa·waneška·hite=wi·na,
wa·waneška·hi +te =wi·na
be.bad +3s/SUBJ =but
But if she[P]'s a bad actor,

161
A a·kwi wi·h=te·pihačini.
a·kwi wi·h= te·pih +ačini
not FUT+ please.by.act +2s-3/NEG
what you do won't make her[P] grateful.

B še·ški=meko_wi·h=ketema·kihehki wi·h-išite·he·wa,'| neteko·pi.
še·ški =meko wi·h= ketema·kih +ehki wi·h= išite·he· +wa
only =EMPH FUT+ ill-treat +3-2s/AOR FUT+ think.{so} +3s/IND

ne+ iN +eko·pi
1+ say.{so}.to +X-1s/IND
All she[P]'ll want to do is make you miserable.'

C i·noki=ča·h=mani i·ni=nene·ta e·ši_wi·tamawiki," netekwa.|
i·noki =ča·hi =mani i·ni ne+ ne·t +a
now =so =as.it.is.now that/INsg 1+ see +1s-0/IND

IC+ iši wi·tamaw +iki ne+ iN +ekwa
xx+ {so}/PV tell +X-1s/PPL(obl) 1+ say.{so}.to +3s-1s/IND
So now today I see the thing that I was told was so."

D ahkwiya·h=meko·='ni=pe·hki ni·na=meko e·h=we·we·ne·netama·ni ke·ko·hi.|
ahkwiya·hi =meko i·ni pe·hki ni·na =meko
especially =EMPH then really 1s/EMPH =EMPH

e·h= we·we·ne·net +ama·ni ke·ko·h +i
AOR+ have.control.over +1s-0/AOR thing +INsg
More than ever, then, it was me that really had say over things.

E nahi_ši·še·wa='yo=ke·hi.
nahi ši·ša· +wa =iyo =ke·hi
know.how.to/PV go.hunting +3s/IND =for =moreover
And he[P] was a good hunter, too.

F ma·ne=meko‿pye·ne·wa| owiye·he·hahi‿ši·ša·čini.
ma·ne =meko pye·N +e·wa owiye·he·h +ahi IC+ ši·ša· +čini
much,many =EMPH bring +3s-3′/IND animal/DIM +OBVpl xx+ go.hunting +3s/ITER
He[P] brought back a good many animals[O] whenever he[P] went hunting.

G a·kwi=ča·h=meko‿nahi-aka·wa·tama·kini mena·škono·ni, e·h=nahi‿ši·ša·či.
a·kwi =ča·hi =meko nahi aka·wa·t +ama·kini mena·škono·n +i
not =so =EMPH given.to/PV desire +1p-0/NEG fresh.meat +INsg

e·h= nahi ši·ša· +či
AOR+ know.how.to/PV go.hunting +3s/AOR
So, with him[P] being a good hunter, we were never in want of meat.

162
A i·na=meko·=’ni e·ye·niwe e·h=taši-onahona·pe·miya·ni.
i·na =meko i·ni e·ye·niwe
that/ANsg =EMPH then staying.the.same

e·h= taši CVCV+ ona·pe·mi +ya·ni
AOR+ {smwh}/PV RED2+ have.O2.as.husband +1s/AOR
Then I stayed there married to that same man[P] right along.

B ma·nwawahi·ne=meko netona·pe·mi.
ma·nwawahi·ne =meko ne+ ona·pe·mi +Ø
many.years =EMPH 1+ have.O2.as.husband +1s/IND
I was married to him for a good many years.

C kapo·twe·=’ni| te·we·hikana e·h=pye·neči.
kapo·twe i·ni te·we·hikan +a e·h= pye·N +eči
at.some.point then drum +ANsg AOR+ bring +X-3/AOR
At some point, then, a drum[P] was brought.

D pa·pekwa=na·hka, “pi·tike·yakwe=wi·na·=’nahi te·we·hikaneki, takwi·yakwe, mama·tomohkakoha,” e·h=išiči.
pa·pekwa na·hka pi·tike· +yakwe =wi·na i·nahi te·we·hikan +eki
right.away also,again go.in +12/SUBJ =but that/LOC drum +LOC

takwi· +yakwe mama·tomo +hkakoha e·h= iN +iči
join.others +12/SUBJ pray,request.aid +12/POT AOR+ say.{so}.to +3s-1s/AOR
And right away he said to me, “If we go into that drum, if we join, we could worship.”

E meše=meko·=’nahi neki·wi‿’šawipena.||
meše=meko·=’nahi ne+ ki·wi išawi +pena
any 1+ around/PV do.{so} +1p/IND
We just went around doing anything we wanted.

163

A a·kwi=meko·=’nahi‿paši‿ki·wi‿nenehke·netama·nini| pešekwa·hiweni,

```
a·kwi =meko =i·nahi    paši        ki·wi      nenehke·net +ama·nini
not   =EMPH =with.that (at.all)/PV around/PV think.about +1s-0/NEG

pešekwa·hiwen +i
divorce       +INsg
```

In those circumstances I had no thoughts at all of divorce,

B e·hpi·hči‿=ta·taki‿-menwa·ko·maki.

```
IC+ ahpi·hči               ta·taki   menwa·ko·m        +aki
xx+ to.{such}.degree/PV in.a.way like.the.ways.of +1s-3/PPL(obl)
```

given how much I liked his[(P)] ways.

* * *

C kapo·twe·=’ni e·h=we·pi-a·hkwaha·hkwamataki.

```
kapo·twe      i·ni e·h= we·pi    CVCV+ a·hkwamat +aki
at.some.point then AOR+ begin/PV RED2+ be.sick   +3s(-0)/AOR
```

Then at some point he[(P)] began to get sick all the time.

D pe·hki=meko neka·htwe·nema·wa.

```
pe·hki =meko ne+ ka·htwe·nem      +a·wa
really =EMPH 1+  feel.sorrow.over +1s-3s/IND
```

I really felt sorry for him[(P)].

E neki·ša·kočite·he=meko.|

```
ne+ ki·ša·kočite·he· +Ø      =meko
1+  feel.terrible    +1s/IND =EMPH
```

I felt just terrible.

F kapo·twe·=’ni pe·hki=meko e·h=we·pi-a·neha·nemesiči.

```
kapo·twe      i·ni pe·hki =meko e·h= we·pi    CVCV+ a·nemesi       +či
at.some.point then really =EMPH AOR+ begin/PV RED2+ be.in.a.plight +3s/AOR
```

Then eventually he[(P)] began to get really desperately sick each time.

G wa·wosa·h=meko| nemayo, e·h=ki·ša·kote·nemaki.‖

```
wa·wosa·hi               =meko ne+ mayo· +Ø      e·h= ki·ša·kote·nem    +aki
it's.(not).expected =EMPH 1+  cry   +1s/IND AOR+ feel.deeply.about +1s-3/AOR
```

I even wept, I felt so terrible about him[(P)].

* * *

164

A o·ni e·h=nepeki=kapo·twe.

```
o·ni     e·h= nep +ki     kapo·twe
and,then AOR+ die +3s/AOR at.some.point
```

And then one day he[(P)] died.

B pe·hki=meko neki·ša·kotesi.
```
pe·hki =meko ne+ ki·ša·kotesi            +Ø
really =EMPH 1+  be.in.a.terrible.state +1s/IND
```
I was really devastated.

C ni·nesani·=’ni e·h=peneškenama·ni,
```
ne+ -i·nes        +ani  i·ni e·h= peneškenama·ni
1+   hair.of.head +INpl then AOR+ unbraid  +1s-0/AOR
```
I unbraided my hair then

D e·h=peneška·nehkwe·noya·ni.
```
e·h= peneška·nehkwe·no +ya·ni
AOR+ unbraid.own.hair  +1s/AOR
```
and mussed my hair to make it completely loose.

E ma·nokoni=meko apina a·kwi kaški|-nepa·ya·nini e·h=ka·htosiya·ni.
```
ma·nokoni     =meko apina a·kwi kaški       nepa· +ya·nini
for.many.days =EMPH even  not   able.to/PV sleep +1s/NEG

e·h= ka·htosi                +ya·ni
AOR+ be.sorrowful.over.loss +1s/AOR
```
For several nights I couldn’t even sleep because of my grief.

F nye·wokonakahki·=’ni e·h=natomaki neniwaki,
```
IC+ nye·wokonakat +ki    i·ni e·h= natom        +aki       neniw +aki
xx+ be.four.days  +0/CC then AOR+ ask.to.come +1s-3/AOR man   +ANpl
```
After four days[P] I asked some men[P] to come over

G “neta·hwi·hemena·nani ma·hani_ki·h=ča·ki-ni·kahama·ti·pwa,” e·h=inaki,
```
ne+ -ta·hwi·hem        +ena·nani ma·hani
1+   thing,possession +1p(INpl) this/INpl

ke+ wi·h= ča·ki  ni·kahama·ti·              +pwa    e·h= iN            +aki
2+  FUT+  all/PV divide.up.for.each.other +2p/IND AOR+ say.{so}.to +1s-3/AOR
```
and told them[P], “Divide up all these possessions of ours among yourselves,”

H či·nawe·makiki‖ neniwaki.
```
IC+ či·nawe·m      +akiki            neniw +aki
xx+ be.related.to +1s-3/PPL(ANpl) man   +ANpl
```
they being men[P] who were my relatives[P].

165

A kaho·ni| e·h=pye·či-penaha·hkwawiwa·či nena·pe·mani=’yo·we| či·nawe·ma·čiki ihkwe·waki.
```
kaho·ni e·h= pye·či     penaha·hkwaw +iwa·či     ne+ -na·pe·m +ani    =iyo·we
so.then AOR+ coming/PV comb.hair.of +3p-1s/AOR 1+   husband +OBVsg =PAST

IC+ či·nawe·m      +a·čiki           ihkwe·w +aki
xx+ be.related.to +3-3′/PPL(ANpl) woman   +ANpl
```
And so then the women[P] who had been relatives[P] of my husband[O] came and combed my hair.

B na·hka=kotakani| pye·to·waki wi·h=ošehki·tama·nini.|
na·hka kotak +ani pye·t +o·waki IC+ wi·h= ošehki·t +ama·nini
also,again other +INpl bring +3p-0/IND xx+ FUT+ wear.(as).clothing +1s-0/PPL(INpl)
And they[P] also brought other clothes for me to wear.

C e·h=mahkate·wišehki·tama·ni.
e·h= mahkate·wišehki·t +ama·ni
AOR+ wear.(as).black.clothing +1s(-0)/AOR
And I dressed in black.

D kapo·twe=na·hka·=’ni i·niye·ka‿neniwaki| či·nawe·makiki mi·nakiki neta·hwi·hemena·nani e·h=pye·to·wa·či wi·seniweni.
kapo·twe na·hka i·ni i·niye·ka neniw +aki
at.some.point also,again then that/ABS(ANpl) man +ANpl

IC+ či·nawe·m +akiki IC+ mi·N +akiki
xx+ be.related.to +1s-3/PPL(ANpl) xx+ give.02.to +1s-3/PPL(ANpl)

ne+ -ta·hwi·hem +ena·nani e·h= pye·t +o·wa·či wi·seniwen +i
1+ thing,possession +1p(INpl) AOR+ bring +3p-0/AOR food +INsg
And also, some time after that, those male relatives[P] of mine that I had given our possessions to brought some food.

166
A ča·ki‿=meko‿-ke·ko·he·hi ihkwe·wanohkya·ni‿takwi‿pye·to·waki.
ča·ki =meko ke·ko·he·h +i ihkwe·wanohkya·n +i
all =EMPH something,anything/DIM +INsg women’s.work +INsg

takwi pye·t +o·waki
along.with.{smth}/PV bring +3p-0/IND
They[P] brought with it all the various things women use for their cooking.

B o·ni=na·hka=ni·na·=’ni i·niye·ka‿pye·či-penaha·hkwawičiki e·h=mawi-a·čimohaki wi·h=na·towa·či i·ni‿wi·seniweni.
o·ni na·hka ni·na i·ni i·niye·ka
and,then also,again 1s/EMPH then that/ABS(ANpl)

IC+ pye·či penaha·hkwaw +ičiki e·h= mawi a·čimoh +aki
xx+ coming/PV comb.hair.of +3-1s/PPL(ANpl) AOR+ go.and/PV inform +1s-3/AOR

wi·h= na·t +wa·či i·ni wi·seniwen +i
FUT+ go.to.get +3p-0/AOR that/INsg food +INsg
And then I, in turn, went and told the ones[P] who had come and combed my hair to go and get that food.

C pe·hki=meko neki·ša·koči-ketema·kite·h.|
pe·hki =meko ne+ ki·ša·koči ketema·kite·he· +Ø
really =EMPH 1+ extremely/PV feel.miserable +1s/IND
I felt absolutely just as miserable as could be.

D nemahkate·wi.
ne+ mahkate·wi· +Ø
1+ fast +1s/IND
I fasted.

E kapo·twe=mek=a·peh nepemi̯-we·pose,
kapo·twe =meko =a·pehe ne+ pemi we·pose· +Ø
at.some.point =EMPH =usually 1+ along/PV start.walking +1s/IND
At times I would just start walking

F atehči e·h=mawi̯-taši̯-mayo·ya·ni,
atehči e·h= mawi taši mayo· +ya·ni
away AOR+ go.and/PV {smwh}/PV cry +1s/AOR
and go off somewhere and cry,

167
A peno·či·me·h=meko wi·h=pwa·wi-kehke·nemiki,
peno·či·me·hi =meko wi·h= pwa·wi kehke·nem +iki
far.away/DIM =EMPH FUT+ NEG/PV know +X-1s/AOR
far enough away so people wouldn't know about me,

B "'na̯-nešiwi=wi·na·='na iši̯-ka·htosi·toke; mehto·či| či·nawe·me·toke," wi·h=pwa·wi-išiki.
ana nešiwi =wi·na i·na iši ka·htosi +wetoke
EMPH terribly =but that/ANsg {so}/PV be.sorrowful.over.loss +3s/DUB

mehto·či či·nawe·m +e·toke wi·h= pwa·wi iN +iki
as.though be.related.to +3s-3′/DUB FUT+ NEG/PV say.{so}.to +X-1s/AOR
and so they wouldn't say about me, "It's really awful how hard she(P) seems to be grieving; you'd think she(P)'d been related to him(O)."

C na·hka apina=meko nena·ni·kihto·hi.
na·hka apina =meko ne+ na·ni·kihto·hi +Ø
also,again even =EMPH 1+ be.lazy +1s/IND
And also I even became lazy.

D še·ški=meko wi·h=šekišekišina·ni nemata·kwe·neta.
še·ški =meko wi·h= CVCV+ šekišin +a·ni ne+ mata·kwe·net +a
only =EMPH FUT+ RED2+ lie.down +1s/AOR 1+ enjoy +1s-0/IND
The only thing I was interested in doing was lying around.

E nene·nepa e·h=ki·wa·tesiya·ni.
ne+ CV+ nepa· +Ø e·h= ki·wa·tesi +ya·ni
1+ RED1+ sleep +1s/IND AOR+ be.lonely +1s/AOR
I slept all the time, since I was lonely.

F kapo·twe·•'ni| i·niya_nešise·ha| e·h•no·ta·ke·teh•ye·toke,

```
kapo·twe         i·ni i·niya         ne+ -šise·h      +a
at.some.point then that/ABS(ANsg) 1+   cross-uncle +ANsg

e·h= no·ta·ke·              +tehe          =ye·toke
AOR+ hear.what.people.say +3s/AOR.PRET =it.seems
```

Then at some point, my uncle(P), that I mentioned before, heard talk, it seems.

168

A "pe·hki•meko mya·nowesiwa ona·pe·mani e·h•nepeniči.

```
pe·hki =meko mya·nowesi  +wa     o+ -na·pe·m +ani    e·h= nep +niči
really =EMPH be.overcome +3s/IND 3+  husband +OBVsg AOR+ die +3′/AOR
```

"She(P)'s really been overcome by the death of her(P) husband(O).

B kotaki•meko išawiwa| i·noki.

```
kotak +i     =meko išawi    +wa     i·noki
other +INsg =EMPH do.{so} +3s/IND now
```

She(P)'s acting different now.

C mehto·či•meko a·hkwamatamwa,"| e·h•inehta·ke·teh,

```
mehto·či  =meko a·hkwamat +amwa        e·h= inehta·ke·              +tehe
as.though =EMPH be.sick   +3s(-0)/IND AOR+ hear.people.say.{so} +3s/AOR.PRET
```

It's just as if she(P) were sick," he(P) apparently heard people say.

D e·h•pye·notawiči.

```
e·h= pye·notaw +iči
AOR+ come.to    +3s-1s/AOR
```

And he(P) came to visit me.

E "e·h•pye·či-wa·pamena·ni, nešemi.

```
e·h= pye·či     wa·pam  +ena·ni     ne+ -šemi·h       +Ø
AOR+ coming/PV look.at +1s-2s/AOR 1+   cross-niece +VOCsg
```

"I've come to see you, niece.

F a·hkwamatakani.

```
a·hkwamat +akani
be.sick   +2s(-0)/PROH
```

You might be sick.

G pe·hki•meko_kena·wisa," netekwa.

```
pe·hki =meko ke+ na·wisa·     +Ø       ne+ iN           +ekwa
really =EMPH 2+  lose.weight +2s/IND 1+  say.{so}.to +3s-1s/IND
```

You've really lost weight," he(P) said to me.

H "a·kwi,"| netena·wa.

```
a·kwi ne+ iN          +a·wa
not   1+  say.{so}.to +1s-3s/IND
```

"No, I'm all right," I said to him(P).

I “kepye·či‿-koh -a·čimohene| wi·h-išawiyani.
ke+ pye·či =kohi a·čimoh +ene IC+ wi·h= išawi +yani
2+ coming/PV =certainly inform +1s-2s/IND xx+ FUT+ do.{so} +2s/PPL(obl)
“Actually, I’ve come to tell you what you should do.

J kekehke·nemene e·h-pe·pesetawiyani na·hina·h‿e·h-pešekwa·hiyani,
ke+ kehke·nem +ene e·h= CV+ pesetaw +iyani na·hina·hi
2+ know +1s-2s/IND AOR+ RED1+ listen.to +2s-1s/AOR time,distance

e·h= pešekwa·hi +yani
AOR+ get.divorced +2s/AOR
I know that you listened to me at the time of your divorce,

169
A e·ši‿wi·tamo·na·ni e·h-te·pwe·htawiyani.
IC+ iši wi·tamaw +ena·ni e·h= te·pwe·htaw +iyani
xx+ {so}/PV tell +1s-2s/PPL(obl) AOR+ believe,agree.to.request.of +2s-1s/AOR

and that you took my advice in what I told you to do.

B i·ni-meko-ke·htena e·h-išawiyani e·šimena·ni.
i·ni =meko ke·htena e·h= išawi +yani IC+ išim +ena·ni
that/INsg =EMPH truly AOR+ do.{so} +2s/AOR xx+ speak.{so}.to +1s-2s/PPL(obl)
And the truth is, you did just what I told you to.

C pe·hki-meko kemenwinawe·hi.
pe·hki =meko ke+ menwinawe·h +i
really =EMPH 2+ please +2s-1s/IND
I was really pleased with you.

D “mani-ča·h wi·h-išawiyani,| nešemi.
mani =ča·hi IC+ wi·h= išawi +yani ne+ -šemi·h +Ø
this/INsg =so xx+ FUT+ do.{so} +2s/PPL(obl) 1+ cross-niece +VOCsg
“So this is what you must do, niece.

E ka·ta asa·mi-kwe·hkwe·wi-a·hpeči|-nenehke·nemiye·kani.
ka·ta asa·mi kwe·hkwe·wi a·hpeči nenehke·nem +iye·kani
don’t too.much/PV going.too.far/PV permanently/PV think.about +2s-3/PROH
Don’t go too far in thinking about him constantly.

F koškoškwa·tota·pi i·ni‿wi·h-išawiki.
koškoškwa·tot +a·pi i·ni wi·h= išawi +eki
tell.of.as.dangerous +X-0/IND that/INsg FUT+ do.{so} +X/AOR
It’s reported to be dangerous to do that.

G ki·hpene wi·hpe·mate ina·hpawa·yane,

```
ki·hpene             wi·hpe·m   +ate         ina·hpawa· +yane
in.the.event.that sleep.with +2s-3/SUBJ dream.{so} +2s/SUBJ
```

If you ever dream that you're sleeping with him[P],

H ma·maya▪meko ki·h▪po·ni‿mehtose·neniwi.

```
ma·maya ▪meko ke+ wi·h▪ po·ni    mehtose·neniwi +Ø
early   ▪EMPH 2+  FUT+  cease/PV be.person      +2s/IND
```

your life will come to an early end.

170

A i·ni▪ča·h we·či-neškiti·ki i·ni‿wi·h▪išawiki.

```
i·ni      ▪ča·hi IC+ oči              neškiti·              +eki
that/INsg ▪so    xx+ from.{smth}/PV admonish.each.other +X/PPL(obl)

i·ni      wi·h▪ išawi   +eki
that/INsg FUT+  do.{so} +X/AOR
```

So that's why it's forbidden to do that.

B "še·ški▪kohi, ka·htosiyane wi·čawiwata,

```
še·ški ▪kohi       ka·htosi                  +yane     IC+ wi·čawiw +ata
only   ▪certainly be.sorrowful.over.loss +2s/SUBJ xx+ be.with  +2s-3/PPL(ANsg)
```

"It's only that, if you grieve for the loss of your husband[P],

C i·noki▪mani e·h▪ši·ka·wiyani,| awita ke·ko·h‿e·nahkiwikini i·tepi▪'ha·hkapa," e·h▪išiči.

```
i·noki ▪mani          e·h▪ ši·ka·wi                          +yani   awita
now    ▪as.it.is.now AOR+ be.widow(er).in.strict.mourning +2s/AOR not/POT

ke·ko·h   +i    IC+ inahkiwi          +ekini   i·tepi    iha·        +hkapa
something +INsg xx+ be.{such}.event +X/ITER to.there go.{smwh} +2s/POT

e·h▪ iN           +iči
AOR+ say.{so}.to +3s-1s/AOR
```

being in strict mourning as you now are, you wouldn't go to any public activities[p]," he[P] said to me.

D "na·hka▪ka·ta aniwetone·mohkani,

```
na·hka      ka·ta aniwetone·mo +hkani
also,again don't talk.a.lot    +2s/PROH
```

"And also don't talk a lot.

E na·hka ka·ta nahi-apahapane·nihkani,

```
na·hka      ka·ta nahi           CVCV+ apane·ni +hkani
also,again don't given.to/PV RED2+ smile    +2s/PROH
```

And also never laugh,

F e·hpi·hči‿ši·ka·wiyani.

```
IC+ ahpi·hči           ši·ka·wi                          +yani
xx+ in.process.of/PV be.widow(er).in.strict.mourning +2s/CC
```

as long as you're in your period of strict mourning.

G še·ški▪meko| ke·ko·h‿ki·h▪ašihašihto mahkwa·či.
še·ški =meko ke·ko·h +i ke+ wi·h= CVCV+ ašiht +o mahkwa·či
only =EMPH thing +INsg 2+ FUT+ RED2+ make +2s-O/IND quietly,calmly
All you should do is to keep making things peacefully.

171
A a·kwi wi·h▪aniwatawa·piyanini.‿
a·kwi wi·h= aniwatawa·pi +yanini
not FUT+ look.around.a.lot +2s/NEG
And you mustn't peer around a lot.

B "me·kwe·he e·h▪pwa·wi‿wi·ke·siyani, ka·hkami▪meko e·h▪pwa·wi‿▪ye·toke -a·čimohehki owiye·ha wi·h▪išawiyani,
me·kwe·he e·h= pwa·wi wi·ke·si +yani ka·hkami =meko
I.believe AOR+ NEG/PV be.careful +2s/AOR from.the.start =EMPH

e·h= pwa·wi =ye·toke a·čimoh +ehki owiye·h +a
AOR+ NEG/PV =it.seems inform +3-2s/AOR someone +ANsg

IC+ wi·h= išawi +yani
xx+ FUT+ do.{so} +2s/PPL(obl)
"I believe your not being careful was because it seems no one instructed you right from the start about what you should do,

C e·ški‿▪meko‿-nepeki| wi·čawiwata.‿
IC+ aški =meko nep +ki IC+ wi·čawiw +ata
xx+ first/PV =EMPH die +3s/CC xx+ be.with +2s-3/PPL(ANsg)
right when your husband[(P)] first died.

D ni·na▪'yo‿netotamesi i·nina·hi,
ni·na =iyo ne+ otamesi +Ø i·nina·hi
1s/EMPH =for 1+ be.busy +1s/IND at.that.time
Like me, I was busy at that time,

E we·či‿pwa·wi‿pya·ya·ni wi·h▪a·čimohena·nehe wi·h▪išawiyani.
IC+ oči pwa·wi pya· +ya·ni wi·h= a·čimoh +ena·nehe
xx+ from.{smth}/PV NEG/PV come +1s/PPL(obl) FUT+ inform +1s-2s/AOR.PRET

IC+ wi·h= išawi +yani
xx+ FUT+ do.{so} +2s/PPL(obl)
which is why I didn't come to instruct you about what you should do.

F "mani▪ke·hi·▪'ni| e·šawiwa·či e·h▪nepeniči wi·čawiwa·čihi.
mani =ke·hi i·ni IC+ išawi +wa·či
this/INsg =moreover that/INsg xx+ do.{so} +3p/PPL(obl)

e·h= nep +niči IC+ wi·čawiw +a·čihi
AOR+ die +3′/AOR xx+ be.with +3s-3′/PPL(OBVpl)
"Specifically, here's what people[(P)] are supposed to do when the ones[(O)] they[(P)]'re married to die.

G na·hina·h‖ e·h=mawi-pi·tahomeči, wi·če·we·waki.
na·hina·hi e·h= mawi pi·tahw +emeči wi·če·we· +waki
time,distance AOR+ go.and/PV bury +X-3′/AOR accompany.people +3p/IND
At the time when the dead(O) are taken to be buried, they(P) go along.

172
A i·ya·h_pye·nečini wa·nakoki,
i·ya·hi IC+ pye·N +ečini wa·nakw +eki
yonder xx+ bring +X-3/ITER hole,grave +LOC
And when the bodies(P) are brought over to the open grave

B ahkwiči ki·ši|-asečini i·niki či·payaki,
ahkwiči IC+ ki·ši aS +ečini i·niki či·pay +aki
on.top xx+ PERF/PV put,have +X-3/ITER that/ANpl corpse,ghost +ANpl
and have been set on top of it,

C e·h=we·pi|-kakano·neči.
e·h= we·pi Ca+ kano·N +eči
AOR+ begin/PV RED1+ speak.to +X-3/AOR
then there are words said to them(P).

D ki·ši-kakano·nečini·=’ni menehta či·nawe·ma·čiki e·h=we·pi_pakisenamawa·wa·či a·hkone·wani,
IC+ ki·ši Ca+ kano·N +ečini i·ni menehta IC+ či·nawe·m +a·čiki
xx+ PERF/PV RED1+ speak.to +X-3/ITER then first xx+ be.related.to +3-3′/PPL(ANpl)

e·h= we·pi pakisenamaw +a·wa·či a·hkone·w +ani
AOR+ begin/PV make.offering.of.02.to +3p-3′/AOR Indian.tobacco +OBVsg
And after the speeches are made to them(P), their(O) relatives(P) begin offering Indian tobacco to them(P) first,

E o·ni kotakaki ahkowi meše·=’nahi.
o·ni kotak +aki ahkowi meše·=’nahi
and,then other +ANpl behind as.may.be
and then others(P) may do so afterwards.

F ki·ši_ča·ki-pakisenamawa·wa·čini,
IC+ ki·ši ča·ki pakisenamaw +a·wa·čini
xx+ PERF/PV all/PV make.offering.of.02.to +3p-3′/ITER
After all of them(P) have offered it to them(O),

G ma·wač_ahkowi·=’ni wi·čawiwa·čiki e·h=pakisenamawa·wa·či.
ma·wači ahkowi i·ni IC+ wi·čawiw +a·čiki
of.all behind then xx+ be.with +3-3′/PPL(ANpl)

e·h= pakisenamaw +a·wa·či
AOR+ make.offering.of.02.to +3p-3′/AOR
then last of all their(O) husbands or wives(P) offer it to them(O).

173

A tetepose·waki e·h=apiniči.
tetepose· +waki e·h= api +niči
circle.walking +3p/IND AOR+ sit +3′/PPL(loc.obl)
They(P) walk around the place where their spouse(O) has been interred.

B o·ni we·ta·paniki e·h=iši̠we·pose·wa·či.
o·ni IC+ ota·pan +niki e·h= iši we·pose· +wa·či
and,then xx+ be.dawn.from.{smth} +0′/PPL(obl) AOR+ {so}/PV start.walking +3p/AOR
And then they(P) start walking to the east(o).

C meše=meko·=’nahi anemihe·waki, na·wi̠sasakanwe.
meše=meko·=’nahi anemiha· +waki na·wi sasakanwe
any go.(some).way +3p/IND in.middle/PP thicket/ECM
They(P) go through anyplace, through the middle of the brush.

D e·h=po·si̠=meko -sasakanikini anemi̠’na·hkwičino·ki.
e·h= po·si =meko sasakan +nikini
AOR+ extreme/PV =EMPH be.thicket +0′/PPL(loc.obl.pl)

anemi ina·hkwičin +waki
go.on/PV be.impeded.{so} +3p/IND
In the very thickest parts of the brush(o) they(P) push right on through.

E a·kwi=ke·h| peteki ina·piwa·čini nana·ši.
a·kwi =ke·hi peteki ina·pi +wa·čini nana·ši
not =moreover back look.{smwh} +3p/NEG (ever)
And another thing, they(P)’re not supposed to ever look back.

F (peteki=ke·h̠ina·piwa·te, ma·maya̠nepowa·sa.)
peteki =ke·hi ina·pi +wa·te ma·maya nep +wa·sa
back =moreover look.{smwh} +3p/SUBJ early die +3p/POT
(If they(P) did look back, they(P) would die an early death.)

G peno·či=meko·=’ni e·h=mawi-oči̠kohki·wa·či,
peno·či =meko i·ni e·h= mawi oči kohki· +wa·či
far.away =EMPH then AOR+ go.and/PV from.{smth}/PV turn.around +3p/AOR
They(P)’re supposed to go way far off then, before they(P) turn around

174

A aya·pami e·h=a·wa·či.
aya·pami e·h= iha· +wa·či
back AOR+ go.{smwh} +3p/AOR
and go back.

B i·ni e·šawiwa·či.

```
i·ni       IC+ išawi   +wa·či
that/INsg xx+ do.{so} +3p/PPL(obl)
```

That's what they[P]'re supposed to do.

C "a·kwi=’yo=me·kwe·h i·ni=’šawiyanini ki·na.

```
a·kwi =iyo me·kwe·he i·ni      išawi   +yanini ki·na
not   =for I.believe that/INsg do.{so} +2s/NEG 2s/EMPH
```

"I say this since I don't believe you did that.

D i·n=e·nehta·ke·ya·ni," netekwa nešise·ha.

```
i·ni      IC+ inehta·ke·             +ya·ni         ne+ iN            +ekwa
that/INsg xx+ hear.people.say.{so} +1s/PPL(obl) 1+  say.{so}.to +3s-1s/IND

ne+ -šise·h      +a
1+   cross-uncle +ANsg
```

That's what I heard," my uncle[P] said to me.

E "a·kwi=koh kehke·netema·nini=ye·toke e·h=išikekehe.

```
a·kwi =kohi        kehke·net +ama·nini =ye·toke  e·h= išiken   +kehe
not   =certainly know       +1s-0/NEG =it.seems AOR+ be.{so} +0/AOR.PRET
```

"No, I definitely didn't know that it was done the way, it seems, it is.

F a·kwi=koči·=’ni| nahi-no·tawakini nekya e·ye·h_ne·se·či e·šawinikwe·ni ši·ka·winičihi.

```
a·kwi =koči      i·ni      nahi          no·taw          +akini    ne+ -ky      +a
not   =you.know that/INsg given.to/PV hear.talk.of +1s-3/NEG 1+   mother +ANsg

IC+ aye·hi           ne·se·  +či
xx+ continue.to/PV live.on +3s/CC

IC+ išawi   +nikwe·ni              IC+ ši·ka·wi                               +ničihi
xx+ do.{so} +3′,0′/INT.PPL(obl) xx+ be.widow(er).in.strict.mourning +3′/PPL(OBVpl)
```

I can only say that, while my mother[P] was alive, I never heard her[P] on the subject of what it is that widowed people[O] do.

G i·ni=ča·h_we·či-pwa·wi-kehke·netama·ni e·še·wi·weniwikwe·ni.

```
i·ni      =ča·hi IC+ oči              pwa·wi kehke·net +ama·ni
that/INsg =so    xx+ from.{smth}/PV NEG/PV know      +1s-0/PPL(obl)

IC+ iše·wi·weniwi      +kwe·ni
xx+ be.{such}.a.custom +3s,0/INT.PPL(obl)
```

So that's why I didn't know what[p] the custom is.

175

A a·kwi i·tepi_iha·ya·nini| e·h=pi·tahoči.

```
a·kwi i·tepi    iha·        +ya·nini e·h= pi·tahw +eči
not   to.there go.{smwh} +1s/NEG  AOR+ bury    +X-3/AOR
```

I didn't go over there when he[P] was buried.

B ayo·h=meko=netawi‿wi·kiya·peki," netena·wa nešise·ha.

```
ayo·hi    =meko ne+ awi        +Ø       wi·kiya·p +eki ne+ iN            +a·wa
this/LOC =EMPH 1+  be.{smwh} +1s/IND house      +LOC 1+  say.{so}.to +1s-3s/IND

ne+ -šise·h      +a
1+   cross-uncle +ANsg
```

I stayed right here at the house," I said to my uncle[P].

C "mani=koči i·ni‿we·či‿'šawiwa·či:

```
mani        =koči       i·ni       IC+ oči                išawi   +wa·či
this/INsg =you.know that/INsg xx+ from.{smth}/PV do.{so} +3p/PPL(obl)
```

Then he[P] said to me, "All I can say is, this is why they[P] do that:

D wi·h=wani·paha·wa·či no·ke·nawani, e·h=sasakaniki we·či‿ki·ki·yose·wa·či," i·n=e·h=išiči.

```
wi·h= wani·pah                 +a·wa·či    no·ke·naw +ani
FUT+  hide.and.escape.from +3p-3'/AOR soul        +OBVsg

e·h= sasakan      +niki
AOR+ be.a.thicket +0'/PPL(loc.obl)

IC+ oči                 Ci·+  ki·yose·    +wa·či       i·ni e·h= iN            +iči
xx+ from.{smth}/PV RED1+ walk.about +3p/PPL(obl) then AOR+ say.{so}.to +3s-1s/AOR
```

the reason they[P] go walking through the brush[O] is to throw the soul[O] off their trail.

E "i·ni=ča·h=ye·hapa we·či-po·site·he·yani.

```
i·ni      =ča·hi =ye·hapa      IC+ oči                po·site·he· +yani
that/INsg =so    =it.turns.out xx+ from.{smth}/PV feel.worse  +2s/PPL(obl)
```

"So that now seems to explain why you feel so bad.

F i·ni=ke·h‿išawiyanehe ‖ e·na·čimohena·ni·='noki,

```
i·ni       =ke·hi     išawi    +yanehe        IC+ ina·čimoh    +ena·ni            i·noki
that/INsg =moreover do.{so} +2s/SUBJ.PRET xx+ inform.{so} +1s-2s/PPL(obl) now
```

In other words, if you'd done the way I'm instructing you now,

176

A awita| i·ni išawihkapa.|

```
awita   i·ni       išawi   +hkapa
not/POT that/INsg do.{so} +2s/POT
```

that wouldn't have happened to you.

B "na·hka ahpene·či=meko wi·seniyanini aškote·ki ki·h=ahtawa·wa.|

```
na·hka       ahpene·či  =meko IC+ wi·seni +yanini
also,again every.time =EMPH xx+ eat     +2s/ITER

aškote·w +eki ke+ wi·h= ahtaw                  +a·wa
fire     +LOC 2+  FUT+  place.O2.{smwh}.for +2s-3s/IND
```

"And also, every time you eat a meal you should put some of it by the fire for him[P].

C ka·ta=meko nana·ši wani·hke·hkani e·hpi·hči‿pwa·wi‿ki·ši‿pakineči.|
ka·ta =meko nana·ši wani·hke· +hkani
don't =EMPH (ever) forget +2s/PROH

IC+ ahpi·hči pwa·wi ki·ši pakiN +eči
xx+ in.process.of/PV NEG/PV PERF/PV discard,release +X-3/CC
Don't ever forget for as long as an adoption feast has still not been held for him[(P)].

D nehki=meko ši·ka·wiwane·ni i·ni| wi·h=išawiyani," netekwa nešise·ha.
nehki =meko IC+ ši·ka·wi +wane·ni
for.{so}.long =EMPH xx+ be.widow(er).in.strict.mourning +2s/INT.PPL(obl)

i·ni IC+ wi·h= išawi +yani
that/INsg xx+ FUT+ do.{so} +2s/PPL(obl)

ne+ iN +ekwa ne+ -šise·h +a
1+ say.{so}.to +3s-1s/IND 1+ cross-uncle +ANsg
For however long you may be in strict mourning that's what you must do," my uncle[(P)] *told me.*

E "nahí·='ni.
nahi´ i·ni
Well! that/INsg
Then he[(P)] *said to me, "Well, that's enough.*

F na·hka=ča·h=kapo·twe ki·h=pye·či-wi·tamo·ne,"|| i·n=e·h=išiči.
na·hka =ča·hi kapo·twe ke+ wi·h= pye·či wi·tamaw +ene
also,again =so at.some.point 2+ FUT+ coming/PV tell +1s-2s/IND

i·ni e·h= iN +iči
then AOR+ say.{so}.to +3s-1s/AOR
So, I'll come back sometime and tell you more."

177

A e·h=na·kwa·či.
e·h= na·kwa· +či
AOR+ leave +3s/AOR
And he[(P)] *left.*

B o·ni=ča·h ahpene·či=meko wi·seniya·nini aškote·ki e·h=ahtawaki wi·čawiwaki.
o·ni =ča·hi ahpene·či =meko IC+ wi·seni +ya·nini
and,then =so every.time =EMPH xx+ eat +1s/ITER

aškote·w +eki e·h= ahtaw +aki IC+ wi·čawiw +aka
fire +LOC AOR+ place.O2.{smwh}.for +1s-3/AOR xx+ be.with +1s-3/PPL(ANsg)
And so then, every time I ate a meal I put some by the fire for my husband[(P)].

C na·hka_nekočawi=meko wi·h=po·ni-a·hpeči-nenehke·nemaki,
na·hka ne+ kočawi +Ø =meko
also,again 1+ try +1s/IND =EMPH

wi·h= po·ni a·hpeči nenehke·nem +aki
FUT+ cease/PV permanently/PV think.about +1s-3/AOR
And also I really tried to stop thinking about him(P) constantly,

D e·h=kohtama·ni wi·h=nepeya·ni ma·maya.
e·h= koht +ama·ni wi·h= nep +ya·ni ma·maya
AOR+ fear +1s-0/AOR FUT+ die +1s/AOR early
as I was afraid of dying an early death.

E aškači·='ni, "katawi_pakita·pi='pi," e·h=inehta·ke·ya·ni.
aškači i·ni katawi pakit +a·pi =ipi
later then almost/PV discard,release +X(-0)/IND =HRSY

e·h= inehta·ke· +ya·ni
AOR+ hear.people.say.{so} +1s/AOR
Then quite some time later I heard people say, "There's supposedly about to be an adoption feast."

F ke·htena·='nahi| kapo·twe nepye·či_natomeko·pi.||
ke·htena =i·nahi kapo·twe ne+ pye·či natom +eko·pi
truly =with.that at.some.point 1+ coming/PV ask.to.come +X-1s/IND
Sure enough, soon after that someone came and invited me.

178

A i·ya·h=e·h=pya·ya·ni, ma·ne·waki| neno·te·waki.
i·ya·hi e·h= pya· +ya·ni ma·ne· +waki neno·te·w +aki
yonder AOR+ come +1s/AOR be.much,many +3p/IND Indian +ANpl
When I got over there, there were a lot of Indians(P).

B ni·na=ke·h i·ya·h_pi·tike·ya·ni,
ni·na =ke·hi i·ya·hi pi·tike· +ya·ni
1s/EMPH =moreover yonder go.in +1s/CC
And when I went in there myself,

C i·nah=či·h we·šehki·hečiki tašisenye·waki.
i·nahi =či·hi IC+ ošehki·h +ečiki tašisenye· +waki
that/LOC =it.was.discovered xx+ clothe,adopt +X-3/PPL(ANpl) eat.{smwh} +3p/IND
there I saw the two who(P) were being adopted, eating.

D e·h=ašamiki,
e·h= ašam +iki
AOR+ give.to.eat.to +X-1s/AOR
And I was fed,

E me·mečine·h=ta·taki e·h=nawači-wi·hpoti·ya·ke‿wi·čawiwaka iši̇we·pi,
me·mečine·hi ta·taki e·h= nawači wi·hpoti· +ya·ke
for.last.time in.a.way AOR+ first,stop.to eat.together +1p/AOR

IC+ wi·čawiw +aka iši̇we·pi
xx+ be.with +1s-3/PPL(ANsg) signifying.{so}
representing, in a way, that my husband[P] and I ate together one last time,

F e·h=peno·hěči.
e·h= peno·h +eči
AOR+ send.on.one's.way +X-3/AOR
sending him[P] on his way.

G ki·ši·seniya·ni·=’ni, “ketenano keto·šehki·ta·kani,” e·h=iši̇ki.|
IC+ ki·ši·seni +ya·ni i·ni keten +ano ke+ ošehki·ta·kan +i
xx+ finish.eating +1s/CC then take.off +2s-0/IMP 2+ clothing +INsg

e·h= iN +iki
AOR+ say.{so}.to +X-1s/AOR
After I had eaten, I was told, “Take off your clothes.”

H kotakani·=’ni e·škikekini e·h=we·pi-nana·heškahiki, ‖
kotak +ani i·ni IC+ aškiken +kini e·h= we·pi nana·heškah +iki
other +INpl then xx+ be.new +0/PPL(INpl) AOR+ begin/PV to.wear.02].cause +X-1s/AOR
Then I began to have other, new clothes[p] given to me to put on,

179
A na·hka e·h=penaha·hkwawiki, na·hka| e·h=kesi·kwe·niki.|
na·hka e·h= penaha·hkwaw +iki na·hka e·h= kesi·kwe·n +iki
also,again AOR+ comb.hair.of +X-1s/AOR also,again AOR+ wash.face.of +X-1s/AOR
and also my hair was combed, and my face was washed.

B o·ni=ča·h,‿“nahi´,‿ka·ta‿peninawi·hkani.
o·ni =ča·hi nahi´ ka·ta peninawi· +hkani
and,then =so Well! don't remove.clothing +2s/PROH
And then when that was done I was told, “Alright now, don't take your clothes off.

C i·ni=meko‿ki·h=ki·wi|-iši̇šehki·ta.
i·ni =meko ke+ wi·h= ki·wi iši̇šehki·t +a
that/INsg =EMPH 2+ FUT+ around/PV wear.(as).clothing.{so} +2s(-0)/IND
You must go around dressed just like that.

D ki·h=we·pi‿mi·ša·tesi.
ke+ wi·h= we·pi mi·ša·tesi +Ø
2+ FUT+ begin/PV dress.up +2s/IND
You must begin to dress up.

E pe·hki=meko| ki·h=we·we·ne·neta‿wi·h=ki·wi‿'šawiyani.
pe·hki =meko ke+ wi·h= we·we·ne·net +a
really =EMPH 2+ FUT+ have.control.over +2s-0/IND

IC+ wi·h= ki·wi išawi +yani
xx+ FUT+ around/PV do.{so} +2s/PPL(obl)
You shall have your own say completely over what you do.

F owiye·ha=ke·h wi·h=wi·čawiwači išite·he·yane, ki·h=wi·čawiwa·wa.
owiye·h +a =ke·hi wi·h= wi·čawiw +ači išite·he· +yane
someone +ANsg =moreover FUT+ be.with +2s-3/AOR think.{so} +2s/SUBJ

ke+ wi·h= wi·čawiw +a·wa
2+ FUT+ be.with +2s-3s/IND
For instance, if you want to get together with someone[P], go ahead and get together with him[P].

G ki·h=pemenekwa=koči, owiye·ha‿wi·čawiwate.
ke+ wi·h= pemen +ekwa =koči owiye·h +a wi·čawiw +ate
2+ FUT+ take.care.of +3s-2s/IND =you.know someone +ANsg be.with +2s-3/SUBJ
After all, if you get together with someone[P], he[P]'ll take care of you.

180
A ka·ta taši|-kosetawihka·ke.
ka·ta taši kosetaw +ihka·ke
don't be.engaged.in/PV fear.to.approach +2-1p/PROH
Don't be shy around us.

B keki·ši‿=koh‿-te·pihipena e·h=menwi‿to·tawači či·nawe·maketa e·ye·h‿ne·se·či.
ke+ ki·ši =kohi te·pih +ipena e·h= menwi to·taw +ači
2+ PERF/PV =certainly please.by.act +2-1p/IND AOR+ well/PV treat.{so} +2s-3/AOR

IC+ či·nawe·m +aketa IC+ aye·hi ne·se· +či
xx+ be.related.to +1p-3/PPL(ANsg) xx+ continue.to/PV live.on +3s/CC
You have certainly pleased us by treating our relative[P] well while he[P] was alive.

C we·kone·h=ča·hi·='nahi wi·h=oči‿ki·wi|-memye·ške·nemena·ke.
we·kone·h +i =ča·hi =i·nahi
what? +INsg =so =with.that

IC+ wi·h= oči ki·wi memye·ške·nem +ena·ke
xx+ FUT+ from.{smth}/PV around/PV plan.trouble.for +1p-2/PPL(obl)
So after that, why would we want to go around making things rough for you?

D "i·ni.
i·ni
that/INsg
"That's all.

E ki·h=te·pwe·htawipena=ča·h i·noki=mani e·nena·ke," e·h=išiki.
ke+ wi·h= te·pwe·htaw +ipena =ča·hi i·noki =mani
2+ FUT+ believe,agree.to.request.of +2–1p/IND =so now =as.it.is.now

IC+ iN +ena·ke e·h= iN +iki
xx+ say.{so}.to +1p–2/PPL(obl) AOR+ say.{so}.to +X–1s/AOR
So you must heed what we're now telling you," I was told.

F o·n=e·h=na·kwa·ya·ni.
o·ni e·h= na·kwa· +ya·ni
and,then AOR+ leave +1s/AOR
And then I left.

G ača·hmeko·='ni e·h=we·pi-‿meše·='nahi -aškišehki·tama·ni, ‖
ača·hmeko i·ni e·h= we·pi meše·='nahi aškišehki·t +ama·ni
only.then then AOR+ begin/PV as.may.be wear.(as).new.clothing +1s(-0)/AOR
And then for the first time in a long time I was free to start wearing new clothes again

181
A na·hka e·h=we·pi‿ke·kesi·kwa·ya·ni.
na·hka e·h= we·pi CV+ kesi·kwa· +ya·ni
also,again AOR+ begin/PV RED1+ wash.own.face +1s/AOR
and also to start washing my face again.

B o·ni=ča·h| e·h=pya·či i·niya=na·hka nešise·ha.
o·ni =ča·hi e·h= pya· +či i·niya na·hka
and,then =so AOR+ come +3s/AOR that/ABS(ANsg) also,again

ne+ -šise·h +a
1+ cross-uncle +ANsg
So then my uncle[(P)] came over for the second time.

C "nahi·='ni=ya·pi=na·hka| e·h=pye·či-a·čimohena·ni, nešemi.|
nahi´ i·ni =ya·pi na·hka e·h= pye·či a·čimoh +ena·ni
Well! then =here.I,we.go also,again AOR+ coming/PV inform +1s–2s/AOR

ne+ -šemi·h +Ø
1+ cross-niece +VOCsg
"Alright, now here I am back again to give you more instructions, niece.

D mani·='noki| i·ni e·h=ki·ši‿pa·ni·yani.
mani i·noki
this/INsg now

i·ni e·h= ki·ši pa·ni· +yani
that/INsg AOR+ PERF/PV be.widow(er).no.longer.in.strict.mourning +2s/AOR
Now, today, is when you've become formally released from your strict mourning.

E **kekehke·neta e·hpi·hči-ki·sa·tesiyani,**
```
ke+ kehke·net +a         IC+ ahpi·hči             ki·sa·tesi      +yani
2+  know      +2s-0/IND xx+ to.{such}.degree/PV have.awful.time +2s/PPL(obl)
```
You know what an awful time you had getting through it,

F **e·h=mehkawatehe‿me·nwawita neniwa‿me·nwi-to·to·hka.**
```
e·h= mehkaw +atehe         IC+ menwawi +ta          neniw +a
AOR+ find   +2s-3/AOR.PRET xx+ do.well +3/PPL(ANsg) man   +ANsg

IC+ menwi   to·taw     +ehka
xx+ well/PV treat.{so} +3-2s/PPL(ANsg)
```
as you had found a well-behaved man[P] who was nice to you.

G **pe·hki=ča·h=meko ki·sa·či| išite·he·no´.**
```
pe·hki =ča·hi =meko ki·sa·či  išite·he·  +no     ´
really =so    =EMPH difficult think.{so} +2s/IMP INTERJ
```
So, by all means consider it a really awful thing.

H **ka·ta=ča·hi‿nahmeko=meko po·ni-nenehke·nemiye·kani.**
```
ka·ta =ča·hi nahmeko         =meko po·ni    nenehke·nem +iye·kani
don't =so    then.and.there =EMPH cease/PV think.about +2s-3/PROH
```
And don't be too quick to just put him out of your mind.

182

A **sanakesiwa=koh=e·yi·ki| neniwa me·nwawita.**
```
sanakesi      +wa     =kohi       e·yi·ki neniw +a    IC+ menwawi +ta
be.difficult +3s/IND =certainly as.well man   +ANsg xx+ do.well +3/PPL(ANsg)
```
There's no doubt a good man[P] is hard to find, as well.

B **keki·ši-='yo| peteki -kehke·neta e·to·to·hki‿menehta wi·čawiwata.**
```
ke+ ki·ši    =iyo peteki kehke·net +a         IC+ to·taw     +ehki
2+  PERF/PV =for back   know      +2s-0/IND xx+ treat.{so} +3-2s/PPL(obl)

menehta IC+ wi·čawiw +ata
first   xx+ be.with  +2s-3/PPL(ANsg)
```
For example, you already came to know previously how your first husband[P] treated you.

C **pe·hki=meko keketema·kihekwa.**
```
pe·hki =meko ke+ ketema·kih +ekwa
really =EMPH 2+  ill-treat  +3s-2s/IND
```
He[P] mistreated you seriously.

D i·ni=ča·h| a·m‿oči- kenwe·ši·me·h -pwa·wi|-wani·hka·nači| ma·hiya a·yahkowi wi·čawiwata.

```
i·ni      =ča·hi
that/INsg =so

IC+ a·mi   oči              kenwe·ši·me·hi pwa·wi wani·hka·N +ači
xx+ POT/PV from.{smth}/PV long.time/DIM  NEG/PV forget     +2s-3/PPL(obl)

ma·hiya                CV+   ahkowi IC+ wi·čawiw +ata
that.recently.present RED1+ behind xx+ be.with  +2s-3/PPL(ANsg)
```

So that's why you shouldn't forget your late second husband[P] for quite a long time.

183

A ki·h=we·pi·hka·ko·ki=’yo=meko neniwaki.

```
ke+ wi·h= we·pi·hkaw          +eko·ki    =iyo =meko neniw +aki
2+  FUT+  begin.dealing.with +3p-2s/IND =for =EMPH man   +ANpl
```

For men[P] are going to start getting after you.

B ka·ta=ča·h pa·pekwa wi·h=we·pi·hka·ti·yani išite·he·hkani.

```
ka·ta =ča·hi pa·pekwa    wi·h= we·pi·hka·ti·                   +yani
don't =so    right.away FUT+  begin.dealing.with.each.other +2s/AOR

išite·he·  +hkani
think.{so} +2s/PROH
```

Well, don't think of starting to get involved right off.

C nye·wawahi·ne kočawino wi·h=pwa·wi|-wani·hka·nači wi·čawiwata| e·h=pana·pamači.

```
nye·wawahi·ne  kočawi +no      wi·h= pwa·wi wani·hka·N +ači
for.four.years try    +2s/IMP FUT+  NEG/PV forget     +2s-3/AOR

IC+ wi·čawiw +ata             e·h= pana·pam      +ači
xx+ be.with  +2s-3/PPL(ANsg) AOR+ lose.sight.of +2s-3/AOR
```

For four years try not to forget that you have lost sight of your husband[P].

D ke·waki=koči=mani‿ketaškiki.

```
ke·waki        =koči       =mani           ke+ aškiki   +Ø
as.yet,still =you.know =as.it.is.now 2+  be.young +2s/IND
```

Remember, you're still young now.

E a·kwi=ča·h=meko| ke·ko·hi kenwe·ši·me·hi pwa·wi|-wi·čawiwate owiye·ha.|

```
a·kwi =ča·hi =meko ke·ko·h   +i
not   =so    =EMPH something +INsg

kenwe·ši·me·hi pwa·wi wi·čawiw +ate        owiye·h +a
long.time/DIM  NEG/PV be.with  +2s-3/SUBJ someone +ANsg
```

So there won't be any problem if you don't get together with someone[P] for quite a long time.

F meči▪'h▪we·na na·hka·▪'ni!?| wi·h▪iši͜menwawiwa!? wi·h▪wi·čawiwa·wate·na!?
meči ▪ihi ▪we·na na·hka i·ni wi·h▪ iši menwawi +wa
quite ▪NEG ▪in.fact also,again that/INsg FUT+ {so}/PV do.well +3s–0/IND

IC+ wi·h▪ wi·čawiw +a·wate·na !?
xx+ FUT+ be.with +2s–3/INT.PPL(ANsg) EN
After all, it's ridiculous to think that whoever you marry[P] will again be a man that good.

184
A "i·ni▪ča·h we·či-pye·či-a·ya·čimohena·ni,
i·ni ▪ča·hi IC+ oči pye·či CV+ a·čimoh +ena·ni
that/INsg ▪so xx+ from.{smth}/PV coming/PV RED1+ inform +1s–2s/PPL(obl)
"Well, that's why I'm over here instructing you,

B e·h▪ka·htwe·netamo·na·ni wi·čawiwata.
e·h▪ ka·htwe·netamaw +ena·ni IC+ wi·čawiw +ata
AOR+ feel.sorrow.over.O2.for +1s–2s/AOR xx+ be.with +2s–3/PPL(ANsg)
because I grieve for your husband[P].

C i·ni wi·h▪iši-kočawiyani.
i·ni IC+ wi·h▪ iši kočawi +yani
that/INsg xx+ FUT+ {so}/PV try +2s/PPL(obl)
That's what you must try and do.

D "na·hka pe·hki▪koči▪wi·na▪meko nemi·ša·te·nemo e·h▪te·pwe·htawiyani e·ši͜menwikeki e·h▪ina·čimohena·ni. ‖
na·hka pe·hki ▪koči ▪wi·na ▪meko ne+ mi·ša·te·nemo +Ø
also,again really ▪you.know ▪but ▪EMPH 1+ be.pleased +1s/IND

e·h▪ te·pwe·htaw +iyani
AOR+ believe,agree.to.request.of +2s–1s/AOR

IC+ iši menwiken +ki e·h▪ ina·čimoh +ena·ni
xx+ {so}/PV be.good +0/PPL(obl) AOR+ inform.{so} +1s–2s/AOR
"And furthermore, you know I'm really very pleased that you heeded me when I instructed you to do what was right.

185
A a·neta▪koči na·hina·h▪meko ne·peničini okiwa·wahi we·pi͜wa·waneška·hiwaki,
a·neta ▪koči na·hina·hi ▪meko IC+ nep +ničini o+ -ky +wa·wahi
some ▪you.know time,distance ▪EMPH xx+ die +3′/ITER 3+ mother +3p(OBVpl)

we·pi wa·waneška·hi +waki
begin/PV be.bad +3p/IND
Let me tell you, some women[P] start to behave badly as soon as their[P] mothers[O] die,

B e·h▪po·ni|- owiye·hani͜-nana·himekowa·či.
e·h▪ po·ni owiye·h +ani nana·him +ekowa·či
AOR+ cease/PV someone +OBVsg give.guidance.to +3′–3p/AOR
since they[P] no longer have anyone[O] to give them guidance.

C kotakah=ke·h‿a·kwi pesetawa·wa·čini e·h=kekye·hkimekowa·či.

```
kotak +ahi    =ke·hi     a·kwi pesetaw    +a·wa·čini e·h= kekye·hkim +ekowa·či
other +OBVpl  =moreover not    listen.to  +3p-3′/NEG AOR+ teach       +3′-3p/AOR
```

And what's more when they[P]'re taught by others[O] they[P] don't listen to them[O].

D i·ni=ča·h=ni·na, 'na·katawe·netisowa nešemi·ha,' we·či‿'šite·he·ya·ni.

```
i·ni       =ča·hi ni·na    na·katawe·netiso       +wa     ne+ -šemi·h       +a
that/INsg  =so    1s/EMPH  follow.self.mentally   +3s/IND 1+  cross-niece   +ANsg

IC+ oči              išite·he·   +ya·ni
xx+ from.{smth}/PV   think.{so}  +1s/PPL(obl)
```

So that's why I thought, 'My niece[P] is watching out for herself.'

E "nahí·='ni, nešemi,‖ e·h=ki·ši-a·ya·čimohena·ni išawiyane wi·h=iši-pešikwiweto·yani ki·yawi."

```
nahi′ i·ni       ne+ -šemi·h      +Ø      e·h= ki·ši   CV+   a·čimoh +ena·ni
Well! that/INsg  1+  cross-niece  +VOCsg  AOR+ PERF/PV RED1+ inform  +1s-2s/AOR

išawi    +yane    IC+ wi·h= iši     pešikwiwet       +o·yani
do.{so}  +2s/SUBJ xx+ FUT+  {so}/PV lead.straight    +2s-0/PPL(obl)

ke+ -i·yaw      +i
2+  body,self   +INsg
```

"Well, now, niece, I've finished instructing you about what to do in order to lead an upright life."

186

A e·šimiči=meko i·n=e·h=išawiya·ni.

```
IC+ išim              +iči              =meko i·ni e·h= išawi   +ya·ni
xx+ speak.{so}.to     +3s-1s/PPL(obl)   =EMPH then AOR+ do.{so} +1s/AOR
```

Then I did just what he[P] told me to do.

B e·h=pwa·wi-kaški·hkawiči owiye·ha e·h=mi·hkemi·hkemiwa·či| neniwaki.

```
e·h= pwa·wi  kaški·hkaw              +iči        owiye·h +a
AOR+ NEG/PV  manage.to.deal.with     +3s-1s/AOR  someone +ANsg

e·h= CVCV+ mi·hkem +iwa·či      neniw +aki
AOR+ RED2+ court   +3p-1s/AOR   man   +ANpl
```

None[P] of the men[P] were able to succeed with me as repeatedly they[P] tried to court me.

C nekehči‿neškima·wa=meko owiye·ha mi·hkemičini.

```
ne+ kehči        neškim               +a·wa        =meko owiye·h +a
1+  greatly/PV   forbid,admonish      +1s-3s/IND   =EMPH someone +ANsg

IC+ mi·hkem +ičini
xx+ court   +3s-1s/ITER
```

Whenever anyone[P] tried to court me I scolded him[P] quite severely.

D nye·wawahi·ne neki·ki·wita,

```
nye·wawahi·ne ne+ Ci·+   ki·wita·      +Ø
four.years    1+  RED1+  stay.around   +1s/IND
```

I stayed single for four years,

E e·hpi·hči=ta·taki -ka·htwe·nemaki wi·čawiwaka.|
IC+ ahpi·hči ta·taki ka·htwe·nem +aki
xx+ to.{such}.degree/PV in.a.way feel.sorrow.over +1s-3/PPL(obl)

IC+ wi·čawiw +aka
xx+ be.with +1s-3/PPL(ANsg)
which was, so to speak, how much I grieved for my husband[P].

187
A oni·ča·nesiya·nehe=wi·na,
oni·ča·nesi +ya·nehe =wi·na
have.child +1s/SUBJ.PRET =but
If I had had children,

B awita| meše·='nahi nana·ši=na·hka ona·pe·mihka·ha.
awita meše·='nahi nana·ši na·hka ona·pe·mi +hka·ha
not/POT as.may.be (ever) also,again have.husband +1s/POT
I probably would never have gotten married again.

C mani=wi·na:
mani =wi·na
this/INsg =but
But the thing was,

D "asa·mi=meko neta·hpeči-ki·wi=nešawi,
asa·mi =meko ne+ a·hpeči ki·wi nešawi +Ø
too.much =EMPH 1+ permanently/PV around/PV be.alone +1s/IND
I kept thinking, "I just go around all the time by myself too much,

E we·či-a·hpeči=ki·wa·tesiya·ni," netešite·h=a·pehe.
IC+ oči a·hpeči ki·wa·tesi +ya·ni
xx+ from.{smth}/PV permanently/PV be.lonely +1s/PPL(obl)

ne+ išite·he· +Ø =a·pehe
1+ think.{so} +1s/IND =usually
which is why I'm lonely all the time."

* * *

F nye·wawahi·makahki a·wasi·me·h i·ni na·hka nekoti neniwa e·h=we·pi=keša·čihaki.
IC+ nye·wawahi·makat +ki a·wasi·me·hi i·ni na·hka nekoti neniw +a
xx+ be.four.years +0/CC more/DIM then also,again one man +ANsg

e·h= we·pi keša·čih +aki
AOR+ begin/PV be.kind.to +1s-3/AOR
After a little more than four years there was again a certain man[P] *I began to be friendly to.*

188

A kapo·twe·=’ni wi·h=owi·weti·ya·ke e·h=išiči.

```
kapo·twe       i·ni wi·h= owi·weti·         +ya·ke  e·h= iN            +iči
at.some.point then FUT+  marry.each.other +1p/AOR AOR+ say.{so}.to +3s-1s/AOR
```

Then at some point he[P] said to me that we should get married.

B “nahi´‿wi·h=wi·čawi·ti·yakwe=kohi we·či‿we·pi·hko·na·ni wi·h=keša·čihena·ni.

```
nahi´ wi·h= wi·čawi·ti·          +yakwe  =kohi      IC+ oči
Well! FUT+  be.with.each.other +12/AOR =certainly xx+ from.{smth}/PV

we·pi·hkaw          +ena·ni          wi·h= keša·čih   +ena·ni
begin.dealing.with +1s-2s/PPL(obl) FUT+  be.kind.to +1s-2s/AOR
```

“Listen, you must know that it was so that we would get together that I took up with you to try and get friendly with you.

C ma·hiya=’yo wi·čawiwata‿netowi·hka·ni.|

```
ma·hiya                =iyo IC+ wi·čawiw +ata
that.recently.present =for xx+ be.with  +2s-3/PPL(ANsg)

ne+ owi·hka·ni          +Ø
1+  have.O2.as.friend +1s/IND
```

After all, your late husband[P] was my friend.

D pe·hki=meko‿neka·kakano·neti·pena.

```
pe·hki =meko ne+ CV+   kakano·neti· +pena
really =EMPH 1+  RED1+ converse     +1p/IND
```

He and I had a lot of talks together.

E i·nina·h=ča·h=a·pehe, ‘nepo·hiya·ne ni·na=menehta,

```
i·ni i·na        =ča·hi =a·pehe  nepo·hi +ya·ne   ni·na    menehta
then that/ANsg =so     =usually die/DIM +1s/SUBJ 1s/EMPH first
```

Well, at those times he used to say to me, ‘If I die first,

F mana=ča·h wi·čawiwaka ki·h=taši·hkawa·wa wi·h=owi·wiyani.

```
mana       =ča·hi IC+ wi·čawiw +aka
this/ANsg =so    xx+ be.with  +1s-3/PPL(ANsg)

ke+ wi·h= taši·hkaw        +a·wa       wi·h= owi·wi            +yani
2+  FUT+  be.dealing.with +2s-3s/IND FUT+  have.O2.as.wife +2s/AOR
```

you must in that case try and take up with my wife[P] here in order to marry her.

G pe·hki‖ asa·mi‿menwawiwa.

```
pe·hki asa·mi       menwawi +wa
really too.much/PV do.well +3s/IND
```

She[P]’s really too good.

189

A ketowi·nemwi=koči e·h=owi·hka·neti·yakwe.
ke+ owi·nemwi +Ø =koči
2+ have.O2.as.sibling-in-law.of.opposite.sex +2s/IND =you.know

e·h= owi·hka·neti· +yakwe
AOR+ have.each.other.as.friend +12/AOR
She's like your sister-in-law, of course, as you and I are friends.

B iše=ma·hi nekekye·škatawe·nema·waki kotakaki neniwaki‿wi·h=owi·wiwa·či,
iše =ma·hi ne+ kekye·škatawe·nem +a·waki kotak +aki neniw +aki
just =you.see 1+ resent,begrudge +1s-3p/IND other +ANpl man +ANpl

wi·h= owi·wi +wa·či
FUT+ have.O2.as.wife +3p/AOR
See, it's just that I resent the thought of any other men[P] marrying her[O],

C e·h=asa·mi‿menwawiči mana‿wi·čawiwaka.
e·h= asa·mi menwawi +či mana IC+ wi·čawiw +aka
AOR+ too.much/PV do.well +3s/AOR this/ANsg xx+ be.with +1s-3/PPL(ANsg)
as my wife[P] is just too good.

D i·ni=ča·h we·či‿=ki·na·=’ni| -inena·ni,
i·ni =ča·hi IC+ oči ki·na i·ni iN +ena·ni
that/INsg =so xx+ from.{smth}/PV 2s/EMPH that/INsg say.{so}.to +1s-2s/PPL(obl)
So that's why I ask you to do that,

E wanimo·či menehta| nepo·hiya·ne.
wanimo·či menehta nepo·hi +ya·ne
perchance first die/DIM +1s/SUBJ
if I should happen to die first.

F a·kwi=koči‿kehke·netamakwini na·hina·h‿wi·h=nepeyakwini,’| netekwa=’yo·we.
a·kwi =koči kehke·net +amakwini
not =you.know know +12-0/NEG

na·hina·hi IC+ wi·h= nep +yakwini ne+ iN +ekwa =iyo·we
time,distance xx+ FUT+ die +12/ITER 1+ say.{so}.to +3s-1s/IND =PAST
We don't know the times when each of us will die, of course.'

190

A “ ‘na·hka ki·h=menwi‿to·tawa·wa=meko ne·h=ki·na.
na·hka ke+ wi·h= menwi to·taw +a·wa =meko ne·hi ki·na
also,again 2+ FUT+ well/PV treat.{so} +2s-3s/IND =EMPH too 2s/EMPH
“ ‘Also, you, too, must really treat her[P] well.

B netepa·na·wa·'yo e·h·menwawiči,' netekwa.
ne+ tepa·N +a·wa =iyo e·h= menwawi +či ne+ iN +ekwa
1+ love +1s-3s/IND =for AOR+ do.well +3s/AOR 1+ say.{so}.to +3s-1s/IND
I say this since I love her[P] for being so good,' he[P] said to me.

C "i·ni=ča·h_we·či- i·ni=meko wi·h=išawiyakwe -taši·hko·na·ni.|
i·ni =ča·hi IC+ oči i·ni =meko wi·h= išawi +yakwe
that/INsg =so xx+ from.{smth}/PV that/INsg =EMPH FUT+ do.{so} +12/AOR

taši·hkaw +ena·ni
be.dealing.with +1s-2s/PPL(obl)
"So that's why I'm after you for us to do just that.

D wa·wosa·hi='h=we·=ke·hi,!? 'ki·h=menwi_to·tawa·wa,' e·h=išiki, nana·hi_we·pi_mya·ši_to·to·naka·ha!?
wa·wosa·hi =ihi =we·na =ke·hi
it's.(not).expected =NEG =in.fact =moreover

ke+ wi·h= menwi to·taw +a·wa e·h= iN +iki
2+ FUT+ well/PV treat.{so} +1s-3s/IND AOR+ say.{so}.to +X-1s/AOR

nana·hi we·pi mya·ši to·taw +enaka·ha !?
get.set.to/PV begin/PV badly,sort.of/PV treat.{so} +1s-2s/POT EN
And after all, being told to treat you well, it's hardly likely that I would be making ready to treat you badly, is it?

E kočawihka·ha=meko e·to·to·hki='yo·we=ni·hka·na,"‖ e·h=išiči.
kočawi +hka·ha =meko IC+ to·taw +ehki =iyo·we ne+ -i·hka·n +a
try +1s/POT =EMPH xx+ treat.{so} +3-2s/PPL(obl) =PAST 1+ friend +ANsg

e·h= iN +iči
AOR+ say.{so}.to +3s-1s/AOR
I would really try to treat you the way my friend[P] did," he[P] said to me.

191

A o·ni e·h=anwa·či·ya·ni.
o·ni e·h= anwa·či· +ya·ni
and,then AOR+ consent +1s/AOR
And then I consented.

B pe·hkote·ki·='ni e·h=wi·hpe·ya·ni=na·hka ača·hmeko.
IC+ pehkote· +ki i·ni e·h= wi·hpe· +ya·ni na·hka ača·hmeko
xx+ be.night +0/CC then AOR+ sleep.with.another +1s/AOR also,again only.then
And that night[P] I slept with a man again for the first time in a long time.

C i·ni=meko na·hka ke·ko·h| e·h=we·pi_'šahišawiya·ke.
i·ni =meko na·hka ke·ko·h +i e·h= we·pi CVCV+ išawi +ya·ke
then =EMPH also,again something +INsg AOR+ begin/PV RED2+ do.{so} +1p/AOR
And also we started making love right then.

D a·kwi‿kenwe·ši taši‿kosetawikini ke·ko·h‿wi·h=to·tawiki.
a·kwi kenwe·ši taši kosetaw +ikini
not long.time be.engaged.in/PV fear.to.approach +X-1s/NEG

ke·ko·h +i wi·h= to·taw +iki
something +INsg FUT+ treat.{so} +X-1s/AOR
There was no long period of shyness about making love to me.

E o=ke·htena=wi·na=meko a·kwi nahi-a·hkwe·čini.
o ke·htena =wi·na =meko a·kwi nahi a·hkwe· +čini
or truly =but =EMPH not given.to/PV be.angry +3s/NEG
And he[(P)] really did never get angry.

F šewe·na‿na·ni·kihto·hiwa=meko=ta·taki,
šewe·na na·ni·kihto·hi +wa =meko ta·taki
but be.lazy +3s/IND =EMPH in.a.way
Still, he[(P)] was sort of lazy

G opye·nesiwa ke·ko·h‿e·h=ašihto·či,
opye·nesi +wa ke·ko·h +i e·h= ašiht +o·či
be.slow +3s/IND something +INsg AOR+ make +3s-0/AOR
and was slow to make anything,

H na·hka‿taneti·neniwiwa.||
na·hka taneti·neniwi +wa
also,again be.gambler +3s/IND
and he[(P)] was also a gambler.

192

A a·kwi=ča·h i·ni ahpi·hči‿tepa·nakini| i·niya ne·peka e·hpi·hči‿tepa·naki.
a·kwi =ča·hi i·ni ahpi·hči tepa·N +akini
not =so that/INsg to.{such}.degree/PV love +1s-3/NEG

i·niya IC+ nep +ka IC+ ahpi·hči tepa·N +aki
that/ABS(ANsg) xx+ die +3/PPL(ANsg) xx+ to.{such}.degree/PV love +1s-3/PPL(obl)
So I didn't love him[(P)] as much as I had loved the one[(P)] who had died.

B o·ni=natawa·či=na·hka| e·h=aka·wa·tama·ni| wi·h=oni·ča·nesiya·ni.
o·ni natawa·či na·hka e·h= aka·wa·t +ama·ni
and,then resolving.accordingly also,again AOR+ desire +1s-0/AOR

wi·h= oni·ča·nesi +ya·ni
FUT+ have.child +1s/AOR
And then I decided that I wanted to have children again.

C “na·pi=ke·h=wi·na| oni·ča·nesiya·ne,| ki·wi-anohka·šiye·ka·ha.
na·pi =ke·hi =wi·na oni·ča·nesi +ya·ne
for.the.better =moreover =but have.child +1s/SUBJ

ki·wi anohka·N +iye·ka·ha
around/PV give.task.to +1s-3/POT
“Besides, the good thing would be that, if I had children, I could give them things to do.

D meči=’h=we·na!?| wa·wosa·hi!? a·hkowi-ča·kine·wa·sa!?” netešite·he.
meči =ihi =we·na wa·wosa·hi a·hkowi ča·kine· +wa·sa !?
quite =NEG =in.fact it’s.(not).expected every.time/PV all.die +3p/POT EN

ne+ išite·he· +Ø
1+ think.{so} +1s/IND
After all, it’s hardly likely that they[P] *would all die each time!” I thought.*

E o·ni‿kapo·twe metemo·he·ha| na·tawino·ni| ke·hke·netaka e·h=nana·tohtawaki.
o·ni kapo·twe metemo·he·h +a
and,then at.some.point old.woman/DIM +ANsg

na·tawino·n +i IC+ kehke·net +aka e·h= nana·tohtaw +aki
medicine +INsg xx+ know +3-0/PPL(ANsg) AOR+ ask.question.of +1s-3/AOR
And then at some point I asked an old lady[P] *who knew about medicine.*

F “ahte·toke na·tawino·ni menoke? a·mi‿kaški-oni·ča·nesiki?”| netena·wa.
ahte· +wetoke na·tawino·n +i meno +eke
be.{smwh} +0s/DUB medicine +INsg drink.02 +X/SUBJ

IC+ a·mi kaški oni·ča·nesi +eki ? ne+ iN +a·wa
xx+ POT/PV able.to/PV have.child +X/PPL(INsg) Q 1+ say.{so}.to +1s-3s/IND
“Is there perhaps a medicine one could drink to be able to have children?” I asked her[P].

193

A “kaši=we·=towi.
kaši =we·na t(o) +wi
what? =in.fact be.{so} +0s/IND
“Yes, of course.

B ni·na=’yo‿nekehke·neta,”‿netekwa.
ni·na =iyo ne+ kehke·net +a ne+ iN +ekwa
1s/EMPH =for 1+ know +1s-0/IND 1+ say.{so}.to +3s-1s/IND
“For instance, I know one myself,” she[P] *said to me.*

C “oni·ča·nesihkapa=meko menoyane.
oni·ča·nesi +hkapa =meko meno +yane
have.child +2s/POT =EMPH drink.02 +2s/SUBJ
“You could indeed have children if you drank it.

D keki·ši-='yo=ke·hi='yo·we -oni·ča·nesi," netekwa.
ke+ ki·ši =iyo =ke·hi =iyo·we oni·ča·nesi +Ø ne+ iN +ekwa
2+ PERF/PV =for =moreover =PAST have.child +2s/IND 1+ say.{so}.to +3s-1s/IND
Bear in mind that you have had children before," she[P] said to me.

E "iše=koči na·tawino·ni nemeno,
iše =koči na·tawino·n +i ne+ meno +Ø
just =you.know medicine +INsg 1+ drink.02 +1s/IND
"Of course it's just that I drank a medicine,

F we·či|-po·ni-oni·ča·nesiya·ni," netena·wa.
IC+ oči po·ni oni·ča·nesi +ya·ni ne+ iN +a·wa
xx+ from.{smth}/PV cease/PV have.child +1s/PPL(obl) 1+ say.{so}.to +1s-3s/IND
why I stopped having children," I said to her[P].

G "a·kwi=ča·hi·='ni_ke·ko·hekini.|
a·kwi =ča·hi i·ni ke·ko·hen +kini
not =so that/INsg be.something +0/NEG
"Well, that[p]'s not a problem.

H oni·ča·nesihkapa=meko=ye·hapa," netekwa.
oni·ča·nesi +hkapa =meko =ye·hapa ne+ iN +ekwa
have.child +2s/POT =EMPH =it.turns.out 1+ say.{so}.to +3s-1s/IND
You could indeed have a child, as we now see," she[P] said to me.

I "na·pi=ma·hi_či·nawe·miye·kapa oni·ča·nesiyane," netekwa.
na·pi =ma·hi či·nawe·m +iye·kapa oni·ča·nesi +yane
for.the.better =you.see be.related.to +2s-3/POT have.child +2s/SUBJ

ne+ iN +ekwa
1+ say.{so}.to +3s-1s/IND
"The good thing would be, obviously, that you'd have some relatives if you had children," she[P] said to me.

194

A e·h=menahiči,
e·h= menah +iči
AOR+ to.drink.02].cause +3s-1s/AOR
She[P] gave it to me to drink,

B ke·htena=meko e·h=we·pi-onihoni·ča·nesiya·ni.
ke·htena =meko e·h= we·pi CVCV+ oni·ča·nesi +ya·ni
truly =EMPH AOR+ begin/PV RED2+ have.child +1s/AOR
and I really did begin to have children.

C ki·ši‿ma·ne·hakeči neni·ča·nesena·naki,

```
IC+ ki·ši    ma·ne·h   +akeči   ne+ -ni·ča·nes +ena·naki
xx+ PERF/PV have.many +1p-3/CC 1+   child      +1p(ANpl)
```

After we'd had a lot of children[P]*,*

D i·n=e·h=nepeki=na·hka wi·čawiwaka.

```
i·ni e·h= nep +ki     na·hka      IC+ wi·čawiw +aka
then AOR+ die +3s/AOR also,again xx+ be.with  +1s-3/PPL(ANsg)
```

my husband[P] *died, the second time that happened.*

E "nahi′, meše·=’nahi·=’ni wi·h=pwa·wi‿=na·hka=nana·ši‿-ona·pe·miya·ni," i·n=e·h=išite·he·ya·ni.

```
nahi′ meše·=’nahi i·ni wi·h= pwa·wi na·hka      nana·ši
Well! as.may.be   then FUT+  NEG/PV also,again (ever)

ona·pe·mi    +ya·ni  i·ni e·h= išite·he·  +ya·ni
have.husband +1s/AOR then AOR+ think.{so} +1s/AOR
```

"Well, now I don't need to ever get married again," I thought then.

F "ma·haki=koči·=’ni wi·h=asemihiwa·či neni·ča·nesaki," netešite·he.‖

```
ma·haki   =koči      i·ni wi·h= asemih +iwa·či    ne+ -ni·ča·nes +aki
this/ANpl =you.know then FUT+  help   +3p-1s/AOR 1+   child      +ANpl

ne+ išite·he·  +Ø
1+  think.{so} +1s/IND
```

"My children[P] *here," I thought, "are bound to help me out now."*

Textual Notes

Several kinds of notes are included in this list.

All emendations of the manuscript are given together with the reading of the original. Manuscript syllabary spellings are given between flat angle brackets (⟨...⟩) in broad phonetic transcription (omitting vowel length and /h/), rather than according to shape. The word divider is transcribed as a period, the bar (|) marks line ends, and the double bar (‖) page ends. An unreadable letter is transcribed as ⟨x⟩.

Page breaks in the middle of words or before enclitics are given here rather than in the edition.

Significant differences in the edition of Michelson (1925) are noted. Michelson's transcriptions, which are here phonemicized, generally reflect the phonetic text that was dictated to him and may not be completely invalid even when they differ from the manuscript. In some cases the correction of the phonemic transcription of words is noted; other corrections of this kind are found in Goddard (1994).

The passages omitted in Michelson (1925) for reasons of taste are noted.

Prosodic and intonational features, which the syllabary cannot write, are noted, with references to Michelson (1925) and field data.

Italicized entries refer to the translation; they give alternative wording, authority for unusual words, and other information that may be of interest.

The sources cited are these:

A = the syllabic original (NAA no. 2999), also referred to as the ms., or its writer.
AW = Adeline Wanatee (b. 1910, d. 1996), pronunciations and interpretations obtained or confirmed during a review of the text in May, 1990.
EK = information obtained from Everett Kapayou in 2001.
HL = Harry Lincoln, linguistic and ethnographic notes recorded by Truman Michelson in NAA ms. 3001.
HP = the English translation by Horace Poweshiek (NAA ms. 3009).
M = the edition and translation of Truman Michelson (Michelson 1925).
ph = the phonetic text dictated by Shapochiwa and Harry Lincoln (NAA ms. 3001).
RM = information from a respected Meskwaki obtained in 1990.
Sak = Sakihtanohkweha, from her manuscript writings.
TM = Truman Michelson.

1B) me·kwe·h=ča·hi A: M me·kwe·he=ča·hi.
1B) e·h=taswipepo·nwe·ya·ni: A seems to have ⟨mwe⟩ for /nwe·/.
1F) e·h=wi·če·nomaki AW: M e·h=wi·če·no·maki.
1G) ⟨kečiniča‖pa⟩ A.

2C) newača·ho·hka·no AW: M newača·hohka·no.
2F) ⟨eta‖swipeponweyani⟩ A.
3A) šewe·=pe·hki AW.
3B) nemayomayo·taneko A, ph, AW: M nemayomayo·tameko, with emendation in ms.
3D) ki·h=nahihto A, HP: M ki·na.
3E) ⟨pwa‖wiašitonani⟩ A.
4D) oto·šehki·ta·kanwa·wi (AW): A ⟨otošikitakanwawi⟩ seems to have ⟨ši⟩ rather than ⟨še⟩, but this is an unclear replacement of a crossed-out and erased syllable, perhaps a ⟨ki⟩; M oto·šihki·taka·nwa·wi.
4F) ⟨neničapa‖ki⟩ A.
5C) e·h=owi·kiya·kini M: for /kini/ ms. seems to have ⟨keni⟩ changed from ⟨kini⟩.
5D) neta·hpeč‿anenwi·pena M: for /nwi·/ ms. has ⟨mwi⟩ replacing an erasure.
5F) ⟨wi‖napee⟩ A.
6A) =meko·=’ni A: M =meko.
7A) ne·škimikini: M neškimikini, in preceding sentence.
7B) pwa·wi‿nenoše·ya·nini: M puts in preceding sentence.
7B) wi·h=ki·wi·‿’te·maki: ms. ⟨wikiwitemaki⟩ with second ⟨ki⟩ added; M wi·h=wi·te·mak(i).
7C) po·si‿wa·waneška·haki: M puts outside quote in preceding sentence.
7D) ⟨anemikiši‖kihiwate⟩ A.
8C) kočihto·yane A: M kočihto·yani.
8F) e·ši‿neškimikini A: M e·šineškimiki.
9B) aya·pami‿pya·no (AW, EK): M pya·no·´; EK prefers *ki·h=pya* for future reference.
9F) ⟨etaswipeponwe‖yani⟩ A.
10C) ahčike·no: M ahčike·no·´.
10G) ⟨netomo‖naakani⟩ A.
12B) tag: “head tag” (HP).
12D) koči‿wača·hono=wi·na=ki·na: M kočiwača·hono·´ wi·na ki·na.
12F) ki·šesama·nini ‘after I had cooked it’: iterative interpretation follows TM.
12F) ⟨ekotatamo‖wači⟩ A, with second ⟨ta⟩ a correction of ⟨kx⟩ in ms.
13B) wi·kese·hkwe·wa: M wi·ke·se·hkwe·wa (translated ‘cook carefully’, as if with wi·ke·t-).
13B) neteko·k=a·pehe A, ph: M neteko·p=a·pehe.
13E) ⟨ei‖šiteeyani⟩ A.
14A) me·ta·swipepo·nwe·ya·ni: M meta·swipepo·nwe·ya·n(i).
14D) ni·h=maw‿anenwi? (AW): M has statement intonation (with a superfluous question mark); this is possible here but not in 15C.
14D) e·nakini A: M e·h=inakini.
14F) ⟨opisekaa‖ni⟩ A.
14F) ‘blouses’: “waists” (HP).
15E) ⟨kokeni‖keyani⟩ A.
17A) ni·na=’yo‿nekya: M ni·n ayo·h neky(a).

17C) e·to·tawiči: M e·h=to·tawič(i).
17C) e·to·to·na·ni: M e·h=to·to·na·ni.
18D) -nahese·hkwe·hiya·ni: M -nahese·hkwe·ya·ni.
18E) e·h=nahikwa·so·hiya·ni: M e·h=nahikwa·so·ya·ni.
18G) ⟨toki‖no⟩ A; M to·hki·no·ʹ.
18G) nepi=ki·h=na·te: nepí=ki·h=na·te (AW); népi kí·h=na·te (TM).
19A) wi·h=peškone·nawačike·yakwini AW: M wi·h=peškono·ne·nawačike·yakwini; ph has [no] or [na].
19E) pye·to·ki PPL: taken as CC by TM
19E) papakye·he·hi A, ph: M papakye·hi.
19G) ⟨mani‖ke.⟩ A.
20B) ki·šahama·nini A, ph: M ki·šahama·ni.
20F) ⟨etaswipepo‖nweyani⟩ A.
21C) 'started' (AW): "fixed it up" (AW), "fastened up" (HP).
22C) o·ni=pe·hki=kapo·twe: A ⟨onipeki|kapotwe⟩.
22E) =ke·h: M =ke.
22G) ⟨nekikikime‖kopimeko⟩ A.
22G) wi·h=ašihašihto·ya·ni: M wi·h=ašihto·ya·ni.
23A) pe·po·kini·=ʼni: M pepo·kinini.
23B) i·nina·h=meko: M ni·na=meko
23G) ⟨ewe‖piasemiakinekya⟩ A.
24E) ⟨ketema‖kienanini|⟩ A.
25D) e·to·tawiči (EK): M e·h=to·tawiči, but translated as if a participle.
25E) ⟨kekoe‖i.⟩ A.
26C) me·nwi̵to·tawitehe: M menwito·tawitehe.
26D) =ča·h=ni·na: M =ča·hi ni·na.
26E) we·nah=: A ⟨.wena|⟩; M hwe·na.
26F) ⟨.oninoki|kina.⟩ A.
26G) =ke·h: M omits.
26G) e·ne·nemiyani: M e·h=ine·nemiyani.
26H) ⟨ne‖ketemakiekwa⟩ A.
26H) ketešite·he·petoke A, ph: M ketešite·ha·petoke.
27B) o=pwa·wi̵=ke·h -tepa·nena·neh (cf. 27C): M o· pwa·wike·htepa·nena·n.
27C) ine·nemena·neh AW: M ine·nemena·ne.
27D) =ča·h : M =ča·hi.
27F) ⟨wena‖menwi⟩ A: M hwe·na menwi.
28A) wa·waneška·hiyane: M wa·waneška·hiyani.
28B) ki·ši|-ašenoya·ne: M ki·šihašenoya·ni.
28G) ⟨makwači‖meko⟩ A.
29E) ki·ši̵nahihto·yane: M ki·šinahihto·yani.

29F) e·šihišihtawači A, ph: M e·šiši·htawači.

29G) ⟨wii‖šitoyani⟩ A.

30B) pe·hčihto·ya·nini: M pehčihto·ya·nini.

30E) ana·hkwa·tamaw-: only here, but phonemicization likely and gloss reasonably clear from context; M a·na·hkwa·tamaw- "put on the sticks for".

30H) ⟨ewe‖pikočiaki⟩ A.

31C) ki·ši‿nahihto·yanini A, ph: M kišinahihto·yani.

31I) ⟨kinakačiwača‖o⟩ A.

32A) sa·kiči awi- *'have a menstrual period': lit., 'stay ouside', the usual polite expression.*

33D) aškihkwe·wi- *'have first menstrual period': lit., 'become a woman for the first time', the usual expression.*

33G) ⟨mya‖netwimaini⟩ A.

34D) e·h▪po·ni‿nenehke·nemekoči: M e·hpo·ninenehke·nemekočini.

34E) wi·ke·sino´: M wi·ke·sino·´.

35A) ki·na▪'yo: A ⟨‖kina.yo.⟩.

35B) e·h▪taši‿▪meko -aškihkwe·wiwane·ni: M e·htašimekohe·škihkwe·wiwane·ni.

35H) ⟨keta‖winawakweki⟩ A.

36C) sa·kiči·- *'urinate': lit. 'go outside', the usual polite expression.*

36G) ača·hmeko▪'yo▪ke·hi·▪'ni i·n▪e·h▪išawiya·ni: M ača·hme·yoke·hi·n i·n e·šawiya·ni.

36H) ⟨ešiwe‖pawiwaneni⟩ A.

37A) e·wotamawiki: M e·hwotamawiki.

37B) i·nah▪meko·▪'ni: M i·nameko·ni.

37B) na·wi‿pi·kwa·we: last letter obscured by dirt in ms. but probably ⟨e⟩.

37F) aškači·meki·h: M aškači·meki.

37F) e·h▪aškačipwi·hiteh: A ⟨eaškačipwiite.⟩ with ⟨wi⟩ written over ⟨i⟩; M, ph e·h▪aškačipwihitehe.

38B) ni·na▪ke·hi·▪'ni‿pe·hki e·h▪kehči-: A ⟨ninakei.|nipekieekeči⟩; M i·nahke·hi·ni pehk e·hkehči-.

38D) iše A: M aše.

38G) i·n▪e·h▪išawiyani: M i·n e·šawiyani, in the following sentence.

38H) ⟨sana‖kitokapa⟩ A.

39E) e·nenwi·wane·ni: M e·hanenwi·wane·ni.

39F) ▪meko: M omits.

41C) M puts in 41B.

41H) ⟨wiinekikwišina‖ke⟩ A.

41H) nekya: M, following HP, puts with what follows.

42B) *'a different old lady': not the mother's mother, who was dead, but an unrelated old woman that the girl called 'grandmother' as a title of respect.*

42F) ⟨wiša‖peneyanini⟩ A.

43C) e·na·kwiki: M e·h▪ana·kwiki.

43E) nepi▪na·hka‿mese·hani: or nepi‿na·hka‿mese·hani (EK).
43F) ⟨ewačao‖yani⟩ A.
44F) e·ši‿pešikwiweto·ki: M e·hpešikwi·weto·ki.
44G) ⟨inoki‖mani⟩ A.
45E) e·nahina·čimohena·nini: M e·nahina·čimohena·ni.
45F) mana▪wi·na: or mana| wi·na.
45G) ⟨newe‖iyaninapee⟩ A.
46F) e·h▪iši‖-aškihkwe·wiya·ke: M e·haškihkwe·wiya·ke.
48A) e·h▪pe·pye·či-nepina·tawiči: or e·h▪pe·pye·či- nepi‿-na·tawiči.
48I) ⟨owipiči‖nawani⟩ A.
49C) neta·ya·čimohekwa: M neta·čimohekw(a).
49G) ⟨.pwawi‖čameko.⟩ A.
50F) ⟨wikeko‖enemekini⟩ A.
51D) ▪ča·h|: perhaps A ⟨▪čai|⟩.
51G) ⟨ke‖koi⟩ A.
52A) e·načini A, ph: M e·hinačini.
52A) 'whenever you ask (them) to do anything': HP "when you ask them something, or tell them something."
52D) o▪mani▪na·hka: o·´‿mani▪na·hka AW, o·´ máni ná·hka M.
52F) i·niki▪ča·h: M i·nikiča·hi.
52F) wa·waneška·haki: apparently A ⟨ške⟩ for /ška·/.
53C) na·hka▪mani (AW, EK): A ⟨.naka.mani.⟩, M ná·hka máni.
53E) maneto·wani▪koh: M manetowanikohi.
53G) ta·tašimiye·kani: ⟨tatašimi‖kani⟩ A, with ⟨ye⟩ added at the end of p. 53 by a second hand.
54G) še·še·hkosiyane▪ke·h: M še·še·hkosiyananeke·hi
54H) ke·ko·h: M ke·ko·hi.
54I) 'aloof and unfriendly toward': HP "wild and unfriendly with."
55F) nahi·▪'ni▪yá·pi: nahí·▪'ni▪ya·péi! (AW).
55G) ⟨si‖poki⟩ A.
56A) ketenano·▪'nahi: AW ketenáno·▪'nahéi!
56C) o·ni: M puts outside quote.
56F) ota·siya·nenano AW: A ⟨otasiyanenono⟩, M ota·siya·ne·nono.
56G) nepwa·meki A: M, ph nepwa·miki.
56H) ⟨mya‖noteyani⟩ A.
57D) i·nini·▪'ni: M i·nin(i).
57F) taši: M puts in following sentence.
57F) 'had to' HP.
57G) me·ta·sokonakahki: M meta·sokonakahki.
57G) na·hka·▪'ni: the ⟨ka⟩ looks more like ⟨ke⟩.
57G) e·h▪mawi-anenwi·ya·ni: ⟨ena‖wianenwiyani⟩ A, with ⟨na⟩ changed to ⟨ma⟩ by a second hand.

57G) 'had to' HP.

58C) neta·hpeči-a·ya·čimohekwa: M neta·hpečiha·čimohekwa.

58G) ⟨pesetawa‖kiče⟩ A.

59D) pe·škiti·han=: M pe·škiti·he·n-; /a/ changed to /e·/ in ph. by TM citing HL, presumably from a confusion with the non-diminutive plural *pe·škitye·ni.*

59F) nya· M: A ⟨mya⟩.

59F) e·h=taswipepo·nwe·ya·ni: ⟨etaswipepo‖weyani⟩ A.

60A) se·nipa·h=ke·hi A, ph.; se·nipa·hi=ke·hi AW; M senipa·hihke·hi, from HL (note in ph.).

60B) ki·h=ašihašihto: M ki·h=ašihašihta·tiso, from the emendation by a second hand in the ms.

60B) nahikwa·soyane: M nahikwa·soyani, with /ne/ changed to /ni/ in ph.

60B) 'sew [those]': cf. HP "If you learn how"; M 'sew' (also in 60C, 60F, 61B); the author already knew how to sew, and the verbs for 'sewing' in these lines refer to the fancy techniques mentioned in 60A; perhaps these verbs should be taken as having pronominal objects.

60C) ki·ši̯-=ke·h -nahikwa·soyane: M ki·šike·hnahikwa·soyani.

60F) ⟨nahikwasoya‖ne⟩ A.

61D) ni·šwawahi·me: in ms. ⟨šwa⟩ is an incomplete ⟨šw⟩ with ⟨a⟩ added by a second hand.

61E) e·h=ašihto·ya·ni: M ⟨yä⟩ is a misprint.

61G) ⟨anakana‖ni⟩ A.

62A) pe·po·kini: M pepo·kini.

62F) ke·ko·h: M ke·ko·hi.

62G) i·na·ma·hani: A ⟨.ina‖maani.⟩, with ⟨na⟩ changed from ⟨ni⟩ by the writer; M i·ni ma·hani.

62G) '[that] you were doing': a guess at the meaning here of the rare and obsolete demonstrative i·na·ma·hani.

63D) ke·ko·h: M ke·ko·hi; ms. has ⟨i⟩ added by a second hand.

63F) ⟨emeseneta‖meki⟩ A.

64: Starting with p. 64 the page-numbering is Michelson's, indicated at the top left of the ms. pages (later, the top right); the original pagination has several errors.

64D) =ča·h: M =ča·hi.

64E) to·hki·no´: M to·hki·no·´.

65C) nenenekapiso: M nenekapis(o); A ⟨nenekapiso⟩ with a third ⟨ne⟩ added by a second hand between the other two.

65F) nekaški̯-kano·na·wa: ⟨ški⟩ changed from ⟨ši⟩ by a second hand in ms.

66B) HP and M take the second aorist as in series rather than as a complement of the first.

66E) ⟨wika‖kanonetiata⟩ A.

67A) we·pi̯-kakano·neti·yane: M we·pikano·neti·yane.

67B) meše=meko·=’nah: M mešemeko·na.

67E) we·na·pe·miwa·čini *'their husbands' (HP): 'when they get married' (AW).*

68D) nekoti·=’ni: M nekot(i).

68E) =ke·h: M omits.

68F) ⟨keteči‖mene⟩ A.

69C) *'that they were well acquainted': similarly HP, AW, EK.*
69E) ▪a·peh: M a·pehe.
69F) ⟨ko‖takanini⟩ A.
71EF) HP puts these together: "Then I began to wish to see him every time I go somewheres, after I had seen him."
71E) i·ni▪meko▪ni·na: ⟨.ini|mekonina.⟩ A.
71F) e·ya·ya·nini: second ⟨ya⟩ changed from ⟨na⟩ by a second hand.
71F) ⟨ekišine‖waki⟩ A.
72D) oškinawe·h: M oškinawe·ha.
72F) ⟨natawači‖meko⟩ A.
73CD) ke·htena·▪'nah▪mani: / i·ni▪meko (cf. 79A): M, ph kehtena·na man(i).
73E) ⟨▪yo‖we⟩ A.
74E) ⟨ine‖šawiniči⟩ A.
75C) owi·wani·▪'na neniwa: M owi·wani. i·na neniwa.
75E) e·ne·nemaki A, ph: M e·h▪ine·nemaki.
75F) ⟨a‖petosewa⟩ A.
77E) ⟨ešiyani‖ni⟩ A.
78D) ne·hihto·ya·ni| ke·ko·hi e·h▪ki·ši̮nahihto·yani: M nahihto·yani.
78D) pe·hki: after this A has ⟨me⟩ crossed out.
79A) ke·htena·▪'nah▪mani: M kehtena·namani (cf. 73C).
79B) we·pi̮ka·ki·wi·̮'te·mači A, AW: we·pi̮ka·ki·wite·mači ph (cf. 51D); M we·pika·ki·wiwi·te·mač(i).
80A) e·ka·wa·na·wa·čih: M e·h▪aka·wa·na·wa·či.
80C) oči̮taši·hkawa·wa·čini: M očitaši·hkawa·wa·či.
80E) ⟨etaswi‖peponweyani⟩ A.
81D) ta·ni·▪'nah: M ta·ninah.
81E) -kakano·neti·hakini: M -kakano·neti·akini (misprint).
81F) ⟨netotetenema‖wameko⟩ A.
82D) *'to his family's house':* owi·kewa·ki *'to their house'.*
82E) ahpene·či▪meko·▪'n▪e·h▪taši·hkawiči: A ⟨apenečimeko.netašikawiči⟩ with ⟨wiči⟩ changed to ⟨kwa⟩ by a second hand; M ahpene·čimeko netaši·hka·kwa, following change in ms.
82E) ⟨wiwi‖temaki⟩ A.
82E) e·taswi̮ne·wakini: M e·htaswine·wakini.
84B) kekehke·neta▪ké·hi: AW kekehké·neta▪ké·h, M kekehké·netake·hi.
84G) e·šimiyanini A, ph: M e·šimiyani.
85D) mani·▪'noki e·nena·ni: M mani·nok e·hinena·ni; HP translates ("of what I said to you") as if in 85C.
85F) pe·hkote·ki·▪'ni: M pehkote·kini.
85G) ⟨eowiki‖yake⟩ A.
86A-D) Omitted from Michelson (1925:312).

86H-89H) Omitted from Michelson (1925:312-314).

86I) e·škačitepehki·niki: ph aškači tepehkiniki.

87C) i·ni=meko=na·hka: A ⟨inimeko|naka⟩.

87D) e·škačitepehki·niki: ph aškači tepehkiniki.

87F) i·ni=ma·h: ph i·ni=ma·hi.

87I) ⟨kina‖nayomani⟩ A; ph ki·na·nayohmani.

88B) ki·h=kehke·neta·pena: ph ki·hkehke·neti·pena.

88G) ⟨wisa‖kamatapi⟩ A.

89A) pe·hki: ph puts at beginning of following sentence.

89H) ⟨kenwe‖šimeko⟩ A.

90E) kapo·twe=na·hka: ⟨kapotwe|naka⟩ A.

90G) ⟨ena‖kwayani⟩ A.

91G) o·ni=na·hka (EK): A ⟨|oni.naka.⟩; M puts na·hka in following quote.

91H) i·nah=ahte·wi: M i·na hahte·wi.

91I) saketone·pičikani·=’nah=ahte·wi: M saketone·pi·čikan i·na ahte·wi.

92G) i·na=’h=we·na=kotaka[!?] (EK): A ⟨inawena.kotaka.⟩.

92H) awata·ke·ko A, ph, HP (“you (both)”): M awata·ke·no, following HL.

93E) nekoti‿=meko‿-maškimote·h=a·pehe ahkwa·wi: M nekoti=meko‿maškimote·h a·peh ahkwa·wi. The edition takes the divider before A ⟨.apee.⟩ as an error, since although non-enclitic *a·pehe* occurs elsewhere, it is not otherwise found in this text. A ⟨maškimote.⟩ is taken as *-maškimote·h=* (for *-maškimote·he* ECM), which presumably can be in construction with *ahkwa·wi* (which is otherwise postposed to a locative noun). If the preceding divider in A ⟨.apee.⟩ is taken as correctly written, the text can be read as *maškimote·h a·pehe*, with the elision of the final vowel after the first /h/, as often with this writer. It is also possible that the writer used †*maškimote* ECM, but this is not otherwise attested.

94C) ayi·ši A, EK, M, Sak: aye·ši AW, Sak, others.

94D) ⟨netaka‖wapamekwameko⟩ A.

95E) i·ni=ča·hi·=’na=kotaka: A ⟨iničaina|kotaka⟩.

95E) a·hpeči A: M ahpene·či.

95G) ⟨eakawapami‖či⟩ A.

95G) kotakah=na·hka A: HP “others”; AW, EK kotakahi=na·hka (or kotakani=na·hka); M kotakana·hka; similarly 144D, 167F, 185C.

96B) e·ya·yanini A, ph: M e·ya·yani.

97A-F) Omitted from Michelson (1925:314).

98H) akote·ki (AW): M ako·te·k (as if with *ako·te·-* ‘hang’.

98H) apeno·haki: M apenohak; A ⟨apenokaki⟩.

99E) wi·čawiwočiki A: M wi·čawi·wačiki.

100A) me·šehkawoči M, ph: A ⟨mešekawači⟩ with ⟨wa⟩ changed to ⟨wo⟩ in light pencil.

100B) ...i·=’n=e·h=iš‿ačihkwiki A: M i·n e·šačihkwiki, following HL’s suggested change of ph. A first wrote ⟨...či|neišawiki⟩ (*i·n=e·h=išawiki* 'when one is like that'), then changed ⟨wiki⟩ to ⟨čikwi⟩ and kept writing with ⟨ki⟩, giving ⟨...či|neišačikwiki|⟩; this is the form in ph. It is possible that simply ⟨eačikwiki⟩ was intended, but for an identical use of *i·ni iši* compare 46F.

100D) i·nah: A ⟨ina|⟩; M i·n.

100G) ⟨ešiti||kinimekoni⟩ A.

101E) e·h=sakakwa·piki A, ph; M e·sasakwa·pik(i).

101F) 'are wall-eyed' (lit. 'have twisted eye(s)'): M 'will be cross-eyed', following HP, but this is wa·wa·ta·naki·kwe·wa.

101G) A ⟨kaoni||naka⟩.

101G) ki·šekwi‿wa·pata·haki *'least bitterns', lit. 'sky-watchers'; for the species identification, cf. Ottawa* waabnigiishwezhiins *'least bittern' (Rhodes 1985:349), Menominee* wa·peki·su^ʔnyah *'shagpoke, green heron' (Bloomfield 1975:265), which both appear to mean 'the one that looks at the sun' and probably both refer to the same species: M, HP 'cranes'.*

102B) ahkiki (HP "down"): M, ph ahki·ki.

102C) owiye·he·ha *'animal': HP 'any thing'; M 'any one'.*

102E) ne·škiti·ki ph: M neškiti·ki.

102F) ⟨wiowiwa||šikimeko⟩ A.

103E) pa·ši AW: M paši.

103F) ⟨ešike||ki⟩ A.

104E) wi·h=išahišawiyakwe A: M wi·h=išawiyakwe.

104G) o=ča·ki‿=ke·h: M o· ča·ki‿=ke·hi.

104H) ⟨eča||ki.kekyawakweni⟩ A.

105E) e·h=pwa·wi‿ki·ši|-kehke·netamani (ph): ⟨epwawikiši|kekenetama||ni⟩ A; M e·h=pwa·wi‿ki·ši‿kehke·netama·n, following HP 'I do not know'; M in ph changes *-an* (2s) to *-a·n* (1s), with the note: "if translation correct"; cf. 106A, 106B.

106A) ⟨akwi| močimeko⟩ A.

106A) wi·h=kaški-kehke·netamanini ph: M wi·h=kaški-kehke·netama·nini, following HP 'I' (see note to 105E).

106B) ki·ši‿no·še·yane ph: M ki·ši‿no·še·ya·ne, following HP 'I' (see note to 105E).

106B) wi·h=kehke·netamani ph: M wi·h=kehke·netama·ni, following HP 'I' (see note to 105E).

106E) i·tepi iha·ya·nini: A ⟨itepi|iayanini⟩; M i·tepi ha·ya·nini.

107D) M has period after *wi·h=tano·še·či*, comma after *we·či‿wa·wotami‿pya·ya·ni.*

107E) 'I thought': HP "thinking".

107G) ki·šike·wa·či·=ʼni ph: M ki·šike·wa·čini.

107H) na·pi·we·=: M na·pi=we·na; A ⟨napiwe⟩ with a following ⟨na⟩ added in light pencil; AW accepted both ways as equivalent.

107H) ⟨akwa||matamokweni⟩ A.

108A) neši·kani (cf. 108F): M nešíhka·n (and implied by HP), accepted as nešihka·=ʼni 'and here

I was alone' (AW, EK); but she was not alone.

108C) a·kwi=ke·h: M a·kw(i).

108D) a·hkwamatakani=wi·na=ne·hi (em. TM, acc. AW, EK): A ⟨akwamataniwinanei⟩, with ⟨ka⟩ added after ⟨ta⟩ by TM; M a·hkwamatakani wi·nane·hi?; a pragmatic question but not with interrogative intonation (AW, EK).

108F) ⟨.netenawa| nekya.⟩ A.

108I) ⟨ni||natomawa⟩ A.

109G) ki·h=ata·hpenama·hkwi AW: M ki·h=ata·hpenama·kwi; same in 110F.

109H) ⟨netanemia||piapitamata⟩ A.

110A) ke·keya·hi·=’ni, "šekišineno (A): M ke·keya·h, "i·ni šekišino; ph šekišino.

110E) i·ni·=’ni: M i·nin(i).

110F) e·h=ata·hpenama·hkwi·ya·n: M e·hata·hpenama·kwiya·n (cf. 109G).

110G) a·kwi=me·h: together and followed by a pause (AW, EK, TM).

110I) ⟨eta||šinanaikawičiki⟩ A.

111G) nawači: *-i* voiced before pause (AW).

112B) ki·ši̯-či·tapihiki·=’ni: M ki·šiči·tapihikini.

112B) newi·šemeki: avoidance of the regularly formed locative *ni·šeki* ([ni·hšékį]), which is homophonous with *ni·h=šeki* 'I will urinate'.

112D) ki·ši̯-menahiči·=’ni: M ki·šimenahičini.

112E) e·h=pemi-nowina·ke·či: M e·hpeminowi·na·ke·či.

112G) pe·mehka·čini AW: M pemeka·čini; AW commented that the woman would not dance (same in 113A).

112I) ⟨naka||pe⟩ A.

113A) pe·mehka·čini AW: M pemeka·čini (cf. 112G).

113B) e·škwe·se·hiwane·ni A: M e·hiškwe·se·hi·wane·ni.

113H) tepina·hi=’ši še·ški: EK tepina·hi=’ší=še·ški.

114A) kwi·yese·he·ha A: M kwi·yese·ha.

114C) paši: M pa·ši.

114E) apeno·he·ha·=’ni: M apeno·he·hani.

114F) nekoti·čiše (RM), perhaps to be written nekoti·-̯’čiše: nekotičiše A, M, nekoti-i·čise (EK).

114F) ⟨akošama||wapi⟩ A.

115A) e·škikeniki M: A ⟨ešikeniki⟩, with ⟨ši⟩ changed to ⟨ški⟩ by a second hand.

115E) owi·ya·se·hi *'small piece of meat' (M, following HP): AW, while accepting this as a possible gloss, thought that what was referred to here was a small piece of the baby's own flesh (from the umbilical cord) that was twisted around the stub of the cord.*

115F) apa·hkwisetawa·pi AW, EK: M ahpa·hkwisetawa·pi.

115G) ⟨kišikašikawisetawa||wa⟩ A.

116B) i·n=e·h=to·tawaki (M): or i·n=e·to·tawaki, with an oblique participle (cf. 17C, 19C, 25D).

116E) ne·sokonakesiči: M nesokonakesič(i).

116F) e·yi·ki A, ph: M ayi·ki, misprint.

116H) ⟨kiapečime‖ko⟩ A.

117B) e·h=inapineči: M starts a new sentence with this word, following HP.

117D) nekotawahi·ne A: M nekotawahi·me.

117G) ⟨wipwawiotami‖iwewači⟩ A.

118A) ne·nesapi·hiwaki A: M ne·nesapiwaki.

118G) Omitted from Michelson (1925:320).

118G) ⟨inime‖ko⟩ A; ⟨ko⟩ begins the text on loose pages of a second notebook.

119A) o·ni=kapo·twe (A, EK): M o·ni kapo·twe.

119B) pye·či-iši‿menwawitehe A: M pye·čišimenwawitehe.

119D) ketaši‿menwi‿to·tawa·wa: ⟨ketašimenwi‖totawawa⟩ A (also ph); M ketašimenwito·tawa.

120C) wi·h=po·ni·hka·ti·yakwini: ⟨ya⟩ changed to ⟨ye⟩ by second hand (=ph), then changed back to ⟨ya⟩ by TM following HL in ph.

121A) e·h=kekye·škatawe·nemiči A: M e·h=kekye·škatawe·nemeči.

121A) we·či-inahina·čimoha·či: M omits (misprint).

121B) e·h=wa·waneška·hiči 'because of her wanton behavior': "because she was bad" (HP).

121D) meše=meko·=’nah: M mešemeko·na.

122E) nekwi·yese·hemena·na A: M nekwisehemena·n(a).

123F) e·h=taši‿se·se·kihe·kwe=’yo·we: A ⟨etašiseseki.ekweyowe⟩.

123G) ⟨oniča‖nesinawaki⟩ A.

124A) iši‿ki·ša·kočite·he·ne·ha: A ⟨išikišakoči.teenea⟩.

124B) e·h=mya·šite·he·ya·ni A: M nemya·šite·he·ya·ni.

124C) e·na·kwiki·=’ni A: M e·h=ana·kwikin(i).

124F) ⟨nečakime‖ko⟩ A.

125D) e·h=anemi‿’ši‿mya·šawiči A: M e·h=anemimya·šawiči.

125F) ⟨neneški‖mekwa⟩ A.

126D) e·nahina·čimohitehe A: M e·h=inahina·čimohitehe.

126G) ⟨aše‖nokini⟩ A.

127B) we·nahi=ke·htena A, AW: EK we·nah=ke·htena.

127C) a·mi‿’šawiwa·ne·ni·=’nah=mani A: M a·mišawiwa·ne·ni ni·na mani, ph a·mišawiwa·ne·ni·na mani.

127D) ⟨pwawikišikekyekimi‖tee⟩ A.

128E) me·no·hkami·kini: M meno·hkami·kin(i).

128G) pe·po·kini=ke·h‖: M pepo·kinike·h.

129D) ⟨ke‖temakiiči⟩ A.

130A) ni·na A, ph: M omits.

130C) kotaka=’yo=ke·h=ni·na A: M kotakayo·weke·h ni·na.

130D) neneškinawa·wa: in A ⟨ški⟩ is changed from ⟨š⟩, perhaps by the first hand.

131C) 'of the quiet type': AW 'who are better'.

131G) neta·šimeko·pi=ki·yawi (EK): ⟨netašimekopi‖kiyawi⟩.

131G) ki·yawi: M puts in following sentence.

132B) wi·h= A: M omits.

132E) menwawihkapa‿koči (M, EK).

132F) 'peacefully': 'dependably' (EK); see 132I.

132GH) HP and M take as one sentence.

132I) 'peacefully' (EK); see 132F.

133DEF) Follows AW; M takes these together.

133F) ni·h= A, ph, AW; M wi·h.

133J) ki·h=we·we·ne·neta A: M ki·h=we·we·neta.

134C) ayi·kwa·mi‿taši‿me·menwa·čimoyane A, ph: M ayi·kwa·mi·tašimenwa·čimoyan(e).

134E) a·kwi=meko A: M a·kwikoh.

134J) ⟨wi‖ayanini⟩ A; M wi·ha·yani.

135D) e·h=nepa·ya·ni A: M, ph e·h=nepa·ya·nini.

135E) wa·paki·=’ni: M wa·pakini.

135F) nama·nike A, ph, AW: M nema·nike, following HL.

136F) ⟨mikečewiyani‖ni⟩ A.

137A) we·pi A: M, ph omit.

137G) ⟨ta‖šitepeneminea⟩ A.

138A) me·mešihka=’yo=meko: M me·mešihk ayo·hmeko; ph me·mešihkayo·meko.

138D) kete·=’nahi: M kehtenahi "Surely," in 138E, but there is no such word.

139C) e·nahina·čimohenokwe·ni A, ph: M e·h=inahina·čimohenokwe·ni.

139D) wa·wosa·hi=’=ča·hi A (with elided |=i| NEG): M wa·wosahiča·hi; AW wa·wasa·hi=ča·hi.

139E) ⟨neni‖waki⟩ A.

140A) mana; mana=we·=me·kwe·he A (⟨mana.ma|nawemekwee⟩): M mana me·kwe·h, with a note in ms. to delete one ⟨mana⟩, following HL; ph ma·nahwe·h deleted following HL.

140A) a·mi|-menwi-to·tawita: A ⟨.ami|menwi totawita.⟩, with extra space in ⟨i t⟩.

140A) e·ne·nema·wate·na A: M e·h=ine·nema·wate·na.

140D) ⟨katanaka|kotaka.⟩ A.

140E) ⟨eikwewiye‖kwe⟩ A.

141A) i·n=e·h=išawiči A: M i·n e·šawiči.

141BC) neniwah.‿ / "i·ni: A ⟨neniwaini⟩, with syllable ⟨i⟩ erased and replaced by ⟨.i⟩; néniwah AW (not neniwahi); M [neni·WAʻ].

141C) e·ne·nemena·ni A: M e·h=ine·nemena·ni.

141D) ⟨.ekišiašenoči|kekya.⟩ A.

141D) e·ši‿kehke·netamo·hiya·ni A: M e·hkehke·netamo·hiya·ni.

141F) kana·h A: M kanahi.

142C) koči·h A (⟨koči|⟩): M koč.

142D) we·te·we A, ph: M we·te·wi, following HL.

142F) ⟨e‖nepeniči⟩ A.

143E) na·hka A: M omits.

143G) ⟨we‖čipešekwaiwaneni⟩ A.

144A) we·či‿pešekwa·hiya·ni A, ph: M omits.

144B) pe·hki=ní·hka (AW, with voiceless [-ḁ]): M pehki ni·hka! (with voiced [-A]) "Well!"; EK pe·hkí=ni·hka ("emphasis").

144C) ona·pe·miwane A, M: ph ona·pe·miwane·ni; TM changed the ms. to follow ph, then erased the change following HL's acceptance of A.

144D) ne·wona·neh= A: AW, EK ne·wona·nehe=, M ne·wona·ne=.

144D) ke·ko·h A: M ke·ko·hi.

145C) wi·h=anwa·či·yani A: M wi·hanwa·čiyane.

145E) ⟨wičawi‖waka⟩ A.

146C) ni·mihete·nikini A: M ni·miheti·nikini.

146D) ⟨iničameko|kina⟩ A.

146G) a·kwi=ke·hi·='nah me·h A: M a·kwike·h i·name·h.

147C) i·nah‿taši‿mi·hketi·te A: M i·n e·htašimi·hketi·te.

147G) ⟨apene‖či⟩ A.

147G) netešite·h A: M netešite·he.

147G) 'I have always wished I could be with you': "live with" (HP); lit., I always think, 'I wish I was (living) with her.'

148D) a·kwi=meko: A first wrote ⟨kwakwi⟩, then this was changed to ⟨kwayakwi⟩ by adding ⟨ya⟩, then this was changed to ⟨akwi⟩ by erasing ⟨kwaya⟩ and writing ⟨a⟩ over the erasure.

148F) paši‿we·te·wi A: M pašiwe·te·we; ms. has A ⟨wi⟩ written over by ⟨we⟩ in a second hand; ph has *wi* changed to *we*; cf. 142D.

149A) =koči A, ph: M omits.

149A) e·h=mya·ši‿to·tawiči A: M e·hmya:šito·tawičini.

149E) na·hina·hi='yo·we‿ke·hkahamawiyani A: M nahinahi yo·we kehkahamawi·yani.

149F) ⟨pe‖koteke⟩ A; M pehkote·ki.

150B) i·ni·='ni e·h=išawiya·ni A: M i·nin e·šawiya·ni.

150D-151E) Omitted from Michelson (1925:326.26).

150D-153B) ph from HL.

150E) ke·ko·h‿e·h=išawiya·ke A: ph ke·ko· e·šawiya·ke.

150F) ke·ko·h‿e·h=išawiya·ke A: ph ke·ko· e·šawiya·ke.

150G) ⟨inine‖tešawipena⟩ A; ph netešawipena.

151G) ⟨ea‖winiči⟩ A.

152A) či·nawe·makiki A: M omits.

152E-153B) Omitted from Michelson (1925:326.31).

152F) o·n‿e·h=a·hkwe·či A: ph o·ni e·ha·hkwe·či.

152G) ⟨tašika‖wiči⟩ A.

153B) nahi A: ph omits.

153D) ki·ši·‿'čawiwaki A: M ki·šiwi·čawiwaki, following the emendation in ms. from HL (adding ⟨wi⟩).

153E) mawi‿ni·mino´: M mawini·mino´.

153E) me·me·nešimihki·ke: M me·me·nešimikike·h.
153F) ⟨i‖šikike.⟩ A; M išikike·h.
154B) mi·ša·tesino´: M mi·ša·tesino´.
154B) netekwa=na·hk=a·pehe A: M netekwa·pehe.
154C) e·h=taši-ka·kakano·neti·ya·ke A (the third ⟨ka⟩ looks like ⟨k⟩ + ⟨w⟩): M e·htašikakano·neti·ya·ke.
154D) 'he asked me': translates netekwa *(154E).*
154E) menehta=ke·h=wi·na=’yo·we A: M menehtake·hwi·nayo·.
154G) ⟨wewenenetí‖soyanini⟩ A.
155C) kotaka·=’ni‿‘... (AW, EK): M kotakani (inside quote); AW did not accept kotakani as the object of the following verb.
155D) keye·hapa: M puts in following sentence.
155E) we·we·ne·netisoya·neh: M we·we·ne·netísoya·n.
156D) 'he then said to me': translates i·n=e·h=išiči *(156E).*
156E) i·n=e·h=išiči A: M i·n e·šiči.
156G) ⟨ne‖pyečiwičawiwawa⟩ A.
157B) iškwe·se·he·ha A: M iškwe·se·ha.
157D) na·tawino·ni A, ph: M na·tawimo·ni, misprint.
158B) mo·hči=meko A: M mo·hčimeki, misprint.
158C) na·ni·mino´: M na·ni·mino´.
158E) aniwe·wi A, ph: M e·niwe·wi.
158E) netešite·h A: M netešite·he, following second hand in ms.
158F) nekotah: M nekota´ (misprint).
158F) ⟨eyači‖ni⟩ A.
159D) ki·šihtawaki·=’ni: M ki·šihtawakini.
159F) ⟨ne‖ki⟩ A.
160B) we·či-ašihto·na·ni: M makes this a separate sentence.
160C) 'he asked me': translates netekwa *(161C).*
160I) ⟨wawaneška‖itewina⟩ A.
161D) =meko·=’ni=pe·hki (EK): ⟨mekoni‖peki⟩ A.
161E) nahi‿ši·še·wa M: A ⟨na‖išewa⟩, with ⟨i⟩ added after A ⟨na⟩ in a light pencil, and ⟨š⟩ added before A ⟨i⟩ in heavy thin pencil, perhaps by TM; ph nahišiše·wa.
161F) owiye·he·hahi‿ši·ša·čini A: M owi·ye·h e·hši·ša·čini; in ms. an additional ⟨ša⟩ is written over A ⟨ai⟩ by a second hand; ph -ye·he·ha (the *-a* is voiced), with note by TM: "error of dictation: see syllabary," referring to the changed text.
161G) ⟨naiakawa‖tamakini⟩ A.
162A) -onahona·pe·miya·ni A, ph: M ona·pe·miya·ni.
162E) 'We just went around doing anything we wanted.' (accepted by AW); "we tried everything" (EK); "We were just going to them." (HP).
163D) neka·htwe·nema·wa M: A ⟨nekatwenemamawa⟩.

163F) kapo·twe·='ni M: A has an extra ⟨pw⟩ after ⟨ka⟩.

163G) nemayo: M nemayo·; A ⟨nema.yo⟩.

164A) e·h=nepeki=kapo·twe (EK): ⟨enepeki|kapotwe⟩ A.

164A) kapo·twe: M puts in 164B.

164H) M puts in 164G as the object, following HP.

165) The text on loose pages from a third notebook begins with *neniwaki* (164H).

165A) či·nawe·ma·čiki: A ⟨|či.nawemačiki.⟩.

165D) e·h=pye·to·wa·či M: because of damage all that can be confirmed in the ms. is ⟨epye|[....]či.wise‖⟩.

165D) ⟨.wise‖niweni.⟩ A.

166A) ča·ki‿=meko‿-ke·ko·he·hi: M puts at the end of the preceding sentence.

166A) ihkwe·wanohkya·ni‿takwi‿pye·to·waki: M ihkwe·wa·no·hkya·nitakwi pye·to·waki; ms. has an emendation by a second hand ⟨ikwewa<ki>nokya<a>nitakwi⟩, which HP follows in translating: "women folks also brought some ground up corn soup," as if this could be *no·hkaha·ni*, a rare word that actually means 'pemmican'.

166A) 'all the various things women use for their cooking': lit. 'every little thing (of, for) woman's work', implying both equipment and staples.

166B) i·niye·ka A, ph: M i·nye·ka (misprint).

166B) e·h=mawi-a·čimohaki: A ⟨emawi.ači.moaki⟩.

166C) neki·ša·koči-ketema·kite·h A: M e·hki·ša·kočiketema·kite·he.

166F) ⟨emawitašimayoya‖ni⟩ A.

167B) 'na=nešiwi=wi·na·='na: M na·nešiwi·wí·na·n, construed as an exclamatory particle.

167F) ⟨enotaketeyeto‖ke⟩ A (contrast 120E); M e·hno·ta·ke·teye·toke; AW, EK e·h=no·ta·ke·tehe=ye·toke.

168F) ⟨akwamatakani⟩ A, a·hkwamatakáni EK: a·hkomatákani? AW, "are you sick?" (HP); M a·hkwamatakini (with previous sentence).

168J) ⟨.e‖pepesetawiyani.⟩ A: syllable ⟨e⟩ has been erased in ms.; M pepesetawiyan i·ni.

169F) koškoškwa·tota·pi: M puts in preceding sentence.

169FG) i·ni ... ina·hpawa·yane: M takes as one sentence.

169H) ⟨mama‖yameko⟩ A.

170E) nahi-apahapane·nihkani M (following HL), AW: A, ph nahi-apahapane·nihkapa.

170G) ⟨kiašia‖šito⟩ A.

172A) i·ya·h‿pye·nečini (new sentence follows HP): M puts with what precedes.

172A) wa·nakoki: M, HP put with what follows.

172D) ki·ši-kakano·nečini·='ni A: M ki·šikakano·nečini.

172D) -senama- A, ph: M -senana- (misprint).

172E) meše·='nahi: M puts at beginning of following sentence.

172G) ⟨wičawi‖wačiki⟩ A.

173F) nepowa·sa A: M nepo·hiwa·sa.

173G) ⟨emawio‖čikokiwači⟩ A.

174F) a·kwi=koči·=ʼni| nahi- A: M a·kwi koči ni·na nahi-, following emendation of ms. by second hand.

174G) ⟨weči.pwawi|kekenetama‖ni⟩ A.

174G) e·še·wi·weniwikwe·ni A: M e·še·wiwenikwe·ni.

175C) 'Then he said to me': translates i·n=e·h=išiči *(175D).*

176E) 'Then he said to me': translates i·n=e·h=išiči *(176F).*

176E) nahí·=ʼni (AW).

178B) ni·na=ke·h A: M i·nahke·h.

178E) wi·čawiwaka išiwe·pi A: M wi·čawiwakišiwe·p(i).

178H) ⟨ewe‖pinanaeškaiki⟩ A; also ph, HL (TM note): M e·h=we·pinanaheškawiki (perhaps wrongly changed when the intention was to correct the form that ph has in 179A).

179A) e·h=penaha·hkwawiki A: M, ph e·hpenaha·hkwa·hiki.

179G) ⟨wi·čawi‖wate⟩ A.

179G) Follows AW, EK: M 'Some one will take care of you if you marry him.' (following HP).

180C) we·kone·h=ča·hi·=ʼnahi A: M we·kone·ča·hi·ninahi.

180E) e·nena·ke A: M e·hinena·ke.

181A) e·h=we·pi‿ke·kesi·kwa·ya·ni A (with first ⟨ke⟩ changed to ⟨wi⟩ by a second hand): M e·hwe·piwi·ke·siya·ni, following the change in the ms. and HP.

181G) išite·he·noˊ: M išite·he·noˊ ([uˊ]).

181H) ka·ta=ča·hi‿nahmeko=meko A: M (following HL) ka·tača·h i·nameko.

182B) e·to·to·hki: M e·hto·to·hki.

182D) ⟨wičawiwa‖ta⟩ A.

183B) wi·h= A: M omits.

183F) ⟨meči‖wena⟩ A.

185A) 'women' (HP): the only ones who would take advice from their mothers.

185A) ne·peničini: M nepeničini.

185C) kotakah=ke·h A, M: AW, EK kotakahi=ke·h.

185E) nahí·=ʼni, nešemi (cf. 176E): AW nahi·=ʼní, nešémi, M nahi·ni, nešemi.

186A) i·n=e·h=išawiya·ni A: M i·n e·šawiya·ni.

186E) ⟨katwenema‖ki⟩ A.

187D) asa·mi=meko: M starts the direct quotation and a new sentence with *we·či* (187E).

187D) 'I kept thinking': translates netešite·h=a·pehe *(187E).*

187F) ⟨ewepikešači‖aki⟩ A.

188B) wi·h=keša·čihena·ni: A ⟨wikešači.enani⟩.

188D) neka·kakano·neti·pena A: M nekakano·neti·pena.

188E) i·nina·h=ča·h=a·pehe A: M i·n i·nača·ha·pehe.

188E) 'he used to say to me': the translation includes netekwa=ʼyo·we *(189F).*

189E) M puts at beginning of following sentence.

189F) ⟨nai‖nawinepeyakwini⟩ A, ph; M omits (misprint).

189F) netekwa=ʼyo·we A, ph: M netekwiyo·we (misprint).

190A) ne·h▪ki·na A: M pehkima·h (following overwriting in ms. by second hand).
190B) netepa·na·wa▪'yo A: M netepa·na·wayo·w(e).
190D) wa·wosa·hi▪'h▪we·▪ke·hi: M wa·wosahiwe·ke·hi, AW wa·wosa·hi=we·▪ke·h.
191A) e·h▪anwa·či·ya·ni A: M omits e·h▪ (misprint).
191B-191D) Omitted from Michelson (1925:334.38).
191B) pe·hkote·ki·▪'ni: ph pehkote·kini.
191E) o▪ke·htena▪wi·na▪meko: M o·´ kéhtena wi·námeko.
192B) o·ni▪natawa·či▪na·hka (EK): A ⟨oni|natawači.naka⟩.
192C) ki·wi-anohka·šiye·ka·ha A: M ki·hano·hka·ši·ye·ka·ha.
192F) ahte·toke ... menoke? a·mi‿kaški-oni·ča·nesiki? (AW, EK); EK gave as an alternative *ahte·toke?* and no interrogative intonation on *menoke* but rejected three interrogative intonations.
192F) ⟨ateto||ke⟩ A.
193B) netekwa A: M netetekwa (misprint).
193D) ▪'yo A: M omits.
193I) ⟨či||nawemiyekapa⟩ A.
194E) i·n▪e·h=išite·he·ya·ni A: M i·ne·šite·he·ya·ni.

References

Bloomfield, Leonard. 1975. *Menomini Lexicon*, ed. by Charles F. Hockett. Milwaukee Public Museum Publications in Anthropology & History 3.

Michelson, Truman. 1925. The autobiography of a Fox Indian woman. *Annual Report of the Bureau of American Ethnology*, vol. 40, pp. 291-349. Washington.

Rhodes, Richard A. 1985. *Eastern Ojibwa-Chippewa-Ottawa dictionary*. Berlin: Mouton.

Appendix

Analysis of Inflections

The inflectional prefixes and suffixes used in the texts "The Autobiography of a Meskwaki Woman" and "The Owl Sacred Pack," and some additional inflections, are explained in this appendix. The analysis follows that in Goddard (2004), which has a full list of abbreviations.

1. *List of prefixes.*

The inflectional prefixes indicated in the interlinear analysis of the texts are listed here. The three pronominal prefixes, the prefix marking unpossessed dependent nouns, and the abstract representation of initial change (**IC+**) are marked with a following plus sign (+). These affixes fuse with the following stem, sometimes irregularly. In contrast, the aorist and future prefixes are marked with a double hyphen (=); although they are not strictly proclitics, as the use of "=" might imply, they are phonologically more independent from the following stem than the prefixes marked with "+", and their demarcation by "=" increases the transparency of inflected forms.

The aorist prefix and initial change have grammatical functions but no specific meaning; hence *e·h=* is simply provided with the label "aor.," and initial change is not glossed.

e·h= aor.: the aorist prefix, which marks aorist conjunct, aorist interrogative, and participles with locative oblique heads (except before *a·mi* POT)
NOTE: dropped before *wi·h=* FUT. (But *e·h=* sometimes appears with a preverb *wi·hi* (often elided to *wi·h*), which has some of the functions of *wi·h=* FUT.)

IC+ initial change; marks the changed modes of the conjunct and interrogative orders (changed conjunct, changed interrogative, changed preterite, iterative, and the participles)

ke+ 2: second person pronominal prefix
→ *k-* before *i·* and *o·* in dependent stems and with *wi·h=* FUT
→ *ket-* before other vowels

ne+ 1: first person pronominal prefix
→ *n-* before *i·* and *o·* in dependent stems and with *wi·h=* FUT
→ *net-* before other vowels

me+ unposs.: unpossessed dependent noun
→ *m-* before *i·* in dependent stems

o+	3: third person animate pronominal prefix → *ow-* before *i·* in dependent stems → Ø before *o·* in dependent stems → *ot-* before other vowels
wi·h=	FUT: future *ne-* (1) + *wi·h=* FUT+ → *ki·h=* *ke-* (2) + *wi·h=* FUT+ → *ni·h=*

2. *List of endings.*

The inflectional endings (ending complexes) indicated in the interlinear analysis with a preceding plus sign (+) are here listed, glossed, and analyzed. Homophonous endings are given separately if at least one component suffix is different. For each ending, each distinctly glossed use in each combination with an associated prefix or initial change is noted, except that combinations with *wi·h=* FUT are omitted; such multiple uses of the same ending are ordered alphabetically by gloss. In the pronominal component of a gloss, categories that are not distinguished are separated by a comma with no space, except that systematically a third person is glossed only as a proximate in an ending that has no obviative counterpart. Thus "3,0" means 'third person animate (3) or inanimate (0)', and "3 – 2s" glosses endings for third person proximate (3) acting on second singular (2s) that are also used for action by third person obviative (3′). In a few cases an ending or use not found in the analyzed texts has been added because it is more basic than an attested use of the ending or otherwise fills out a paradigm. Still, this is by no means a complete list of all endings used in the language.

The endings are analyzed into their separate component suffixes as an aid to understanding the function of the forms. A template for the verbal suffixes arranged by position class is in Goddard (2004:104). Pronominal suffixes of position 6 and combined suffixes of positions 6 and 7 that are used after only one theme sign are glossed for both arguments. No claim is made about the synchronic viability of these elements; in reality much of this morphology is presumably inaccessible to speakers except as points of contrast within paradigms. In many cases analyses of different levels of abstraction are possible. The citation of elements in the interlinear analysis of the texts tends toward less abstract representations, ones that more nearly resemble the shape of elements in actual forms. The discussion of phonological rules in some cases presents rules that account for some segments in these less abstract forms.

The aorist prefix (*e·h=*) and the initial change vowel ablaut (IC) are included in the analytical affix complex even when they are not overtly present in the occurring forms. Specifically, *e·h=* aor. is specified here even for forms that lack it overtly because it is displaced by the future prefix (*wi·h=*); and initial change is specified, as in the interlinear glosses, even if the actual inflected form does not indicate it overtly because the first stem vowel is long.

The individual suffixes that make up the endings are also listed separately, together with information on irregular combinations with stems or other suffixes. The endings (ending complexes) are marked with "+" and in bold type; a suffix that is the unique component of an ending is given in italics as a subentry. Suffixes that are not also endings are listed separately in normal type, marked with a hyphen.

Glosses with numbers in parentheses are placed after the corresponding gloss without the parentheses. Endings beginning with a raised dot (·) are alphabetized by their first consonant. The endings with the shape -Ø (zero) are at the end of the list.

+a ANsg: animate singular on nouns
-a anim. sg.: animate singular in ending complexes

+a *ne–a* 1s–0/IND: ne- (1) -am (TI(1) th.) -Ø (sg.)
1s(-0)/IND: same on an objectless TI(1)
ke–a 2s–0/IND: ke- (2) -am (TI(1) th.) -Ø (sg.)
2s(-0)/IND: same on an objectless TI(1)

-a 1s proh.: first singular prohibitive

+ači *e·h·–ači* 2s–3/AOR: e·h· (aor.) -Ø (TA th. 1) -at (2s–3) -i (conj.)
IC–ači 2s–3/CC: IC+ -Ø (TA th. 1) -at (2s–3) -i (conj.)

+ači *IC–ači* 2s–3/PPL(obl): IC+ -Ø (TA th. 1) -at (2s–3) -i (inan. sg.)

+ačiki *IC–ačiki* 2s–3/PPL(ANpl): IC+ -Ø (TA th. 1) -at (2s–3) -iki (anim. pl.)

+ačini *IC–ačini* 2s–3/ITER: IC+ -Ø (TA th. 1) -at (2s–3) -ini (neg.-iter.)
–ačini 2s–3/NEG: -Ø (TA th. 1) -at (2s–3) -ini (neg.-iter.)

+ahi OBVpl: obviative plural on nouns
-ahi obv. pl.: obviative plural in ending complexes

-ak 1s–3: first singular acting on third animate, conjunct and interrogative

+aka *IC–aka* 1s–3/PPL(ANsg): IC+ -Ø (TA th. 1) -ak (1s–3) -a (anim. sg.)

+aka *IC–aka* 3–0/PPL(ANsg): IC+ -am (TI(1) th.) -k (3) -a (anim. sg.)
3(-0)/PPL(ANsg): same on an objectless TI(1)

+akani 2s–0/PROH: -am (TI(1) th.) -hk (proh.) -an (2s) -i (conj.)
2s(-0)/PROH: same on an objectless TI(1)

+ake 1s–3/SUBJ: -Ø (TA th. 1) -ak (1s–3) -e (subj.)

+ake 3s–0/SUBJ: -am (TI(1) th.) -k (3) -e (subj.)
3s(-0)/SUBJ: same on an objectless TI(1)

+akeči *e·h·–akeči* 1p–3/AOR: e·h· (aor.) -Ø (TA th. 1) -aket (1p–3) -i (conj.)
IC–akeči 1p–3/CC: IC+ -Ø (TA th. 1) -aket (1p–3) -i (conj.)

+akeči *IC–akeči* 1p–3/PPL(obl): IC+ -Ø (TA th. 1) -aket (1p–3) -i (inan. sg.)

+akečini 1p–3/NEG: -Ø (TA th. 1) -aket (1p–3) -ini (neg.-iter.)

+akehe *IC–akehe* 1s–3/PRET.PPL(obl): IC+ -Ø (TA th. 1) -ak (1s–3) -ehe (pret.)

-aket 1p–3: first plural exclusive acting on third animate, conjunct and interrogative

+aketa *IC–aketa* +1p–3/PPL(ANsg): IC+ -Ø (TA th. 1) -aket (1p–3) -a (anim. sg.)

+ake·ko 2p–0/PROH: -am (TI(1) th.) -hk (proh.) -e·ko (2p proh.)

+ake·koha 2p–0/POT: -am (TI(1) th.) -hk (proh.) -e·kw (2p) -ehe (pret.)

+aki ANpl: animate plural on nouns
-aki anim. pl.: animate plural in ending complexes

+aki	*e·h·–aki* 1s–3/AOR: e·h· (aor.) -Ø (TA th. 1) -ak (1s–3) -i (conj.)
	IC–aki 1s–3/CC: IC+ -Ø (TA th. 1) -ak (1s–3) -i (conj.)
	–aki 1s–3/CONJ: -Ø (TA th. 1) -ak (1s–3) -i (conj.)
+aki	*IC–aki* 1s–3/PPL(obl): IC+ -Ø (TA th. 1) -ak (1s–3) -i (inan. sg.)
+aki	*e·h·–aki* 3s–0/AOR: e·h· (aor.) -am (TI(1) th.) -k (3) -i (conj.)
	3s(-0)/AOR: same on an objectless TI(1)
	IC–aki 3s–0/CC: IC+ -am (TI(1) th.) -k (3) -i (conj.)
	3s(-0)/CC: same on an objectless TI(1)
	–aki 3s–0/CONJ: -am (TI(1) th.) -k (3) -i (conj.)
+aki	*IC–aki* 3s–0/PPL(INsg): IC+ -am (TI(1) th.) -k (3) -i (inan. sg.)
	3s–0/PPL(obl): same
+akiče	3s–0/PROH: -am (TI(1) th.) -hk (proh.) -če (3,0 imp.)
	3s(-0)/PROH: same on an objectless TI(1)
+akiki	*IC–akiki* 1s–3/PPL(ANpl): IC+ -Ø (TA th. 1) -ak (1s–3) -iki (anim. pl.)
+akiki	*IC–akiki* 3–0/PPL(ANpl): IC+ -am (TI(1) th.) -k (3) -iki (anim. pl.)
	3(-0)/PPL(ANpl): same on an objectless TI(1)
+akini	*IC–akini* 1s–3/ITER: IC+ -Ø (TA th. 1) -ak (1s–3) -ini (neg.-iter.)
	–akini 1s–3/NEG: -Ø (TA th. 1) -ak (1s–3) -ini (neg.-iter.)
+akini	*IC–akini* 3s–0/ITER: IC+ -am (TI(1) th.) -k (3) -ini (neg.-iter.)
	–akini 3s–0/NEG: -am (TI(1) th.) -k (3) -ini (neg.-iter.)
	3s(-0)/NEG: same on an objectless TI(1)
+akini	*IC–akini* 3s–0/PPL(INpl): IC+ -am (TI(1) th.) -k (3) -ini (inan. pl.)
-ako·w	1s–2p: first singular on second plural, conjunct
	NOTE: after *-ako·w* 1s–2p all suffixes are replaced by *-e* (< *-i* conj.)
-akw	12: first plural inclusive in conjunct, interrogative, potential, and prohibitive
	→ *-yakw* after a vowel
+akwa	*IC–akwa* 12–3/PPL(ANsg): IC+ -Ø (TA th. 1) -akw (12) -a (anim. sg.)
+akwe	*e·h·–akwe* 12–3/AOR: e·h· (aor.) -Ø (TA th. 1) -akw (12) -i (conj.)
	IC–akwe 12–3/PPL(obl): IC+ -Ø (TA th. 1) -akw (12) -i (inan. sg.)
+akwe	*–akwe* 12–3/SUBJ: -Ø (TA th. 1) -akw (12) -e (subj.)
+akwiki	*IC–akwiki* 12–3/PPL(ANpl): IC+ -Ø (TA th. 1) -akw (12) -iki (anim. pl.)
+akwini	12–3/NEG: -Ø (TA th. 1) -akw (12) -ini (neg.-iter.)
-am	TI(1) th.: theme sign of TI class 1
	→ *-a·* before *p* in independent
	→ *-a* word-finally and before *-k*, *-hk*, *-n*, and *č*.
+amakwe	*e·h·–amakwe* 12–0/AOR: e·h· (aor.) -am (TI(1) th.) -akw (12) -i (conj.)
	IC–amakwe 12–0/PPL(obl): IC+ -am (TI(1) th.) -akw (12) -i (inan. sg.)
+amakwe	*–amakwe* 12–0/SUBJ: -am (TI(1) th.) -akw (12) -e (subj.)
+amakwini	12–0/NEG: -am (TI(1) th.) -akw (12) -ini (neg.-iter.)
+amane	2s–0/SUBJ: -am (TI(1) th.) -an (2s) -e (subj.)

+amani *e·h▪–amani* 2s–0/AOR: e·h▪ (aor.) -am (TI(1) th.) -an (2s) -i (conj.)
2s(-0)/AOR: same on an objectless TI(1)

+amanini *IC–amanini* 2s–0/ITER: IC+ -am (TI(1) th.) -an (2s) -ini (neg.-iter.)
2s(-0)/ITER: same on an objectless TI(1)
–amanini 2s–0/NEG: -am (TI(1) th.) -an (2s) -ini (neg.-iter.)

+ama·kini 1p–0/NEG: -am (TI(1) th.) -a·k (1p) -ini (neg.-iter.)

+ama·nehe 1s/PRET.SUBJ: -am (TI(1) th.) -a·n (1s) -ehe (pret.)

+ama·ni *e·h▪–ama·ni* 1s–0/AOR: e·h▪ (aor.) -am (TI(1) th.) -a·n (1s) -i (conj.)
1s(-0)/AOR: same on an objectless TI(1)
IC–ama·ni 1s–0/CC: IC+ -am (TI(1) th.) -a·n (1s) -i (conj.)
1s(-0)/CC: same on an objectless TI(1)

+ama·ni *e·h▪–ama·ni* 1s–0/PPL(loc.obl): e·h▪ (aor.) -am (TI(1) th.) -a·n (1s) -i (inan. sg.)
1s(-0)/PPL(loc.obl): same on an objectless TI(1)
IC–ama·ni 1s–0/PPL(obl): IC+ -am (TI(1) th.) -a·n (1s) -i (inan. sg.)

+ama·nini *IC–ama·nini* 1s–0/ITER: IC+ -am (TI(1) th.) -a·n (1s) -ini (neg.-iter.)
–ama·nini 1s–0/NEG: -am (TI(1) th.) -a·n (1s) -ini (neg.-iter.)
1s(-0)/NEG: same on an objectless TI(1)

+ama·nini *IC–ama·nini* 1s–0/PPL(INpl): IC+ -am (TI(1) th.) -a·n (1s) -ini (inan. pl.)

+ameke X–0/SUBJ: -am (TI(1) th.) -ek (X) -e (subj.)

+ameki *e·h▪–ameki* X–0/AOR: e·h▪ (aor.) -am (TI(1) th.) -ek (X) -i (conj.)
X(-0)/AOR: same on an objectless TI(1)
–ameki X–0/CONJ: -am (TI(1) th.) -ek (X) -i (conj.)

+ameki *IC–ameki* X–0/PPL(INsg): IC+ -am (TI(1) th.) -ek (X) -i (inan. sg.)
X–0/PPL(obl): same
X(-0)/PPL(obl): same on an objectless TI(1)

+amekini *IC–amekini* X–0/ITER: IC+ -am (TI(1) th.) -ek (X) -ini (neg.-iter.)
–amekini X–0/NEG: -am (TI(1) th.) -ek (X) -ini (neg.-iter.)

-amet 3–1p: first plural exclusive (as object of third person animate)
→ *-yamet* after a vowel (which is always the case)
NOTE: combines with modal markers, sometimes after metathesis:
-(y)amet (3–1p) + *-w* (irr.) → *-(y)amekw* (3–1p irr.)
-(y)amet (3–1p) + *-hk* (proh.) + *-če* (3,0 imp.) → *-(y)amehkiče* (3–1p proh.)
-(y)amet (3–1p) + *-sa* (3,0 pot.) → *-(y)amesa* (3–1p pot.)
-(y)amet (3–1p) + *-če* (3,0 imp.) → *-(y)ameče* (3–1p imp.)

+ame·kwe *e·h▪–ame·kwe* 2p–0/AOR: e·h▪ (aor.) -am (TI(1) th.) -e·kw (2p) -i (conj.)

+ame·kwe *IC–ame·kwe* 2p–0/PPL(obl): IC+ -am (TI(1) th.) -e·kw (2p) -i (inan. sg.)

+ame·kwe *–ame·kwe* 2p–0/SUBJ: -am (TI(1) th.) -e·kw (2p) -e (subj.)

+ame·kwini *IC–ame·kwini* 2p–0/ITER: IC+ -am (TI(1) th.) -e·kw (2p) -ini (neg.-iter.)
–ame·kwini 2p–0/NEG: -am (TI(1) th.) -e·kw (2p) -ini (neg.-iter.)

+aminiči *e·h▪–aminiči* 3′–0/AOR: e·h▪ (aor.) -am (TI(1) th.) -ni (obv.) -t (3) -i (conj.)

+aminičihi *IC–aminičihi* 3′–0/PPL(OBVpl): IC+ -am (TI(1) th.) -ni (obv.) -t (3) -ihi (obv. pl.)
3′(-0)/PPL(OBVpl): same on an objectless TI(1)

+amoko 2p–0/IMP: -am (TI(1) th.) -ko (2p imp.)

+amokwe·na *IC–amokwe·na* 3s–0/INT.PPL(ANsg): IC+ -am (TI(1) th.) -kw (3,0 irr.) -e·n (int.) -a (anim. sg.)

+amokwe·ni *IC–amokwe·ni* 3s–0/CH.INT: IC+ -am (TI(1) th.) -kw (3,0 irr.) -e·n (int.) -i (conj.)
3s(-0)/CH.INT: same on an objectless TI(1)

+amowa·či *e·h=–amowa·či* 3p–0/AOR: e·h= (aor.) -am (TI(1) th.) -wa· (pl.) -t (3) -i (conj.)
3p(-0)/AOR: same on an objectless TI(1)

+amowa·či *IC–amowa·či* 3p–0/PPL(obl): IC+ -am (TI(1) th.) -wa· (pl.) -t (3) -i (inan. sg.)
3p(-0)/PPL(obl): same on an objectless TI(1)

+amowa·čini *IC–amowa·čini* 3p–0/ITER: IC+ -am (TI(1) th.) -wa· (pl.) -t (3) -ini (neg.-iter.)
–amowa·čini 3p–0/NEG: -am (TI(1) th.) -wa· (pl.) -t (3) -ini (neg.-iter.)

+amowa·sa 3p–0/POT: -am (TI(1) th.) -wa· (pl.) -sa (3,0 pot.)

+amowečini *IC–amowečini* X–0/REL/ITER: IC+ -am (TI(1) th.) -wet (X rel.) -ini (neg.-iter.)

+amowe·kwe·ni *e·h=–amowe·kwe·ni* 2p–0/AOR.INT: e·h= (aor.) -am (TI(1) th.) -w (irr.) -e·kw (2p) -e·ni (int.)

+amo·hkani 2s–0/FUT.IMP: -am (TI(1) th.) -hk (fut. imp.) -an (2s) -i (conj.)

+amo·hiyakwe *IC–amo·hiyakwe* 12–0/DIM/PPL(INsg): IC+ -am (TI(1) th.) -·hi (dim.) -akw (12) -i (inan. sg.)

+amo·hiya·ni 1s–0/DIM/PPL(INsg): IC+ -am (TI(1) th.) -·hi (dim.) -a·n (1s) -i (inan. sg.)
1s–0/DIM/PPL(obl): same

+amo·hiye·kwe *e·h=–amo·hiye·kwe* 2p–0/DIM/AOR: e·h= (aor.) -am (TI(1) th.) -·hi (dim.) -e·kw (2p) -i (conj.)

+amo·ki 3p–0/IND: -am (TI(1) th.) -w (3,0) -aki (anim. pl.)

+amwa 3s–0/IND: -am (TI(1) th.) -w (3,0) -a (anim. sg.)
3s(-0)/IND: same on an objectless TI(1)

-an 2s: second singular in conjunct, interrogative, and prohibitive
→ *-yan* after a vowel

+ane 2s/SUBJ: -an (2s) -e (subj.)

+ane·ha X–0/POT: -am (TI(1) th.) -ene·ha (X pot.)

+ani INpl: inanimate plural on nouns
-ani inan. pl.: inanimate plural in ending complexes

+ani OBVsg: obviative singular on nouns
-ani obv. sg.: obviative singular in ending complexes

+ano 2s–0/IMP: -am (TI(1) th.) -no (2s imp.)

-apa 2s pot.: second singular, potential

+asa 3s–0/POT: -am (TI(1) th.) -sa (3,0 pot.)

-at 2s – 3: second singular acting on third animate in conjunct

+ata *IC – ata* 2s – 3/PPL(ANsg): IC+ -Ø (TA th. 1) -at (2s – 3) -a (anim. sg.)

+ate 2s – 3/SUBJ: -Ø (TA th. 1) -at (2s – 3) -e (subj.)

+atehe *e·h· – atehe* 2s – 3/AOR.PRET: e·h· (aor.) -at (2s – 3) -ehe (pret.)

-a· TA th. 1 (direct theme sign): action on an animate that is lower than the actor in the hierarchy: 1,2 > X > 3 > 3′ > 3″

→ Ø before a vowel

NOTE:

-a· (TA th. 1) + *-w* (3,0) → *-e·w*, (with contraction) *-e·*

-a· (TA th. 1) + *-·hi* (dim.) → *-e·hi*

+a·či *e·h· – a·či* 3s – 3′/AOR: e·h· (aor.) -a· (TA th. 1) -t (3) -i (conj.)

IC – a·či 3s – 3′/CC: IC+ -a· (TA th. 1) -t (3) -i (conj.)

– a·či 3s – 3′/CONJ: -a· (TA th. 1) -t (3) -i (conj.)

IC – a·či 3s – 3′/PPL(obl): IC+ -a· (TA th. 1) -t (3) -i (inan. sg.)

+a·čihi *IC – a·čihi* 3s – 3′/PPL(OBVpl): IC+ -a· (TA th. 1) -t (3) -ihi (obv. pl.)

+a·čiki *IC – a·čiki* 3 – 3′/PPL(ANpl): IC+ -a· (TA th. 1) -t (3) -iki (anim. pl.)

+a·čini *IC – a·čini* 3s – 3′/ITER: IC+ -a· (TA th. 1) -t (3) -ini (neg.-iter.)

– a·čini 3s – 3′/NEG: -a· (TA th. 1) -t (3) -ini (neg.-iter.)

-a·ha 1s pot.: first singular potential

+a·hkani 2s – 3/FUT.IMP: -a· (TA th. 1) -hk (fut. imp.) -an (2s) -i (conj.)

+a·hke·ko 2p – 3/FUT.IMP: -a· (TA th. 1) -hk (fut. imp.) -e·ko (2p proh.)

+a·hkiče 3s – 3′/FUT.IMP: -a· (TA th. 1) -hk (fut. imp.) -če (3,0 imp.)

-a·k 1p: first plural exclusive in conjunct, interrogative, potential, and prohibitive

→ *-ya·k* after a vowel

+a·ke *IC – a·ke* 1p/PPL(obl): IC+ -a·k (1p) -i (inan. sg.)

-a·kw 3,X – 2p: second plural as object of third person animate or indefinite, conjunct and interrogative

-a·n 1s: first singular, conjunct and interrogative

→ *-ya·n* after a vowel

+a·ni *e·h· – a·ni* 1s/AOR: e·h· (aor.) -a·n (1s) -i (conj.)

+a·ničihi *IC – a·ničihi* 3′ – 3″/PPL(OBVpl): IC+ -a· (TA th. 1) -ni (obv.) -t (3) -ihi (obv. pl.)

+a·pena *ne – a·pena* 1p – 3/IND: ne- (1) -a· (TA th. 1) -pena (1p,12)

ke – a·pena 12 – 3/IND: ke- (2) -a· (TA th. 1) -pena (1p,12)

+a·pena *ke – a·pena* 12 – 0/IND: ke- (2) -am (TI(1) th.) -pena (1p,12)

+a·petoke *ne – a·petoke* 1s – 0/DUB: ne- (1) -am (TI(1) th.) -p (sg.) -etoke (dub.)

ke – a·petoke 2s – 0/DUB: ne- (2) -am (TI(1) th.) -p (sg.) -etoke (dub.)

+a·pi X – 0/IND: -am (TI(1) th.) -pi (X)

X(-0)/IND: same on an objectless TI(1)

+a·pi X – 3/IND: -a· (TA th. 1) -pi (X)

+a·pwa *ke – a·pwa* 2p – 0/IND: ke- (2) -am (TI(1) th.) -pwa (2p)

+a·pwa *ke – a·pwa* 2p – 3/IND: ke- (2) -a· (TA th. 1) -pwa (2p)

+a·sa	3s–3′/POT: -a· (TA th. 1) -sa (3,0 pot.)
+a·ta	*IC–a·ta* 3–3′/PPL(ANsg): IC+ -a· (TA th. 1) -t (3) -a (anim. sg.)
+a·te	3s–3′/SUBJ: -a· (TA th. 1) -t (3) -e (subj.)
+a·tehe	*e·h▪–a·tehe* 3s–3′/AOR.PRET: e·h▪ (aor.) -a· (TA th. 1) -t (3) -ehe (pret.)
	IC–a·tehe 3s–3′/CH.PRET: IC+ -a· (TA th. 1) -t (3) -ehe (pret.)
+a·te·ni	X–3/INT: -a· (TA th. 1) -w (irr.) -et (X–3) -e·ni (int.)
+a·wa	*ne–a·wa* 1s–3s/IND: ne- (1) -a· (TA th. 1) -w (sg.) -a (anim. sg.)
	ke–a·wa 2s–3s/IND: ne- (2) -a· (TA th. 1) -w (sg.) -a (anim. sg.)
+a·waki	*ne–a·waki* 1s–3p/IND: ne- (1) -a· (TA th. 1) -w (sg.) -aki (anim. pl.)
	ke–a·waki 2s–3p/IND: ke- (2) -a· (TA th. 1) -w (sg.) -aki (anim. pl.)
+a·wate·na	2s–3/INT.PPL(ANsg): -a· (TA th. 1) -w (irr.) -at (2s–3) -e·ni (int.) -a (anim. sg.)
+a·wa·či	*e·h▪–a·wa·či* 3p–3′/AOR: e·h▪ (aor.) -a· (TA th. 1) -wa· (pl.) -t (3) -i (conj.)
	–a·wa·či 3p–3′/CONJ: -a· (TA th. 1) -wa· (pl.) -t (3) -i (conj.)
+a·wa·či	*IC–a·wa·či* 3p–3′/PPL(obl): IC+ -a· (TA th. 1) -wa· (pl.) -t (3) -i (inan. sg.)
+a·wa·čihi	3p–3′/PPL(OBVpl): IC+ -a· (TA th. 1) -wa· (pl.) -t (3) -ihi (obv. pl.)
+a·wa·čini	*IC–a·wa·čini* 3p–3′/ITER: IC+ -a· (TA th. 1) -wa· (pl.) -t (3) -ini (neg.-iter.)
	–a·wa·čini 3p–3′/NEG: -a· (TA th. 1) -wa· (pl.) -t (3) -ini (neg.-iter.)
+a·wa·sa	3p–3′/POT: -a· (TA th. 1) -wa· (pl.) -sa (3,0 pot.)
+če	3s,0/IMP: -če (3,0 imp.)
	-če 3,0 imp.: third person animate and inanimate, imperative; also in the prohibitive
	→ *-iče* after *-hk* proh., fut. imp.
+či	*e·h▪–či* 3s/AOR: e·h▪ (aor.) -t (3) -i (conj.)
	3s–0/AOR: same on a Class 3 TI
	IC–či 3s/CC: IC+ -t (3) -i (conj.)
	–či 3s/CONJ: -t (3) -i (conj.)
+či	*e·h▪–či* 3s/PPL(loc.obl): e·h▪ (aor.) -t (3) -i (inan. sg.)
+či	*IC–či* 3s/PPL(obl): IC+ -t (3) -i (inan. sg.)
	3s–0/PPL(INsg): same on a Class 3 TI with inan. sg. head
+čiki	*IC–čiki* 3/PPL(ANpl): IC+ -t (3) -iki (anim. pl.)
+čini	*IC–čini* 3s/ITER: IC+ -t (3) -ini (neg.-iter.)
	–čini 3s/NEG: -t (3) -ini (neg.-iter.)
+čini	3s/PPL(obl.pl): IC+ -t (3) -ini (inan. pl.)
	3s–0/PPL(INpl): same on a Class 3 TI
+e	VOCsg: vocative singular on nouns
-e	conj.: see *-i* conj.
-e	inan. sg.: *-i* inan. sg.
-e	subj.: subjunctive mode
-e	voc.: vocative as head of participle; cf. **+e** VOCsg

+eči	*e·h·–eči* X–3/AOR: e·h· (aor.) -Ø (TA th. 1) -et (X–3) -i (conj.)
	IC–eči X–3/CC: IC+ -Ø (TA th. 1) -et (X–3) -i (conj.)
	–eči X–3/CONJ: -Ø (TA th. 1) -et (X–3) -i (conj.)
+eči	*IC–eči* X–3/PPL(INsg): IC+ -Ø (TA th. 1) -et (X–3) -i (inan. sg.)
	X–3/PPL(obl): same with oblique head
+ečiki	*IC–ečiki* X–3/PPL(ANpl): IC+ -Ø (TA th. 1) -et (X–3) -iki (anim. pl.)
+ečini	*IC–ečini* X–3/ITER: IC+ -Ø (TA th. 1) -et (X–3) -ini (neg.-iter.)
	–ečini X–3/NEG: -Ø (TA th. 1) -et (X–3) -ini (neg.-iter.)
+ečini	*IC–ečini* X–3/PPL(obl.pl): IC+ -Ø (TA th. 1) -et (X–3) -ini (inan. pl.)
-ehapa	con.: conclusive mode
	→ *-ehapan* before *-iki* (anim. pl.)
-ehe	pret.: preterite of aorist, subjunctive, negative, and participle; also in some potential endings
	→ *-eha* after *-kw*: *-kw-eha* → *-koha*
	NOTE: Modal and participial suffixes do not appear after *-ehe* (pret.).
+ehka	*IC–ehka* 3–2s/PPL(ANsg): IC+ -eN (TA th. 4) -k (3) -a (anim. sg.)
+ehke	3–2s/SUBJ: -eN (TA th. 4) -k (3) -e (subj.)
+ehki	*e·h·–ehki* 3–2s/AOR: e·h· (aor.) -eN (TA th. 4) -k (3) -i (conj.)
+ehki	*IC–ehki* 3–2s/PPL(obl): IC+ -eN (TA th. 4) -k (3) -i (inan. sg.)
+ehkini	3–2s/NEG: -eN (TA th. 4) -k (3) -ini (neg.-iter.)
+ehko	2p–3/IMP: -Ø (TA th. 1) -ehko (2p–3 imp.)
	-ehko 2p–3 imp.: second plural on third, imperative
-ek	X: indefinite subject in conjunct and interrogative
+eke	X/SUBJ: -ek (X) -e (subj.)
+eki	LOC: locative on nouns
	-eki loc.: locative in ending complexes
+eki	*e·h·–eki* X/AOR: e·h· (aor.) -ek (X) -i (conj.)
	X–0/AOR: same on a Class 3 TI
	–eki X/CONJ: -ek (X) -i (conj.)
+eki	*IC–eki* X/PPL(INsg): IC+ -ek (X) -i (inan. sg.)
	X/PPL(obl): same
	X–0/PPL(INsg): same on a Class 3 TI
	X–0/PPL(obl): same
+ekini	*IC–ekini* X/ITER: IC+ -ek (X) -ini (neg.-iter.)
	X–0/ITER: same on a Class 3 TI
	–ekini X/NEG: -ek (X) -ini (neg.-iter.)
	X–0/NEG: same on a Class 3 TI
+ekini	*e·h·–ekini* X/PPL(loc.obl.pl): e·h· (aor.) -ek (X) -ini (inan. pl.)
	IC–ekini X/PPL(obl.pl): IC+ -ek (X) -ini (inan. pl.)
+ekoči	*e·h·–ekoči* 3′–3s/AOR: e·h· (aor.) -ekw (TA th. 2) -t (3) -i (conj.)
+ekoči	*IC–ekoči* 3′–3s/PPL(obl): IC+ -ekw (TA th. 2) -t (3) -i (inan. sg.)

+ekočihi	*IC–ekočihi* 3′–3s/PPL(OBVpl): IC+ -ekw (TA th. 2) -t (3) -ihi (obv. pl.)
+ekočiki	*IC–ekočiki* 3′–3/PPL(ANpl): IC+ -ekw (TA th. 2) -t (3) -iki (anim. pl.)
+ekočini	3′–3s/NEG: -ekw (TA th. 2) -t (3) -ini (neg.-iter.)
+ekočini	*IC–ekočini* 3′–3s/PPL(OBVsg): IC+ -ekw (TA th. 2) -t (3) -ini (obv. sg.)
+ekona·na	*ne–ekona·na* 3s–1p/IND: ne- (1) -ekw (TA th. 2) -ena·n (1p,12) -a (anim. sg.) *ke–ekona·na* 3s–12/IND: ke- (2) -ekw (TA th. 2) -ena·n (1p,12) -a (anim. sg.)
+ekosa	3′–3s/POT: -ekw (TA th. 2) -sa (3,0 pot.)
+ekota	*IC–ekota* 3′–3/PPL(ANsg): IC+ -ekw (TA th. 2) -t (3) -a (anim. sg.)
+ekowa·či	*e·h▪–ekowa·či* 3′–3p/AOR: e·h▪ (aor.) -ekw (TA th. 2) -wa· (pl.) -t (3) -i (conj.)
+ekowa·či	*IC–ekowa·či* 3′–3p/CC: IC+ -ekw (TA th. 2) -wa· (pl.) -t (3) -i (conj.)
+ekowa·či	*IC–ekowa·či* 3′–3p/PPL(obl): IC+ -ekw (TA th. 2) -wa· (pl.) -t (3) -i (inan. sg.)
+ekowa·či	*e·h▪–ekowa·či* 3′–3p/PPL(loc.obl): e·h▪ (aor.) -ekw (TA th. 2) -wa· (pl.) -t (3) -i (inan. sg.)
+ekowa·čini	3′–3p/NEG: -ekw (TA th. 2) -wa· (pl.) -t (3) -ini (neg.-iter.)
+ekowa·sa	3′–3p/POT: -ekw (TA th. 2) -wa· (pl.) -sa (3,0 pot.)
+ekowa·wa	*ke–ekowa·wa* 3s–2p/IND: ke- (2) -ekw (TA th. 2) -wa·w (2p,3p) -a (anim. sg.)
+eko·ki	*ne–eko·ki* 3p–1s/IND: ne- (1) -ekw (TA th. 2) -w (sg.) -aki (anim. pl.) *ke–eko·ki* 3p–2s/IND: ke- (2) -ekw (TA th. 2) -w (sg.) -aki (anim. pl.)
+eko·ki	*–eko·ki* 3′–3p/IND: -ekw (TA th. 2) -w (3,0) -aki (anim. pl.)
+eko·pena	*ne–eko·pena* X–1p/IND: ne- (1) -ekw (TA th. 2) -pena (1p,12)
+eko·pi	*ne–eko·pi* X–1s/IND: ne- (1) -ekw (TA th. 2) -pi (X) *ke–eko·pi* X–2s/IND: ke- (2) -ekw (TA th. 2) -pi (X)
+eko·pwa	*ke–eko·pwa* X–2p/IND: ke- (2) -ekw (TA th. 2) -pwa (2p)
+eko·toke	*ke–eko·toke* 3s–2s/DUB: ke- (2) -ekw (TA th. 2) -w (sg.) -etoke (dub.)
-ekw	TA th. 2 (inverse theme sign): action on an animate that is higher than the actor in the hierarchy: 1,2 > X > 3 > 3′ > 3″ > 0 NOTE: Selected by different combinations of subject and object in different orders. → *-eko* before *t, s* → *-eko·* before *p* (|-ekw-p| → |-ekwe-p| → *-eko·p*) (indefinite subject, independent order) Variant: *-ekwi* (TA th. 2a): inanimate subject
+ekwa	*ne–ekwa* 3s–1s/IND: ne- (1) -ekw (TA th. 2) -w (sg.) -a (anim. sg.) *ke–ekwa* 3s–2s/IND: ke- (2) -ekw (TA th. 2) -w (sg.) -a (anim. sg.)
+ekwa	*–ekwa* 3′–3s/IND: -ekw (TA th. 2) -w (3,0) -a (anim. sg.)
-ekwi	TA th. 2a: see *-ekw* TA th. 2
+ekwičini	0–3s/NEG: -ekwi (TA th. 2a) -t (3) -ini (neg.-iter.)
+ekwihka·ha	0–1s/POT: -ekwi (TA th. 2a) -hk (proh.) -a·ha (1s pot.)
+ekwihke·koha	0–2p/POT: -ekwi (TA th. 2a) -hk (proh.) -e·kw (2p) -ehe (pret.)
+ekwipena	*ne–ekwipena* 0–1p/IND: ne- (1) -ekwi (TA th. 2a) -pena (1p,12)

+ekwita *IC–ekwita* 0–3/PPL(ANsg): IC+ -ekwi (TA th. 2a) -t (3) -a (anim. sg.)

+ekwiwa·či *IC–ekwiwa·či* 0–3p/PPL(INsg): IC+ -ekwi (TA th. 2a) -wa· (pl.) -t (3) -i (inan. sg.)

+ekwiyakwe *IC–ekwiyakwe* 0–12/PPL(INsg): IC+ -ekwi (TA th. 2a) -akw (12) -i (inan. sg.)

+ekwiye·kwe *IC–ekwiye·kwe* 0–2p/PPL(INsg): IC+ -ekwi (TA th. 2a) -e·kw (2p) -i (inan. sg.)
0–2p/PPL(obl): same

-em obv.: marks object as obviative with first, second, or indefinite subject

-em poss. th.: makes the possessed theme of some nouns

+ema *ne–ema* 1s(ANsg): ne- (1) -em (poss. th.) -a (anim. sg.)

+emaki *e·h▪–emaki* 1s–3′/AOR: e·h▪ (aor.) -em (obv.) -Ø (TA th. 1) -ak (1s–3) -i (conj.)

+emakini *IC–emakini* 1s–3′/PPL(OBVsg): IC+ -em (obv.) -Ø (TA th. 1) -ak (1s–3) -ini (obv. sg.)

+emani *o–emani* 3s(INpl): o- (3) -em (poss. th.) -ani (inan. pl.)

+emani *o–emani* 3s(OBVsg): o- (3) -em (poss. th.) -ani (obv. sg.)

+emeči *e·h▪–emeči* X–3′/AOR: e·h▪ (aor.) -em (obv.) -et (X–3) -i (conj.)

+emeči *e·h▪–emeči* X–3′/PPL(loc.obl): e·h▪ (aor.) -em (obv.) -et (X–3) -i (inan. sg.)

+emeči *IC–emeči* X–3′/PPL(obl): IC+ -em (obv.) -et (X–3) -i (inan. sg.)

+emečini *IC–emečini* X–3′/PPL(OBVsg): IC+ -em (obv.) -et (X–3) -ini (obv. sg.)

+emeki *ne–emeki* 1s(LOC): ne- (1) -em (poss. th.) -eki (loc.)

+emena·na *ne–emena·na* 1p(ANsg): ne- (1) -em (poss. th.) -ena·n (1p,12) -a (anim. sg.)
ke–emena·na 12(ANsg): ke- (2) -em (poss. th.) -ena·n (1p,12) -a (anim. sg.)

+emena·ni *ke–emena·ni* 12(INsg): ke- (2) -em (poss. th.) -ena·n (1p,12) -i (inan. sg.)

+emete X–3′/SUBJ: -em (obv.) -et (X–3) -e (subj.)

+emi *ne–emi* 1s(INsg): ne- (1) -em (poss. th.) -i (inan. sg.)
o–emi 3s(INsg): o- (3) -em (poss. th.) -i (inan. sg.)

+eminawaki *o–eminawaki* X(ANpl): o- (3) -em (poss. th.) -inaw (X) -aki (anim. pl.)

+emwa·wahi *o–emwa·wahi* 3p(OBVpl): o- (3) -em (poss. th.) -wa·w (2p,3p) -ahi (obv. pl.)

+emwa·waki *ke–emwa·waki* 2p(ANpl): ke- (2) -em (poss. th.) -wa·w (2p,3p) -aki (anim. pl.)

+emwa·wani *o–emwa·wani* 3p(INpl): o- (3) -em (poss. th.) -wa·w (2p,3p) -ani (inan. pl.)

-eN TA th. 4: action on second person or first person inclusive
NOTE: Selected by different combinations of subject and object in different orders.
→ *en* except as follows:
→ *-ene* word-finally and before *p*, *s*
→ *-eh* before *-k*

+enaka·ha 1s–2s/POT: -eN (TA th. 4) -hk (proh.) -a·ha (1s pot.)

+enakiče 3–2s/PROH: -eN (TA th. 4) -hk (proh.) -če (3,0 imp.)

+enaki·ke X–2s/PROH: -eN (TA th. 4) -hk (proh.) -i·ke (X proh.)

+enakoha *e·h▪–enakoha* 3,X–12/AOR.PRET: e·h▪ (aor.) -eN (TA th. 4) -akw (12) -ehe (pret.)

+enako·we — *e·h·–enako·we* 1s–2p/AOR: e·h· (aor.) -eN (TA th. 4) -ako·w (1s–2p) -i (conj.)
IC–enako·we 1s–2p/CC: IC+ -eN (TA th. 4) -ako·w (1s–2p) -i (conj.)
1s–2p/PPL(1s): same
1s–2p/PPL(2p): same
1s–2p/PPL(INsg): same
1s–2p/PPL(obl): same
–enako·we 1s–2p/NEG: -eN (TA th. 4) -ako·w (1s–2p) -i (conj.)

+enakwa — *IC–enakwa* 3,X–12/PPL(ANsg): IC+ -eN (TA th. 4) -akw (12) -a (anim. sg.)

+enakwe — *e·h·–enakwe* 3,X–12/AOR: e·h· (aor.) -eN (TA th. 4) -akw (12) -i (conj.)
IC–enakwe 3,X–12/PPL(obl): IC+ -eN (TA th. 4) -akw (12) -i (inan. sg.)

+enakwini — *IC–enakwini* 3,X–12/ITER: IC+ -eN (TA th. 4) -akw (12) -ini (neg.-iter.)
–enakwini 3,X–12/NEG: -eN (TA th. 4) -akw (12) -ini (neg.-iter.)

+ena·ke — *e·h·–ena·ke* 1p–2/AOR: e·h· (aor.) -eN (TA th. 4) -a·k (1p) -i (conj.)

+ena·ke — *IC–ena·ke* 1p–2/PPL(obl): IC+ -eN (TA th. 4) -a·k (1p) -i (inan. sg.)

+ena·kini — *–ena·kini* 1p–2/NEG: -eN (TA th. 4) -a·k (1p) -ini (neg.-iter.)

+ena·kwa — *IC–ena·kwa* 3,X–2p/PPL(ANsg): IC+ -eN (TA th. 4) -a·kw (3,X–2p) -a (anim. sg.)

+ena·kwe — *e·h·–ena·kwe* 3,X–2p/AOR: e·h· (aor.) -eN (TA th. 4) -a·kw ((3,X–2p) -i (conj.)
IC–ena·kwe 3,X–2p/CC: IC+ -eN (TA th. 4) -a·kw ((3,X–2p) -i (conj.)

+ena·kwe — *IC–ena·kwe* 3,X–2p/PPL(obl): IC+ -eN (TA th. 4) -a·kw ((3,X–2p) -i (inan. sg.)

+ena·kwe — *–ena·kwe* 3,X–2p/SUBJ: -eN (TA th. 4) -a·kw ((3,X–2p) -e (subj.)

+ena·kwiki — *IC–ena·kwiki* 3,X–2p/PPL(ANpl): IC+ -eN (TA th. 4) -a·kw ((3,X–2p) -iki (anim. pl.)

+ena·kwini — *IC–ena·kwini* 3,X–2p/ITER: IC+ -eN (TA th. 4) -a·kw ((3,X–2p) -ini (neg.-iter.)

+ena·kwini — *–ena·kwini* 3,X–2p/NEG: -eN (TA th. 4) -a·kw ((3,X–2p) -ini (neg.-iter.)

-ena·n — 1p,12: pluralizes the first person for possessors of nouns and for subjects of inverse verbs in the independent order; used with ne- (1) to mark first person exclusive, and with ke- (2) to mark first person inclusive.
→ *-ena·* before *-eki* loc. and *-etoke* dub.

+ena·na — *IC–ena·na* 1s–2s/PPL(ANsg): IC+ -eN (TA th. 4) -a·n (1s) -a (anim. sg.)

+ena·na — *ne–ena·na* 1p(ANsg): ne- (1) -ena·n (1p,12) -a (anim. sg.)
ke–ena·na 12(ANsg): ke- (2) -ena·n (1p,12) -a (anim. sg.)

+ena·naki — *ne–ena·naki* 1p(ANpl): ne- (1) -ena·n (1p,12) -aki (anim. pl.)
ke–ena·naki 12(ANpl): ke- (2) -ena·n (1p,12) -aki (anim. pl.)

+ena·nani — *ne–ena·nani* 1p(INpl): ne- (1) -ena·n (1p,12) -ani (inan. pl.)
ke–ena·nani 12(INpl): ke- (2) -ena·n (1p,12) -ani (inan. pl.)

+ena·nani — *ke–ena·nani* 12(OBVsg): ke- (2) -ena·n (1p,12) -ani (obv. sg.)

+ena·ne — 1s–2s/SUBJ: -eN (TA th. 4) -a·n (1s) -e (subj.)

+ena·nehe — *e·h·–ena·nehe* 1s–2s/AOR.PRET: e·h· (aor.) -eN (TA th. 4) -a·n (1s) -ehe (pret.)
IC–ena·nehe 1s–2s/PRET.PPL(obl): IC+ -eN (TA th. 4) -a·n (1s) -ehe (pret.)
–ena·nehe 1s–2s/SUBJ.PRET: -eN (TA th. 4) -a·n (1s) -ehe (pret.)

+ena·ni — *e·h·–ena·ni* 1s–2s/AOR: e·h· (aor.) -eN (TA th. 4) -a·n (1s) -i (conj.)
IC–ena·ni 1s–2s/CC: IC+ -eN (TA th. 4) -a·n (1s) -i (conj.)

+ena·ni — *IC–ena·ni* 1s–2s/PPL(obl): IC+ -eN (TA th. 4) -a·n (1s) -i (inan. sg.)

+ena·ni — *ne–ena·ni* 1p(INsg): ne- (1) -ena·n (1p,12) -i (inan. sg.)
ke–ena·ni 12(INsg): ke- (2) -ena·n (1p,12) -i (inan. sg.)

+ena·nini — *–ena·nini* 1s–2s/NEG: -eN (TA th. 4) -a·n (1s) -ini (neg.-iter.)

+ena·nini — *IC–ena·nini* 1s–2s/PPL(INpl): IC+ -eN (TA th. 4) -a·n (1s) -ini (inan. pl.)
1s–2s/PPL(obl.pl): same

+ene — *ke–ene* 1s–2s/IND: ke- (2) -eN (TA th. 4) -Ø (sg.)

+eneke — *–eneke* X–2s/SUBJ: -eN (TA th. 4) -ek (X) -e (subj.)

+enene·ha — X–2s/POT: -eN (TA th. 4) -ene·ha (X pot.)

+enepena — *ke–enepena* 1p–2/IND: ke- (2) -eN (TA th. 4) -pena (1p,12)

+enepwa — *ke–enepwa* 1s–2p/IND: ke- (2) -eN (TA th. 4) -pwa (2p)

+eneče — 3–2s/IMP: -eN (TA th. 4) -če (3,0 imp.)

+enesa — 3–2s/POT: -eN (TA th. 4) -sa (3,0 pot.)

+ene·ha — X/POT: -ene·ha (X pot.)
-ene·ha X pot.: indefinite subject, potential
NOTE: *-am* (TI(1) th.) + *-ene·ha* (X pot.) → **+ane·ha** X–0/POT

+ene·ha — X–3/POT: -Ø (TA th. 1) -ene·ha (X pot.)

+enokwe·ni — *IC–enokwe·ni* 3s–2s/INT.PPL(obl): IC+ -eN (TA th. 4) -kw (3,0 irr.) -e·ni (int.)

+enowakwe·ni — 3,X–12/INT: -eN (TA th. 4) -w (irr.) -akw (12) -e·ni (int.)

+enowakwe·ni — *IC–enowakwe·ni* 3,X–12/INT.PPL(obl): IC+ -eN (TA th. 4) -w (irr.) -akw (12) -e·ni (int.)

+enowa·ne·ni — 1s–2s/INT: -eN (TA th. 4) -w (irr.) -a·n (1s) -e·ni (int.)

+eno·ke·ni — X–2s/INT: -eN (TA th. 4) -w (irr.) -ek (X) -e·ni (int.)

+enwa·če — 3–2p/IMP: -eN (TA th. 4) -wa· (2p) + -če (3,0 imp.)

+enwa·sa — 3–2p/POT: -eN (TA th. 4) -wa· (2p) + -sa (3,0 pot.)

-epani — ast.: assertive mode

-et — X–3: indefinite acting on third animate, conjunct

+eta — *IC–eta* X–3/PPL(ANsg): IC+ -Ø (TA th. 1) -et (X–3) -a (anim. sg.)

+ete — X–3/SUBJ: -Ø (TA th. 1) -et (X–3) -e (subj.)

+etike — VOCpl: vocative plural on noun

-etoke — dub.: dubitative mode
→ *-etoke·h* before *-iki* (anim. pl.), *-ini* (inan. pl.)

+e·hiyakwa — *IC–e·hiyakwa* 12–3.DIM/PPL(ANsg): IC+ -a· (TA th. 1) -·hi (dim.) -akw (12) -a (anim. sg.)

+e·hiyakwiki	*IC−e·hiyakwiki* 12−3.DIM/PPL(ANpl): IC+ -a· (TA th. 1) -·hi (dim.) -akw (12) -iki (anim. pl.)
+e·hiya·nini	*IC−e·hiya·nini* 1s−3/DIM/ITER: IC+ -a· (TA th. 1) -·hi (dim.) -a·n (1s) -ini (neg.-iter.)
+e·hiye·kwiki	*IC−e·hiye·kwiki* 2p−3.DIM/PPL(ANpl): IC+ -a· (TA th. 1) -·hi (dim.) -iki (anim. pl.)
-e·ko	2p proh.: second plural, prohibitive Compare *-e·kw* (2p) and *-ko* (2p imp.).
-e·kw	2p: second plural in the conjunct, interrogative, and potential → *-ye·kw* after a vowel
+e·kwe	*e·h▪−e·kwe* 2p−3/AOR: e·h▪ (aor.) -Ø (TA th. 1) -e·kw (2p) -i (conj.) *IC−e·kwe* 2p−3/PPL(obl): IC+ -Ø (TA th. 1) -e·kw (2p) -i (inan. sg.)
+e·kwe	2p−3/SUBJ: -Ø (TA th. 1) -e·kw (2p) -e (subj.)
+e·kwiki	*IC−e·kwiki* 2p−3/PPL(ANpl): IC+ -Ø (TA th. 1) -e·kw (2p) -iki (anim. pl.)
+e·kwini	*IC−e·kwini* 2p−3/ITER: IC+ -Ø (TA th. 1) -e·kw (2p) -ini (neg.-iter.) *−e·kwini* 2p−3/NEG: -e·kw (2p) -ini (neg.-iter.)
-e·ni	interrog.: interrogative mode → *-e·n* before *-a* anim. sg. → *-e·h* before *-iki* anim. pl., *-ini* obv. sg., *-ihi* obv. pl. NOTE: *-e·ni* (int.) + *-i* (inan. sg.), *-ini* (inan. pl.) → *-e·ni*
+e·toke	3s−3′/DUB: -a· (TA th. 1) -w (3,0) -etoke (dub.)
+e·wa	3s−3′/IND: -a· (TA th. 1) -w (3,0) -a (anim. sg.)
+e·waki	3p−3′/IND: -a· (TA th. 1) -w (3,0) -aki (anim. pl.)
-·hi	dim.: diminutive in verbs → *-o·hi* after a consonant → *-o·h* before *-ena·n* (1p,12) and *-wa·w* (2p,3p)
-hk	proh.: in all endings of the prohibitive mode and some endings of the potential → *-k* after a deleting *n* in an AI stem NOTE (contrast *-hk* fut. imp.): *-am* (TI(1) th.) + *-hk* (proh.) → *-ak* *-a·* (TA th. 1) + *-hk* (proh.) → *-iye·k* *-eN* (TA th. 4) + *-hk* (proh.) → *-enak*
-hk	fut. imp.: makes distinct future imperative forms with two theme signs NOTE (contrast *-hk* proh.): *-am* (TI(1) th.) + *-hk* (fut. imp.) → *-amo·hk* *-a·* (TA th. 1) + *-hk* (fut. imp.) → *-a·hk*
+hka	1s/PROH: -hk (proh.) -a (1s proh.)
+hkakoha	12/POT: -hk (proh.) -akw (12) -ehe (pret.)
+hkani	2s/PROH: -hk (proh.) -an (2s) -i (conj.)
+hkapa	2s/POT: -hk (proh.) -apa (2s pot.)
+hka·ha	1s/POT: -hk (proh.) -a·ha (1s pot.)

+hke·ko	2p/PROH: -hk (proh.) -e·ko (2p proh.)
+hke·koha	2p/POT: -hk (proh.) -e·kw (2p) -ehe (pret.)
+hkiče	0/PROH: -hk (proh.) -če (3,0 imp.) 3s/PROH: same
+i	*ke−i* 2s−1s/IND: ke- (2) -i (TA th. 3) -Ø (sg.)
+i	2s−3/IMP: -Ø (TA th. 1) -i (2s−3 imp.) *-i* 2s−3 imp.: second singular acting on third, imperative
+i	INsg: inanimate singular on nouns *-i* inan. sg.: inanimate singular in endings; marks inanimate singular or oblique singular head of participle → *-e* (after first plural and second plural suffixes except the two-syllable first exclusive suffixes, *-aket*, *-amet*, and *-·namek*)
-i	TA th. 3: action on first person singular or first plural exclusive
-i	conj.: used in conjunct modes not marked by a specific modal suffix; also in other modes after pronominal suffixes that are identical to those of the conjunct → *-e* (after first plural and second plural suffixes except the two-syllable first plural exclusive suffixes *-aket*, *-amet*, and *-·namek*)
+iči	*e·h▪−iči* 3s−1s/AOR: e·h▪ (aor.) -i (TA th. 3) -t (3) -i (conj.) *IC−iči* 3s−1s/CC: IC+ -i (TA th. 3) -t (3) -i (conj.)
+iči	*IC−iči* 3s−1s/PPL(obl): IC+ -i (TA th. 3) -t (3) -i (inan. sg.)
+ičiki	*IC−ičiki* 3−1s/PPL(ANpl): IC+ -i (TA th. 3) -t (3) -iki (anim. pl.)
+ičini	*IC−ičini* 3s−1s/ITER: IC+ -i (TA th. 3) -t (3) -ini (neg.-iter.) *−ičini* 3s−1s/NEG: -i (TA th. 3) -t (3) -ini (neg.-iter.)
-ihi	obv. pl.: obviative plural (head of participle)
+ihkapa	2s−1s/POT: -i (TA th. 3) -hk (proh.) -apa (2s pot.)
+ihka·ke	2−1p/PROH: -i (TA th. 3) -hk (proh.) -a·k (1p) -i (conj.)
+ihke·ko	2p−1s/PROH: -i (TA th. 3) -hk (proh.) -e·ko (2p proh.)
+ihki·ke	X−1s/PROH: -i (TA th. 3) -hk (proh.) -i·ke (X proh.)
+ika	*IC−ika* X−1s/PPL(ANsg): IC+ -i (TA th. 3) -ek (X) -a (anim. sg.)
+ikehe	*IC−ikehe* X−1s/CH.PRET: IC+ -i (TA th. 3) -ek (X) -ehe (pret.) X−1s/PRET.PPL(obl): same
+ikini	*IC−ikini* X−1s/ITER: IC+ -i (TA th. 3) -ek (X) -ini (neg.-iter.) *−ikini* X−1s/NEG: -i (TA th. 3) -ek (X) -ini (neg.-iter.)
+ikini	*IC−ikini* X−1s/PPL(obl.pl): IC+ -i (TA th. 3) -ek (X) -ini (inan. pl.)
+iki	*e·h▪−iki* X−1s/AOR: e·h▪ (aor.) -i (TA th. 3) -ek (X) -i (conj.) *IC−iki* X−1s/CC: IC+ -i (TA th. 3) -ek (X) -i (conj.)
+iki	*IC−iki* X−1s/PPL(INsg): IC+ -i (TA th. 3) -ek (X) -i (inan. sg.) X−1s/PPL(obl): same
-iki	anim. pl.: animate plural (head of participle and in the assertive, conclusive, dubitative, and interrogative modes)
+iko	2p−1s/IMP: -i (TA th. 3) -ko (2p imp.)

+ikwe·na *IC–ikwe·na* 3s–1s/INT.PPL(ANsg): IC+ -i (TA th. 3) -kw (3,0 irr.) -e·ni (int.) -a (anim. sg.)

+ikwe·ni *–ikwe·ni* 3s–1s/INT: -i (TA th. 3) -kw (3,0 irr.) -e·ni (int.)
IC–ikwe·ni 3s–1s/CH.INT: IC+ -i (TA th. 3) -kw (3,0 irr.) -e·ni (int.)

-inaw X: indefinite possessor

+inawaki *o–inawaki* X(ANpl): o- (3) -inaw (X) -aki (anim. pl.)

+inawani *o–inawani* X(INpl): o- (3) -inaw (X) -ani (inan. pl.)

+inawi *o–inawi* X(INsg): o- (3) -inaw (X) -i (inan. sg.)

+ine·ha X–1s/POT: -i (TA th. 3) -ene·ha (X pot.)

-ini inan. pl.: inanimate plural (head of participle and in dubitative mode)

-ini neg.-iter.: negative and iterative modes

-ini obv. sg.: obviative singular (head of participle)

+iniči *e·h·–iniči* 3′–1s/AOR: e·h· (aor.) -i (TA th. 3) -ni (obv.) -t (3) -i (conj.)

+ino 2s–1s/IMP: -i (TA th. 3) -no (2s imp.)

+ipena *ke–ipena* 2–1p/IND: -i (TA th. 3) -pena (1p,12)

+ipwa *ke–ipwa* 2p–1s/IND: -i (TA th. 3) -pwa (2p)

+isa 3s–1s/POT: -i (TA th. 3) -sa (3,0 pot.)

+ita *IC–ita* 3–1s/PPL(ANsg): IC+ -i (TA th. 3) -t (3) -a (anim. sg.)

+ite 3s–1s/SUBJ: -i (TA th. 3) -t (3) -e (subj.)

+itehe *e·h·–itehe* 3s–1s/AOR.PRET -i (TA th. 3) -t (3) -ehe (pret.)
IC–itehe 3s–1s/CH.PRET: IC+ -i (TA th. 3) -t (3) -ehe (pret.)
3s–1s/PRET.PPL(obl): same
–itehe 3s–1s/SUBJ.PRET: -i (TA th. 3) -t (3) -ehe (pret.)

+iwa·či *e·h·–iwa·či* 3p–1s/AOR: e·h· (aor.) -i (TA th. 3) -wa· (pl.) -t (3) -i (conj.)

+iwa·čini *IC–iwa·čini* 3p–1s/ITER: IC+ -i (TA th. 3) -wa· (pl.) -t (3) -wa· (pl.) -t (3) -ini (neg.-iter.)

+iyameči *e·h·–iyameči* 3–1p/AOR: e·h· (aor.) -i (TA th. 3) -amet (3–1p) -i (conj.)
IC–iyameči 3–1p/CC: IC+ -i (TA th. 3) -amet (3–1p) -i (conj.)

+iyameči *IC–iyameči* 3–1p/PPL(obl): IC+ -i (TA th. 3) -amet (3–1p) -i (inan. sg.)

+iyamečini 3–1p/NEG: -i (TA th. 3) -amet (3–1p) -ini (neg.-iter.)

+iyamehkiče 3–1p/PROH: -i (TA th. 3) -amet (3–1p) -hk (proh.) + -če (3,0 imp.)

+iyamekwe·ni 3–1p/: -i (TA th. 3) -amet (3–1p) -w (irr.) -e·ni (int.)

+iyamesa 3–1p/POT: -i (TA th. 3) -amet (3–1p) -sa (3,0 pot.)

+iyameta *IC–iyameta* 3–1p/PPL(ANsg): IC+ -i (TA th. 3) -amet (3–1p) -a (anim. sg.)

+iyane 2s–1s/SUBJ: -i (TA th. 3) -an (2s) -e (subj.)

+iyani *e·h·–iyani* 2s–1s/AOR: e·h· (aor.) -i (TA th. 3) -an (2s) -i (conj.)

+iyani *IC–iyani* 2s–1s/PPL(INsg): IC+ -i (TA th. 3) -an (2s) -i (inan. sg.)
2s–1s/PPL(obl): same

+iyanini *IC–iyanini* 2s–1s/ITER: IC+ -i (TA th. 3) -an (2s) -ini (neg.-iter.)
–iyanini 2s–1s/NEG: -i (TA th. 3) -an (2s) -ini (neg.-iter.)

+iyanini *IC–iyanini* 2s–1s/PPL(obl.pl): IC+ -i (TA th. 3) -an (2s) -ini (inan. pl.)

-iye·k	TA th. 1 proh.: -a· (TA th. 1) -hk (proh.) → -iye·k
+iye·kani	2s – 3/PROH: -a· (TA th. 1) -hk (proh.) -an (2s) -i (conj.)
+iye·kapa	2s – 3/POT: -a· (TA th. 1) -hk (proh.) -apa (2s pot.)
+iye·ka·ha	1s – 3/POT: -a· (TA th. 1) -hk (proh.) -a·ha (1s pot.)
+iye·ka·ke	1p – 3/PROH: -a· (TA th. 1) -hk (proh.) -a·k (1p) -i (conj.)
+iye·ke·ko	2p – 3/PROH: -a· (TA th. 1) -hk (proh.) -e·ko (2p proh.)
+iye·kwe	*e·h*= – *iye·kwe* 2p – 1s/AOR: e·h= (aor.) -i (TA th. 3) -e·kw (2p) -i (conj.)
+iye·kwini	2p – 1s/NEG: -i (TA th. 3) -e·kw (2p) -ini (neg.-iter.)
-i·ke	X proh.: indefinite subject in prohibitive
+i·ke·ni	*IC* – *i·ke·ni* X – 1s/INT.PPL(obl): IC+ -i (TA th. 3) -w (irr.) -ek (X) -e·ni (int.)
+i·nameki	*IC* – *i·nameki* X – 1p/PPL(obl): IC+ -i (TA th. 3) -·namek (X – 1p) -i (inan. sg.)
+i·nami·ke·ni	X – 1p/INT: -i (TA th. 3) -·namek (X – 1p) + -w (irr.) -e·ni (int.)
+i·namehki·ke	X – 1p/PROH: -i (TA th. 3) -·namek (X – 1p) + -hk (proh.) -i·ke (X proh.)
+i·namene·ha	X – 1p/POT: -i (TA th. 3) -·namek (X – 1p) + -ene·ha (X pot.)
-k	0: inanimate in conjunct modes
-k	3: replaces *-t* (3) after a consonant
	NOTE: retaining consonant stems select *-k* (3) and insert *-e-*
-·k	X irr.: indefinite subject, irrealis (interrogative and prioritive)
	Analyzed as: *-w* (irr.) + *-ek* (X).
+ka	*IC* – *ka* 3/PPL(ANsg): IC+ -k (3) -a (anim. sg.)
+ke	0/SUBJ: -k (0) -e (subj.)
+kehe	*e·h*= – *kehe* 0/AOR.PRET: e·h= (aor.) -k (0) -ehe (pret.)
	– *kehe* 0/SUBJ.PRET: -k (0) -ehe (pret.)
+ki	*e·h*= – *ki* 0/AOR: e·h= (aor.) -k (0) -i (conj.)
	IC – *ki* 0/CC: IC+ -k (0) -i (conj.)
+ki	*IC* – *ki* 0/PPL(INsg): IC+ -k (0) -i (inan. sg.)
	0/PPL(obl): same
	e·h= – *ki* 0/PPL(loc.obl): e·h= (aor.) -k (0) -i (inan. sg.)
+ki	*e·h*= – *ki* 3s/AOR: e·h= (aor.) -k (3) -i (conj.)
	IC – *ki* 3s/CC: IC+ -k (3) -i (conj.)
+kiki	*IC* – *kiki* 3/PPL(ANpl): IC+ -k (3) -iki (anim. pl.)
+kini	*IC* – *kini* 0/ITER: IC+ -k (0) -ini (neg.-iter.)
	– *kini* 0/NEG: -k (0) -ini (neg.-iter.)
+kini	*IC* – *kini* 0/PPL(INpl): IC+ -k (0) -ini (inan. pl.)
+kini	3s/NEG: -k (3) -ini (neg.-iter.)
+ko	2p/IMP: second plural, imperative
	-ko 2p imp.: second plural imperative in endings
	→ **+oko**, *-oko* after a consonant
-kw	3,0 irr.: equivalent to *-w* (irr.) + *-k*<*-t* (3) and *-w* (irr.) + *-k* (0)
	→ *-okw* after a consonant
+kwe·hiki	*IC* – *kwe·hiki* 3p/INT.PPL(obl): IC+ -kw (3,0 irr.) -e·ni (int.) -iki (anim. pl.)

+kwe·na *IC – kwe·na* 3s/INT.PPL(ANsg): IC+ -kw (3,0 irr.) -e·ni (int.) -a (anim. sg.)

+kwe·ni *e·h· – kwe·ni* 3s,0/AOR.INT: e·h· (aor.) -kw (3,0 irr.) -e·ni (int.)
– kwe·ni 3s,0/INT: -kw (3,0 irr.) -e·ni (int.)

+kwe·ni *IC – kwe·ni* 3s,0/INT.PPL(IN): IC+ -kw (3,0 irr.) -e·ni (int.)
3s,0/INT.PPL(obl): same
e·h· – kwe·ni 3,0/INT.PPL(loc.obl): e·h· (aor.) -kw (3,0 irr.) -e·ni (int.)

-·namek X – 1p: indefite acting on first plural exclusive
-i (TA th. 3) + *-·namek* (X – 1p) → *-i·namek* (X – 1p)
NOTE: combines with modal markers, sometimes after metathesis:
-i-·namek (X – 1p) + *-w* (irr.) → *-i-·nami·k* (X – 1p irr.)
-i-·namek (X – 1p) + *-hk* (proh.) → *-i-·namehk* (X – 1p proh.)
-i-·namek (X – 1p) + *-ene·ha* (X pot.) → *-i-·namene·ha* (X – 1p pot.)

-ni obv.: obviative animate or inanimate central participant in verbal endings
→ *-ini* after *-am* (TI(1) th.)

+niči *e·h· – niči* 3′/AOR: e·h· (aor.) -ni (obv.) -t (3) -i (conj.)
IC – niči 3′/CC: IC+ -ni (obv.) -t (3) -i (conj.)

+niči *e·h· – niči* 3′/PPL(loc.obl): e·h· (aor.) -ni (obv.) -t (3) -i (inan. sg.)
IC – niči 3′/PPL(obl): IC+ -ni (obv.) -t (3) -i (inan. sg.)

+ničihi *IC – ničihi* 3′/PPL(OBVpl): IC+ -ni (obv.) -t (3) -ihi (obv. pl.)

+ničini *IC – ničini* 3′/ITER: IC+ -ni (obv.) -t (3) -ini (neg.-iter.)
– ničini 3′/NEG: -ni (obv.) -t (3) -ini (neg.-iter.)

+ničini *IC – ničini* 3′/PPL(OBVsg): IC+ -ni (obv.) -t (3) -ini (obv. sg.)

+ničini *e·h· – ničini* 3′/PPL(loc.obl.pl): e·h· (aor.) -ni (obv.) -t (3) -ini (inan. pl.)

+nike 0′/SUBJ: -ni (obv.) -k (0) -e (subj.)

+nikehe *IC – nikehe* 0′/PRET.PPL(obl): IC+ -ni (obv.) -k (0) -ehe (pret.)

+niki *e·h· – niki* 0′/AOR: e·h· (aor.) -ni (obv.) -k (0) -i (conj.)

+niki *IC – niki* 0′/CC: IC+ -ni (obv.) -k (0) -i (conj.)

+niki *– niki* 0′/CONJ: -ni (obv.) -k (0) -i (conj.)

+niki *IC – niki* 0′/PPL(INsg): IC+ -ni (obv.) -k (0) -i (inan. sg.)
0′/PPL(obl): same
e·h· – niki 0′/PPL(loc.obl): e·h· (aor.) -ni (obv.) -k (0) -i (inan. sg.)

+nikiki *IC – nikiki* 0′/PPL(ANpl): IC+ -ni (obv.) -k (0) -iki (anim. pl.)

+nikini *IC – nikini* 0′/ITER: IC+ -ni (obv.) -k (0) -ini (neg.-iter.)

+nikini *– nikini* 0′/NEG: -ni (obv.) -k (0) -ini (neg.-iter.)

+nikini *IC – nikini* 0′/PPL(INpl): IC+ -ni (obv.) -k (0) -ini (inan. pl.)

+nikini *e·h· – nikini* 0′/PPL(loc.obl.pl): e·h· (aor.) -ni (obv.) -k (0) -ini (inan. pl.)

+nikwe *IC – nikwe* 3′/CH.PRI: IC+ -ni (obv.) -kw (3,0 irr.) -e (subj.)

+nikwe·ni *e·h· – nikwe·ni* 0′/INT.PPL(loc.obl): e·h· (aor.) -ni (obv.) -kw (3,0 irr.) -e·ni (int.)

+nikwe·ni *IC – nikwe·ni* 0′/INT.PPL(obl): IC+ -ni (obv.) -kw (3,0 irr.) -e·ni (int.)
3′/INT.PPL(obl): same

+nisa 3′,0′/POT: -ni (obv.) -sa (3,0 pot.)

+nite	3′/SUBJ: -ni (obv.) -t (3) -e (subj.)
+nitehe	*e·h·–nitehe* 3′/PRET.PPL(loc.obl): e·h· (aor.) -ni (obv.) -t (3) -ehe (pret.)
+niwahi	3′p/IND: -ni (obv.) -w (3,0) -ahi (obv. pl.)
+niwani	0′p/IND: -ni (obv.) -w (3,0) -ani (inan. sg.)
+niwani	3′s/IND: -ni (obv.) -w (3,0) -ani (obv. sg.)
+niwi	0′s/IND: -ni (obv.) -w (3,0) -i (inan. sg.)
+no	2s/IMP: second singular, imperative
	-no 2s imp.: second singular imperative in endings
+o	*ne–o* 1s–0/IND: ne- (1) -o· (TI(2) th.) -Ø (sg.)
	ke–o 2s–0/IND: ke- (2) -o· (TI(2) th.) -Ø (sg.)
-oko	2p imp.: see **+ko** 2p/IMP
-owa·	pl.: see *-wa·* pl.
-owa·w	2p,3p: see *-wa·w* 2p,3p
-owet	X rel.: see *-wet* X rel.
-o·	TI(2) th.: theme sign of Class 2 TI
+o·či	*e·h·–o·či* 3s–0/AOR: e·h· (aor.) -o· (TI(2) th.) -t (3) -i (conj.) 3s(-0)/AOR; same on an objectless TI(2)
	IC–o·či 3s–0/CC: IC+ -o· (TI(2) th.) -t (3) -i (conj.)
+o·či	*IC–o·či* 3s–0/PPL(INsg): IC+ -o· (TI(2) th.) -t (3) -i (inan. sg.) 3s–0/PPL(obl): same
+o·čiki	*IC–o·čiki* 3–0/PPL(ANpl): IC+ -o· (TI(2) th.) -t (3) 3(-0)/PPL(ANpl): same on an objectless TI(2)
+o·čini	*IC–o·čini* 3s–0/ITER: IC+ -o· (TI(2) th.) -t (3) -ini (neg.-iter.)
+o·hiya·ni	*IC–o·hiya·ni* 1s–0/DIM/PPL(obl): IC+ -o· (TI(2) th.) -·hi (dim.) -a·n (1s) -i (inan. sg.)
+o·hkapa	2s–0/POT: -o· (TI(2) th.) -hk (proh.) -apa (2s pot.) 2s(-0)/POT: same on an objectless TI(2)
+o·hke·koha	2p–0/POT: -o· (TI(2) th.) -hk (proh.) -e·kw (2p) -ehe (pret.)
+o·ke	X–0/SUBJ: -o· (TI(2) th.) -ek (X) -e (subj.)
+o·kini	X–0/NEG: -o· (TI(2) th.) -ek (X) -ini (neg.-iter.)
+o·kini	*IC–o·kini* X–0/PPL(INpl): IC+ -o· (TI(2) th.) -ek (X) -ini (inan. pl.)
+o·ki	*e·h·–o·ki* X–0/AOR: e·h· (aor.) -o· (TI(2) th.) -ek (X) -i (conj.) X(-0)/AOR: same on an objectless TI(2)
+o·ki	*IC–o·ki* X–0/CC: IC+ -o· (TI(2) th.) -ek (X) -i (conj.)
+o·ki	*IC–o·ki* X–0/PPL(INsg): IC+ -o· (TI(2) th.) -ek (X) -i (inan. sg.) X–0/PPL(obl): same
+o·ko	2p–0/IMP: -o· (TI(2) th.) -ko (2p imp.)
+o·kwe·ni	3s–0/INT: -o· (TI(2) th.) -kw (3,0 irr.) -e·ni (int.)
+o·ne·ha	X–0/POT: -o· (TI(2) th.) -ene·ha (X pot.)
+o·ničini	*IC–o·ničini* 3′–0/PPL(OBVsg): IC+ -o· (TI(2) th.) -ni (obv.) -t (3) -ini (obv. sg.)
+o·no	2s–0/IMP: -o· (TI(2) th.) -no (2s imp.)

+o·pena *ne–o·pena* 1p–0/IND: ne- (1) -o· (TI(2) th.) -pena (1p,12)
ke–o·pena 12–0/IND: ke- (2) -o· (TI(2) th.) -pwa (2p)
12(-0)/IND: same on an objectless TI(2)

+o·pi X–0/IND: -o· (TI(2) th.) -pi (X)

+o·pwa *ke–o·pwa* 2p–0/IND: ke- (2) -o· (TI(2) th.) -pwa (2p)

+o·ta *IC–o·ta* 3–0/PPL(ANsg): IC+ -o· (TI(2) th.) -t (3) -a (anim. sg.)

+o·te 3s–0/SUBJ: -o· (TI(2) th.) -t (3) -e (subj.)

+o·wa 3s–0/IND: -o· (TI(2) th.) -w (3,0) -a (anim. sg.)

+o·waki 3p–0/IND: -o· (TI(2) th.) -w (3,0) -aki (anim. pl.)

+o·wane·ni *IC–o·wane·ni* 2s–0/INT.PPL(obl): IC+ -o· (TI(2) th.) -w (irr.) -an (2s) -e·ni (int.)

+o·wa·či *e·h▪–o·wa·či* 3p–0/AOR: e·h▪ (aor.) -o· (TI(2) th.) -wa· (pl.) -t (3) -i (conj.)

+o·wa·čini 3p–0/NEG: -o· (TI(2) th.) -wa· (pl.) -t (3) -ini (neg.-iter.)

+o·wa·ne·ni *IC–o·wa·ne·ni* 1s–0/INT.PPL(obl): IC+ -o· (TI(2) th.) -w (irr.) -a·n (1s) -e·ni (int.)

+o·wa·sa 3p–0/POT: -o· (TI(2) th.) -wa· (pl.) -sa (3,0 pot.)
3p(-0)/POT: same on an objectless TI(2)

+o·wa·te 3p–0/SUBJ: -o· (TI(2) th.) -wa· (pl.) -t (3) -e (subj.)

+o·weči *IC–o·weči* X–0/REL/PPL(obl): IC+ -o· (TI(2) th.) -wet (X rel.) -i (inan. sg.)

+o·yakwe 12–0/SUBJ: -o· (TI(2) th.) -akw (12) -e (subj.)

+o·yane 2s–0/SUBJ: -o· (TI(2) th.) -an (2s) -e (subj.)

+o·yani *e·h▪–o·yani* 2s–0/AOR: e·h▪ (aor.) -o· (TI(2) th.) -an (2s) -i (conj.)

+o·yani *IC–o·yani* 2s–0/PPL(INsg): IC+ -o· (TI(2) th.) -an (2s) -i (inan. sg.)
2s–0/PPL(obl): same

+o·yanini 2s–0/NEG: -o· (TI(2) th.) -an (2s) -ini (neg.-iter.)
2s(-0)/NEG: same on an objectless TI(2)

+o·ya·ke *e·h▪–o·ya·ke* 1p–0/AOR: e·h▪ (aor.) -o· (TI(2) th.) -a·k (1p) -i (conj.)
IC–o·ya·ke 1p–0/CC: IC+ -o· (TI(2) th.) -a·k (1p) -i (conj.)

+o·ya·kini 1p–0/NEG: -o· (TI(2) th.) -a·k (1p) -ini (neg.-iter.)

+o·ya·ni *e·h▪–o·ya·ni* 1s–0/AOR: e·h▪ (aor.) -o· (TI(2) th.) -a·n (1s) -i (conj.)
1s(-0)/AOR: same on an objectless TI(2)
IC–o·ya·ni 1s–0/CC: IC+ -o· (TI(2) th.) -a·n (1s) -i (conj.)

+o·ya·ni *IC–o·ya·ni* 1s–0/PPL(INsg): IC+ -o· (TI(2) th.) -a·n (1s) -i (inan. sg.)
1s–0/PPL(obl): same

+o·ya·nini *IC–o·ya·nini* 1s–0/ITER: IC+ -o· (TI(2) th.) -a·n (1s) -ini (neg.-iter.)

+o·ya·nini *IC–o·ya·nini* 1s–0/PPL(INpl): IC+ -o· (TI(2) th.) -a·n (1s) -ini (inan. pl.)

+o·ye·kwe *e·h▪–o·ye·kwe* 2p–0/AOR: e·h▪ (aor.) -o· (TI(2) th.) -e·kw (2p) -i (conj.)

+o·ye·kwe *IC–o·ye·kwe* 2p–0/PPL(INsg): IC+ -o· (TI(2) th.) -e·kw (2p) -i (inan. sg.)
2p–0/PPL(obl): same

-p sg.: first and second singular in the dubitative and conclusive
NOTE: -p (sg.) appears as -Ø (sg.) word-finally.

+pena	*ne–pena* 1p/IND: ne- (1) -pena (1p,12)
	ke–pena 12/IND: ke- (2) -pena (1p,12)
	12–0/IND: same with Class 3 TI
	-pena 1p,12: first plural exclusive and inclusive in the independent order
	→ *-pena·* before modal suffixes
+petoke	*ke–petoke* 2s/DUB: ke- (2) -p (sg.) -etoke (dub.)
+pi	X/IND: -pi (X)
	X–0/IND: same with Class 3 TI
	-pi X: indefinite subject in the independent order
	→ *-p* before dubitative and conclusive modal suffixes
+pwa	*ke–pwa* 2p/IND: ke- (2) -pwa (2p)
	-pwa 2p: second plural in the independent order.
	→ *-pwa·* before modal suffixes
+sa	3s,0/POT: -sa (3,0 pot.)
	-sa 3,0 pot.: third person animate or inanimate subject, potential mode
	NOTE: As if *-t* (3), *-k* (3), *-k* (0) + *-sa* (pot.) → *-sa* (3,0 pot.)
-t	3: third person animate in the conjunct
	→ *-k* after a consonant-final stem or suffix
-t	X–3 irr.: indefinite acting on third animate, irrealis (interrogative and proritive)
	Analyzed as: *-w* (irr.) + *-et* (X–3).
+ta	*IC–ta* 3/PPL(ANsg): IC+ -t (3) -a (anim. sg.)
	3–0/PPL(ANsg): same with Class 3 TI
+te	3s/SUBJ: -t (3) -e (subj.)
+tehe	*e·h▪–tehe* 3s/AOR.PRET: e·h▪ (aor.) -t (3) -ehe (pret.)
	IC–tehe 3s/PRET.PPL(obl): IC+ -t (3) -ehe (pret.)
-w	3,0: third person animate and inanimate in the independent order
	NOTE: *-w* 3,0 umlauts stem-final *a·* or TA Theme 1 *a·* to *e·* (except in *-ka·pa·* 'stand', *nepwa·hka·-* 'be smart')
	NOTE: *-w* 3,0 contracts leaving a long vowel in the dubitative, assertive, and conclusive; after a consonant, *-w* 3,0 contracts with nonfinal *-a-* and *-e-* to *-o·-*
-w	irr.: irrealis; marks interrogative and prioritive modes
	→ *-ow* after a consonant
	Contracts with *-e-* leaving a long vowel:
	-w (irr.) + *-et* (X–3) → *-t* (X–3 irr.)
	-w (irr.) + *-ek* (X) → *-·k* (X irr.)
	NOTE: some combinations show metathesis and fusion:
	-w (irr.) + *-k*<*-t* (3), *-k* (0) → *-kw* (3,0 irr.)
	-w (irr.) + *-amet* (3–1p) → *-amet* (1p) + *-w* (irr.) → *-amekw* (3–1p irr.)
	-w (irr.) + *-·namek* (X–1p) → *-·namek* (1p) + *-w* (irr.) → *-·nami·k* (X–1p irr.)

-w — sg.: first and second singular on TA themes 1 and 2 in the independent indicative
→ -Ø after *-ekw* TA th. 2
NOTE: not used in direct diminutive forms

+wa — 3s/IND: -w (3,0) -a (anim. sg.)
3s – 0/IND: same with Class 3 TI

+waki — 3p/IND: -w (3,0) -aki (anim. pl.)

+wakwe·ni — *e·h▪ – wakwe·ni* 12/AOR.INT: e·h▪ (aor.) -w (irr.) -akw (12) -e·ni (int.)

+wakwe·ni — *IC – wakwe·ni* 12/INT.PPL(obl): IC+ -w (irr.) -akw (12) -e·ni (int.)

+wane — *IC – wane* 2s/CH.PRI: IC+ -w (irr.) -an (2s) -e (subj.)

+wane·na — *IC – wane·na* 2s/INT.PPL(ANsg): IC+ -w (irr.) -an (2s) -e·ni (int.) -a (anim. sg.)

+wane·ni — *e·h▪ – wane·ni* 2s/AOR.INT: e·h▪ (aor.) -w (irr.) -an (2s) -e·ni (int.)
IC – wane·ni 2s/CH.INT: IC+ -w (irr.) -an (2s) -e·ni (int.)

+wane·ni — *e·h▪ – wane·ni* 2s/INT.PPL(loc.obl): e·h▪ (aor.) -w (irr.) -an (2s) -e·ni (int.)
IC – wane·ni 2s/INT.PPL(obl): IC+ -w (irr.) -an (2s) -e·ni (int.)

+wani — 0p/IND: -w (3,0) -ani (inan. pl.)

-wa· — pl.: pluralizes the animate third person proximate in the conjunct, potential, and prohibitive, and in some forms of the interrogative participle
→ *-owa·* after a consonant stem or after a consonant-final theme
NOTE: not used in conjunct participles with *-iki* anim. pl.

-wa· — 2p: pluralizes certain second person objects in the potential and imperative

+wa·či — *e·h▪ – wa·či* 3p/AOR: e·h▪ (aor.) -wa· (pl.) -t (3) -i (conj.)
3p – 0/AOR: same with Class 3 TI
IC – wa·či 3p/CC: IC+ -wa· (pl.) -t (3) -i (conj.)
– wa·či 3p/CONJ: -wa· (pl.) -t (3) -i (conj.)

+wa·či — *e·h▪ – wa·či* 3p/PPL(loc.obl): e·h▪ (aor.) -wa· (pl.) -t (3) -i (inan. sg.)
IC – wa·či 3p/PPL(INsg): IC+ -wa· (pl.) -t (3) -i (inan. sg.)
3p – 0/PPL(INsg): same with Class 3 TI
3p/PPL(obl): same
3p – 0/PPL(obl): same with Class 3 TI

+wa·čini — *IC – wa·čini* 3p/ITER: IC+ -wa· (pl.) -t (3) -ini (neg.-iter.)
– wa·čini 3p/NEG: -wa· (pl.) -t (3) -ini (neg.-iter.)
3p – 0/NEG: same with Class 3 TI

+wa·čini — *e·h▪ – wa·čini* 3p/PPL(loc.obl.pl): e·h▪ (aor.) -wa· (pl.) -t (3) -ini (inan. pl.)
IC – wa·čini 3p/PPL(obl.pl): IC+ -wa· (pl.) -t (3) -ini (inan. pl.)
3p – 0/PPL(INpl): same with Class 3 TI and inanimate plural head

+wa·čini — *IC – wa·čini* 3p/PPL(OBVsg): IC+ -wa· (pl.) -t (3) -ini (obv. sg.)

+wa·ke·ni — *IC – wa·ke·ni* 1p/INT.PPL(obl): IC+ -w (irr.) -a·k (1p) -e·ni (int.)

+wa·ki — *o – wa·ki* 3p(LOC): o- (3) -wa·w (2p,3p) -eki (loc.)

+wa·ne·ni — *IC – wa·ne·ni* 1s/INT.PPL(obl): IC+ -w (irr.) -a·n (1s) -e·ni (int.)

-wa·t	X rel. irr.: indefinite subject, relational, irrealis (interrogative and prioritive) Analyzed as: *-w* (irr.) + *-wet* (X rel.).
+wa·če	3p/IMP: -wa· (pl.) -če (3,0 imp.)
+wa·sa	3p/POT: -wa· (pl.) -sa (3,0 pot.)
+wa·te	3p/SUBJ: -wa· (pl.) -t (3) -e (subj.)
+wa·tehe	*IC–wa·tehe* 3p/CH.PRET: IC+ -wa· (pl.) -t (3) -ehe (pret.) 3p/PRET.PPL(obl): same
+wa·te·ni	X/REL/INT: -w (irr.) -wet (X rel.) -e·ni (int.)
-wa·w	2p,3p: pluralizes second- and third-person possessors of nouns, and second-person subjects of inverse verbs in the independent order → *-owa·w* after stems and themes in *-Cw* → *-(o)wa·* before *-eki* loc. and *-etoke* dub.
+wa·wa	*ke–wa·wa* 2p(ANsg): ke- (2) -wa·w (2p,3p) -a (anim. sg.)
+wa·wahi	*o–wa·wahi* 3p(OBVpl): o- (3) -wa·w (2p,3p) -ahi (obv. pl.)
+wa·waki	*ke–wa·waki* 2p(ANpl): ke- (2) -wa·w (2p,3p) -aki (anim. pl.)
+wa·wani	*o–wa·wani* 3p(INpl): o- (3) -wa·w (2p,3p) -ani (inan. pl.)
+wa·wani	*o–wa·wani* 3p(OBVsg): o- (3) -wa·w (2p,3p) -ani (obv. sg.)
+wa·wi	*ke–wa·wi* 2p(INsg): ke- (2) -wa·w (2p,3p) -i (inan. sg.) *o–wa·wi* 3p(INsg): o- (3) -wa·w (2p,3p) -i (inan. sg.)
+weči	*e·h·–weči* X/REL/AOR: e·h· (aor.) -wet (X rel.) -i (conj.) *IC–weči* X/REL/CC: IC+ -wet (X rel.) -i (conj.)
+weči	*IC–weči* X/REL/PPL(INsg): IC+ -wet (X rel.) -i (inan. sg.) X/REL/PPL(obl): same *e·h·–weči* X/REL/PPL(loc.obl): e·h· (aor.) -wet (X rel.) -i (inan. sg.)
+wečini	*IC–wečini* X/REL/ITER: IC+ -wet (X rel.) -ini (neg.-iter.)
+wehapa	3s,0s/CON: -w (3,0) -ehapa (con.)
+wehapaniki	3p/CON: -w (3,0) -ehapa (con.) -iki (anim. pl.)
+wepani	3s,0s/AST: -w (3,0) -epani (ast.)
+wepaniki	3p/AST: -w (3,0) -epani (ast.) -iki (anim. pl.)
-wet	X rel.: indefinite subject, relational → *-owet* after a consonant NOTE: *-w* (irr.) + *-wet* (X rel.) → *-wa·t* (X rel. irr.)
+wete	X/REL/SUBJ: -wet (X rel.) -e (subj.)
+wetoke	3s,0s/DUB: -w (3,0) -etoke (dub.)
+wetoke·hiki	3p/DUB: -w (3,0) -etoke (dub.): -iki (anim. pl.)
+we·kwe·ni	*IC–we·kwe·ni* 2p/CH.INT: IC+ -w (irr.) -e·kw (2p) -e·ni (int.)
+we·kwe·ni	*IC–we·kwe·ni* 2p/INT.PPL(obl): IC+ -w (irr.) -e·kw (2p) -e·ni (int.)
+wi	0s/IND: -w (3,0) -i (inan. sg.)
+yakwe	*e·h·–yakwe* 12/AOR: e·h· (aor.) -akw (12) -i (conj.)

+yakwe *e·h·–yakwe* 12/PPL(loc.obl): e·h· (aor.) -akw (12) -i (inan. sg.)
IC–yakwe 12/PPL(obl): IC+ -akw (12) -i (inan. sg.)
+yakwe 12/SUBJ: -akw (12) -e (subj.)
+yakwini *IC–yakwini* 12/ITER: IC+ -akw (12) -ini (neg.-iter.)
–yakwini 12/NEG: -akw (12) -ini (neg.-iter.)
+yakwini *IC–yakwini* 12/PPL(INpl): IC+ -akw (12) -ini (inan. pl.)
12/PPL(obl.pl): same
+yana *IC–yana* 2s/PPL(ANsg): IC+ -an (2s) -a (anim. sg.)
+yane 2s/SUBJ: -an (2s) -e (subj.)
+yanehe 2s/SUBJ.PRET: -an (2s) -ehe (pret.)
+yani *e·h·–yani* 2s/AOR: e·h· (aor.) -an (2s) -i (conj.)
2s–0/AOR: same with Class 3 TI
+yani *IC–yani* 2s/PPL(INsg): IC+ -an (2s) -i (inan. sg.)
2s/PPL(obl): same
e·h·–yani 2s/PPL(loc.obl): e·h· (aor.) -an (2s) -i (inan. sg.)
+yanini *IC–yanini* 2s/ITER: IC+ -an (2s) -ini (neg.-iter.)
–yanini 2s/NEG: -an (2s) -ini (neg.-iter.)
+yanini *IC–yanini* 2s–0/PPL(INpl): IC+ -an (2s) -ini (inan. pl.)
+ya·ke *e·h·–ya·ke* 1p/AOR: e·h· (aor.) -a·k (1p) -i (conj.)
IC–ya·ke 1p/CC: IC+ -a·k (1p) -i (conj.)
+ya·ke *IC–ya·ke* 1p/PPL(INsg): IC+ -a·k (1p) -i (inan. sg.)
1p/PPL(obl): same
e·h·–ya·ke 1p/PPL(loc.obl): e·h· (aor.) -a·k (1p) -i (inan. sg.)
+ya·kini *IC–ya·kini* 1p/ITER: IC+ -a·k (1p) -ini (neg.-iter.)
–ya·kini 1p/NEG: -a·k (1p) -ini (neg.-iter.)
+ya·kini *e·h·–ya·kini* 1p/PPL(loc.obl.pl): e·h· (aor.) -a·k (1p) -ini (inan. pl.)
+ya·na *IC–ya·na* 1s/PPL(ANsg): IC+ -a·n (1s) -a (anim. sg.)
+ya·ne 1s/SUBJ: -a·n (1s) -e (subj.)
+ya·nehe 1s/SUBJ.PRET: -a·n (1s) -ehe (pret.)
+ya·ni *e·h·–ya·ni* 1s/AOR: e·h· (aor.) -a·n (1s) -i (conj.)
IC–ya·ni 1s/CC: IC+ -a·n (1s) -i (conj.)
+ya·ni *IC–ya·ni* 1s/PPL(INsg): IC+ -a·n (1s) -i (inan. sg.)
1s/PPL(obl): same
e·h·–ya·ni 1s/PPL(loc.obl): e·h· (aor.) -a·n (1s) -i (inan. sg.)
+ya·nini *IC–ya·nini* 1s/ITER: IC+ -a·n (1s) -ini (neg.-iter.)
–ya·nini 1s/NEG: -a·n (1s) -ini (neg.-iter.)
+ya·nini *IC–ya·nini* 1s/PPL(INpl): IC+ -a·n (1s) -ini (inan. pl.)
+ye·kwe *e·h·–ye·kwe* 2p/AOR: e·h· (aor.) -e·kw (2p) -i (conj.)

+ye·kwe	*e·h·–ye·kwe* 2p/PPL(loc.obl): e·h· (aor.) -e·kw (2p) -i (inan. sg.)
	IC–ye·kwe 2p/PPL(obl): IC+ -e·kw (2p) -i (inan. sg.)
	IC–ye·kwe 2p/PPL(loc.obl): IC+ -e·kw (2p) -i (inan. sg.) (With *a·mi* PV [2.270].)
+ye·kwe	2p/SUBJ: -e·kw (2p) -e (subj.)
+ye·kwini	*IC–ye·kwini* 2p/ITER: IC+ -e·kw (2p) -ini (neg.-iter.)
	–ye·kwini 2p/NEG: -e·kw (2p) -ini (neg.-iter.)
+Ø	*ne–Ø* 1s/IND: ne- (1) -Ø (sg.)
	ke–Ø 2s/IND: ke- (2) -Ø (sg.)
	2s – 0/IND: same with Class 3 TI
	NOTE: -Ø (sg.) appears as -p (sg.) before a modal suffix.
+Ø	VOCsg: vocative singular on nouns
	NOTE: indicated after stems in *-h* and with irregular kinship terms
-Ø	sg.: first and second singular in the independent
	NOTE: not indicated for singular possessors of nouns
-Ø	TA th. 1: see -a· (TA th. 1)